salt pans SP   KK Khon, Pak Talay
Kaeng Krachan   KK
Khao Yai   KY
Doi Inthanon   DI
Doi Angkhang   DA

A guide to the
Birds of Thailand

Boonsong Lekagul
Philip D. Round

Foreword by
Ben King

Illustrated by
Mongkol Wongkalasin
Kamol Komolphalin

A Guide to the Birds of Thailand

ISBN 974-85673-6-2

Published by Saha Karn Bhaet Group
Typesetting and Page Make up : IPEC Bangkok
Colour Separations : 71 Film
Printed in Thailand : Darnsutha Press

All orders should be placed with Saha Karn Bhaet Group
Kasetsart University Alumni Association Building,
50 Phaholyothin Road, Ladyao, Jatujak, Bangkok 10900 Thailand
Tel/Fax: 66-2-940-5262   E-mail: birdguidethailand@yahoo.com

CONTENTS

FOREWORD

The publication of this first-class field guide to the birds of Thailand is a significant milestone in Thai ornithology. It is the culmination of Dr. Boonsong Lekagul's pioneering efforts to produce guides to Thailand's wildlife as part of his program to conserve natural resources. The first two versions (1968 and 1974) of this book, his *Bird Guide of Thailand*, helped immensely to raise interest in the birds of Thailand, thereby kindling a desire to protect them and their habitat.

The text of this completely new book employs the latest in field techniques for identifying Thailand's more than 900 species of birds. Research carried out by Philip Round in the course of working on this bird guide led to the collation of much new bird distribution data, collected by both Thai and foreign observers, and the addition of over 60 species to the Thai list as well as a comprehensive evaluation of the conservation status of the country's avifauna. The compilation of this data on computer at Mahidol University, Bangkok, under a World Wide Fund for Nature-sponsored project, now forms the basis for a comprehensive monitoring system for the protected areas, habitats and regions of the country. This work, done during 1986–1989, made it possible to prepare completely updated text and distribution maps for most species.

The illustrations are the best ever produced by any south Asian wildlife artist. The accuracy and 'birdiness' of the plates is remarkable considering that there is no history and accumulated expertise in representational bird art in Thailand. The work of these two Thai artists, Kamol Komolphalin and Mongkol Wongkalasin, ranks very favourably with that of artists from other countries with long traditions and experience in bird illustration. Both artists have daytime jobs and did their work for this guide in their spare time, mostly evenings.

When I first visited Thailand for a few weeks in July 1961, the skies above Bangkok were filled with birds at all hours of the day: storks, vultures, darters, cormorants, herons, egrets, etc. At that time, there were no identification books on the birds of Thailand. Then, and during my subsequent three-and-a-half years' stay in Thailand (1964–1967), I used Deignan's *Birds of Northern Thailand* and Smythies' *Birds of Burma* and other regional works, none of which were written with a view toward field identification. To say that identifications were difficult then would be a gross understatement — often it just wasn't possible. Many hours were spent trying to identify mist-netted birds in the hand — species which can now be confidently and instantly identified at some distance.

In the 1960s and 1970s, Dr. Boonsong Lekagul pioneered conservation in Thailand. His enjoyment of Thailand's forests and wildlife led him to become a formidable force in conservation, spending every penny he had and even risking his life for the cause of conserving Thailand's natural resources. His approach was comprehensive and awesome for a single man: media articles; his own conservation bulletin and organization; lobbying in government circles; discussions with Thailand's revered King and Queen; production of guides in English and/or Thai on birds, butterflies, mammals, etc; involvement with foreign conservation organizations, and so on. He received the prestigious Getty Award in 1979 and much other international recognition for his work. Money received from these awards was promptly plowed back into conservation. Dr. Boonsong wrote the text and painted most of the illustrations for the first two editions of his bird guide. Unfortunately, his illness during the past few years has prevented him from following this new guide through to completion.

Dr. Boonsong's family have been very supportive in seeing this bird guide project through to its conclusion. They recognize the importance of Dr. Boonsong's life's work and recently took the initiative to produce a reprint of Dr. Boonsong's and Jeffrey McNeely's much-acclaimed *Mammals of Thailand*.

Times have changed in Thailand. The birds are mostly gone from Bangkok's skies and the threats to Thailand's forests and wildlife are greater than ever. Thailand's population continues to grow and its demands on the environment increase: illegal logging and poaching still occur; commercial forestry puts pressure on native forest areas; the lives and livelihood of the nation's rural poor are threatened by the degradation of watersheds, etc. However, the conservation movement has also grown rapidly and a number of highly effective non-government organizations (NGO's) dedicated to conservation now exist. These NGO's, combined with a very strong grass roots movement, recently defeated the ecologically unsound Nam Choan hydroelectric project while their growing influence also contributed to the government's recent decision to ban most logging in Thailand. The park and sanctuary network has expanded enormously offering a considerable protection to much remaining forest.

While the English language edition of this book will be well-received worldwide, a Thai language version is essential in order to promote conservation among the people of Thailand. I hope that a way will be found to produce a Thai edition of this guide, as Dr. Boonsong had always planned.

That such positive developments in conservation should have occurred and this fine bird guide be produced are a testament to Dr. Boonsong's genius, effectiveness and foresightedness. Because of his fierce dedication and perseverance, there is still much to be saved and savored by those he nurtured.

BEN KING

ACKNOWLEDGMENTS

The past decade, during which this guide was in preparation, has been an exciting period during which much new information on the status and distribution of birds has been added, thanks to the contributions of a great many individuals and institutions.

Foremost among these we must thank the Ecological Research Division, Thailand Institute of Scientific and Technological Research. We are indebted to Dr. Niphan Ratanaworobhan, the director of the division, and her staff, Porntip Angkapreechases, Preecha Luecha, Jarujin Nabhitabhata and Nivesh Nadee, all of whom have assisted us in innumerable ways. They have generously shared with us the results of their many field surveys and have granted ready access to the bird specimens in the National Reference Collection.

In the Royal Forest Department, we owe a special debt of gratitude to the many persons who have helped us gain access to national parks, wildlife sanctuaries and other areas or who have provided information on bird distribution. We must especially thank Boonlerd Angsirijinda, Bubphar Amget, Tanya Chunarch, Suvimolmanee Dobias, Jira Jintanugool, Bussabong Kanchanasaka, the late Seub Nakhasathien, Wichai Panjamanont, Pramote Saiwichian, Suvat Singhapant, Withya Songkakul, Siriporn Thongaree, Dr. Schwann Tunhikorn, Seri Vejaboosakorn and Sawat Wongteirawat. Boonchana Klankamsorn provided information on forest cover.

Jira Mekvichai, director of the Dusit Zoo, Bangkok kindly allowed us to photograph and sketch the birds in his care.

The late Dr. Salim Ali arranged a loan of specimens from the collection of the Bombay Natural History Society as did the late Dr. Yoshimaro Yamashina from the Yamashina Institute of Ornithology. Dr. David Wells loaned us many specimens from the collection of the Department of Zoology, University of Malaya, Kuala Lumpur. We also thank the trustees of the British Museum (Natural History) and Dr. Thosaporn Wongratana of the Chulalongkorn University Museum of Zoology, Bangkok for permission to examine and photograph specimens. Craig Robson and Frank Rozendaal allowed us to make notes from their sketches and paintings of South-east Asian birds.

We are very grateful to E.C. Dickinson and Dr. R.E. Elbel for access to copies of correspondence between Elbel and the late H.G. Deignan. Dr. Bruce Beehler, National Museum of Natural History, Washington, D.C. and Dr. Raymond A. Paynter Jr., Museum of Comparative Zoology, Cambridge, Massachusetts, provided information on some specimens in their care.

The following helped us greatly by reading and commenting on sections of the draft text, often at some length: Arnoud van den Berg; Steen Christensen; Jon Dunn; Ben King; Richard Lair; Dr. Joe T. Marshall Jr.; Jelle Scharringa; Claudia Wilds. Dr. David Wells read through the entire species text and made a great many useful suggestions.

Jarujin Nabhitabhata and Uthai Treesucon provided an updated list of Thai language bird names and prepared the index of Thai names. Others who have particularly assisted us with information, discussion of identification points or taxonomy, or by providing access to photographs, sketches or sound recordings of birds are:

Peter Alexander-Marrack, Per Alström, Surapol Ardseungnern, Kevin Baker, Erik Bos, Warren Brockelman, Murray Bruce, Mike Chalmers, Virach Chantrasmi, Peter Coe, Peter Colston, David M. Cottridge, Ian Dawson, Surapon Duangkhae, David Eades, Roland Eve, David Fisher, Charles Francis, the late P.J. Grant, Rod Hall, Dr. Chris Hails, Peter Harrison, Carol and Tim Inskipp, Surachit Jamonman, Peter Kennerley, Obhas Khopkhaet, Wichian Kongtong Frank Lambert, Paul Leader, Scott Mandeville, John Marchant, David Melville, Killian Mullarney, Somtob Norapuckprutikorn, David Ogle, Richard Ollington, Urban Olsson, Somsak Pakdeephuvadol, John Parr, Pisit na Patalung, Naris Phumpakapun, Santana Pleumshoosak, Pilai Poonswad, Richard Porter, Dr. Ookaew Prakobvitayakit Beaver, Tirapat Prayurasiddhi, Pratheep Rojanadilok, Nukul Rutanadukul, Dr. Derek Scott, Dr. Lucia Severinghaus, Dr. Lester Short, David Simon, Graham Speight, Belinda Stewart-Cox, Protpimol Sukhavanija, Dennis Tidwell, David Tomlinson, Arpha Triyan, Atsuo Tsuji, Mick Turton, M.R. Parcharjakorn Voravan, Grahame Walbridge, John Wall, Gary Wiles, James Wolstencroft, Wu Sen-Hsiong, Dennis Yong.

We thank the many other birdwatchers who have sent us details of their bird sightings, thereby allowing much new distributional information to be incorporated into this book.

We should like to thank Anukit Norakitborihan for introducing us to some of the less accessible birding areas; Nopparat Naksatit for his assistance and hospitality in the most exciting wilderness area in Thailand; and Beung Sukmechai who helped us find some of southern Thailand's most exciting and elusive rainforest birds.

Bird topography drawings in the introduction are based, with permission, on those of P.J. Grant and K. Mullarney (*The New Approach to Identification*) published in *Birding World* 1988–1989.

Philip Round would especially like to thank Kamol Komolphalin and Uthai Treesucon for their companionship in the field on numerous occasions and for sharing their expertise with him.

Many friends have encouraged us at various times during the gestation of this book. Chief among these, we should like to mention Peter Alexander-Marrack, Dr. Rauf Ali, Bob Dobias, Noritaka Ichida, Ben King, Patcharee Komolphalin, Jeffrey McNeely, David Melville, Dr. S. Dillon Ripley, Dr. J.T.R. Sharrock, Sonapa Wongrattana, Dr. David Wells and, above all, Richard Lair whose advice and expertise has been invaluable.

Dararat Sirisingkarn helped type the manuscript; Raman Kaewphakdee and Valasinee Trangasetsin helped prepare the distribution maps and index. Kanita Lekhakula assisted with book production.

A comprehensive updating of both distribution data and text was made possible when Philip Round was supported by the World Wide Fund for Nature (Project WWF 3713 – Development of a monitoring system for species, habitats and protected areas in Thailand). We are grateful to the Biology Department, Mahidol University for providing working space and facilities.

We are grateful to Mr. Bancha Lamsam, President and Chief Executive Officer, Thai Farmers Bank, for permission to reproduce the sunbird illustration on the title page.

Both authors would like to thank Arnold and Vera Round, Philip's parents, and the Lekagul family, for their support and encouragement.

INTRODUCTION

A Guide to the Birds of Thailand arose from the need to update the highly successful *Bird Guide of Thailand* (second edition) which appeared in 1974. What was originally intended as a mere revision, however, grew into a major project entailing the compilation of a completely new book. *A Guide to the Birds of Thailand* not only treats in full all of the 915 bird species recorded from the country up to March 1989 (an increase of 66 over the previous edition) but all the plates are new and both text and distribution maps have been fully revised in order to incorporate much new information gained during the past decade. Many recently discovered field characters and behavioural features of South-east Asian birds are reported.

HISTORY OF ORNITHOLOGY IN THAILAND

The history of ornithology in Thailand may be divided into three periods. Although classical Thai poets and writers mentioned some of the larger and more conspicuous birds, and early Western visitors such as Sir John Bowring and Sir Robert Schomburgk made many generalized observations on natural history, bird studies gained real momentum only after the turn of the century. At this time, a number of collectors such as C.J. Aagaard, Dr. W.L. Abbott, Emil Eisenhofer, Count Nils Gyldenstope, E.C. Herbert, Baron Rodolphe Meyer de Schauensee, the ichthyologist H.M. Smith, Sir Walter Williamson and others were active and despatched large numbers of specimens to museums in Europe and the United States. Another major contributor was H.C. Robinson, Director of Museums for the Federated Malay States, whose joint exploration of the southern provinces with C. Boden Kloss led to the publication of the *Birds of South-west and Peninsular Siam* in 1921–1924.

The foundations of modern Thai ornithology and, indeed, of much of South-east Asian bird taxonomy, were laid down by Herbert G. Deignan who arrived in Chiang Mai in 1928 in order to teach at the Prince Royal's College. During two periods of residence, 1928–1932 and 1935–1937, he quickly consolidated his knowledge of northern Thai birds and culture. Two major papers on the birds of Chiang Mai and many shorter papers culminated in the production of his *Birds of Northern Thailand* in 1945. Deignan's work in Thailand greatly contributed to his definitive taxonomic revisions of some passerine bird families, most notably bulbuls and babblers. His *Checklist of the Birds of Thailand*, a detailed synthesis of his own research and that of his predecessors and collaborators, remains the standard taxonomic work on Thai birds.

We may define the second period as spanning the mid-1960s to the mid-1970s, when the United States military presence contributed much funding for biological field research through the vehicle of the Migratory Animal Pathological Survey (MAPS). The primary purpose of MAPS was to study pathogenic organisms which might be transmitted to humans through the agency of wildlife such as rodents and birds. Ornithologists, wisely, used the available funds to mount major ringing and migration studies, ecological studies and to explore and collect further specimens from the remote forested mountains which were just then being opened up by Thailand's expanding road network. Some of the key figures during this period were Dr. H. E. McClure, director of the MAPS programme; Ben King, whose expeditions to the four corners of the Kingdom added 34 new species to the Thai list; and Dr. Joe T. Marshall who is particularly renowned for his highly original work on the vocalizations, systematics and taxonomy of nightbirds, particularly the scops-owls and frogmouths. Mention must also be made of Thailand's most outstanding vertebrate taxonomist, the late Kitti Thonglongya. It was the senior author's privilege to have encouraged the young Kitti's interest, which led to his joining the government's Applied Scientific Research Corporation. Kitti died at the tragically early age of 44 years though during his brief but remarkable span, he discovered a species of bird new to science, the White-eyed River-Martin *Pseudochelidon sirintarae*.

It was during this period that the first and second editions of the *Bird Guide of Thailand* were produced, followed by Ben King, Edward Dickinson and Martin Woodcock's *Field Guide to the Birds of South-East Asia*.

If this second era belonged mostly to the professional ornithologist, then the third and most recent period of Thai ornithology, dating from the mid-1970s and continuing to the present, surely belongs to the conservationist, the world traveller and the enthusiastic and highly competent amateur birdwatcher. The growth of Thailand's national park and wildlife sanctuary network has encouraged ever more birdwatchers and nature enthusiasts to visit the nation's tropical forests, wetlands and seashores. While many of these birdwatchers are visitors from abroad, a nucleus of skilled Thai observers has also developed. Many observers keep detailed field notes so that, through the medium of the sight record, the amount of information on Thai birds is increasing as never before. As well as collecting distributional information, today's birdwatchers are also making observations on seasonality, breeding, ecology, feeding behaviour, vocalizations, and so on.

PHYSIOGRAPHY

Thailand lies in the Indo-Chinese Peninsula of the Oriental (or Indo-Malayan) faunal region, covering a land area of approximately 513,115 sq km. It extends from 5°37′ N latitude to 20°30′ N latitude and between 97°20′ and 105°39′ E longitude (approximately 1,500 km from north to south and 800 km from east to west).

The country may be divided into four principal geological provinces. The first, the mainly mountainous north and west, is divided by four major rivers which drain into the second region, the marshy, alluvial Central Plains, which extends to the Gulf of Thailand. The third region is the north-east, an area of dry, poor soils, derived from sands, clays and salt deposits, (usually referred to as the Khorat Plateau) which drains into the River Mekong dividing Thailand from Laos. The mountain spine which extends down the west of the country continues south as the backbone of the fourth region, the Peninsula. Throughout, we refer to the main body of the country (including the Peninsula north of roughly 11°40′ N latitude) as continental Thailand.

CLIMATE

Thailand has a tropical monsoonal climate, showing distinct wet and dry seasons. Over most of the country, 80 percent of the rain falls during the south-west monsoon, from May to October, so that the months November to April constitute the dry season. The wettest parts of the country, in the Peninsula and in the extreme south-eastern provinces, also receive a good deal of rain from the north-east monsoon, during November to January, and the far southern provinces of Yala and Narathiwat, bordering Malaysia, actually receive over half of their annual rainfall at this time.

The driest, most seasonal areas lie in the very centre of the Khorat Plateau, in the country's north-eastern 'bulge', and in some parts of the west, which lie in the rain shadow of the mountains along the Burmese border. The average annual rainfall of some of these areas is only 1000 mm or a little less. The wettest areas lie in the extreme south-east, and on the west coast of the Peninsula, where the average rainfall is 3000 to 4000 mm per year.

The average annual temperature over most of the country lies in the region of 26–29°C, but there is considerable variation, with the more landlocked parts of the country displaying more variation than the coastal regions. In the hottest month, usually April, daytime temperatures in the lowlands may rise to over 40°C. In the coolest months of December and January, ground frosts are frequently recorded on exposed ridges on the higher mountains of the North.

HABITATS

Terrestrial Forests

The majority of bird species in Thailand are associated with forests, which once covered most of the country's land area. Basically, broad-leaved forests in Thailand may be divided into *deciduous forests*, in which a majority of the trees shed their leaves in response to water stress during the annual dry season, and *evergreen forests* which remain in leaf throughout the year. Trees of the tropical Asian family Dipterocarpaceae usually predominate in most forest types, at least in the lowlands.

The distribution of different forest types is extremely complex and is influenced locally by such factors as topography, exposure, drainage, proximity to watercourses and so on, so that two or three different forest types, with intergradations between them, may occur locally in a mosaic pattern, even in a relatively small area.

Forest cover in Thailand has been very greatly reduced during a prolonged phase of commercial logging and also because of clearance and conversion to agricultural land by the country's predominantly rural population. While lowland forests have been disproportionately affected, populations of ethnically distinct upland shifting cultivators, often referred to collectively as hilltribes, have had a major impact on forest cover in the mountains of the north and west.

Estimates of remaining forest vary, depending upon one's definition of forest, but cover probably lies in the region of 15–20% of the country's land area. The overwhelming proportion of that which remains has been selectively logged or otherwise disturbed.

Deciduous forests

Deciduous forests formerly occupied most of the lowlands and lower hill slopes throughout continental Thailand, much of which is subject to a dry season of five months. Deciduous forests may be further divided into two major easily recognisable subtypes.

Dry dipterocarp forest, sometimes referred to as *savanna forest*, is dominated by up to four species of dipterocarp trees and tends to be a relatively uniform, low and open forest type, with a grassy ground storey. It occurs on the poorest, stoniest soils. Though dry dipterocarp forests are often rich in medium-sized arboreal birds, especially woodpeckers and some members of the crow family, smaller birds are scarcer because of the lack of middle storey and understorey foraging niches. Prinias and munias haunt the grassy ground storey vegetation.

Mixed deciduous forest is a richer, more diverse forest type in which a greater variety of trees occur in a mixed association. Teak (*Tectona grandis*) is co-dominant in one of the sub-types of mixed deciduous forest. The trees are generally taller and the forest more layered than in dry dipterocarp forest, and consequently there are more foraging opportunities for understorey birds. Bamboo is a frequent component of mixed deciduous forests but is usually a sign of a human disturbance, chiefly through the use of fire.

The structure of the bird community in mixed deciduous forests is similar to that found in evergreen forests, and representatives of most landbird families occur.

Evergreen forests

Evergreen forests predominate whenever wetter conditions prevail. In much of continental Thailand, they are chiefly confined to the hill slopes of moderate elevation, where rainfall is higher, or along watercourses, where the soil may be moister, as so-called *gallery forests*. But in the wettest areas of the country, such as the South-east and in the Peninsula, they predominate throughout both the lowlands and the hills. Many authors have used the term *dry evergreen forest* or *semi-evergreen forest* to distinguish the somewhat more seasonal evergreen forests of continental Thailand from *rainforest* in the Peninsula while others use the term *semi-evergreen rainforest* for both the peninsular forests as well as the type of evergreen forests found in the mountains of Khao Yai and elsewhere in continental Thailand. We have therefore used the term *evergreen forest* to refer to all such forest types (including *hill evergreen forest*, mentioned below), while recognising that there are many subtle gradations between them. By and large, *evergreen forests* support the most diverse bird communities of any terrestrial habitat, the species composition of each community varying according to its geographical location.

Hill Evergreen forest

While the lowland terrestrial forests in South-east Asia are dominated by the tree family Dipterocarpaceae, at higher elevations, particularly above ca. 1000 m, other families such as oaks and chestnuts predominate, and form a distinctly different forest type usually referred to as *hill evergreen forest* or more properly as *lower montane forest.* Such forests occur right up to the highest summits, where native rhododendrons and other trees or shrubs of the families Ericaceae and Magnoliaceae are frequent. The largest areas of this habitat are found in northern Thailand, while smaller areas extend along the mountains of the west, down into the Peninsula and in the mountains of the north-east. Hill evergreen forests vary greatly: they may be open, low stature on drier ridges, or tall and dense, with lush understorey vegetation in moist valleys.

Hill evergreen forest is a very important habitat for many species of montane birds, including a host of babblers, resident and wintering warblers, thrushes, and flycatchers.

Pines

Two species of native pines, *Pinus kesiya* and *P. merkusii*, are found in Thailand but pure stands are very limited in extent. Pines most often occur on dry plateaux or ridges and are most often mixed with hill evergreen forests at the higher elevations and with dry dipterocarp forests at lower to moderate elevations.

No species of bird in Thailand is entirely restricted to pines, although one, the Giant Nuthatch, usually occurs where pines and broad-leaved evergreen trees grow in proximity. The Great Tit appears to be restricted to pines in continental Thailand, though it occurs in mangroves in the Peninsula.

Swamp forest

Freshwater swamp forests may once have been widespread in Thailand, but have been almost entirely lost. From the birdwatcher's perspective, they are perhaps best regarded as a special sub-type of lowland evergreen forest with which they share many bird species. An 80 sq km remnant of tall, species-rich peat swamp forest at Pa Phru in the far south, for example, supports a rich variety of arboreal forest birds, much as would be found in terrestrial rainforest. The relative abundance of some understorey and canopy species differs and, understandably, Galliformes and other ground-feeding birds are absent.

Most swamp forests have already been cleared entirely or are now replaced by uniform stands of fire-resistant *Melaleuca* scrub which support many fewer bird species.

Mangrove Forests

Mangroves consitute a distinct forest type composed of trees with a number of specialised adaptations which enable them to survive inundation by saline or brackish waters. They are found in silt-rich sheltered inlets and near the mouths of rivers, often in association with areas of extensive intertidal mudflats. A small number of bird species, such as Brown-winged Kingfisher and Mangrove Pitta, are entirely restricted to mangroves while many other species are shared between mangroves and terrestrial forest or cultivation.

Limestone outcrops

Limestone crags are frequent in many regions of the country and, because of their precipitous topography, they usually remain forested, forming important refuges for a few species of birds which may have disappeared from the deforested, cultivated lowlands. Sheer rock faces may also support a few cliff-nesting birds, such as Peregrine Falcon and Dusky Crag-Martin, while associated caves may support nesting swiftlets. In some parts of the country, the Limestone Wren-Babbler is found among such rocky, wooded outcrops.

Bamboo

Bamboo usually occurs where the original forest has been destroyed or disturbed, especially through the use of fire. While uniform stands of bamboo are generally much less rich in bird species than broad-leaved forest, a number of species are associated with bamboo where it occurs as a component of deciduous or evergreen forest. These include the piculets, Bamboo Wood-pecker, Yellow-bellied Warbler and the Pin-tailed Parrotfinch.

Tree Plantations

Tree plantations in Thailand consist chiefly of monocultures of fire-resistant trees, such as teak, pine or non-native *Eucalyptus*. In the wetter parts of the country such as the Peninsula and the south-east, there are large areas of rubber and oil-palm. Such 'tree crops' have little wildlife conservation importance, supporting few, if any, native forest birds. Generally speaking, the only species which can utilise these habitats are those which are already common in open country and dry farmland.

Untended rubber plantations in which a moist understorey of native forest plants has been allowed to regenerate will sometimes support a number of smaller, more tolerant forest birds.

Farmland

A number of ecologically tolerant, deciduous forest and savanna birds can survive in intensively cultivated farmland provided that some native trees and rough scrub or grassland remain. Some of the typical resident birds of drier open country habitats include the Barred Buttonquail, Barred Owlet, Indian Nightjar, Coppersmith Barbet, Rufous-winged Bushlark, Sooty-headed Bulbul, Grey-breasted Prinia and Ashy Wood-swallow, together with various species of myna and munia. The only babblers common in such open-country habitats are the Yellow-eyed Babbler and Chestnut-capped Babbler, both of which favour tall grass and scrub.

Freshwater wetlands

Wetlands are of major importance for birds, supporting a variety of both breeding and wintering waterfowl such as cormorants, herons, egrets, storks, ducks and waders together with birds of prey and many small birds such as warblers.

Most freshwater wetlands have been very greatly modified. The large expanses of reeds and *Saccharum* grasslands along riverine floodplains have been almost entirely lost, and extensive marshlands have been drained and canalised and turned into rice paddy. A few marshes have been dammed in order to create lakes, some of which still support a good variety of birds, such as Bung Boraphet in central Thailand. Lowland reservoirs often support smaller breeding waterbirds as well as a great many winter visitors and passage migrants. Thailand's large rivers are another important wetland habitat, but have been much changed by intensive human use, including settlement, and deforestation of their banks. A few birds, such as Little Ringed Plovers and Small Pratincoles, still nest on sand and shingle banks of the larger rivers, though larger, more conspicuous birds such as Great Thick-knee and River Tern may have been lost.

In the past 20–30 years, a number of large reservoirs have been created in once forested, steep-sided valleys for hydro-electric power generation. Such reservoirs usually support very few birds, probably because they are too deep and steep-sided, and possess no adjoining marshes.

Rice paddy itself is an important wetland habitat, supporting many birds, especially when newly flooded and being ploughed. Species which prefer rank marsh grasses, however, tend to avoid large expanses of standing rice and are chiefly confined to the grassy margins of the paddies.

Seacoasts, islands

Intertidal mudflats are of very great importance for a host of migrant waders and terns. Many of these species winter in Thailand, but a great many also occur as spring and autumn passage migrants, feeding and 'refuelling' along Thailand's coasts during migration between their Siberian breeding areas and their wintering areas in Indonesia or even Australasia. Sand beaches support small numbers of nesting Malaysian Plovers and Little Terns and, at least formerly, supported the rare Beach Thick-knee.

Small rocky islets, most of which lie off the west coast of the Peninsula and in the inner gulf, are important as nesting areas for a small number of tern species. Larger seabirds such as the Brown Booby almost certainly once nested on such islets off the Thai coasts but the collection of eggs and young by fishermen has led to their extirpation.

Forests on islands are, on the whole, very poor in birds, supporting only a small number of the more ecologically tolerant and edge species. Two pigeons, however, are specifically adapted to live on small forested islands: the Pied Imperial Pigeon particularly favours islands with steep cliffs, while the largely terrestrial Nicobar Pigeon inhabits the forest interior.

ZOOGEOGRAPHY

At the time of writing, 915 species of birds (roughly 10% of the world's bird species) are known from Thailand. Such a high level of diversity can be partly explained by the country's geographical position, at the zoogeographical 'crossroads' of South-east Asia. The lowlands of continental Thailand, a mosaic of dry deciduous and moister evergreen forests, support a fauna which shares affinity either with India and Burma to the west or with Indo-China to the east. In peninsular Thailand, the lowland fauna is predominantly Sundaic, having affinity with Malaysia and with the more westerly islands of Indonesia, the Greater Sundas. The mountains of the North are low outliers of the Tibetan Plateau and support a great diversity of montane birds which are shared with the eastern Himalayas and south-west China.

In addition to the resident species there are a great many visitors and passage migrants from the Palearctic and from the Sino-Himalayan region. The many wintering and migrant species together occupy almost the whole gamut of habitats, lowland and montane, including marshes, paddies, seacoasts, open country and scrub, as well as forests.

We have followed Deignan (1963) in dividing the country into six principal zoogeographic regions. The features of each are set out briefly below.

The North

The North is a mainly mountainous region divided by a number of north–south hilly ridges and drains via the Rivers Ping, Wang, Yom and Nan, southward into the Chao Phraya River of Thailand's Central Plains. Small areas in the north of this region drain into the Mekong River while parts of the west lie in the watershed of the Salween River. Virtually the whole area lies above 200 m elevation, and there are large areas of uplands above 1000 m. Among the few peaks above 2000 m is Doi Inthanon, Thailand's highest mountain (2565 m). Average annual rainfall in the lowlands varies from 1000–1500 mm over most of the region, so that the lower elevations are dominated chiefly by deciduous forests.

The climax vegetation of the higher mountains (above 1000 m) is broad-leaved hill evergreen forest. Native pines are also fairly frequent. The area of both lowland and montane forests has been much reduced and most of what remains is heavily disturbed.

It is in the North that the diversity of montane birds is at its highest, and roughly 50 breeding species appear to be restricted to this region. Babblers, thrushes and flycatchers are particularly well represented, both as breeding birds and as migrant visitors and a great many scarce residents or winter visitors are known only from a small number of peaks in the north of this region.

The majority of lowland birds are shared either with those of western or north-eastern Thailand.

The West

The West is chiefly hilly, extending along the Burmese border, from roughly 16°30' N to 11°40' N. Covering such a great north–south span, the west is an area of great zoogeographical interest, in which northern montane and lowland birds merge with southern lowland forms, including those characteristic of the drier forests of northern Tenasserim as well as a small number of peninsular rainforest species. The mountains are on average lower than those of the North, even though there is one peak over 2000 m, so that there are slightly fewer montane species than in the North.

Much of the area is hot and dry, although rainfall increases further west and south and may be over 2000 mm in some areas fringing the Burmese border. The West is of great conservation importance because it supports the largest remaining expanses of forest and woody secondary growth in Thailand. The lowlands and lower hills are chiefly dominated by mixed deciduous forests, including some large areas of little disturbed valley bottom along the upper reaches of the Khwae river system, the famed 'River Kwai'. Such valley bottoms today still support some of the larger, more sensitive species (such as White-winged Duck and Green Peafowl) which, though once widespread, have vanished from most of their former Thai ranges. In recent years, a small number of Sundaic bird species have been found in patches of evergreen forest, a few hundred kilometres north of their previous known distributional limits, so that there is clearly still much to discover concerning the avifauna of this region.

The North-east

North-east Thailand is a dry plateau at 100 to 200 m elevation which drains into the Mekong River which forms its northern and eastern border. To the west, the plateau is bordered by the flat-topped mountains of the Dong Phaya Yen mountain range and to the south, along the border with Cambodia, by the Phanom Dongrak range. The rainfall is mostly very low (less than 1000 mm in some parts of the centre of the region) and highly seasonal, so that most of the area once supported open deciduous woodlands, chiefly dry dipterocarp, and savanna, with evergreen forests being mostly confined to the mountain slopes. Some lowland evergreen forest formerly occurred in the extreme north-east, bordering the Mekong River, where the rainfall is higher, but has now been almost completely cleared.

The North-east has a long history of intensive human use, and a sophisti-cated, rice-growing culture may have existed as long as 6,500 years ago, so that all of the lowland forests had probably been altered by man long before the twentieth century. Today, the North-east supports a higher human population density than any part of the country except the Central Plains. Because of the generally poor soils and low rainfall, a great many people live at subsistence level. Cutting of wood for fuel has removed almost all of the natural cover and such deforestation, together with the hunting of wildlife for food, has resulted in the almost complete disappearance of many lowland birds, including most larger open country species and even many of the small and ecologically tolerant species which would normally inhabit secondary growth. The former distribution patterns of such species will probably never be elucidated. A number of natural and semi-natural wetlands remain, and are of considerable importance for wintering waterfowl.

The most important forests are found on the flanks of the Dong Phaya Yen range, and form a chain of forest patches extending southwards to Khao Yai in the south-west corner of the region and at the western extremity of the Phanom Dongrak range. The mountains are chiefly flat-topped and rise to a maximum elevation of only a little over 1500 m. The northernmost mountains, such as Phu Luang (1571 m) appear to have a close affinity with the mountains of Nan province in the northern zoogeographic region with which they share many species and subspecies, and, in fact, were treated by Deignan (1963) as belonging to the North. Progressively fewer montane birds are found south-wards towards Khao Yai.

The South-east

The South-east is a predominantly lowland area, bordered to the south and west by the Gulf of Thailand and to the east by the Cambodian border. A belt of dry lowlands along the Bang Pakong River, which runs east–west, separates this region from the North-east. The rainfall in this region is generally higher than in most other regions of continental Thailand, some parts receiving as much as 3000 – 4000 mm of rain per year, and hence most of the lowlands were once covered with evergreen forest. The mountains of Khao Soi Dao, an outlier of the Cardamom Mountains of South-west Cambodia, rise to 1670 m elevation.

The bird fauna of the South-east shows a strong affinity with that of the moist rainforest regions of southern Indo-China, and there are many shared subspecies, both among montane and lowland forms. Additionally there are eight subspecies of lowland or submontane forest birds which are thought to be endemic to this region. Though the mountains of the South-east support a less diverse resident bird fauna than do those of the North and North-east, there are nonetheless apparently four species whose Thai range is entirely restricted to this region: Chestnut-headed Partridge, Blue-rumped Pitta, Eastern Green Magpie and Mountain Fulvetta. The South-east is therefore of great biological and conservation importance.

The Central Plains

This region comprises the alluvial basin of the Chao Phraya River, which enters the Gulf of Thailand at Bangkok. Other major rivers (the Mae Klong and Tachin to the west and the Pa Sak and Bang Pakong to the east) flow through the Central Plains. Most of the area lies below 50 m elevation and some parts in the south are less than 10 m above sea level. The only significant uplands are jagged limestone outcrops and low spurs extending from hill ridges of the surrounding regions. The average annual rainfall may reach 1400 mm on the coast around Bangkok, though rainfall is substantially less (around 1100 mm) in the north of the region, towards Nakhon Sawan.

The formerly extensive swamps and lowland forests of the Central Plains were mostly lost by the early twentieth century as rice became a major export crop. Many of the smaller and more ecologically tolerant marsh-living birds nonetheless continue to survive in marginal growth along canals and around paddies and in other small marshy patches. The wetter southern part of this region, extending north from the coast towards Ayutthaya and Ang Thong, probably supports most of Thailand's significant breeding colonies of cormorants, herons, and egrets. The larger, more strictly swamp-dwelling birds — such as the Spot-billed Pelican, storks (with the exception of the Asian Openbill) and ibises — have been lost as breeding birds though many species still occur as scarce migrant visitors.

The Central Plains have probably long been a barrier to the dispersal of forest birds and there are many instances where the race of a bird in the lowlands of South-east or North-east Thailand differs from that occurring on the west side. A small number of forest birds until recently inhabited moist woody vegetation in the vicinity of the major rivers in the heart of the Central Plains. Now, the only woodland birds which remain are a few of the more ecologically tolerant species which may still be found in larger orchards, wooded gardens and in the grounds of temples where isolated stands of tall *Dipterocarpus alatus* trees remain.

The Central Plains supports many winter visitors from the Palearctic. Ducks roost in large concentrations on a few large water bodies which are protected from disturbance. Many wintering herons, egrets, chats and warblers utilise paddies, other flooded areas, scrub, tall grass and reeds. Although very little mangrove scrub remains around the coast, extensive areas of coastal mudflats extending east and west of Bangkok support large concentrations of wintering and passage shorebirds.

The Peninsula

Peninsular Thailand is considered to extend southwards from roughly 11°40' N latitude. Many continental Thai forms have been recorded this far south on the flanks of the mountain of Khao Luang (1251 m), in Prachuap Khiri Khan province. From then on, southwards, there is a rapid transition to a predominantly Sundaic bird fauna. The Peninsula varies in width from roughly 50 km to 220 km and a mountainous backbone runs its full length. The highest mountain is Khao Luang (1835 m), in Nakhon Si Thammarat province.

The rainfall is less seasonal than in continental Thailand: annual rainfall is over 2000 mm for most of the area and exceeds 3000 mm in some parts. Rainforest is the natural climax vegetation of the Peninsula and formerly covered almost the entire area, the lowlands as well as the hill slopes. Most of the Thai Peninsula being rather more seasonal than Malaysia, many of the subspecies of lowland forest birds differ and many are endemic to peninsular Thailand or are shared with the extreme south of Burma, which supports a similar, somewhat seasonal, type of rainforest vegetation. About 130 species of Thai birds are confined to the Peninsula and while a small number of these are apparently restricted to the extreme southern provinces, the great majority occur (or formerly occurred) throughout, extending almost as far as the northern boundary of the region. The lowland bird community lacks only a few peninsular Malaysian species. In addition, there are a few Indo-Chinese species in peninsular Thailand which either do not cross into Malaysia or which are found only in the far north of that country.

One species, Gurney's Pitta, is entirely restricted to peninsular Thailand and extreme southern Burma. There are a number of others, such as the Fulvous-chested Flycatcher, which are found in both peninsular Thailand and Sumatra, but not in the intervening forests of peninsular Malaysia. The forests in the least seasonal, southernmost provinces of Yala and Narathiwat more closely resemble peninsular Malaysian forests in tree species composition and many birds are of the Malaysian, rather than the penisular Thai, subspecies.

The montane bird fauna is not very rich, since the mountains are very steep and the mountaintop areas very small. None of the endemic, Sundaic montane bird species are known from peninsular Thailand, and relatively few of the mountain bird species found in continental Thailand occur: nonetheless, a number of these (such as the Blue-throated and Golden-throated Barbets; Green-tailed and Black-throated Sunbirds) have diverged into endemic peninsular Thai subspecies.

Almost all of the remaining forest lies on steep hill slopes. A great many lowland rainforest birds, which seem to be wholly or largely confined to the level plains, have therefore disappeared from most of their former range in peninsular Thailand, so that there is probably no single remaining rainforest area which supports a full complement of even the small songbird species. Nevertheless, a few areas of critical conservation importance remain and are protected.

Mangrove forests are an important habitat in the Peninsula, the most extensive and species-rich areas occurring on the west coast. There are also a great many islands, which are important for such island forest species as Nicobar Pigeon as well as for nesting terns.

CONSERVATION

Of the 915 bird species recorded for Thailand, at least 8 (and probably more) species have already been extirpated, while a further 159 or so resident species and 23 migrants (totalling more than 20% of the entire bird fauna) are thought to be at risk, being either endangered or vulnerable. This is an alarmingly high proportion and begs the question of why this should be so, considering that Thailand has relatively good conservation legislation: national parks and wildlife sanctuaries already cover 9% of the land area, and the great majority of bird species have been legally protected from hunting or trade since 1960.

One of the chief reasons for the large number of threatened species is that lowland habitats, whether forests or wetlands, are very poorly represented in the park and sanctuary network; most were cleared and settled before the 1970s, when most of the largest and more significant protected areas were established. At least 70 species of birds are at risk because of the destruction of lowland forests, while another 56 threatened species are associated with wetlands. Lakes are still an important wetland habitat but, because lakes are usually cultivated right to their very shores, they nearly always have lost the adjoining, shallow freshwater swamps and swamp woodlands which would enable large wading birds to feed and to breed.

Even today, the majority of birds are still present in protected areas but particularly for some of the more sensitive lowland species, the areas of habitat remaining may be too small to sustain viable populations. There are also many wetland and open-country birds which are probably prevented from recolonising areas from which they have disappeared through persecution, chiefly hunting for food and capture for the avicultural trade. Hunting is still a major threat to wildlife even in national parks and wildlife sanctuaries, as local people living around protected area margins are very poor and supplement their income by collecting and selling various forest products collected within. Hunters and villagers routinely shoot such large and conspicuous birds as hornbills, and trap ground-living birds such as pheasants, for food. All such hunting and capture is illegal but the efforts of government officials to prevent it are wholly inadequate, so that even such a widespread species as the Great Hornbill, for example, though it occurs in the majority of protected forest areas, may not necessarily have a secure future.

The Thai government suspended logging activities in Thailand in May 1989, so perhaps for the forseeable future, the threat from legal timber extraction may no longer exist. Clearance of forests by landless settlers and illegal logging continue to be major problems, as is the replacement of disturbed or degraded forest (which may still be capable of supporting much wildlife) with monocultures of *Eucalyptus*. In particular, the threats posed by plantation forestry have increased very rapidly over the past few years, partly because Thailand's National Forest Policy fails to distinguish between natural forests and plantations. As native forest cover has been reduced, however, so villagers' awareness of the critical importance of forested watersheds has grown; in some cases, villagers themselves have adopted measures to protect forests.

A further threat to forest birds, the importance of which has been greatly overlooked, is the deliberate burning of forests. Fire has undoubtedly been a most important tool for man in the seasonal tropics for many thousands of years and is still widely used by upland shifting cultivators as well as by lowland Thai farmers to prepare areas for planting each dry season. However, local people also routinely set fires in standing forest, well away from cultivated plots, and this has so far received little attention. Villagers may set forest fires to encourage the growth of mushrooms or bamboo, keep trails open or improve visibility for hunting. Even in parks and sanctuaries, it is not unusual to encounter forest guards intentionally setting fire to the undergrowth either because they mistakenly believe that burning is beneficial to the forest or in order to encourage new grass shoots which may be grazed by large herbivores such as deer and wild cattle.

Undoubtedly, the use of fire in management can be useful should it be necessary to maintain a particular vegetational subclimax. Many of the areas we assume to be natural dry dipterocarp forests may actually be fire-climaxes which have replaced the original moist forest cover. But such burning is carried out even in the moister evergreen forests where natural fires must seldom, if ever, occur. Repeated burning almost certainly prevents the regeneration of the huge dipterocarps, and other larger trees. As a result, large expanses of forest in Thailand are being steadily degraded by fire and are perhaps in a state of transition from high diversity, moist evergreen to low diversity, dry deciduous forest and savanna. This could have very serious consequences for the future of bird communities, and indeed, for many other forest plants and animals. The majority of insectivorous birds are nesting at the height of the dry season, when most fires occur, so that many eggs and young must perish.

In spite of the many problems, there is today a rapidly growing awareness of their severity and a much increased determination to search for solutions. The high level of technical expertise and commitment among the many young Thais working in conservation, both inside and outside government, indicates that many of the critical management issues are now being addressed. Thailand may have already lost a good deal of its native biota, and will doubtless lose some more, but it nonetheless has a good chance of saving much of what remains.

BIRDWATCHING IN THAILAND

FINDING BIRDS

One of the first things that often strikes the casual visitor to Thailand is the apparent scarcity of birds in cities and in open country. Indeed, even the more knowledgeable visitor may think it ironic that birds should be so difficult to find in a country with such a rich fauna. The scarcity of large, conspicuous birds in open areas may be attributed largely to human persecution: possession of firearms is widespread and a great many birds are shot for food or caught for sale as pets. Further, Thailand's lowland areas are so intensively cultivated that patches of semi-natural vegetation which support wildlife are few and far between.

Nevertheless, Thailand remains one of the most exciting countries in Asia for birdwatchers. The more persistent observer will find that there are still a great many birds to see—they are simply rather good at being unobtrusive. Trees in temple grounds or larger gardens, even those in the middle of cities, support a number of small, colourful, birds, such as Coppersmith Barbets, Olive-backed Sunbirds and Scarlet-backed Flowerpeckers. Some smaller marshbirds may be found practically anywhere that has shallow standing water. Mynas are abundant along roadsides in the early morning, but retire to perch quietly in the shade during the heat of the day.

Inevitably, however, the birdwatcher will be drawn to Thailand's forests, with which the majority of resident species are associated. Birdwatching in a tropical forest, though an exciting experience, can also be both daunting and frustrating for the beginner, because the forest is such an unfamiliar environment and one in which it is intrinsically difficult to observe wildlife. In spite of the great variety of bird and insect sounds all around, it is extremely difficult to get clear views of the species from which they emanate. When you do see a bird, apparently well enough to identify it, you may well find, upon opening this book, that it is only one of four or five similar species and that you have overlooked the particular field marks which would have enabled a firm identification. On some occasions, birding can be a sheer delight with a bewildering variety of species in view. Equally, it is sometimes possible to walk for a full hour without seeing a single bird. Because of the special difficulties encountered in forests, therefore, it may be worthwhile devoting some attention to methods of birdwatching in this environment.

Birds are usually more abundant near vegetational breaks of one sort or another, such as the edge of roads, along streams, or where different forest types merge. When entering a new area for the first time, therefore, it is often best to start your birding along the forest edge, as it is here you will encounter the greatest variety of birds for a given period of time. The birds you see may be heavily biased towards the more abundant edge-loving species, but, particularly where tall trees come right up to the road on both sides, there may also be a chance of observing shy species of the forest interior. Even pheasants, which are normally extremely shy, will emerge on to the narrower dirt roads through the forest, especially after rain.

Having gained some familiarity with the commoner edge species, you will want to venture into the forest interior along trails, where these have been established. Although Khao Yai National Park and a small number of other sites have reasonably well-marked trails, the majority of sites still lack properly maintained footpaths so care should always be exercised to avoid getting lost. If one has the slightest doubt about one's ability to follow a trail, one should be accompanied by a park guard. A compass should always be carried, since there will be times when it becomes necessary to stray off a trail while following a bird.

Well-trodden trails tend to have less leaf litter than other parts of the forest floor so that, with care, it is possible to walk silently. One's initial inclination may be to walk extremely slowly, peering under every bush, searching for skulking forest floor species. While this may work well for babblers and warblers, it is much less successful for the shyer species such as pheasants and pittas, which are usually aware of the observer's presence before the observer is aware of them. By walking swiftly and silently along a trail in order to cover as much ground as possible, you often stand a better chance of catching such birds unawares and obtaining views. You should always be ready to lift your binoculars in response to the slightest movement in the undergrowth or on the forest floor. Overall, perhaps, the best technique for birding the forest interior is to alternate between periods of slow-walking and more rapid walking and periods spent standing or sitting wherever any particular features liable to attract birds are present. Sitting down on a fallen log for a few minutes in order to relax and take stock of what you have seen will restore flagging energy and ensure that you are alert when starting out again.

You should look out for flowering or fruiting trees, which can sometimes attract large numbers of feeding birds. In particular, red-flowered trees of the genera *Acrocarpus*, *Bombax*, *Butea* and *Erythrina*, which usually bloom in the dry months, during the early part of the year, support large numbers of Vernal Hanging Parrots, Hair-crested Drongos, starlings and mynas as well as Asian Fairy-bluebirds.

Of the wealth of fruiting trees which can be found throughout the year, the many species of figs (Moraceae) are particularly important. Flocks of green-pigeons *Treron* spp. feed chiefly on the fruits of figs, as do many hornbills, barbets, flowerpeckers and a host of other birds. It is often worthwhile to creep up beneath a towering fig, lying prone on the forest floor and scanning the branches above to watch the comings and goings of the many species feeding there. Some pheasants are also known to feed under figs, taking fallen fruits on the forest floor.

Another useful technique, particularly in the dry season when water supplies are limited, is to sit quietly by a stream, in order to watch birds coming down to drink or bathe. This is best done during the heat of midday or during the afternoon, when feeding activity has declined.

Many insectivorous birds associate in mixed-species flocks or *bird waves*, so actively searching out such bird waves by listening for bird calls is helpful. Sometimes, it is possible to attract small birds by *pishing*: that is, making a squeaking or rasping sound which imitates birds' alarm calls, or by imitating the calls of small owls. The species which works best in this regard is the Collared Owlet, at least in those forests in which it occurs.

In forest, your hearing becomes very important for detecting and identifying birds as, more often than not, you hear a bird calling before seeing it. Once you have learnt to recognise the calls of the majority of species, your perception of their relative abundance may be turned upside-down: some which you previously thought of as rare may turn out to be relatively frequent. Listening for the rustling of leaves on the forest floor is also a good way to detect ground birds.

A word of caution should be added concerning the use of taped bird songs and calls, a practice which is becoming increasingly frequent in Asia. Playing back a bird's territorial call may bring it into view but will also disrupt its behaviour and perhaps also cause some distress to the bird. For this reason we would urge the utmost restraint. We especially wish to discourage the use of tapes on the more heavily frequented trails, particularly those in national parks which may be visited be a great many birdwatchers. If a tape is used at all, then it should be used sparingly, with consideration for the welfare of the bird. In any case, the strongest response to a tape is usually given upon first use. With repeated playbacks, the bird may continue to respond but, because it will by then have detected the observer, it may subsequently give only fleeting views.

In forests, as in other habitats, the early morning, immediately after daybreak, is a particularly good time for detecting birds. Activity declines sharply from late morning onwards and never really picks up again in the late afternoon.

Most forest birds are rather shy, so that it is always better to birdwatch on your own or with one or two others rather than in a large group. Nonetheless, organised nature tour groups do manage to birdwatch very successfully in forest by following certain routines. You should always keep conversation to the minimum and speak only softly. Drab-coloured clothing should be worn and white garments avoided. When walking, it is helpful to deliberately lift your feet at each step in order to avoid shuffling noisily through the leaf-litter. Avoid sudden movements and, if it is necessary to point out a bird to a colleague, raise the arm steadily and smoothly, keeping it close to the body rather than extending it fully.

Another aspect of behaviour which we should mention with regard to birdwatching in national parks and other protected areas concerns the disposal of litter. Very few parks possess proper means for litter disposal so that, even if the visitor places rubbish in litter bins provided, the chances are that it will eventually find its way into the forest, since the contents of litter bins are usually dumped in open pits near park headquarters and periodically burnt. The volume of litter generated by the many visitors to Thailand's parks is such that there is a very real risk of the fires generated by burning rubbish damaging surrounding trees. The conscientious birdwatcher should therefore take the very minimum of plastic or paper wrapping into the forest, and should not dispose of any rubbish within the park but carry it home. Leave the forest exactly as you found it so that others may enjoy it after you.

MAKING OBSERVATIONS

Although the avifauna of Thailand is relatively well-known, there is still a great deal to discover and the birdwatcher who keeps reliable and comprehensive field notes may be in a position to greatly enhance existing knowledge.

1. Distribution

Although many of the richest sites have been well-observed, the majority of protected areas in Thailand are still relatively little known, seldom visited by bird-watchers and lack even simple lists of the species present. The birdwatcher can contribute by visiting these sites and also by visiting those parts of the country which have previously received scant attention, such as the north-east. Although this region is relatively impoverished, it must support great numbers of winter visitors, the distributions of which are poorly known. Another part of the country which has been greatly under-watched is the south-western provinces, where there may be a possibility of discovering northwards range extensions for some peninsular moist forest species.

2. Breeding and seasonality

Although we know in general terms that the majority of insectivorous birds breed during the late dry season and first half of the wet season (from February to July), while most waterbirds breed during the late wet season and early dry season (July to January), we have too little information to carry out any statistical analysis. All records of nesting or other confirmed breeding activity are there-fore extremely important. Although repeated visits to nests can also provide much information on bird biology and behaviour, the duration of incubation and fledging periods and so on, great care needs to be exercised to ensure that the observer does not unwittingly disturb the birds, disrupting their behaviour or exposing the nest to the unwelcome attentions of predators.

3. Feeding behaviour

There is still a great deal to learn concerning the feeding behaviour of birds in the tropics. Which fruiting and flowering trees are used by birds and during which season? Or if a bird takes insects or other animal prey, how does it forage?

4. Migration

Relatively little information exists on the precise timing of migration. When do the first individuals of a given species arrive and when do the last ones depart? When is the timing of peak passage? The observer who repeatedly watches the same limited area, such as the grounds of a temple, a small marsh or similar site, keeping daily or weekly records of the birds seen, is in a particularly good position to contribute to our understanding of migration.

5. **Numbers**

Trying to estimate the absolute numbers or density of birds in forest is fraught with difficulty, and meaningful information can perhaps be gathered only by carrying out detailed mapping, adopting line-transect or other sampling procedures which may be too time-consuming for the birdwatcher. But there are many other instances where counts are easily made and much needed: colonies of nesting or roosting waterbirds; flocks of wintering waterfowl or waders, or unusually large concentrations of any species are all worth reporting. Such counts supplied by birdwatchers are often of crucial importance in formulating plans for the conservation of birds and their habitats.

KEEPING NOTES AND SUBMITTING RECORDS

King et al. (1975) considered that *no new record should be accepted for any part of SE Asia (on any but a hypothetical list) unless supported by a specimen or a recognizable photograph by a reliable observer.* Taking into account recent advances in field identification skills, this would now be regarded as an extreme view especially since collecting may no longer be acceptable. It can also be difficult to obtain identifiable photographs of unusual species. An experienced birdwatcher should, however, be able to take field descriptions of birds which will usually allow their subsequent identification. Good field descriptions are needed not only to validate sight records of species which are new to Thailand but also those of birds which occur infrequently or which are seen in an unexpected region of the country. Observers should first get into the habit by making field notes on some of the more common species. Then, when an unusual bird is encountered, it will be easier to write a good description. A description should include:

> Date
> Time
> Location
> Habitat (including elevation)
> Light and weather conditions
> Details of binoculars/telescope used
> Distance between observer and bird
> Detailed description of bird (size, shape and structure;
>   colour of plumage and bare parts)
> Description of behaviour (posture, flight, gait, feeding, etc.)
> Notes on associated species, if any
> Additional supporting notes, including the observer's familiarity
>   with bird and similar species, and details of unusual
>   weather conditions which could have resulted in the
>   bird's appearance (e.g., a typhoon)

Do not expect to identify every bird which you see. Distance and poor light may make identification difficult and often a bird is seen for only a very short time. Additionally, plumage aberrations (melanism, leucism and albinism) and changes in appearance caused by moult and wear may lead to confusion.

Unusual or significant sightings of birds in Thailand should be submitted either to the the Conservation Data Centre of Mahidol University, or to the Editor, Bangkok Bird Club Bulletin (see below).

ORNITHOLOGICAL AND CONSERVATION BODIES

The following bodies are all concerned with ornithology or with the conservation of Thai birds.

The Bangkok Bird Club promotes birdwatching, information gathering and conservation education throughout Thailand, publishing the monthly *Bangkok Bird Club Bulletin* and organising monthly birdwatching field trips. Address: P.O. Box 13, Ratchathevi Post Office, Bangkok 10401.

The Conservation Data Centre maintains a computerised data base for monitoring the conservation status of birds, mammals and habitats throughout Thailand. It makes this information available to both government and non-government agencies, international conservation bodies, researchers and others. In collaboration with a panel of professional Thai scientists, it serves to evaluate records of birds and other vertebrates and then promotes their publication in appropriate scientific journals. Address: Department of Biology, Mahidol University, Rama 6 Road, Bangkok 10400.

The International Council for Bird Preservation monitors and protects endangered birds and their habitats throughout the world, working through a network of local contacts and scientists to promote awareness, collate information and initiate conservation projects. It produces the *International Bird Red Data Book* in collaboration with IUCN. Address: 32 Cambridge Road, Girton, Cambridge CB3 0PJ, United Kingdom.

The IPT Asian Wetland Bureau is an independent international organization which aims to promote the protection and sustainable utilization of wetland resources in Asia, in conjunction with both governmental and non-governmental agencies. It publishes a regional newsletter, *Asian Wetland News*. Address: Institute of Advanced Studies, University of Malaya, 59100 Kuala Lumpur, Malaysia.

The Oriental Bird Club serves to promote interest in, and the conservation of, birds of the entire Oriental Region. It produces one issue of its journal, *Forktail*, and two bulletins per year. Address: c/o The Lodge, Sandy, Bedfordshire SG19 2DL, United Kingdom.

The Siam Society (Natural History Section) publishes a scientific journal, the *Natural History Bulletin of the Siam Society*, which appears twice per year and usually contains papers on birds, including updates on status and distribution. Address: G.P.O. Box 65, Bangkok 10501.

Wildlife Fund Thailand is an associate of the World Wide Fund for Nature (WWF) concerned with promoting the conservation of all Thai wildlife through conservation education, implementing and administering projects, fundraising and supporting the activities of government conservation agencies. It publishes a monthly newsletter and organises regular field outings to protected areas. Address: 255 Soi Asoke, Sukhumvit 21, Bangkok 10110.

SOME IMPORTANT BIRDWATCHING SITES

The following sites (identified on the map on page 31) are considered to be representative of a variety of different habitats and geographical areas and include many, but by no means all, of the sites of key importance for bird conservation in Thailand. Although some of these sites may be visited during one-day trips, official permission for longer stays should be sought from the Royal Forest Department for those sites which are national parks (NP), wildlife sanctuaries (WS) and non-hunting areas (NHA). Special restrictions apply to wildlife sanctuaries, in which, generally speaking, tourism is not actively encouraged. Maximum elevation (m above sea level) is given for sites which encompass mountains.

1. **Chiang Saen**   Sandbars on the Mekong River, low deforested hills, paddy basins and a nearby lake support a good variety of open country wintering birds, including many scarcer species.

2. **Doi Pha Hom Pok**   2,285 m.   Thailand's second highest mountain. A number of smaller montane forest birds are restricted to this site.

3. **Doi Ang Khang**   1,928 m.   Chiefly deforested, though still fairly rich in smaller montane forest birds, sharing some of the northern specialities found on Doi Pha Hom Pok.

4. **Doi Chiang Dao**   WS. 2,175 m.   Spectacular mountain scenery. Supports a rich variety of montane birds associated with the more open hill evergreen forest and pines.   Relatively dense, submontane evergreen forest extends down to the foothills in some parts.

5. **Doi Suthep-Pui**   NP.   1,685 m.   Fairly rich in montane forest birds; easy access from Chiang Mai.

6. **Doi Inthanon**   NP.   2,565 m.   Montane and submontane forest birds. One of the richest birdwatching sites in the entire country, with a unique patch of forest around the summit extending almost 300 m higher than that on any other mountain. Dry dipterocarp woodland on the lower slopes still supports many birds. Easy access, with a road leading to the summit.

7. **Umphang** WS. 2,152 m. Higher elevation forest remnants are still fairly rich in montane forest birds, including a few species which either do not extend into northern Thailand or which are much scarcer there. Transected by a metalled road.

8. **Huai Kha Khaeng** WS. 1,554 m. One of the richest sites for birds remaining anywhere in continental Thailand and certainly the best single site for lowland deciduous forest birds. Also supports both submontane and montane evergreen forest.

9. **Phu Luang** WS. 1,571 m. A flat-topped mountain which is among the richest known sites for montane forest birds in north-east Thailand. Good submontane evergreen and deciduous forests are present on the mountain flanks.

10. **Phu Wua** WS. 449 m. One of the last remnant patches of lowland forest in the north-east. Still relatively little-known.

11. **Nong Han Kumphawapi** Freshwater lake and marsh; good for wintering waterfowl and marsh birds.

12. **Nam Nao** NP. 1,271 m. Supports a good variety of deciduous and evergreen forest birds.

13. **Phu Khieo** WS. 1,310 m. Together with Nam Nao NP, constitutes part of a large, contiguous forest block supporting a rich variety of deciduous and evergreen forest birds.

14. **Nong Lahan** Freshwater lake and associated marshland. Good for wintering waterbirds.

15. **Khao Yai** NP. 1,351 m. Some of the least disturbed and most accessible tall forest anywhere in the country, supporting a good variety of lowland and submontane forest birds.

16. **Khao Ang Ru Nai** WS. 777 m. Situated in the last true lowland forest remnant in south-east Thailand and supporting a number of species which are scarce or absent elsewhere.

17. **Khao Soi Dao** WS. 1,670 m. Montane and submontane forest; the principal station in Thailand for a small number of Indochinese montane birds.

18. **Ban Lung Tua** (Nong Nam Khao NHA). Ponds protected by a local farmer. One of the best sites for wintering waterfowl in the entire country.

19. **Bung Boraphet** NHA. One of the most important wetlands in the country, supporting large numbers of breeding and wintering waterfowl.

20. **Bung Kroeng Kavia** NHA. 1,739 m. Mixed deciduous and evergreen forests which support a rich variety of resident and migrant birds. This is the most northerly known station for a small number of resident species which are otherwise known only in the Peninsula.

21. **Gulf of Thailand** Extensive intertidal mudflats which support spectacular concentrations of wintering and passage shorebirds. The best observation points are at Bang Poo and between the mouths of the Tachin and Mae Klong Rivers.

22. **Kaeng Krachan** NP. 1,513 m. Thailand's largest national park; still comparatively little-known, but exceedingly rich, supporting lush evergreen forest.

23. **Khao Sam Roi Yot** NP. 605 m. The largest reedswamp in the country. Sand beaches and mudflats support wintering and passage shorebirds.

24. **Khlong Nakha** WS. 1,395 m. Dense rainforest on hill slopes. Supports a fair variety of lowland forest birds in small areas of valley bottom forest.

25. **Khao Luang** NP. 1,835 m. An important site for montane and submontane rainforest species in the Peninsula.

26. **Khanab Nam, Krabi.** Supports an extremely rich variety of mangrove birds. Accessible by boat hired in the town of Krabi.

27. **Khao Pra-Bang Khram** NHA. 650 m. Small remnant patches of lowland forest at the foot of forested hills constitute one of the foremost remaining birdwatching sites in peninsular Thailand.

28. **Khao Banthad** WS. 1,350 m. Submontane and montane rainforest birds.

29. **Thalae Noi** NHA. A freshwater lake and marsh supporting a good variety of smaller breeding waterfowl and many wintering egrets.

30. **Ko Libong** NHA. One of the most important sites for wintering and passage shorebirds in the Peninsula.

31. **Ton Nga Chang** WS. 932 m. Tall forest on hill slopes is still rich in many lowland or submontane forest species.

32. **Pa Phru** NHA. The last remnant of primary peat swamp forest in Thailand. Extremely rich in many arboreal lowland forest birds, and may be the last remaining site in the Peninsula for a number of species.

33. **Mu Ko Surin** NP. Among the best and least disturbed of forested islands, supporting a relatively rich avifauna.

LIST OF NATIONAL PARKS AND WILDLIFE SANCTUARIES

(Survey level: 2 = fairly comprehensive bird list; 1 = preliminary bird list available;
0 = not surveyed or very little information)

National Parks	Survey Level	Land Area [sq km]
1. Khao Yai	2	2168
2. Phu Kradeung	1	348
3. Thung Salaeng Luang	1	1317
4. Khao Sam Roi Yot	2	98
5. Nam Nao	2	962
6. Doi Inthanon	2	482
7. Phu Phan	0	665
8. Tarutao	1	260
9. Khao Luang	1	570
10. Doi Khun Tan	1	255
11. Khao Sabap (Namtok Phriu)	1	135
12. Erawan	0	550
13. Khao Chamao-Khao Wong	1	84
14. Khao Kitchakut	1	59
15. Lansang	0	104
16. Phu Rua	0	120
17. Chaloem Rattanakosin	1	59
18. Ramkhamhaeng	1	341
19. Sai Yok	1	500
20. Thaleban	2	101
21. Mu Ko Ang Thong	1	18
22. Khao Sok	2	645
23. Tat Ton	0	217
24. Doi Suthep-Pui	2	261
25. Ao Phangnga	1	53
26. Sri Satchanalai	1	213
27. Khao Sam Lan	2	45
28. Kaeng Krachan	1	2910
29. Mu Ko Surin	1	33
30. Khao Phanom Bencha	2	50
31. Hat Nai Yang	2	22
32. Mae Ping	0	1003
33. Kaeng Tana	0	80
34. Mu Ko Samet	2	8
35. Wiang Kosai	1	410
36. Hat Chao Mai	0	94
37. Namtok Mae Surin	0	397
38. Sri Nakarin	0	1532
39. Thap Lan	0	2240
40. Taksin Maharat	0	149
41. Pang Sida	0	844
42. Khao Pu-Khao Ya	1	694
43. Mu Ko Similan	1	14
44. Khlong Lan	1	300
45. Mu Ko Chang	1	192
46. Laem Son	1	48

National Parks	Survey Level	Land Area [sq km]
47. Mu Ko Pi Pi	2	64
48. Phu Hin Rong Kla	1	307
49. Mu Ko Phetra	0	26
50. Phu Kao-Phu Phan Kham	1	322
51. Mae Yom	1	455
52. Khao Lam Pi	1	72
53. Phu Jong Na Yoi	0	686
54. Mae Wong	0	941
55. Namtok Chatakan	0	543
56. Sri Phangnga	1	283
57. Huai Huad	0	829
58. Jaeson	1	592
59. Mukdahan	0	49
60. Sri Lanna	0	1406

Wildlife Sanctuaries	Survey Level	Land Area [sq km]
1. Salak Phra	1	859
2. Khlong Nakha	2	480
3. Phu Khieo	1	1560
4. Khao Soi Dao	2	745
5. Huai Kha Khaeng	2	2575
6. Lum Nam Pai	1	1194
7. Thung Yai Naresuan	2	3200
8. Khao Khieo-Khao Chomphu	2	145
9. Khlong Saeng	2	1155
10. Phu Luang	1	848
11. Phu Wua	1	187
12. Khao Banthad	2	1267
13. Yot Dom	0	203
14. Khao Ang Ru Nai	2	108
15. Phu Miang-Phu Thong	0	545
16. Ton Nga Chang	1	182
17. Maenam Phachi	0	489
18. Mae Tuen	0	1173
19. Doi Chiang Dao	2	521
20. Salawin	1	875
21. Khao Phanom Dongrak	0	316
22. Doi Pha Muang	1	583
23. Khlong Phraya	2	95
24. Doi Pha Chang	1	577
25. Om Koi	2	1224
26. Doi Luang	1	97
27. Khao Sanam Phriang	0	101
28. Mae Yuam Fang Khwa	1	292
29. Sap Langka	1	154
30. Rap Ro	2	455
31. Umphang	1	2548

Other categories of protected area (e.g., non-hunting areas and forest parks) are not listed. Further information about protected areas is available from the National Parks Division and the Wildlife Conservation Division of the Royal Forest Department.

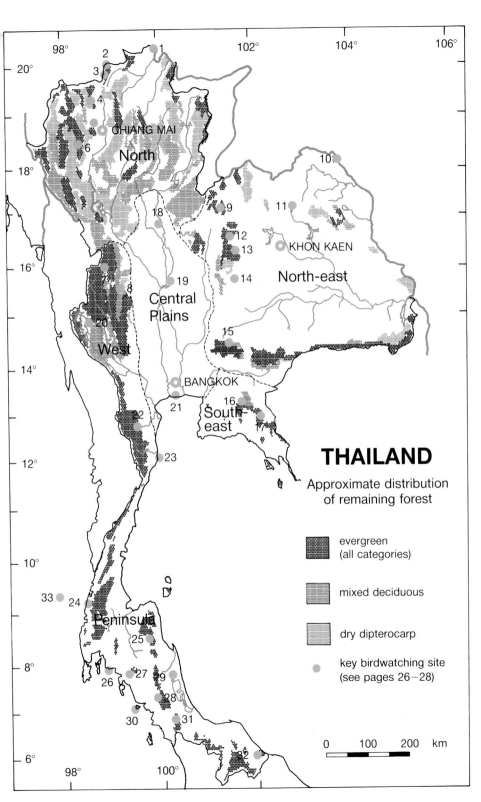

98°   100°   102°   104°   106°

20°

2   1

3

4

CHIANG MAI

North

6

18°   10

18   11

9   KHON KAEN

16°   12
                                             13
                     19   North-east
7   14
8

Central
Plains
20

15

West

14°
                     BANGKOK
                 21   South-
16   east
                            22   17

THAILAND

12°   23

Approximate distribution
of remaining forest

evergreen
(all categories)

10°

mixed deciduous

dry dipterocarp

33   24   key birdwatching site
Peninsula   (see pages 26–28)

25

8°

27
26   29

28

0   100   200   km

30   31

6°   32

98°   100°

HOW TO USE THIS BOOK

NOMENCLATURE AND TAXONOMIC ORDER

Common names are based chiefly on King, Dickinson, and Woodcock (1975) *Field Guide to the Birds of South-East Asia.* This book was the first serious effort to standardise English vernacular names for South-East Asian birds, and it seems certain to remain the best field reference for the entire region for many years. Where we differ, either because of the need to recognise recent taxonomic revisions, or because we consider that other, more widely used names are more suitable, we have given King's name in parentheses. Other sources for English names used are King (in litt.) and Voous (1977). Some names have been adopted following discussion with the nomenclature committee of the Oriental Bird Club.

The species are numbered sequentially in the order in which they appear. The basic order usually follows Deignan (1963), but since this is primarily an identification manual we have felt free to depart from taxonomic sequence where this either facilitates comparison between physically similar, but unrelated species (e.g., swifts and swallows; larks and pipits) or because of the constraints of layout.

While we are aware of the recent revision of the classification of birds brought about by the DNA-DNA hybridisation studies of Professor Charles Sibley and his collaborators, we have adopted revised family headings only where this was possible without necessitating major changes in sequence.

SPECIES ACCOUNTS

Size
Approximate total body length in centimetres follows the scientific name. Where there is a marked variation in size, as for example in sexually dimorphic species, the size range is given.

Description
The text aims to complement the illustrations, concentrating principally upon field marks rather than on comprehensive plumage descriptions. The reader is referred to the glossary and to the bird topography drawings for a definition of any technical terms used. Male, female and immature plumages are described where these are distinctively different, as are differences between subspecies where these may be readily separated in the field. The symbol ◆ indicates that the text referring to a particular age or sex class has ended and that further description refers to the species as a whole.

Voice
Voice descriptions are those assigned by the authors on the basis of field experience or after listening to their own tapes or those provided by others, except where stated. In some cases we have either quoted voice descriptions provided by Arnoud van den Berg (AvdB); Ben King (BK); Jelle Scharringa (JS); Uthai Treesucon (UT) or D.R. Wells (DRW); or have followed published descriptions in Medway and Wells, 1976 (M&W) or Smythies, 1986.

Habitat

The occurrence of every species by vegetation type, together with its altitudinal range is described. Where we say that a species occurs from plains to 1000 m, this indicates that the species normally occurs in the level lowlands and also ascends the hill slopes up to a limit of about 1000 m elevation.

The term *secondary growth* has been used to indicate the mid-successional stages which characterise an area in which the forest has been cut, and subsequent cultivation abandoned; it implies a degree of recolonisation by pioneer or secondary forest trees which yields some understorey shade. For recently cleared and open areas which support only low bushes and tangles, we have used the term *scrub*.

Abundance

Each species is assigned to one of six categories: very rare, rare, uncommon, fairly common, common and very common. It is frequently very difficult to apply these categories uniformly across species. The size disparity and different trophic level (position in the food chain) of, say, an eagle and a warbler are such that the former would normally be much scarcer than the latter, even should both occur at optimal density in a given piece of habitat. The great majority of small resident birds tend to be common or even very common in their preferred habitat and geographical range. Should a species be classified as *rare* if it is restricted to a single mountaintop, even if it is abundant there? Since the range of the species is evident from the maps, we have not used *rare* in this context, and instead have opted for the term *locally common*.

Another difficulty in describing abundance is that species are not always uniformly abundant throughout their entire geographical ranges or through the whole spectrum of habitats which they occupy. Where a species' abundance varies greatly in different parts of the country, this is usually mentioned.

We have reserved the term *very rare* for those species for which there are fewer than five records or those which, even though they may once have been common, appear to be on the brink of extinction.

Seasonality and distribution

The following terms are used to categorize seasonal status.

Resident: a species which is present throughout the year and which breeds or is presumed to breed.

Non-breeding visitor: most non-breeding visitors are referred to as *winter visitors* since they normally enter Thailand for the duration of the Palearctic winter, from September to May. A few, such as the Grey Wagtail, for example, may begin to arrive as early as July; in other winter visitors, such as some shorebirds, a small proportion of birds, (probably those which are too young to breed or too unfit to migrate back north), may linger on in Thailand for the Palearctic summer.

Passage migrant: a species which occurs as a transient visitor, chiefly in spring (March to May) or autumn (August to November) while on migration between its breeding grounds to the north of Thailand and its wintering grounds to the south. Occasionally, a few individuals may linger throughout the winter though the bulk of the population clearly does not winter in Thailand.

Breeding visitor: a species which migrates into Thailand for part of the year in order to breed. Most such breeding visitors (such as the Blue-winged Pitta) arrive to nest during the wet season, from late April or early May onwards. A few breeding visitors, however, such as the Asian Openbill, arrive to nest in the dry season.

In many species, different populations have different patterns of seasonality. The Grey-headed Flycatcher, for example, is resident in the north, west and in the Peninsula. But in some parts of the east, it is known only as a winter visitor. Such species might be described as *partial migrants*.

We have purposely refrained from using the term *vagrant* since this implies that the species is of accidental occurence, having strayed well outside its usual range. Among the birds known for Thailand, some are undoubtedly genuine vagrants but there are also many more which, although they may have only been recorded once or twice, must occur more frequently than is presently known. With increased coverage, patterns of occurrence among Thai birds will become much better understood.

RANGE

The distributions depicted in the maps represent, as far as possible, the known contemporary distribution, based on reliable sight records, museum specimens and published records. Where widely scattered records are apparently linked by suitable habitat for the species, the intervening area is shaded in. Historical records are included where the habitat in which a particular species was found still remains. Asterisks have been used to indicate the approximate ranges of those species which are thought to have been extirpated or which have apparently vanished from large segments of their former range.

Even the most recent forest cover maps continue to depict northern Thailand as being mainly wooded and therefore many of the forest birds which occur in the north are shown in the distribution maps as occurring throughout. In reality, their distribution may be extremely patchy within a total range, especially for those species depending on moister, less disturbed forest, since much of the forest area is now comprised of drier, secondary deciduous forest and scrub.

Where both breeding and wintering populations occur in the same area, we have not been able to display this in the distribution maps, which are shaded as for a resident. Where it is uncertain whether a species is a resident or winter visitor, the species is shaded as for a winter visitor.

KEY TO DISTRIBUTION MAPS

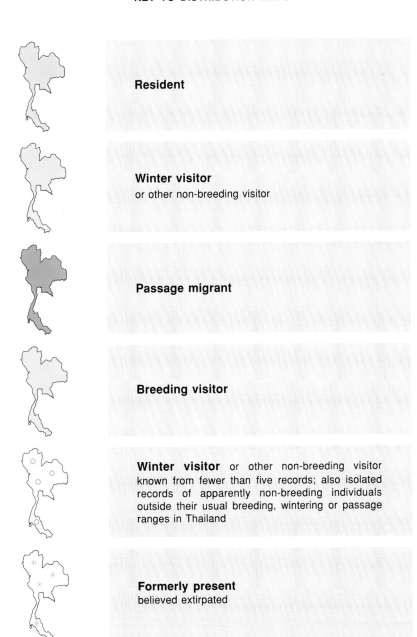

Resident

Winter visitor
or other non-breeding visitor

Passage migrant

Breeding visitor

Winter visitor or other non-breeding visitor
known from fewer than five records; also isolated
records of apparently non-breeding individuals
outside their usual breeding, wintering or passage
ranges in Thailand

Formerly present
believed extirpated

BIRD TOPOGRAPHY DIAGRAMS

(Reproduced from Grant and Mullarney 1988—1989. The New Approach to Identification.)

HEAD: plumage marks

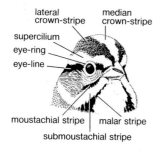

lateral crown-stripe · median crown-stripe · supercilium · eye-ring · eye-line · moustachial stripe · malar stripe · submoustachial stripe

PASSERINE: wing-feather tracts

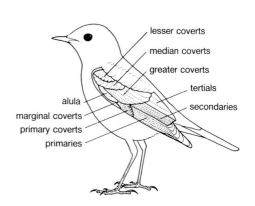

lesser coverts · median coverts · greater coverts · tertials · secondaries · alula · marginal coverts · primary coverts · primaries

HEAD: bare parts

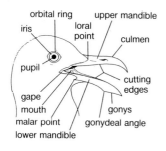

orbital ring · upper mandible · iris · loral point · culmen · pupil · cutting edges · gape · mouth · gonys · malar point · gonydeal angle · lower mandible

PASSERINE: body-plumage tracts

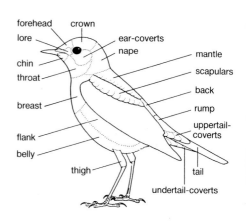

forehead · crown · lore · ear-coverts · nape · mantle · chin · throat · scapulars · back · breast · rump · uppertail-coverts · flank · belly · thigh · tail · undertail-coverts

WADER: mantle, scapulars and wing

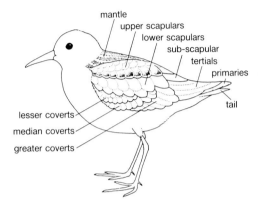

mantle
upper scapulars
lower scapulars
sub-scapular
tertials
primaries
tail
lesser coverts
median coverts
greater coverts

UPPERWING

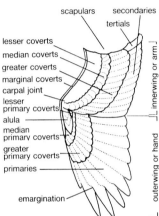

scapulars
secondaries
tertials
lesser coverts
median coverts
greater coverts
marginal coverts
carpal joint
lesser primary coverts
alula
median primary coverts
greater primary coverts
primaries
emargination
innerwing or arm
outerwing or hand

WADER: head, underparts and leg

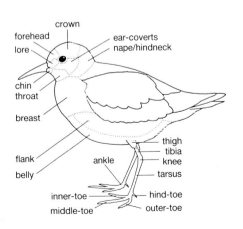

crown
forehead
lore
ear-coverts
nape/hindneck
chin
throat
breast
thigh
tibia
knee
flank
ankle
belly
tarsus
inner-toe
middle-toe
hind-toe
outer-toe

UNDERWING

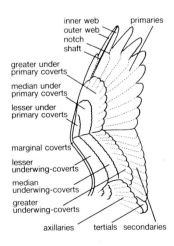

inner web
outer web
notch
shaft
primaries
greater under primary coverts
median under primary coverts
lesser under primary coverts
marginal coverts
lesser underwing-coverts
median underwing-coverts
greater underwing-coverts
axillaries
tertials
secondaries

SYSTEMATIC SECTION

40

GREBES: Family *Podicipedidae*. Strictly aquatic, swimming and diving birds with pointed bills and lobed toes. Weak fliers; patter along the surface of the water before taking flight. Feed on small aquatic animals; nest on floating vegetation. Sexes similar. Cosmopolitan distribution. World: 20 species. Thailand: 2 species.

1. Little Grebe *Tachybaptus ruficollis* S: 25   นกเป็ดผีเล็ก

The smallest duck-like bird, with a thin, pointed bill and a truncated, tailless appearance. In flight, shows mainly dark wings with narrow white trailing edge to secondaries. **Non-breeding:** upperparts dark grey-brown; sides of head and underparts paler, grading to whitish on flanks and belly. **Breeding:** dark chestnut sides to head and neck. Shows conspicuous yellow-green spot at base of bill; yellow eye. **Juvenile:** shows bold, blackish stripes on head and neck. ◆ Seldom flies, preferring to dive when alarmed. Can be very secretive when breeding, though often seen in large flocks on open water outside the breeding season. **Voice:** a shrill, whinnying trill, rather like the calls of some crakes, *Porzana* spp. **Habitat:** marshes, ponds, lakes and canals. Very common resident.

2. Great Crested Grebe *Podiceps cristatus* S: 48   นกเป็ดผีใหญ่

A duck-like swimming bird but with a long, slender neck and a dagger-like bill. In flight, shows white leading edge to wing and a square white patch on secondaries; neck held slightly drooped. Dives. **Non-breeding:** white face and neck, with blackish crown and white stripe over eye. Upperparts and narrow line down back of neck dark grey-brown. Bill dull pinkish at base. **Breeding:** prominent chestnut and black frills on sides of head. **Habitat:** lakes, reservoirs. Very rare winter visitor.

CORMORANTS: Family *Phalacrocoracidae*. Large, blackish, aquatic birds with webbed feet, and strong, hook-tipped bills. Bill often held slanted upwards when swimming on surface; dive beneath surface for fish. Strong and direct flight on short broad wings; neck held outstretched. Roost and nest in colonies in trees; frequently perch with wings held outstretched in order to dry them. Sexes similar. World: 27–28 species. Thailand: 3 species.

3. Great Cormorant *Phalacrocorax carbo* S: 82   นกกาน้ำใหญ่

Distinguished by large size and by heavy bill; white throat. Rest of plumage blackish with bronze sheen on back. **Breeding:** shows a white thigh patch and a whitish sheen around head and neck. **Immature:** dark brown above and whitish below. Underparts become progressively darker with age. **Habitat:** marshes, rivers and seacoasts. May formerly have bred; now rare winter visitor.

Plate 1 Grebes, Cormorants, Oriental Darter

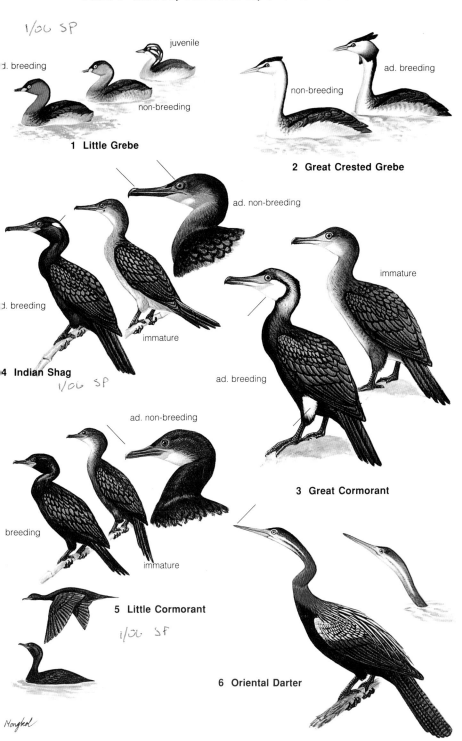

1/06 SP

juvenile

d. breeding

non-breeding

1 Little Grebe

non-breeding

ad. breeding

2 Great Crested Grebe

ad. non-breeding

immature

d. breeding

immature

4 Indian Shag

1/06 SP

ad. breeding

ad. non-breeding

3 Great Cormorant

breeding

immature

5 Little Cormorant

1/06 SP

6 Oriental Darter

Mongkol

4. Indian Shag *Phalacrocorax fuscicollis* S: 64 นกกาน้ำปากยาว

Intermediate in size between Great and Little Cormorants. Head and bill much less heavy than Great; bill much longer than that of Little. Sometimes shows whitish border to yellow-green gular pouch. **Adult:** blackish plumage; breeding birds show a tuft of white feathers behind bright green eye. **Immature:** brownish above, scaled with black; underparts dirty whitish. **Habitat:** inland waters, especially the larger rivers; mangroves and coastal fish ponds. Local and uncommon resident.

5. Little Cormorant *Phalacrocorax niger* S: 52 นกกาน้ำเล็ก

Smaller than other cormorants, with a distinctive short bill, and a comparatively short neck with a heavy jowl. **Adult:** blackish plumage with a small, diffuse whitish throat patch in winter. Shows a silky white sheen on head and neck in breeding plumage. **Immature:** paler and browner than adult; extent of whitish on underparts confined to neck and upper breast. **Habitat:** inland waters, canals and flooded paddyfields; mangroves and coastal areas. Common resident.

วงศ์นกอ้ายงั่ว

DARTERS: Family *Anhingidae*. Similar to cormorants, but differ in having slender, dagger-like bills and thinner, snake-like necks. Sexes similar. World: 4 species. Thailand: one species.

6. Oriental Darter *Anhinga melanogaster* S: 91 นกอ้ายงั่ว

Diagnostic long, snaky neck and slender, pointed bill. Head and neck brown; wings and body blackish. Whitish streaks on sides of neck and on upperparts. In flight, shows peculiar kink in outstretched neck and long tail. Spears fish underwater with pointed bill; swims with body submerged and outstretched head and neck protruding. Occasionally in soaring flight. **Habitat:** slow flowing rivers, canals, lakes and marshes. Rare resident; may no longer breed and now endangered.

วงศ์นกจมูกหลอด

TUBENOSES: Family *Procellariidae*. Pelagic seabirds which usually come inland only when nesting or when storm-driven. Bill shows tubular nostrils and a hooked tip; long, narrow wings. Usually fly close to the ocean surface. Feed on small fish, squid or plankton. Sexes similar. World: 93 species. Thailand: 3 species. (See under Additions, page 397.)

7. Streaked Shearwater *Calonectris leucomelas* S: 48 นกจมูกหลอดลาย

Diagnostic whitish facial area and forecrown, contrasting with darker streaked hindcrown and nape. Upperparts brownish; underparts white and underwing white with broad dark hind margin and usually some dark carpal markings. Flies with short bursts of wing flaps interspersed with long periods of banking on rigid wings. **Habitat:** oceans, coastal waters. Very rare visitor; one found in Maha Sarakham Province, presumably blown inland, after a typhoon in October 1967.

Plate 2 Shearwaters, Boobies

upperwing

underwing

upperwing

underwing

7 Streaked Shearwater

8 Short-tailed Shearwater

ad. upperwing

juv. upperwing

juv. underwing

9 Masked Booby

ad. upperwing

ad. underwing

juv. underwing

10 Brown Booby

Mongkol

8. Short-tailed Shearwater *Puffinus tenuirostris* S: 42   นกจมูกหลอดหางสั้น

A medium size, all sooty-brown shearwater with a greyish wing lining. Fast flight, short bursts of rapid wingbeats alternating with stiff-winged glides. **Habitat:** oceans, coastal waters. Visitor of uncertain status; has once been captured at sea off Phuket Island by fishermen.

วงศ์นกบู๊บบี้

BOOBIES: Family *Sulidae*. Large seabirds with long, pointed wings and wedge-shaped tails; long pointed bills and webbed feet. Feed on fish by plunge-diving. Strong, graceful flight. Sexes similar. World: 9 species. Thailand: 2 species.

9. Masked Booby *Sula dactylatra* S: 86   นกบู๊บบี้หน้าดำ

Adult: easily identified by white body and coverts, black flight feathers of wings and tail and black face with yellowish bill. **Juvenile:** from Brown Booby by paler brown upperparts, whitish collar across back of neck and by less brown on the foreneck. **Habitat:** seacoasts, islands. Very rare visitor.

10. Brown Booby *Sula leucogaster* S: 74   นกบู๊บบี้สีน้ำตาล

Adult: entire upperparts, head, neck and upper breast chocolate-brown and contrasting sharply with white belly, underwing coverts and under tail coverts. **Juvenile:** contrast muted, with white parts of plumage washed pale brownish. ◆ Bill bluish white or greenish yellow; usually dull pinkish in juvenile. **Habitat:** seacoasts, islands. Rare visitor; probably once bred on islets in the Gulf and off the Peninsula, but now believed extirpated due to theft of eggs and young by fishermen.

วงศ์นกโจรสลัด

FRIGATEBIRDS: Family *Fregatidae*. Oceanic birds with angular, pointed wings and long, forked tails which are capable of soaring for hours without flapping. Never land on the water surface. Feet only partially webbed. Feed on fish or squid, picked from the surface or pirated from other seabirds. In breeding displays, the males inflate their red gular pouches, sometimes even in flight. Juveniles have pale, either white or rufous heads and usually a dark breast band. Nest in colonies on islands, though no species breed in Thai waters. World: 5 species. Thailand: 3 species.

11. Christmas Frigatebird *Fregata andrewsi* S: 95   นกโจรสลัดเกาะคริสต์มาส

Adult male: shows diagnostic white patch on lower belly, contrasting with black head and upper breast. **Female and immature:** combination of extensively white underparts, extending to lower abdomen; dark spurs on sides of upper breast and prominent white spurs on underwing are diagnostic. Adult female has black head and throat. **Juvenile:** differs from female in having head always pale tawny and usually a complete breast band. **Habitat:** coastal, offshore waters. Uncommon, non-breeding visitor; may be present all year.

Plate 3 Frigatebirds

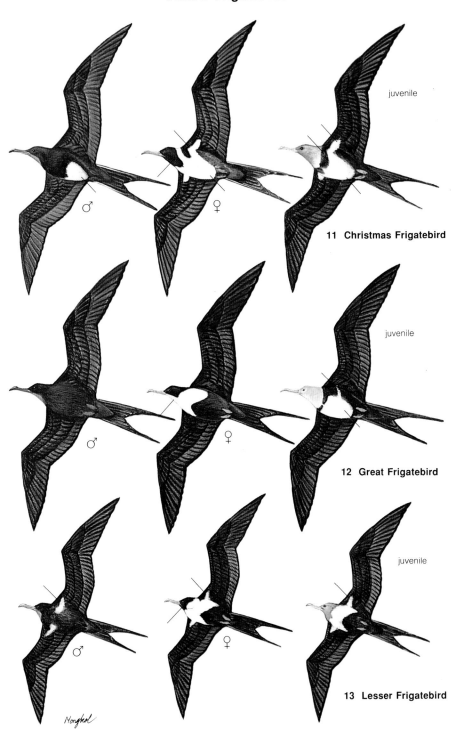

♂
♀
juvenile
11 Christmas Frigatebird

♂
♀
juvenile
12 Great Frigatebird

♂
♀
juvenile
13 Lesser Frigatebird

Mongkol

12. Great Frigatebird *Fregata minor* S: 95   นกโจรสลัดใหญ่

Adult male: all dark apart from red gular pouch (which usually invisible in the field). **Female and immature:** white belly patch extensive, recalling Christmas Frigatebird but white spurs on base of underwing are usually lacking or, if present, are very faint. Adult female shows black head and dusky throat. **Juvenile:** shows either dark russet, tawny or whitish head and partial or complete breast band. **Habitat:** coastal, offshore waters. Rare visitor (the rarest frigatebird in Thai waters).

13. Lesser Frigatebird *Fregata ariel* S: 78   นกโจรสลัดเล็ก

Smaller than the other frigatebirds. **Adult male:** all dark, with white underwing spurs and axillaries. **Female and immature:** show white spurs on base of underwing, but have a less extensive white area on underbody than Christmas, with a concave hind border. **Adult female:** black head and throat. **Juvenile:** rusty head and partial or complete breast band. **Habitat:** coastal, offshore waters. Uncommon visitor; probably the most numerous frigatebird in Thai waters.

วงศ์นกยาง

HERONS: Family *Ardeidae.* Long-legged, long-necked wading birds with dagger-like bills. Fly slowly with regular wingbeats, on broad, rounded wings; head and neck held folded close to body and legs trailing. Many utter harsh, deep croaking notes. Feed on small fish, aquatic animals, insects, etc., caught with a stab of the bill while wading in shallow water or stalking in reedbeds or grassland. Many species nest in colonies (sometimes with cormorants or storks) and build shallow stick platforms in trees. Some species are crepuscular or nocturnal. Sexes similar or nearly so. Some species develop ornamental plumes on head, neck and scapulars during the breeding season. World: 62 species. Thailand: 19 species.

14. Great-billed Heron *Ardea sumatrana* S: 114   นกกระสาใหญ่

Larger than the Grey Heron, with darker, more uniformly grey plumage which lacks any sharp contrasts. Larger bill with angled gonys. In flight, wings uniform both above and below. **Adult breeding:** whitish plumes on nape, scapulars and breast. **Immature:** slightly browner with rufous to buff tips to feathers of upperparts; lacks the whitish plumes of the adult. ◆ Legs and bill dark. **Habitat:** coastal islands, mangroves. Very rare resident; much reduced due to persecution and habitat destruction.

15. Grey Heron *Ardea cinerea* S: 102   นกกระสานวล

A large, mainly light grey heron; in flight shows pronounced contrast between pale grey upperwing coverts and blackish flight feathers. Uniform greyish underwing. **Adult:** white head and neck, black line through eye and crest, black streaks on neck. **Juvenile:** greyer head and neck, with reduced contrast. **Habitat:** inland and coastal marshes, mangroves, mudflats, lakes and paddyfields. Fairly common winter visitor; formerly bred.

Plate 4 Large Herons

14 Great-billed Heron

15 Grey Heron

adult

juvenile

adult

juvenile

16 Purple Heron

adult

juvenile

Mongkol

16. Purple Heron *Ardea purpurea* S: 97 นกกระสาแดง

Darker plumage than Grey Heron with rufous neck and underparts. More angular appearance with thinner bill and more pronounced downward neck bulge and longer trailing legs in flight. **Adult:** greyish upperwing coverts and darker flight feathers, but less contrasting than in Grey Heron; rufous wing lining. Black line down side of neck and black cheek bar. **Juvenile:** brownish upperwing coverts; sandy-rufous neck lacks any strong markings. **Habitat:** marshes, lakes and rivers; also occasionally intertidal areas. Breeds in the larger reedswamps. Local and uncommon resident. Common migrant and winter visitor.

17. Chinese Pond-Heron *Ardeola bacchus* S: 46 นกยางกรอกพันธุ์จีน

A comparatively short-necked and compact heron which shows white wings contrasting with dark mantle in flight, with legs projecting only a short way beyond tail. Possibly inseparable from Javan Pond-Heron in winter and immature plumages, although may show more obvious dusky tips to outermost primaries. **Non-breeding:** at rest, appears brownish with buffy, dark-streaked head, neck and breast. **Breeding:** from early March until spring departure, shows uniformly dark chestnut-maroon head, neck and breast and blackish back. Facial skin yellow-green; legs may be flushed red. **Habitat:** open areas, usually near water, including marshes, paddyfields, mangroves and intertidal mudflats. Very common winter visitor.

18. Javan Pond-Heron *Ardeola speciosa* S: 46 นกยางกรอกพันธุ์ชวา

Probably inseparable from Chinese Pond-Heron in non-breeding and immature plumages. **Breeding:** many are in breeding dress from late January to mid-July, when head and neck pale brownish buff to creamy-white; breast bright cinnamon and back blackish. Facial skin grey-blue; legs may be flushed red. **Habitat:** freshwater marshes, ponds, paddyfields; mangroves and intertidal mudflats. Very common resident.

19. Cattle Egret *Bubulcus ibis* S: 51 นกยางควาย

Smaller, shorter-necked and shorter-billed than other egrets with characteristic heavy-jowled appearance. When extended, neck appears thick at base and tapers markedly towards head. In flight, more compact appearance than other egrets with slightly shorter trailing legs. **Non-breeding:** plumage all white or with small spot of rufous-buff on forecrown. Yellow bill, greenish yellow facial skin and usually dark feet and legs. **Breeding:** shows highly distinctive rufous-buff head, neck and back; bill, facial skin and sometimes legs pinkish red. ◆ Gregarious; often seen feeding on insects disturbed by cattle. **Habitat:** lowland cultivated fields, marshes. Fairly common resident.

Plate 5 Pond-Herons, Egrets

non-breeding

breeding

breeding

17 Chinese Pond-Heron
1/06 SP

18 Javan Pond-Heron
1/06 SP

non-breeding

breeding

19 Cattle Egret
1/06 KK

dark morph

white morph

20 Pacific Reef-Egret

Mongkol

20. Pacific Reef-Egret *Egretta sacra* S: 58   นกยางทะเล

Dimorphic. Size and proportions recall Little Egret though shows noticeably shorter leg projection in flight. Legs greenish; facial skin grey. **Dark morph:** dark slaty grey, usually with inconspicuous whitish throat. Bill colour usually blackish, though often with varying amounts of yellow on lower mandible; occasionally entire bill is yellow, apart from dark culmen. **White morph:** all white, though sometimes with greyish mottling on neck and back. Bill usually yellow or with greenish tip and upper mandible. **Habitat:** rocky seacoasts and islets, sand beaches. Common resident.

21. Chinese Egret *Egretta eulophotes* S: 69   นกยางจีน

Size and proportions recall Little or Intermediate Egrets. **Non-breeding:** shows greenish legs and feet, blackish bill with lower mandible basally yellow and greenish facial skin. Easily confused with white morph Pacific Reef-Egret but bill tapers more towards tip and shows longer leg projection in flight. **Breeding:** legs black and feet greenish yellow. From Little Egret by yellow bill, blue facial skin and by shorter, shaggy crest. **Habitat:** intertidal mudflats. Very rare winter visitor or passage migrant; possibly much overlooked.

22. Great Egret *Egretta alba* S: 90   นกยางโทนใหญ่

From Intermediate Egret by larger size, which is obvious both at rest and in flight; longer, more dagger-like bill and longer neck which shows a more pronounced kink. When neck is extended, looks extremely thin and snaky. **Non-breeding:** yellow bill; blackish legs and feet. **Breeding:** black bill; usually bright blue-green facial skin; lower parts of legs often reddish. Long plumes from lower back only. **Habitat:** lowland marshes, lakes, paddyfields; also mangroves and intertidal mudflats. Common resident and winter visitor.

23. Intermediate Egret (Plumed Egret) *Egretta intermedia* S: 71   นกยางโทนน้อย

At all times of year, shows yellow bill sometimes tipped brownish; yellowish to green facial skin and black legs and feet. From Cattle Egret by longer, thinner neck. From Great Egret by smaller size; proportionately shorter, thicker neck with a less marked kink; heavier jowl and shorter bill. Often raises the feathers of the forecrown. **Breeding:** shows plumes on both upper breast and lower back. **Habitat:** mostly found around the larger freshwater marshes, but also frequents paddyfields. Less often in intertidal areas than Great or Little Egrets. Fairly common winter visitor; may not breed.

24. Little Egret *Egretta garzetta* S: 61   นกยางเปีย

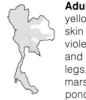

Adult: distinguished from all but breeding plumage Chinese Egret by yellow feet, contrasting with black legs. Long, thin black bill; facial skin greyish to greenish yellow though may be bright blue or even violet in breeding dress. **Breeding:** shows two long plumes on nape and plumes on both breast and back. **Immature:** dark, greyish olive legs, feet and base of bill. ◆ Highly gregarious. **Habitat:** lowland marshes and paddyfields, intertidal mudflats, salt pans and fish ponds. Occasionally on beaches and rocky coasts. Common resident and winter visitor.

Plate 6 White Egrets

22 Great Egret

23 Intermediate Egret

24 Little Egret

non-breeding

breeding

non-breeding

breeding

22 Great Egret

non-breeding

breeding

21 Chinese Egret

non-breeding

breeding

23 Intermediate Egret

non-breeding

breeding

immature

breeding

24 Little Egret

1/06 SP

1/06 SP

Mongkol

52

25. Little Heron *Butorides striatus* S: 46 นกยางเขียว

Small and dark. Can be confused only with Black Bittern, from which differs by contrast between dark crown and greyer mantle, uniformly greyish sides of neck and yellowish legs. In flight, greyish upperwing coverts contrast with blackish flight feathers; more compact appearance than Black Bittern. **Juvenile:** shows brownish scaling on wing coverts and streaked underparts. **Voice:** a harsh *keyow.* **Habitat:** resident birds inhabit mudflats, mangroves. Winter visitors often found along forest streams inland, up to 900 m. Common resident and winter visitor.

26. Black Bittern *Dupetor flavicollis* S: 54 นกยางดำ

In flight, from Little Heron by less compact shape, slightly longer, trailing dark legs and by more uniformly dark appearance but with contrasting yellow-buff patch on sides of neck. Upperparts and upperwing vary from uniformly blackish to dark rufous-brown. Secretive; keeps to dense grass and reeds and most often seen in flight. **Habitat:** marshes, paddyfield margins, mangroves. Breeding visitor; very common throughout central Thailand during the wet season, wintering mainly in the south.

27. Black-crowned Night-Heron *Nycticorax nycticorax* S: 61 นกแขวก

Adult: distinctive black cap and mantle, uniform pale grey wings and greyish white underparts. Legs yellow (often flushed red in breeding season). **Immature:** youngest stages brown, with bold, whitish buff spots and streaks on upperparts; later stages resemble adult, but cap and mantle dark grey-brown. ◆ Has a characteristic stocky, compact shape in flight with only a short leg projection. Gregarious and mainly nocturnal, except in the breeding season. **Voice:** a deep, harsh *kwok.* **Habitat:** marshes, paddies, mangroves. Common resident and winter visitor.

28. Malayan Night-Heron *Gorsachius melanolophus* S: 48 นกยางลายเสือ

Blackish flight feathers, white-tipped primaries and short, stout bill. Shows a broad white stripe along bases of flight feathers of the underwing. **Adult:** dull chestnut upperparts, densely and finely vermiculated with black; crown and nape blackish. Underparts buffy, streaked blackish. Bright blue-green facial skin. **Juvenile:** upper parts duller brown, finely spotted with white. ◆ Highly secretive. **Voice:** a sequence of 10 or 11 deep *oo* notes, about 1.5 seconds apart. Calls at dusk and dawn from high forest canopy. **Habitat:** dense evergreen and mixed deciduous forest, secondary growth, close to streams, chiefly of lowlands or level plateaux; rarely up to 1200 m. Uncommon resident, passage migrant and winter visitor.

29. Yellow Bittern *Ixobrychus sinensis* S: 38 นกยางไฟหัวดำ

In flight, by distinctive wing pattern of pale, buffy wing coverts contrasting with blackish grey flight feathers. **Adult:** blackish cap, light brownish mantle, yellow-buff underparts and wing coverts. **Juvenile:** dark brown streaks on both upperparts and underparts. ◆ Like all bitterns, usually shy and difficult to observe at rest; most often seen in flight. **Habitat:** tall reeds of marshy areas; less often in grassy habitats than Cinnamon Bittern. **Voice:** often gives a staccato *kak-kak-kak* in flight. Very common resident and winter visitor.

Plate 7 Little Heron, Black Bittern, Night-Herons

25 Little Heron

adult

juvenile

adult

26 Black Bittern

27 Black-crowned Night-Heron

adult

juvenile

28 Malayan Night-Heron

adult

juvenile

Mongkol

54

30. Schrenck's Bittern *Ixobrychus eurhythmus* S: 38　　　นกยางไฟหัวเทา

From Yellow Bittern by paler, greyer primaries in flight. **Adult male:** chestnut mantle, sides of head and neck; black cap. Shows pale, yellow-buff upperwing coverts in flight. **Adult female:** upperparts spotted with white; dark streaks on underparts. **Juvenile:** similar to female, but browner and more heavily streaked. Both female and immature lack sharply defined pale upperwing coverts in flight; from Cinnamon Bittern by greyish instead of rufous primaries and secondaries. **Habitat:** swampy areas in forest or secondary growth. Uncommon or rare passage migrant and perhaps winter visitor.

31. Cinnamon Bittern *Ixobrychus cinnamomeus* S: 38　　　นกยางไฟธรรมดา

Identified in all plumages by dark cinnamon-rufous primaries and secondaries when seen in flight. **Adult male:** upperwing and upperparts uniform, bright cinnamon-rufous; prominent white malar streak. Underparts paler. **Adult female:** differs only in having streaked underparts. **Juvenile:** mantle and upperwing coverts barred brownish; heavy dark streaks on underparts. **Habitat:** long grass and reeds of marshes, paddyfield margins, ponds, up to 1800 m. Very common resident.

32. Great Bittern *Botaurus stellaris* S: 76　　　นกยางแดงใหญ่

Large size. From immature Black-crowned Night-Heron by delicately mottled, buff, black and brown upperparts; also by contrast between sandy brown upperwing coverts and darker, barred, primaries. Black cap and moustache. Very secretive. **Habitat:** marshy areas of lowlands. Uncommon winter visitor.

　　　　　　　　　　　　　　　　　　　　　　วงศ์นกกระสา

STORKS: Family *Ciconiidae*. Very large wading birds with long, heavy bills, long necks and legs. Fly with head and neck extended (except for adjutants, *Leptoptilos* spp.), and legs trailing. Frequently soar. Feed on a variety of small animals, both aquatic and terrestrial. In courtship, make loud clattering noises with bill. Many species nest colonially, building untidy stick platforms. Sexes similar. Most Thai species are now threatened or endangered due to drainage and destruction of nesting and feeding areas and the direct persecution of both adults and young. World: 19 species. Thailand: 10 species. (See under Additions, pages 397–398.)

33. Painted Stork *Mycteria leucocephala* S: 102　　　นกกาบบัว

Distinctive long, tapering and slightly decurved orange-yellow bill. In flight, underwing appears mainly blackish. **Adult:** mainly white plumage with black breast band, black tail, and black and white wings tinged pinkish on greater coverts, scapulars and secondaries. In flight, upperwing blackish with a broad, white band across greater coverts. Legs brown or reddish; facial skin red in breeding season. **Juvenile:** head, neck, mantle and upperwing coverts brownish. Bare parts of head duller, greyish pink. **Habitat:** freshwater marshes, lakes; occasionally in paddyfields. Very rare breeding visitor, passage migrant and probably winter visitor. Formerly much more common and widespread.

Plate 8 Bitterns

adult

juvenile

29 Yellow Bittern

i/oc SP

♂

♀

♂

♀

30 Schrenck's Bittern

31 Cinnamon Bittern

i/oc SP

adult

juvenile

32 Great Bittern

Mongkol

56

34. Asian Openbill *Anastomus oscitans* S: 81 นกปากห่าง

Open space between mandibles diagnostic. **Adult:** black scapulars and flight feathers of wings and tail; white body plumage which becomes greyish during the course of the breeding season. **Immature:** pattern as adult, but white parts of plumage slightly darker, more grey-brown. ◆ Bill horn-coloured to reddish in adult; brownish in juvenile. Legs and feet greyish to pinkish brown. Feeds mainly on molluscs, including apple snails, *Pila* spp., and some bivalves. **Habitat:** marshes, paddyfields. Common breeding visitor, nesting in a few colonies in the Central Plains during November-April. Most migrate to the Brahmaputra and Ganges Deltas of Bangladesh during the wet season, though a few birds remain throughout the year.

35. White Stork *Ciconia ciconia* S: 102 นกกระสาขาว

Larger than the Asian Openbill, from which distinguished by conical, reddish bill, white tail and usually cleaner white body plumage. **Habitat:** marshes, paddyfields. Very rare winter visitor; only one sight record.

36. Black Stork *Ciconia nigra* S: 100 นกกระสาดำ

Shape as White Stork, but easily identified by glossy black head, neck and upper breast; white lower breast, belly and under tail coverts. Bill and legs red. In flight, underwing appears black with a small white triangle close to the leading edge. **Immature:** same pattern as adult, but black areas are browner; legs and bill grey-green. **Habitat:** marshes, rivers. Rare winter visitor.

37. Woolly-necked Stork *Ciconia episcopus* S: 91 นกกระสาคอขาว

All glossy black, except for entirely white neck, lower belly and under tail coverts. Bill blackish and legs red. **Immature:** black parts browner. **Habitat:** open lowlands, including marshes and pools in the more open forests. Rare resident; extirpated from most of the country.

38. Black-necked Stork *Ephippiorhynchus asiaticus* S: 132 นกกระสาคอดำ

Huge size; tall and slender-necked. Glossy black head, neck and tail, with white upper back and entire underparts. In flight, wings are mainly white with a broad black bar on both upperwing and underwing coverts, scapulars and tertials. Bill black; legs red. Iris of eye brown in male, yellow in female. **Immature:** has browner dark parts and sullied white parts of plumage. **Habitat:** marshes, coastal areas, open woodlands. Very rare resident; no longer breeds and is close to extinction.

Plate 9 Storks

adult   juvenile

ad. upperwing

ad. underwing

33 Painted Stork

juv. upperwing

34 Asian Openbill

i/06
road to KY
rice field

underwing

35 White Stork

underwing

underwing

36 Black Stork

underwing

37 Woolly-necked Stork

Mongkol

39. Greater Adjutant *Leptoptilos dubius* S: 145 นกตะกราม

Unlike other storks, both adjutants fly with neck retracted; their heads and necks are unfeathered. Greater Adjutant is distinguished by its huge size, and pale upperwing panel formed by grey greater coverts and inner secondaries. Also shows a prominent white neck ruff and a hanging neck pouch. In flight, underwing coverts mainly whitish, mottled brown. Shows a narrow pale grey band along the upperwing coverts. Head and neck reddish in the breeding season; yellowish at other times. **Immature:** shows some brownish feathering on neck; black replaced by dark brown. **Habitat:** marshes, paddies larger rivers; sometimes in open, dry woodlands of the plains. Rare but almost annual visitor.

40. Lesser Adjutant *Leptoptilos javanicus* S: 114 นกตะกรุม

Noticeably smaller and thinner-billed than Greater Adjutant. Upperwing entirely blackish, though may show white scalloping on scapulars and tertials. Lacks white ruff and neck pouch. In flight, underwing appears uniformly dark, apart from small white triangle at base of wing. **Habitat:** chiefly mangroves, coastal brackish and freshwater swamps; occasionally inland. Rare resident and occasional visitor.

วงศ์นกกระเรียน

CRANES: Family *Gruidae*. Very large birds with long necks and legs, and straight, pointed bills. From storks and herons by elongate inner secondaries which droop over the tail at rest. From herons in flight by neck held outstretched. Distinctive loud, trumpeting calls. Omnivorous. Nest on the ground or in shallow water by building bulky pad of vegetation. World: 15 species. Thailand: one species.

41. Sarus Crane *Grus antigone* S: 152 นกกระเรียน

Sexes similar. Light grey body plumage and bare red skin of head and upper neck. Primaries and primary coverts black, all secondaries whitish grey. Legs reddish; bill pale greenish horn. **Immature:** has feathered, buffy head and upper neck and slightly browner overall appearance. **Habitat:** marshes and paddyfields. Former resident; now extinct in Thailand.

วงศ์นกกระทุง

PELICANS: Family *Pelecanidae*. Very large aquatic birds with distinctive long, pouched bills and webbed feet. Gregarious; a group of birds will often fish in a coordinated effort. Nest in trees; sexes similar. World: 7 species. Thailand: one species.

42. Spot-billed Pelican *Pelecanus philippensis* S: 140 นกกระทุง

Overall greyish appearance with diagnostic whitish spectacle around eye; flesh-coloured bill and dull, purplish pink pouch. At close range, shows bluish spots along rim of upper mandible and brown-tinged neck. In flight, shows relatively little contrast between flight feathers and coverts of mainly greyish underwing. **Breeding:** lower back and underparts tinged pinkish. **Immature:** head, neck, body and upperwing tinged brownish. **Habitat:** marshes, lakes, rivers and seacoasts; occasionally visits nesting colonies of other waterbirds. Rare and endangered visitor; formerly much commoner and probably used to breed.

Plate 10 Larger Storks, Sarus Crane

38 Black-necked Stork

underwing

upperwing

39 Greater Adjutant

40 Lesser Adjutant

underwing

upperwing

41 Sarus Crane

Mongkol

วงศ์นกช้อนหอยและนกปากช้อน

IBISES AND SPOONBILLS: Family *Threskiornithidae*. Large wading birds with long, thin, decurved bills (ibises) or flattened bills with spatulate tip (spoonbills). Flight is characterised by fairly rapid wingbeats and outstretched, slightly drooped necks. Feed on fish, crabs and other small aquatic animals. Nest arboreally in colonies, often with herons or storks. Sexes similar. World: 33 species. Thailand: 6 species.

นกช้อนหอยขาว, นกกุลา

43. Black-headed Ibis *Threskiornis melanocephalus* S: 76

Adult: easily identified by long, decurved bill; by black naked skin of head and neck and by white body and wings with grey tertials. Bill and legs black; shows a bright red patch of naked skin near leading edge of underwing. **Juvenile:** some brownish feathers on neck; black tips to outer primaries. Bare skin of underwing is blackish. **Habitat:** marshes, paddyfields; roosts colonially with other large waterbirds in clumps of trees. Formerly resident but now an uncommon, usually annual, winter visitor.

44. White-shouldered Ibis *Pseudibis davisoni* S: 76   นกช้อนหอยดำ

Dark brown plumage with glossy blue-black wings and tail. Naked skin of head slaty blackish with striking pale blue nape and neck collar. Legs pinkish red. Has a white patch on inner lesser wing coverts which is not usually visible when bird is at rest. **Voice:** a harsh, ringing *kyee-aah*, very like the contact call of Great Barbet (378). **Habitat:** lakes, rivers, marshes. Formerly resident, but now extinct in Thailand.

45. Giant Ibis *Pseudibis gigantea* S: 104   นกช้อนหอยใหญ่

Large, almost stork-sized. Lacks white wing patch. Plumage dark grey-brown, glossed greenish. Naked skin of head and upper neck greyish, with black bars on nape. In flight, black primaries contrast with dull, silvery, black-scaled wing coverts. Legs red. **Habitat:** marshes and open wooded plains. Formerly rare resident; now extinct in Thailand.

46. Glossy Ibis *Plegadis falcinellus* S: 64   นกช้อนหอยดำเหลือบ

Smaller than White-shouldered and Giant Ibises, with feathered head and neck. **Adult:** appears all blackish, though upperparts glossed greenish and underparts tinged dark chestnut. Lacks white in wing. **Juvenile:** duller, browner plumage than adult, with dusky whitish streaking on head and neck. **Habitat:** marshy areas. Very rare visitor.

Plate 11 Pelican, Ibises, Spoonbills, Bar-headed Goose

42 Spot-billed Pelican

upperwing

underwing

43 Black-headed Ibis

44 White-shouldered Ibis

45 Giant Ibis

46 Glossy Ibis

non-breeding

immature

48 Black-faced Spoonbill

breeding

immature

breeding

47 White Spoonbill

adult

immature

49 Bar-headed Goose

KAMOL BANGKOK

47. White Spoonbill *Platalea leucorodia* S: 84   นกปากช้อนหน้าขาว
Distinctive broad, spatulate bill and whitish plumage. **Adult:** black bill with contrasting yellow spoon tip; yellowish facial skin. Shows yellowish breast patch and bushy crest in breeding dress. **Immature:** bill and facial skin usually greyish pink; shows small blackish tips to primaries. **Habitat:** marshes, lakes, mudflats. Very rare winter visitor.

48. Black-faced Spoonbill *Platalea minor* S: 76   นกปากช้อนหน้าดำ
Adult and immature plumages similar to White Spoonbill. Distinguished by black facial skin and more or less uniformly dark grey bill at all times of year. Underside of tip of spoon may be dull yellowish. **Habitat:** coastal mudflats. Very rare winter visitor.

วงศ์นกเป็ดน้ำ

DUCKS AND GEESE: Family *Anatidae*. Water birds with plump bodies, broad, flattened bills and webbed feet. Excellent swimmers; most feed on aquatic plants and animals, though some species graze vegetable food on the land. Flight strong and direct, with rapid beats of usually pointed wings; neck held extended. Sexes differ; females are usually dull-coloured while the males have colourful breeding dress, though many species have an eclipse (non-breeding) plumage in which the male resembles the female. In both sexes, simultaneous moult of the flight feathers prevents flight for a few weeks after breeding. Social; the commoner species are found in large flocks on the less disturbed water bodies during the winter. Most build simple, down-lined nests on the ground in thick waterside vegetation though a few species nest in tree holes or crevices. All but four species are exclusively winter visitors. (Note: the Lesser Whistling-Duck is sometimes placed in a separate family, *Dendrocygnidae*.) World: 154 species. Thailand: 21 species. (See under Additions, page 398.)

49. Bar-headed Goose *Anser indicus* S: 76   ห่านหัวลาย
Easily identified by very large size, white head, and stripe down side of neck (two black bars on nape). Grey body with barred flanks and orange-yellow bill. Sexes similar. In flight, shows pale greyish forewing, whitish rump and blackish nape. **Immature:** uniformly dark hindcrown and nape, lacking black bars. **Habitat:** large lowland rivers, marshes. Very rare winter visitor.

เหล่าเป็ดน้ำที่ว่ายหากินบนผิวน้ำ

DABBLING DUCKS: Genus *Anas*. Associated with shallow waters, feeding mainly by up-ending or dabbling on the surface. Shape generally elongated, with slightly upturned tail. Many species have a prominent speculum (coloured wing patch). Take off vertically from the water surface.

Plate 12 Ducks I

50 Northern Pintail
♀ upperwing
♂ upperwing

♀ upperwing
♀ underwing
♂ upperwing

51 Common Teal
♀
♂

52 Spot-billed Duck
upperwing
underwing

♀ upperwing
♂ upperwing

53 Gadwall
♀
♂

♀ underwing
ad. upperwing ♂
♂ imm. upperwing

♀ upperwing
♀ upperwing
♀
♂

54 Eurasian Wigeon

♀ upperwing
♀ underwing
♂ upperwing

55 Garganey
♀
♂ breeding

Mongkol

50. Northern Pintail (Common Pintail) *Anas acuta* S: 56   เป็ดหางแหลม

Distinctive long, slender neck and pointed tail visible both at rest and in flight. Bill grey. **Male:** white foreneck and breast contrasts with chocolate-brown head. Conspicuous white streak extends up the sides of the neck on to the head. Body mainly grey, with pale creamy-yellow patch on rear flank and black under tail. **Female:** mottled brown. Best identified by shape, bill colour and in flight by white line along trailing edge of secondaries and whitish belly. **Habitat:** lowland marshes and lakes, seacoasts. Common winter visitor.

51. Common Teal *Anas crecca* S: 38   เป็ดปีกเขียว

Rather small. **Male:** shows prominent long, white horizontal stripe along mainly grey body; yellow patch on under tail and chestnut head with a broad green eye patch. **Female:** identified by small size; from Garganey by more uniform sides of head, lacking dark cheek bar. In flight, both sexes show a bright green speculum, edged by creamy white bars and a whitish patch on the belly. **Habitat:** marshes, lakes, larger rivers and seacoasts. Uncommon winter visitor.

52. Spot-billed Duck *Anas poecilorhyncha* S: 61   เป็ดเทา

A large, pale brownish duck with a dark cap and a dark line through the eye. Large white patch on tertials is almost always visible at rest. Sexes similar. In flight, shows white-bordered, green speculum and gleaming white underwing coverts which contrast sharply with blackish underside of flight feathers. Bright yellow subterminal spot on dark bill; legs bright red. **Habitat:** marshes, lakes and larger, slow-moving rivers. Rare winter visitor.

53. Gadwall *Anas strepera* S: 51   เป็ดเทาก้นดำ

Distinguished in flight by large, square white patch on secondaries and whitish belly patch. **Male:** blue-grey body, pale brownish head and black under tail coverts. Bill blackish. **Female:** mottled brown; from Northern Pintail by more compact shape and from Eurasian Wigeon by duller brown plumage. From both by yellowish patch on sides of bill. Feet yellowish. **Habitat:** freshwater marshes, lakes. Very rare winter visitor.

54. Eurasian Wigeon *Anas penelope* S: 48   เป็ดปากสั้น

Rather short blue-grey bill, rounded head, and compact, short-necked appearance at rest. **Male:** mainly greyish body, usually showing broad white horizontal bar formed by folded wing coverts; creamy white patch on flank next to black under tail coverts. Chestnut head with yellowish creamy forehead and vinous breast. In flight, shows white triangular patch on the forewing and green speculum. **Immature male:** differs from adult in lacking white forewing and creamy forehead. **Female:** a richer, more rufous-brown than females of other surface-feeding ducks, especially on breast. Shows a clear white belly patch and a dull-coloured speculum in flight. **Voice:** male calls with a clear whistle, *wheeoo*. **Habitat:** marshes and lakes. Uncommon winter visitor.

Plate 13 Ducks II

56 Northern Shoveler

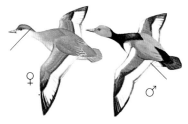

57 Red-crested Pochard

58 Common Pochard

59 Ferruginous Pochard

60 Baer's Pochard

61 Tufted Duck

66

55. Garganey *Anas querquedula* S: 41   เป็ดลาย

Only a little larger than Common Teal, with a slightly heavier bill. In flight, speculum dull-coloured in both sexes but male always shows pale blue-grey forewing. **Male breeding:** brown head with broad, crescentic white eyebrow. Grey flanks, brown breast and elongate black and white scapulars. **Male eclipse:** for most of winter resembles female except for flight pattern. **Female:** from female Common Teal by more striped face pattern and duller speculum. **Habitat:** marshes, lakes, ponds and seacoasts. Common winter visitor; sometimes in flocks of several thousand.

56. Northern Shoveler *Anas clypeata* S: 51   เป็ดปากพลั่ว

Easily identified by long, unwieldy-looking, spatulate bill (blackish in male; orange-brown in female). **Male:** shows white breast contrasting with rich chestnut flanks and dark green head. **Female:** mottled brown and best recognised by bill shape. ◆ In flight, both sexes show dark belly, green speculum and pale bluish forewing, brighter in the male. **Habitat:** lakes, marshes and occasionally coastal areas. Uncommon winter visitor.

เหล่าเป็ดน้ำที่ดำน้ำหากิน

DIVING DUCKS: Genera *Netta*, *Aythya*. Generally found on deeper waters than the preceding group, where they dive for food. Have shorter, heavier bodies and down-curved tails. Usually patter along surface of water before taking flight.

57. Red-crested Pochard *Netta rufina* S: 56   เป็ดปากแดง

Larger than other diving ducks. **Male:** red bill and golden-chestnut head; black neck, breast and belly patch, unmarked white flanks. **Eclipse and immature male:** from female by red bill and small white mark on side of neck. **Female:** brownish; dark brown cap contrasts with whitish sides to head. Red patch near tip of dark bill. Broad whitish wing bar in flight; male also shows whitish forewing. **Habitat:** marshes, lakes and ponds. Very rare winter visitor.

58. Common Pochard *Aythya ferina* S: 44   เป็ดโป๊ะช๊าดหลังขาว

Shows distinctive peaked crown and sloping forehead and has blue-grey band near tip of otherwise dark bill. **Male:** reddish head, pale grey body plumage with black breast and tail. **Female:** patterned like male, but dark brown head and breast which has a more subdued contrast with the paler, grey-brown body. Ill-defined pale marks around eyes and base of bill. ◆ In flight, from other diving ducks by pale greyish (instead of white) wing bar. **Habitat:** ponds and lakes. Very rare winter visitor.

Plate 14 Ducks III

62 Mandarin Duck

63 Cotton Pygmy-Goose

64 Comb Duck

65 White-winged Duck

66 Ruddy Shelduck

67 Lesser Whistling-Duck

68

59. Ferruginous Pochard (White-eyed Pochard) *Aythya nyroca* S: 41 เป็ดดำหัวสีน้ำตาล

Bold white wing bar in flight. **Male:** head, breast and most of body deep chestnut, contrasting with white under tail coverts. White eye. **Female:** duller than male, with brown eye. Separated from female Baer's Pochard by slightly smaller bill; head and neck concolorous with breast. **Habitat:** marshes, ponds and lakes. Rare winter visitor.

60. Baer's Pochard *Aythya baeri* S: 44   เป็ดดำหัวดำ

Bold white wing bar in flight. At rest, bill appears heavier than in Ferruginous Pochard. **Male:** blackish, green-glossed head contrasts with chestnut-brown breast; paler brownish flanks and white under tail coverts. Upperparts blackish brown. Eye white or yellow. **Female:** duller; similar to female Ferruginous Pochard, but head and neck blackish brown, slightly darker than rufous-brown breast. Eye brown. **Habitat:** marshes, ponds and lakes; occasionally seacoasts. Uncommon winter visitor.

61. Tufted Duck *Aythya fuligula* S: 43   เป็ดเปีย

Both sexes show a slight crest (though often difficult to discern) and a bold white wing bar in flight. **Male:** glossy blackish head, black back, breast and tail contrast with clean white flanks. Yellow eye. **Female:** black of male replaced by dark brown, with slightly paler brownish flanks. Often shows small whitish patch at base of bill. From female Ferruginous and Baer's Pochards by (usually) lack of white on under tail coverts and by yellow eye. **Habitat:** lakes, ponds and large, slow moving rivers. Rare winter visitor.

เหล่าเป็ดน้ำที่ทำรังในโพรงไม้สูงและอื่นๆ

PERCHING DUCKS: Genera *Aix, Nettapus, Sarkidiornis, Cairina, Tadorna, Dendrocygna.* A heterogeneous grouping, not easily placed with the preceding forms.

62. Mandarin Duck *Aix galericulata* S: 48   เป็ดแมนดาริน

Male: easily recognised by broad white eyebrow, red bill, orange-rufous cheeks and by wing sails. Two white bands on sides of breast; rufous flanks. **Male eclipse:** resembles female save for red bill. **Female:** dark grey-brown plumage with bold white spectacles, white mark at base of bill, white belly and under tail coverts. Bill blackish. **Habitat:** marshes, lakes. Very rare winter visitor.

63. Cotton Pygmy-Goose *Nettapus coromandelianus* S: 33   เป็ดคับแค

Small size. **Male:** white face, neck and underparts, blackish cap, upperparts and neck collar. Black parts are glossed greenish. In flight, black wings show a broad white band along flight feathers. **Female:** duller; black areas replaced by brown and white parts suffused brownish. Shows a prominent dark eye-line. In flight, white is limited to a narrow trailing edge along secondaries. ◆ Frequently perches on derelict temples and other buildings and nests in crevices, tree holes. **Voice:** a soft, musical laughing or quacking. **Habitat:** freshwater marshes, lakes, ponds. Locally common resident.

Plate 15 Osprey, Kites

upperwing

head-on

68 Osprey

underwing

upperwing

underwing

head-on

hovering

69 Black-shouldered Kite

1/06 KY

upperwing

head-on

underwing

70 Black Kite

1/06 SP

ad. underwing

juv. underwing

1/06 SP

juvenile

adult

ad. upperwing

juv. upperwing

71 Brahminy Kite

Mongkol

64. Comb Duck *Sarkidiornis melanotos* S: male 76; female 61.　เป็ดหงส์
Very large size. In flight, rather rounded wings and small-headed appearance. Wings, black above and below, contrast with all whitish neck and underparts. **Male:** diagnostic comb and whitish, black-speckled head and neck. Upperparts glossy black with whitish area on lower back; underparts white. **Female:** smaller and lacks comb. Similarly coloured, but lower back is grey-brown. ◆ Walks well on land, where it often feeds. Roosts in trees and nests in tree-hollows, occasionally far from water. **Habitat:** marshes, woodland ponds, flooded fields. Rare resident and winter visitor; may no longer breed.

65. White-winged Duck *Cairina scutulata* S: 76 ·　เป็ดก่า
Very large. Blackish body plumage with whitish head and neck; dull reddish bill and yellow legs. In flight, shows white forewing, underwing coverts and border to inner secondaries; blue-grey median coverts and speculum. Sexes similar but male has slightly thicker bill and glossier plumage. Partly nocturnal; roosts in lofty forest trees and nests in tree hollows. **Voice:** a series of short, mournful honks. **Habitat:** streams and ponds in evergreen and mixed deciduous forests of flat lands and plateaux, up to 1500 m. Very rare and endangered resident.

66. Ruddy Shelduck *Tadorna ferruginea* S: 64　เป็ดพม่า
Large size and goose-like shape. In flight, white coverts of both upperwing and underwing contrast sharply with blackish flight feathers. Orange-chestnut body plumage and buffy head; green speculum. **Male:** shows thin black neck collar in breeding dress. **Female:** slightly darker body plumage and whiter head than male. ◆ Walks well on land and often grazes. **Voice:** a nasal, goose-like honking. **Habitat:** lakes, marshes, rivers and flooded paddies. Rare winter visitor.

67. Lesser Whistling-Duck (Lesser Treeduck) *Dendrocygna javanica* S: 41 เป็ดแดง
Sexes similar. In flight, wings broader and more rounded than in other ducks; extended neck and head held drooped slightly lower than body. Generally dark appearance, though chestnut upperwing and upper tail coverts contrast with blackish flight feathers at close range. At rest, pale, buffy-brown head with dark brown cap; warm rufescent brown flanks and rufous-scaled, darker brown back. Long-necked appearance when alert. Mainly nocturnal, keeping to the safety of the larger water bodies during the day and flighting out to feed in ricefields at dusk. Often in flocks of several thousand outside the breeding season. Nests in tree hollows or occasionally in waterside vegetation. **Voice:** high-pitched, wheezy whistling notes. **Habitat:** flooded fields, marshy areas and lakes. Common resident and winter visitor.

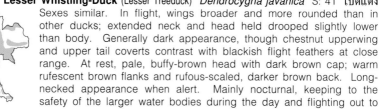

วงศ์เหยี่ยวและนกอินทรี

HAWKS: Family *Accipitridae*. Familiar shape, characterised by sharp, hooked bills, strong feet and sharp claws, and long wings. Plumage often highly variable but shape and markings in flight usually important for identification. Frequently soar or glide. Most species are predatory, but some are scavengers. Usually build untidy stick nests or take over the nests of other species. Females are usually considerably larger than males. World: 224 species. Thailand: 43 species. (See also Additions, page 398.)

68. Osprey *Pandion haliaetus* S: 55–61   เหยี่ยวออสเปร

 Long thin wings held angled at carpal joint, bowed below horizontal; often hovers over water with heavy wingbeats. Dark brown upperparts, white crown and broad blackish eye-line; white underparts and usually dark breast band. In flight, shows striking white underwing and black carpal patches, blackish flight feathers and band along margin of coverts. Underside of tail whitish with dark bars. **Immature:** lighter brown upperparts, feathers fringed creamy white; lacks broad terminal tail band of adult. ◆ Feeds exclusively on fish, caught by plunge-diving. **Habitat:** sea coasts, lakes, rivers and marshes. Uncommon winter visitor; a few birds (probably immatures) remain throughout the year.

เหล่าเหยี่ยวไคท์

KITES: Genera *Elanus, Milvus, Haliastur.* Medium-sized, with long wings and buoyant flight, inhabiting open country.

69. Black-shouldered Kite *Elanus caeruleus* S: 28–35   เหยี่ยวขาว

 Slender, pointed wings which held in a steep V while gliding. Frequently hovers. Pale ashy-grey plumage with black shoulder patch; white underwing with black underside to primaries and sometimes dark-based secondaries. **Juvenile:** upperparts tinged brownish and scaled whitish; slight dark streaking on underparts, nape and hindneck. **Habitat:** open country, including cultivated areas, from plains to 1500 m. Common resident.

70. Black Kite *Milvus migrans* S: 61–66   เหยี่ยวดำ

 Identified by forked tail, which appears almost straight-ended when broadly fanned. Long angular wings held arched below horizontal in flight; wingbeats slow and floppy, tail constantly flexed. Plumage dark brown; whitish patch at base of primaries on underwing; upperwing with rusty or buffy brown band on coverts and diffuse pale patch in primaries. Resident race *M. m. govinda* (now rare) has yellow legs and cere; richer, more reddish brown plumage than migrant race *M. m. lineatus* (which has blue-grey legs and cere). Wintering birds often frequent large communal roosts. **Voice:** shrill whinnying notes. **Habitat:** open country, cultivated areas, marshes, chiefly of lower elevations. Also coasts. Common winter visitor; rare resident.

71. Brahminy Kite *Haliastur indus* S: 43–51   เหยี่ยวแดง

Adult: distinctive bright chestnut upperwing and belly, contrasting with white head, neck and breast, black wing-tips. **Immature:** dull brownish plumage with white patch on underside of primaries. Appears longer-tailed than adult. From Black Kite by unforked tail which rounded when fanned; shorter, broader wings and less angular appearance. Wings usually held horizontal when gliding or soaring. See Eastern Marsh-Harrier, Booted Eagle. ◆ Often scavenges on floating debris. **Voice:** a nasal, drawn-out, slightly undulating *kyerrh*. **Habitat:** coastal areas, mangroves, larger rivers and around the edges of towns. Now very much reduced away from the coast. Common resident.

72

BAZAS: Genus *Aviceda*. Small to medium, long-winged hawks with prominent crests, which take small prey items by snatching them from among foliage or from the ground.

72. Jerdon's Baza *Aviceda jerdoni* S: 46   เหยี่ยวกิ้งก่าสีน้ำตาล

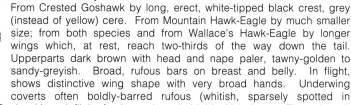

From Crested Goshawk by long, erect, white-tipped black crest, grey (instead of yellow) cere. From Mountain Hawk-Eagle by much smaller size; from both species and from Wallace's Hawk-Eagle by longer wings which, at rest, reach two-thirds of the way down the tail. Upperparts dark brown with head and nape paler, tawny-golden to sandy-greyish. Broad, rufous bars on breast and belly. In flight, shows distinctive wing shape with very broad hands. Underwing coverts often boldly-barred rufous (whitish, sparsely spotted in Crested Goshawk) and flight feathers show bold blackish bars. Three broad, dark bands on tail (usually 4 in Crested Goshawk). **Immature:** whiter underparts with sparse, brownish streaks. **Voice:** an airy *pee-weeeow*, the second note falling away. **Habitat:** evergreen forests of low to moderate elevation; up to 1400 m on passage. Uncommon resident and passage migrant or winter visitor.

73. Black Baza *Aviceda leuphotes* S: 33   เหยี่ยวกิ้งก่าสีดำ

An unmistakable, accipiter-sized, black and white bird with a long, erect crest. In flight, black underwing coverts, blackish body and blackish grey secondaries contrast with paler grey primaries and tail. Under tail coverts blackish. Usually active, flapping, crow-like flight; glides on flattish wings. Frequently sits on exposed perches and feeds by making short dashes through dense foliage to seize prey (mainly larger insects). Often in large flocks on migration. **Voice:** a single, airy note. **Habitat:** deciduous and evergreen forests, secondary growth from plains to 1500 m. Sometimes in gardens, orchards on passage or in winter. Uncommon resident; common passage migrant and winter visitor.

เหล่าเหยี่ยวนกเขา

SPARROWHAWKS: Genus *Accipiter*. Small to medium-sized hawks, with rather broad wings and relatively long tails. Show conspicuous white under tail coverts which are expanded laterally, often covering the base of the upper tail coverts, in buoyant display flight on winnowing wings. Plumages are confusingly similar and immatures are often impossible to separate with certainty. Hunt with active, dashing flight, usually inside wooded areas, preying particularly on smaller birds.

74. Crested Goshawk *Accipiter trivirgatus* S: 40–46   เหยี่ยวนกเขาหงอน

At rest, from all other accipiters by short crest. In addition, from Jerdon's Baza by yellow cere and much shorter wings. In flight, underwing coverts whitish, sparsely spotted. Well protruding head; wings very rounded and relatively short, incurved at the base. Long tail well spread while soaring, showing 4 dark bands. **Adult:** upperparts dark brown with slate-grey crown, crest and sides of head. Lacks both whitish supercilium and nape spot shown by some other accipiters. Bold mesial throat streak; rufous-brown streaks on breast and dark bars on belly which become progressively narrower and denser towards thighs. **Juvenile:** browner head, streaked whitish buff on crown; white belly with bold but sparse spots (not bars). ◆ Eye yellow in adult; brown in juvenile. **Habitat:** evergreen and deciduous forests from plains up to 1800 m. Common resident.

Plate 16 Bazas, Accipiters

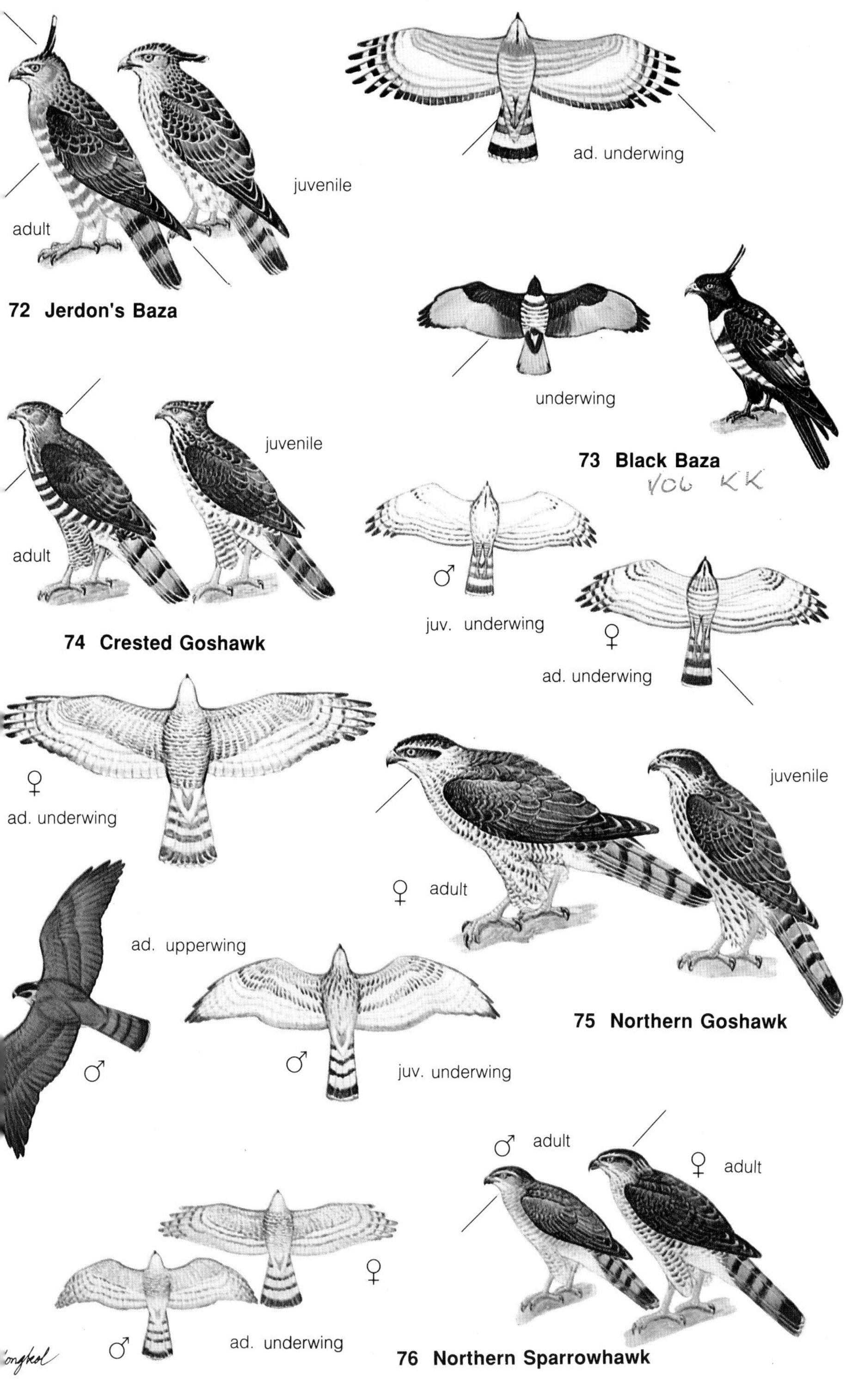

juvenile

ad. underwing

adult

72 Jerdon's Baza

underwing

73 Black Baza

VOG KK

juvenile

adult

74 Crested Goshawk

♂ juv. underwing

♀ ad. underwing

♀ ad. underwing

juvenile

♀ adult

ad. upperwing

♂ juv. underwing

75 Northern Goshawk

♂ adult

♀ adult

♀

ad. underwing

longkol ♂

76 Northern Sparrowhawk

74

75. Northern Goshawk *Accipiter gentilis* S: 48–61　　เหยี่ยวนกเขาท้องขาว

Much larger than other accipiters (though female Crested Goshawk and Northern Sparrowhawk can approach male Northern Goshawk in size). Long, relatively pointed and broad-based wings and well protruding head in flight. Rounded tail-tip. **Adult:** dark, slaty-brown upperparts and whitish, finely dark-barred underparts. Prominent whitish supercilium, lacking in Crested Goshawk. Bold dark eye patch and crown give a hooded appearance. **Juvenile:** browner upperparts with buffy patch on centre of upperwing coverts; warmer, buffy underparts with dark brown streaks. **Habitat:** mountainous, wooded country. Rare winter visitor.

76. Northern Sparrowhawk *Accipiter nisus* S: 33–38　　เหยี่ยวนกกระจอกใหญ่

In flight from Northern Goshawk by smaller size, less pointed wings with straighter trailing edge, and by more square-cut tail. Proportionately longer, more slender wings and longer tail than the following species. In all plumages shows barred breast and belly with never more than faint streaks on throat. Lacks mesial throat streak. **Male:** dark blue-grey upperparts and rufous-barred underparts. From adult Shikra by more strongly barred underwing and tail; from male Besra and Japanese Sparrowhawk by (usually) paler grey upperparts; from all by rufous cheeks. **Female:** dark brown upperparts; underparts whitish with dark brown bars. From female Japanese Sparrowhawk by larger size, paler sides of head and crown, bold whitish supercilium and larger white spot on nape. **Juvenile:** brownish upperparts, resembling female. From other juvenile accipiters by entirely fine-barred underparts. ◆ Iris of eye yellow to orange. **Habitat:** both open and wooded country from plains to 1800 m. Rare winter visitor.

77. Chinese Goshawk *Accipiter soloensis* S: 30–36　　เหยี่ยวนกเขาพันธุ์จีน

Adult: whitish underwing, lacking any barring on coverts of flight feathers, with extensive blackish wing-tips. Upperparts darker, more slaty-grey than in Shikra; underparts whitish, usually unbarred, with vinous-grey to pinkish orange suffusion on breast. Central tail feathers uniform dark slaty, though some females may show 3–4 dark bands. **Juvenile:** similar to immatures of other small accipiters but darker slaty crown and nape and whiter underwing. ◆ Eye dark brown, dark red or yellow. Sometimes in flocks on migration. **Habitat:** open forests and scrub country, chiefly of the lowlands and lower hills. Uncommon passage migrant and winter visitor.

Plate 17 Smaller Accipiters

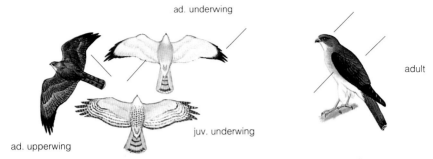

ad. underwing

adult

ad. upperwing

juv. underwing

77 Chinese Goshawk

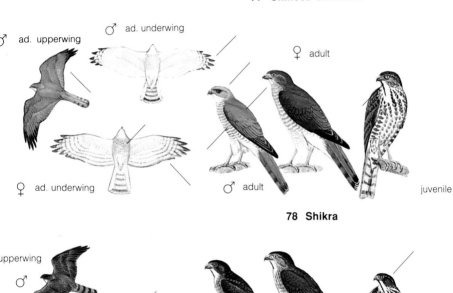

♂ ad. upperwing

♂ ad. underwing

♀ adult

♀ ad. underwing

♂ adult

juvenile

78 Shikra

upperwing

♂

underwing

♂ adult

♀ adult

juvenile

79 Besra

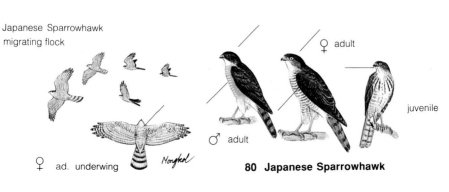

Japanese Sparrowhawk
migrating flock

♀ adult

juvenile

♂ adult

♀ ad. underwing

Mongkol

80 Japanese Sparrowhawk

78. Shikra *Accipiter badius* S: 30–36   เหยี่ยวนกเขาชิครา

Male: paler, more bluish grey upperparts than any other accipiter, with entirely grey cheeks. Underparts narrowly and densely-barred pale rufous. In flight, underwing whitish with dark tips and slight barring on undersides of flight feathers (can sometimes appear almost unbarred). Central tail feathers unbarred (apart from faint dark subterminal band). **Female:** like male, but upperparts tinged slightly brownish; underparts with broader cinnamon-brown barring and underwing barring slightly bolder. More distinct subterminal band on central tail feathers. **Juvenile:** blackish brown to dark grey-brown above, with white and rufous streaks on nape and whitish supercilium. Broad, spot-like streaks on breast and short broad bars on sides of breast, flanks and thighs. Bold dark mesial throat streak. Probably indistinguishable from juvenile Besra in the field. ◆ Often feeds by dropping to the ground from a perch, in order to take larger insects and small reptiles. Eye dark red to yellow. **Voice:** a high-pitched piping *kyeew* (recalling some notes of Ashy Drongo) and other varied notes. Very vocal while displaying. **Habitat:** deciduous and the more open evergreen forests, plantations and open country. Often in or near towns from plains up to 1500 m. Common resident.

79. Besra *Accipiter virgatus* S: 30–36   เหยี่ยวนกกระจอกเล็ก

Both sexes show dark upperparts and a bold dark mesial throat streak. **Male:** very dark slaty above with blackish head and deep rufous underparts, slightly streaked on upper breast and barred on belly. **Female:** dark brown upperparts and brownish-barred underparts, with streaks limited to upper breast. **Juvenile:** from most juvenile Japanese Sparrowhawks by broad mesial throat streak; possibly indistinguishable from immature Shikra, though crown and nape darker. **Habitat:** mixed deciduous and evergreen forests of hilly country up to 2000 m. Uncommon resident.

80. Japanese Sparrowhawk *Accipiter gularis* S: 25–30   เหยี่ยวนกเขาพันธุ์ญี่ปุ่น

The smallest accipiter. In all plumages, from Besra by mesial throat stripe either faint or lacking. **Male:** upperparts much darker grey than Shikra; underparts pale rufous, faintly barred. From Chinese Goshawk by bold barring on underwing; from Besra also (usually) by lack of streaking on upper breast. **Female:** upperparts dark grey-brown, with crown slightly darker. Entire underparts whitish, narrowly barred dark brown. Smaller than Northern Sparrowhawk and lacking white supercilium. **Juvenile:** mesial throat streak usually thin or lacking (always distinct in immature Besra). Upper breast boldly streaked or spotted. Usually whiter belly than immatures of either Shikra or Besra, with slightly narrower brown bars. ◆ Often in flocks on migration. **Habitat:** forest, secondary growth, plantations and open country, chiefly of lowlands and lower hills. Fairly common passage migrant and winter visitor.

Plate 18 Buzzards

Oriental Honey Buzzard 1/06 KY

head-on

typical

dark morph

immature

1/06 DA

(Eurasian)

81 Crested Honey-Buzzard

head-on

hovering

underwing

upperwing

82 Common Buzzard

underwing

upperwing

1/06 DA

83 Rufous-winged Buzzard

head-on

upperwing

juvenile

underwing

adult

84 Grey-faced Buzzard

78

เหล่าเหยี่ยวใหญ่

BUZZARDS: Genera *Pernis, Buteo, Butastur.* A heterogeneous grouping of medium-sized hawks, which frequently soar. Have smaller heads and bills than do eagles. Some species are gregarious outside the breeding season and occur in large flocks on migration. Crested Honey-Buzzard and Common Buzzard are large and broad-winged; the so-called 'buzzard-eagles' (*Butastur* spp.) are smaller with narrower wings and proportionately longer, more slender tails. They look almost intermediate in shape between buzzards and harriers.

เหยี่ยวผึ้ง

81. **Crested Honey-Buzzard** (Eurasian Honey-Buzzard) *Pernis ptilorhyncus* S: 51–61

In flight from Common Buzzard and from hawk-eagles by wings which held level, seldom above horizontal (except in undulating, butterfly-like display flight which is rarely seen). Thinner, more protruding head than Common Buzzard and longer tail, with carpal joints thrust well forward in gliding flight. Closed tail shows slightly rounded corners. Plumage is highly variable, but flight silhouette, once learned, is usually diagnostic. **Adult:** boldly-banded flight feathers from below. At rest, shows short crest and usually a dark moustache, bordering a pale gorget. Upperparts brownish with greyer sides to head. May be uniform dark brown, rusty-brown, or creamy-white on body and underwing coverts, though body often streaked or barred. Some individuals may be blackish brown with whitish wing patches, or have strikingly white head and unmarked whitish underparts. Tail pattern variable; most often three bold dark bands, unequally spaced, but a few birds show a black tail with a broad white central bar, recalling Crested Serpent-Eagle. **Immature:** very variable. Underparts and underwing coverts vary from dark brown to creamy-buff or whitish. Underwing and tail barring usually finer than in adults. Often show a large pale patch on the upper primaries. ◆ Cere dark grey in adults; yellow in juvenile. Feeds chiefly on larvae of wasps and honeybees, breaking open their nests. **Habitat:** deciduous and evergreen forests, open wooded country, usually below 1200 m. Fairly common winter visitor and passage migrant; uncommon resident.

82. **Common Buzzard** *Buteo buteo* S: 50–56

เหยี่ยวทะเลทราย

More compact than Crested Honey-Buzzard with slightly shorter tail which has sharper corners; head shorter and broader, protruding less. Flies with stiffer wing beats and soars with wings in a shallow V. Plumage somewhat variable, but the race which winters in Thailand (*B. b. japonicus*) is usually creamy-buff or whitish below, with large blackish carpal patches, a prominent dark trailing edge to the wing and a dark brown belly patch (lacking in some immatures). Underside of tail appears very pale, almost unbarred. Occasionally hovers. **Habitat:** paddyfields, drier open country, deciduous forests, evergreen forest edges or clearings from plains to the tops of the highest mountains. Fairly common winter visitor.

79

83. Rufous-winged Buzzard *Butastur liventer* S: 38–43   เหยี่ยวปีกแดง

When perched, long wings cover tail-tip. Dull brownish upperwing coverts partly obscure rufous flight feathers. Extensive bright orange-yellow on cere and base of bill. In flight, shows whitish underwing and tail, with no more than faint barring; bright rufous upperwing and upper tail. Shape similar to Grey-faced Buzzard, but is more compact, with slightly shorter wings and tail. Wing-tips appear pointed in fast gliding posture. Both glides and soars on flattish wings, but these strongly flexed downwards in display. **Adult:** grey head and breast. **Immature:** browner head and breast, with whitish supercilium. **Voice:** a shrill *pit-piu*, the first note higher. **Habitat:** open dry dipterocarp woodlands, scrub country of plains and foothills to at least 800 m. Uncommon resident.

84. Grey-faced Buzzard *Butastur indicus* S: 41–46   เหยี่ยวหน้าเทา

Long wings almost reach tail-tip when perched. When soaring and gliding, appears intermediate between a slender harrier and a small, slender Crested Honey-Buzzard. Long, narrow wings; long tail which broadly fanned in soaring. Soars on flattish wings; wings slightly flexed downwards in fast gliding posture. From Rufous-winged Buzzard by bold tail bars and more heavily barred underwing; upperwing with no more than a small rufous patch at base of primaries. **Adult:** rufous-brown or grey-brown breast and belly, with whitish barring. White throat is clearly demarcated from grey sides of head; dark mesial throat streak. **Immature:** browner head, streaked whitish; whitish supercilium and white-streaked nape (may form a pale collar in some individuals). Entire underparts whitish, narrowly streaked brown. ◆ One of the commonest migrant raptors, forming large flocks on migration. **Habitat:** forests, secondary growth, plantations, open areas with scattered trees. From plains up to 1800 m. Common passage migrant and winter visitor.

เหล่าเหยี่ยวปลา

FISH-EAGLES: Genera *Haliaeetus, Ichthyophaga*. Large and usually broad-winged, with massive bills. Show distinctly contrasting wing or tail patterns. Usually close to water. Adopt upright posture when perched in trees.

85. Pallas's Fish-Eagle *Haliaeetus leucoryphus* S: 68–81   นกอินทรีหัวนวล

Rounded or slightly wedge-shaped tail; soars and glides on level wings. Wings almost parallel-sided, tapering less near wing-tips than in White-bellied Sea-Eagle, but longer, narrower than Grey-headed Fish-Eagle. **Adult:** white tail with black terminal band. Dark body plumage; pale head and neck. Underwing appears almost uniformly dark, apart from slightly paler grey bases to primaries. **Immature:** body plumage paler brown with dark patch behind eye. In flight, shows broad pale band across underwing coverts and pale patches on under primaries. Upperwing more uniformly dark, with a narrower whitish band through mid-wing. Tail dark brown. **Habitat:** open country, near water. Very rare winter visitor; only one sight record.

80

86. White-bellied Sea-Eagle *Haliaeetus leucogaster* S: 60–69 นกออก

Short, strongly wedge-shaped tail; wings narrow towards tip and are lifted in a pronounced shallow V while soaring. Pale body and underwing coverts contrast with dark flight feathers. (See Booted Eagle). **Adult:** grey upperparts; pure white head, neck, underparts, and lesser and median underwing coverts, contrast with blackish flight feathers and greater underwing coverts. Tail white, with black base. **Immature:** pale brownish body and creamy underwing coverts (with scattered brownish markings) which become progressively paler with age. Greater coverts remain dark. White patch at base of primaries is also reduced with age. Tail creamy whitish, often mottled brownish at base, grading into brownish distal third. Subadult shows white tail with narrow black terminal band. ◆ Often scavenges on refuse, picked from water's surface or uses long talons to gaff fish just below surface. **Habitat:** rugged seacoasts, islands; occasionally inland. Uncommon resident; now much reduced in numbers.

เหยี่ยวปลาใหญ่หัวเทา

87. Grey-headed Fish-Eagle *Ichthyophaga ichthyaetus* S: 61–74

Tail short and rounded; short, broad wings. Uniformly dark brownish grey wings and body, greyer head, contrasting with white lower belly and under tail coverts. From Lesser Fish-Eagle by mainly white tail with clear-cut black terminal band. **Immature:** paler, browner than adult with some creamy-whitish markings on underwing coverts and bases of flight feathers; darker wing-tips. Pale brown head and breast, with buffy supercilium. Rear body creamy with scattered brownish mottling. Tail shows variable pale mottling on basal third. From Lesser Fish-Eagle by more distinct whitish shaft streaks on breast. **Habitat:** lakes, marshes, seacoasts and larger rivers in wooded country of the level lowlands or occasionally on plateaux. Very rare resident; much reduced and now endangered.

88. Lesser Fish-Eagle *Ichthyophaga humilis* S: 51–64 เหยี่ยวปลาเล็กหัวเทา

Smaller than previous species, but similar in shape. **Adult:** from Grey-headed by mainly dark tail, which shows only slight white mottling at base and a slight suggestion of a darker terminal band. **Immature:** very like immature Grey-headed, but distinguished by less prominent white shaft-streaking on breast feathers and by darker, mottled brownish underwing coverts. **Habitat:** forested streams of lower hills. Rare resident.

เหล่าเหยี่ยวรุ้ง

SERPENT-EAGLES: Genera *Circaetus, Spilornis.* Have long, unfeathered tarsi and proportionately large heads. They specialise in feeding on snakes.

89. Short-toed Eagle *Circaetus gallicus* S: 60–81 เหยี่ยวนิ้วสั้น

Very long wings, held only slightly lifted while soaring. Underwing whitish with dark speckling and barring; lacks the dark carpal patches of some Crested Honey-Buzzards and most Common Buzzards. Tail shows 3 broad, widely and evenly spaced dark bars; head is often dusky brownish. Well protruding head, broad neck; medium to long tail with narrow base, sharp corners and square-cut tip. Soft, elastic wing beats; frequently hovers. **Habitat:** open wooded country. Rare passage migrant or winter visitor.

Plate 19 Fish-Eagles

85 Pallas's Fish-Eagle

adult

immature

86 White-bellied Sea-Eagle

adult

immature

87 Grey-headed Fish-Eagle

adult

immature

88 Lesser Fish-Eagle

adult

immature

Mongkol

82

90. Crested Serpent-Eagle *Spilornis cheela* S: 51–71 เหยี่ยวรุ้ง

Much shorter, broader wings than Short-toed, recalling hawk-eagles, but tail somewhat shorter. Soars with wings in a shallow V. Tail strongly flexed upwards in display, accentuating its shortness. Stocky build, with large head and nuchal crest visible at rest. **Adult:** dark brown underparts and underwing coverts, spotted white. In flight, shows a single broad white band along flight feathers of wing and across tail, contrasting with otherwise dark plumage. **Immature:** whitish head and underparts; underwing boldly barred like hawk-eagles but, like adult, usually shows two short dark lines forming a loop marking in the carpal region. From Changeable Hawk-Eagle by black line through eye; heavier outline, broader wings and clearly shorter tail with bolder bars and by wings held more consistently in a V. **Voice:** an airy, ringing, *pe-wheew-wheew*. **Habitat:** deciduous and evergreen forests, secondary growth up to 1500 m. Common resident.

เหล่าเหยี่ยวภูเขา

HAWK-EAGLES: Genus *Spizaetus*. Medium to large, with broad wings and long tails. Usually glide on level wings and soar with wings in a shallow V. Hind margin of wings appear 'pinched in' where they join body. Feathered tarsi.

91. Mountain Hawk-Eagle *Spizaetus nipalensis* S: 66–75 เหยี่ยวภูเขา

Both adults and immatures show long, erect crest. Much larger than Blyth's or Wallace's Hawk-Eagles and slightly larger than Changeable. When soaring, hands broader than in Changeable, somewhat recalling Black Eagle wing shape; wings noticeably lifted above horizontal, pressed forward slightly. **Adult:** streaks limited to upper breast only; broad, rufous-brown bars on lower breast and flanks. Ground colour of breast and underwing coverts is tawny (white in pale morph of Changeable). Usually shows 4 dark tail bands which are broader and bolder than those of pale morph Changeable. **Immature:** head and underparts unmarked, tawny-buff as opposed to almost pure white in Changeable. Tail bars are narrower, less bold than in adult. **Voice:** 3 shrill notes, *tlueet-weet-weet*, reminiscent of the calls of Green Magpie. **Habitat:** evergreen and deciduous forests, secondary growth, up to the highest elevations. Local and uncommon resident breeding from about 600 m to over 2500 m. More widespread in distribution outside the breeding season, occurring down to the plains and foothills.

Plate 20 Serpent-Eagles, Hawk-Eagles

underwing

upperwing

89 Short-toed Eagle

ad. underwing

juv. underwing

juvenile

adult

90 Crested Serpent-Eagle

juvenile

ad. underwing

adult

91 Mountain Hawk-Eagle

adult dark morph underwing

ad. pale morph

adult pale morph underwing

ad. dark morph

Mongkol

juvenile

92 Changeable Hawk-Eagle

92. Changeable Hawk-Eagle *Spizaetus cirrhatus* S: 56–75   เหยี่ยวต่างสี

Distinguished from other hawk-eagles by short crest. In flight, from Mountain by relatively narrower wings and proportionately longer tail. Usually glides and soars with wings level, (except while displaying, when both wings and tail may be flexed markedly upwards, recalling Crested Serpent-Eagle). **Adult pale morph:** dark brown upperparts; breast and belly whitish with bold black streaks. Five dark tail bands, narrower than those of Mountain Hawk-Eagle (in many birds, so fine that tail appears almost unbarred). Whiter underwing coverts and flight feathers less heavily barred; extreme wing-tips blackish. **Adult dark morph:** (possibly more frequent in the south). Blackish brown plumage, lacking barring in flight and tail feathers. From Black Eagle by different wing shape; by contrast between dark ventral region and paler greyish under-tail, grading into a diffuse dark terminal band; by paler flight feathers of wing (particularly under primaries) contrasting with dark underwing coverts and wing-tips. **Juvenile:** unmarked, pure white head and underparts. See immature Crested Serpent-Eagle. **Voice:** an ascending series of shrill whistles, *kri-kri-kri-kri-kree-ah*; also a *kreeee-krit*, with much stress on the elongate first syllable. The last note may be either higher or lower. **Habitat:** evergreen and deciduous forest, secondary growth, up to 2000 m. Uncommon resident.

93. Blyth's Hawk-Eagle *Spizaetus alboniger* S: 51–58   เหยี่ยวดำท้องขาว

Erect crest. **Adult:** From other hawk-eagles by single broad white band across dark tail. Blackish upperparts and face mask, with black-barred belly and streaked breast. See Crested Serpent-Eagle. **Juvenile:** brownish upperparts, buffy underparts (unmarked in youngest stages; becoming sparsely-streaked later) and narrowly barred tail. Possibly inseparable from juvenile Wallace's, but older immatures usually start to moult in some black feathers on both upperparts and underparts even before attaining adult tail pattern. **Voice:** variable shrill whistles: *kee-kew-kew* (highest first note stressed); *kreee-krit*, recalling Changeable Hawk-Eagle, but last note lower. Also a single, upward-inflected scream. **Habitat:** evergreen forests of the hill slopes, up to 1700 m. Uncommon to fairly common resident.

94. Wallace's Hawk-Eagle *Spizaetus nanus* S: 51–58 เหยี่ยวหงอนสีน้ำตาลท้องขาว

The smallest hawk-eagle; has erect crest. **Adult:** like subadult Blyth's, but upperparts uniformly dark brown, lacking any black feathering; three dark tail bands. **Juvenile:** probably indistinguishable in the field from juvenile Blyth's but has more extensive feathering on middle toe. **Voice:** a shrill, high-pitched *yik-yee*; second note inflected upwards (JS). **Habitat:** evergreen forests, chiefly of lowlands and lower hill slopes. Uncommon or rare resident; may be threatened due to habitat destruction.

เหล่านกอินทรีขนาดกลาง

OTHER MEDIUM-SIZED EAGLES: Genus *Hieraaetus*. Longer-winged than hawk-eagles, with striking flight patterns. Usually soar on level wings.

Plate 21 Hawk-Eagles

adult

juvenile

93 Blyth's Hawk-Eagle

adult

juvenile

94 Wallace's Hawk-Eagle

adult

juvenile

juvenile

adult

95 Rufous-bellied Eagle

ad. upperwing

ad. underwing

adult

juv. underwing

96 Bonelli's Eagle

dark morph
underwing

dark morph

pale morph underwing

pale morph

Mongkol

upperwing

97 Booted Eagle

95. Rufous-bellied Eagle *Hieraaetus kienerii* S: 51–61   เหยี่ยวท้องแดง

Short crest when perched. **Adult:** conspicuous black hood, contrasting with white throat and upper breast. Lower breast, belly and underwing coverts pale to dark rufous; often shows dark border to underwing coverts. Flight feathers of underwing mainly whitish. Usually shows conspicuous white patch on upperwing at base of primaries. **Juvenile:** unmarked whitish underwing coverts and breast; dark brownish flanks. Head pattern is of black eye patch, white supercilium and pale brownish crown. ◆ Usually glides and soars on level wings, only occasionally raised above the horizontal. Sometimes dives vertically in display, wings swept back close to body. **Habitat:** evergreen and occasionally deciduous forests from foothills up to 2000 m. Uncommon resident.

96. Bonelli's Eagle *Hieraaetus fasciatus* S: 64–69   นกอินทรีแถบปีกดำ

Soars on level, rather narrow wings. When gliding, carpal joints thrust well forward, recalling Crested Honey-Buzzard. Differs in more square-cut and straight-sided tail. **Adult:** distinctive pattern of blackish underwing coverts (leading coverts bordered white) and only slightly paler flight feathers, contrasting with whitish underbody. Broad black terminal band to otherwise pale tail. From above, usually shows whitish patch on upper back. **Juvenile:** rufous to creamy buff underbody and underwing coverts, the latter often dark-bordered. Finely barred flight feathers of wing and tail. Shows a large translucent cinnamon-buff patch at base of primaries, visible both from above and below and contrasting with the clear blackish wing-tip. **Habitat:** forests, often close to rocky cliffs. Rare; status uncertain.

97. Booted Eagle *Hieraaetus pennatus* S: 48–56   นกอินทรีเล็ก

A small, slim eagle which soars on level wings; somewhat recalls Black Kite in shape and actions, but tail square-cut (rounded when fanned). Sometimes dives vertically like Rufous-bellied Eagle. **Dark morph:** from Black Kite also by white neck patches and, usually, whitish buff upper tail coverts (seldom coloured so in Black Kite). From young Brahminy Kite by these features and also by broad, creamy band across centre of upperwing coverts. Underparts and underwing more or less uniformly dark with a translucent wedge formed by 3 inner primaries. Tail appears cinnamon in strong light, unbarred unless seen at very close range. **Pale morph:** diagnostic whitish underwing coverts and underbody contrasts with blackish primaries and secondaries. Other features as in dark morph. See White-bellied Sea-Eagle, Common Buzzard. **Habitat:** wooded areas of both plains and hills. Rare passage migrant or winter visitor.

เหล่านกอินทรีขนาดใหญ่

LARGE, DARK EAGLES: Genera *Ictinaetus*, *Aquila*. *Ictinaetus* is a resident forest bird, with a medium to long tail and a diagnostic wing shape. *Aquila* are all winter visitors, mainly frequenting open areas, and all are somewhat similar in appearance, soaring on flattish wings, with the hand often slightly lowered. Tails medium to long, but shape often unreliable due to wear.

Plate 22 Black Eagle, Aquila Eagles

98 Black Eagle

juvenile

adult

Greater Spotted Eagle

ad. underwing

ad. upperwing

juv. upperwing

99 Greater Spotted Eagle

juvenile

adult

Tawny Eagle

pale morph   upperwing

dark morph underwing

Tawny Eagle juvenile underwing

ad. dark morph

ad. pale morph

juvenile

100 Tawny Eagle

Imperial Eagle

ad. underwing

juv. underwing

juvenile

101 Imperial Eagle

ad. upperwing   juv. upperwing

adult

Mongkol

98. Black Eagle *Ictinaetus malayensis* S: 69-78 นกอินทรีดำ

Distinguished from other dark eagles by wings broadest on inner primaries, slightly narrowing inwards. Glides and soars on level or slightly bowed wings; tail usually held closed, appearing narrow, square-cut. **Adult:** all blackish plumage, with little or no contrast between flight feathers and coverts of underwing, though usually slight pale crescents at base of primaries and indistinct tail barring. Upper tail coverts sometimes show a small pale area. **Juvenile:** browner. Paler underwing coverts and body are streaked dark brown.
◆ Hunts by slow quartering, low over canopy; robs bird nests. **Habitat:** evergreen forest of mountains, from the foothills to the highest summits. Uncommon resident.

99. Greater Spotted Eagle *Aquila clanga* S: 66-74 นกอินทรีปีกลาย

Distinguished from both Black and Imperial Eagles by shorter, less square-cut tail. From adult Imperial by absence of yellowish white hindneck. Wings held slightly bowed below horizontal, both when gliding and soaring. Underwing coverts darker than flight feathers; usually shows a slightly translucent area in inner primaries and a whitish crescent at base of primaries on underwing. **Adult:** almost entirely dark brown with slight or no white primary patch on upperwing; little or no white on upper tail coverts. (A scarce colour morph shows pale creamy-buff body and underwing coverts.) **Juvenile:** large whitish spots on upperwing coverts and scapulars, appear as whitish bands across upperwing in flight; also shows a diffuse whitish patch at base of primaries on upperwing, whitish trailing edge of variable width to both wings and tail. Often wholly white upper tail coverts forming a U-shaped patch. **Habitat:** open areas, especially marshes; sometimes frequents nesting colonies of larger waterbirds. Usually in the plains, but seen in mountainous areas on passage. Uncommon winter visitor and passage migrant; the most frequently observed *Aquila*.

100. Tawny Eagle *Aquila rapax* S: 64-71 นกอินทรีสีน้ำตาล

A. r. vindhiana is only race so far known for Thailand. Flight silhouette differs from that of Greater Spotted Eagle by wings which are longer in the hand and more angled at the carpal joint. In gliding, wings less obviously bowed than in Spotted. From Imperial Eagle by smaller size, less protruding head and neck and shorter tail. At rest, shows larger bill and baggier 'trousers' than Greater Spotted. Plumage variable, but usually shows creamy lower back and upper tail coverts irrespective of age or morph. **Adult:** two colour morphs. Dark brown, with hind crown and hindneck sometimes tawny yellowish, and underwing coverts of similar shade to flight feathers (may be slightly darker or paler). Upperwing shows a diffuse pale primary patch. Pale morph is bright rufous on body and coverts, bleaching to creamy-whitish and contrasting sharply with dark flight and tail feathers. Primaries of underwing often paler than secondaries, especially in pale morph. **Juvenile:** plumage like pale morph adult. Older immatures are confusingly variable. See juvenile Imperial Eagle. **Habitat:** well watered, open plains. Very rare visitor; only one record. (Note: Steppe Eagle, *A. r. nipalensis*, — sometimes treated as a separate species — which is larger and has distinctively different immature plumages, showing a white band on greater coverts of underwing, should also occur in Thailand.)

Plate 23 Vultures

adult

immature

underwing

102 Red-headed Vulture

underwing

103 Cinereous Vulture

juvenile

ad. underwing

adult

juv. underwing

ad. upperwing

104 Long-billed Vulture

ad. underwing

adult

juvenile

ad. upperwing

juv. underwing

105 White-rumped Vulture

Mongkol

101. Imperial Eagle *Aquila heliaca* S: 79–84   นกอินทรีหัวไหล่ขาว

Longer-tailed than Greater Spotted and Tawny Eagles; when perched, shows large, greenish yellow bill. Soars and glides holding wings level or no more than slightly lifted. **Adult:** blackish brown, with yellowish white crown and hindneck; bicoloured tail, silvery with a broad blackish subterminal band. Flight feathers of underwing paler than coverts; has white scapular patches which are difficult to see. **Juvenile:** pale sandy body, upper and underwing coverts contrast with strikingly dark flight feathers. Shows a conspicuous pale wedge in three innermost primaries, whitish band to trailing edges of wing and tail (except when worn) and a large creamy area on lower back and rump, together with whitish upper tail coverts. Prominent dark streaks on breast. **Habitat:** marshy open plains. Rare but annual winter visitor.

เหล่าอีแร้ง

VULTURES: Genera *Sarcogyps*, *Aegypius*, *Gyps*. Huge soaring birds with naked or partly naked heads. Can cover large distances in order to locate and scavenge on the bodies of dead animals. Gregarious.

102. Red-headed Vulture *Sarcogyps calvus* S: 81   พญาแร้ง

Glides on level wings, hand slightly lowered; soars on wings only slightly raised. Short, wedge-shaped tail and well protruding head and neck; broad-based wings narrow towards tip, more obviously so in adult than in juvenile. **Adult:** red head and neck, and black plumage with oval white thigh patches. Shows a greyish white band at base of secondaries on underwing; white at base of neck is usually visible in flight at close range. **Juvenile:** browner than adult, with whitish lower belly and under tail coverts; head and neck greyish pink. ◆ Often shows a whitish area on lower back. Less gregarious than other vultures; tree-nesting. **Habitat:** wooded areas of lowlands and lower hills, especially along river valleys. Now confined to the most remote areas which still support populations of native large mammals. Rare resident.

103. Cinereous Vulture *Aegypius monachus* S: 104   อีแร้งดำหิมาลัย

Huge size. Soars on flatter wings than other vultures (sometimes wings even held slightly bowed). Wings also more parallel-sided, without bulging secondaries; individual feathers of secondaries pointed, giving saw-toothed appearance to trailing edge of wing. Tail slightly wedge-shaped. Uniformly blackish plumage, with pale feet; head pale with blackish eye-mask. **Juvenile:** slightly browner than adult, with blackish head. **Habitat:** open and wooded country. Rare winter visitor.

104. Long-billed Vulture *Gyps indicus* S: 89   อีแร้งสีน้ำตาล

Glides on more level wings than White-rumped; wings sometimes bowed. Body, upper and underwing coverts sandy or creamy brown; much paler than in juvenile White-rumped. **Adult:** white neck ruff. Dark head and neck contrasts with rosy-yellow cere and bill. **Juvenile:** browner, darker than adult, but still noticeably paler than juvenile White-rumped. Lacks neck ruff; bill mainly dark with yellowish culmen. **Habitat:** open and partly wooded country. Very rare resident; possibly now extinct in Thailand.

105. White-rumped Vulture *Gyps bengalensis* S: 89 อีแร้งเทาหลังขาว

Soars with wings in shallow V. Trailing edge to wing is more curved than in Long-billed Vulture. **Adult:** mainly blackish, with white lower back and rump, white underwing coverts and neck ruff. In perched birds, bill appears pale with dark tip and dark cere. **Juvenile:** body, upper and underwing coverts grey-brown, contrasting with blackish brown flight feathers and tail. Appears uniform at a distance, but at close range, shows whitish shaft streaks to feathers of underparts and (less obviously) on upperparts. No white on lower back or rump. Bill and cere blue-black. Older immatures gradually develop whitish bars on underwing coverts but never have the uniform sandy underwing coverts of Long-billed Vulture. **Habitat:** open and partly wooded country, from plains to at least 1600 m. Very rare resident and occasional winter visitor. Once common but now almost extinct.

เหล่าเหยี่ยวทุ่ง

HARRIERS: Genus *Circus*. Slim, long-winged birds of prey which hunt low over open country. From Black and Brahminy Kites by wings consistently held in shallow V.

106. Eastern Marsh-Harrier *Circus spilonotus* S: 48–56 เหยี่ยวทุ่ง

Larger and broader-winged than other harriers, with slightly bulging secondaries and more protruding head. **Adult male:** blackish, grey and white plumage; from male Pied Harrier by throat, neck, breast, mantle and upperwing coverts streaked black and white instead of being solid black. Never shows any pure white upperwing coverts. Usually shows some narrow dark bands on outer tail feathers. Younger males have brown mantle and brownish fringes on upper-wing coverts. Underwing and tail may be as boldly banded as female Pied. **Adult female:** dark rufous-brown with dark-streaked, creamy white cap, leading edge to wing and upperwing coverts, and frequently upper breast and upper back. Breast blotched rufous-brown (never streaked). Usually shows some whitish mottling on upper tail coverts. Underwing uniformly dark, apart from whitish patch at base of primaries; may show slight banding on tail. **Juvenile:** darker than female with pale markings reduced or lacking, and cap usually dark; probably indistinguishable from Western Marsh-Harrier, *C. aeruginosus*, which may possibly occur in Thailand and which is sometimes considered conspecific. **Habitat:** marshes and low-lying open country. Common winter visitor.

107. Northern Harrier *Circus cyaneus* S: 43–51 เหยี่ยวทุ่งแถบเหนือ

Male: upperparts pale grey with white rump; underparts whitish apart from greyish head and upper breast. Black outer primaries. **Female and juvenile:** strongly barred underwing and large white rump patch. Tail usually shows 4 broad dark bands (5 narrower bands in female Pied). Paler upperwing coverts contrast with darker brown mantle and flight feathers. Underparts like female Pied Harrier but more heavily streaked on upper breast. Has a pale buffy hind border to the facial disc. **Habitat:** dry and marshy open country of both mountains and plains. Rare winter visitor.

92

108. Pied Harrier *Circus melanoleucos* S: 43–46   เหยี่ยวด่างดำขาว

Smaller and narrower-winged than Eastern Marsh, but difficult to separate on size and shape from Northern. **Male:** distinguished from male Eastern Marsh by solid black parts of plumage and by pure white lesser upperwing coverts. See Black-shouldered Kite. **Female:** more sparsely streaked upper breast and whiter underwing coverts than female and juvenile Northern Harrier. Greater and primary coverts, and flight feathers of upperwing, greyish, fringed brick-red, with some dark barring showing through; bars on upper and underside of tail and on underwing (when visible) slightly narrower than in Northern Harrier. Relatively plain brown facial disc and darker brown mark through eye, but lacks a pale hind border. From subadult male Eastern Marsh by broader banding on flight feathers of upperwing and bolder bands on tail which extend on to central tail feathers. **Juvenile:** rather uniformly rich cinnamon-brown below and dark brown above. From juvenile Eastern Marsh-Harrier by usually bolder white patch on upper tail coverts, heavy dark barring on underwing and tail (visible usually only at fairly close range); dark line through eye and by smaller, slimmer appearance. **Habitat:** marshes, open plains. Uncommon to fairly common winter visitor.

วงศ์เหยี่ยวปีกแหลม

FALCONS: Family *Falconidae*. Long, usually slender and pointed wings and strong, rapid flight. Many species snatch their bird or insect prey from the air. When soaring, wings of some species can appear slightly more rounded, leading to possible confusion with the *Accipiter* hawks. The White-rumped Falcon and the falconets are hole-nesters; most other species nest either on ledges or by taking over the old nests of other birds. Females are usually larger than the males. World: 62 species. Thailand: 8 species.

109. White-rumped Falcon *Polihierax insignis* S: 25–28   เหยี่ยวเล็กตะโพกขาว

Larger and much longer-tailed than falconets with more rounded wing-tips. White rump and upper tail coverts and unmarked white underparts; grey upperparts. **Male:** whitish, grey-streaked head and upper back. **Female:** chestnut head and upper back. **Juvenile:** head and upper back dark grey, almost concolorous with rest of upperparts, but usually separated by a whitish collar. Often sits on exposed perches, dropping to the ground to seize prey. **Voice:** a long, reedy falling tone whistle. **Habitat:** open deciduous woodlands, clearings, from plains to 700 m. Uncommon resident.

110. Collared Falconet *Microhierax caerulescens* S: 19   เหยี่ยวแมลงปอขาแดง

Tiny; blackish upperparts with white forehead, supercilium and white collar across back of neck. Broad black line through the eye. Underparts mainly white, with rufous suffusion on throat, thighs, flanks and under tail coverts. **Juvenile:** throat whitish; forehead and supercilium suffused rufous. ◆ Sits on exposed perches, darting out with great speed and agility to snatch flying insects. Gregarious; often in small groups. **Habitat:** deciduous forests, clearings and edge of evergreen forests from plains up to 1800 m. Common resident.

Plate 24 Harriers

♀ upperwing

♂

♂ upperwing

♂ upperwing

♀

106 Eastern Marsh-Harrier

♀ upperwing

♂ upperwing

♀ underwing

♂ underwing

♂

♀

107 Northern Harrier

♂ upperwing

♀ upperwing

♀ underwing

♂

♂ underwing

juv. underwing

♀

108 Pied Harrier

94

111. **Black-thighed Falconet** *Microhierax fringillarius* S: 16   เหยี่ยวแมลงปอขาดำ

Distinguished from Collared Falconet by lack of white collar, narrower white supercilium which extends only behind eye and does not join with smaller white forehead patch. Underparts similar to Collared Falconet, but has black flanks and outside to thighs (usually difficult to discern in the field). **Habitat:** forest clearings, secondary growth from plains to 1500 m. Fairly common resident.

112. **Eurasian Kestrel** *Falco tinnunculus* S: 31–35   เหยี่ยวเคสเตรล

Longer-tailed than other falcons, with less dashing flight. Rapid, winnowing wingbeats; frequently hovers, dropping to the ground to catch small animals. Facial pattern lacks strong contrast but shows a diffuse dark moustache. Underwing mainly whitish with faint barring on flight feathers and spotting on coverts. Rufous brown mantle and upperwing coverts contrast with blackish primaries and outer secondaries. **Male:** black-spotted, rufous back contrasts with grey head and tail. **Female and immature:** entirely rufous brown upperparts, heavily barred and spotted blackish; barred tail. More profusely spotted on underparts and underwing coverts than adult male. **Habitat:** grassland, scrub country, marshes, towns and even cities from plains to 2000 m. Fairly common winter visitor.

113. **Amur Falcon** *Falco amurensis* S: 28–31   เหยี่ยวตีนแดง

Intermediate in shape between Eurasian Kestrel and Northern Hobby. Sometimes hovers; often catches insects on the wing. **Male:** dark slaty upperparts and paler grey underparts with striking white wing lining and reddish thighs and ventral region. Subadult males like adult, though often retain dark spotting on white underwing coverts. **Female and immature:** from Northern Hobby by slightly longer tail and slightly less pointed wings; by entirely barred upperparts (usually visible only at close range), less distinct moustache and by whiter underwing, often showing a suggestion of a dark trailing edge. ◆ Feet, cere and orbital ring are bright orange-red in male, orange in female. **Habitat:** mainly wooded country of both lowlands and hills. Very rare passage migrant.

114. **Northern Hobby** *Falco subbuteo* S: 31–35   เหยี่ยวฮอบบี้ยุโรป

Strikingly long, pointed, scythe-like wings and relatively short tail; does not normally hover. **Adult:** sharply contrasted face pattern of black moustache and white cheeks recalls migratory races of Peregrine Falcon, but white cheek patch larger. Underparts broadly streaked black (never barred) and thighs and under tail coverts chestnut. Central tail feathers are unbarred, giving plain appearance to closed tail from above. **Juvenile:** browner upperparts; thighs and under tail coverts buffy. **Habitat:** both open and wooded country from plains to 2000 m. Rare winter visitor and probably passage migrant.

Plate 25 Smaller Falcons

White-rumped Falcon

♂ upperwing

110 Collared Falconet

109 White-rumped Falcon

♂ upperwing

♀ upperwing

111 Black-thighed Falconet

♀ underwing

♂ hovering

112 Eurasian Kestrel

♂   ♀

♀ underwing

♂ underwing

113 Amur Falcon

Mongkol

96

115. Oriental Hobby *Falco severus* S: 28–33 เหยี่ยวฮอบบี้

A small dark falcon; stockier and shorter-winged than Northern Hobby. Black hood, without obviously contrasting white cheeks. **Adult:** unmarked dark rufous underparts and underwing coverts; slaty upperparts, becoming almost blackish on head, hindneck and mantle; somewhat paler on lower back and upper tail coverts. **Juvenile:** slightly paler, rufous-brown below with bold drop-like spots or streaks on body and dense spots and bars on underwing coverts. **Habitat:** deciduous and evergreen forests, secondary growth from foothills to at least 1500 m; often in the vicinity of crags and cliffs. Uncommon resident.

116. Peregrine Falcon *Falco peregrinus* S: 38–48 เหยี่ยวเพเรกริน

A large, but compact falcon; broad-based wings with a narrow, pointed hand. Broad, blackish moustache and white cheek patch. **Adult:** upperparts slaty grey; underparts buffy, narrowly dark-barred. **Juvenile:** dark brown upperparts; underparts with bold dark streaks. ◆ Above descriptions refer to wintering race, *F. p. japonensis.* Resident birds with characteristics resembling *F. p. ernesti* have been recorded. Adults of this form show more of a hood than a moustache, with reduced area of white on cheek; underparts deeper vinous or lavender-grey, with heavier dark bars. There has also been at least one sighting of a bird showing the bright rufous underparts of race *F. p. peregrinator.* **Habitat:** both open and wooded country, often near crags; seacoasts. From plains to 2000 m. Uncommon resident and winter visitor.

เหล่าเหยี่ยวค้างคาว

BAT HAWK: Genus *Macheiramphus.* Actually an aberrant hawk placed with falcons for convenience because of similar long, pointed wings. Crepuscular habits, hunts bats.

117. Bat Hawk *Macheiramphus alcinus* S: 46 เหยี่ยวค้างคาว

Falcon-like. In flight, distinguished by dark appearance combined with long, broad-based wings which are more pointed than those of Peregrine Falcon. Flies with deep wingbeats. Blackish plumage with white throat patch; sparse, wispy crest hangs horizontally behind head when perched. Bright yellow eye and whitish eyelids. Roosts during the day in lofty forest trees. **Voice:** a series of up to 7 short, piercing whistles given at roost trees during daylight hours. **Habitat:** evergreen forest of the level lowlands and foothills. Rare resident, probably threatened by habitat destruction.

วงศ์ไก่ฟ้าและนกกระทา

PHEASANTS: Family *Phasianidae.* Terrestrial birds with plump bodies; strong, unfeathered legs; and short, strong bills. Can fly strongly on broad, rounded wings, although most species prefer to run from danger. Highly secretive and difficult to observe, though some species have distinctive calls. Feed on seeds, fruits, insects, etc. Nest on the ground. Many species are threatened due to destruction or fragmentation of their forest habitats, combined with illegal hunting or capture. World: 189 species. Thailand: 23 species.

Plate 26 Falcons, Bat Hawk

ad. underwing

juv. underwing

114 Northern Hobby

adult

juvenile

ad. underwing

juv. underwing

115 Oriental Hobby

adult

juvenile

ad. underwing

juv. underwing

adult

juvenile

116 Peregrine Falcon

Peregrine Falcon
adult, resident form

117 Bat Hawk

Mongkol

98

GALLOPHEASANTS: Genera *Lophura, Gallus.* Chicken-like, with long, heavy tails. Show strong sexual dimorphism. Have noisy, wing-whirring displays but calls of most species (other than the Red Junglefowl) are usually quiet and unobtrusive. Often found in small parties.

118. Kalij Pheasant *Lophura leucomelana* S: 51–74 ไก่ฟ้าหลังเทา

Male: upperparts finely vermiculated, appearing uniformly grey and lacking the bold chevron markings of male Silver Pheasant. Shows bold white streaks on sides of breast and a longer, straighter crest than male Silver. **Female:** distinguished from female Silver by straighter crest and coarser pattern of white, V-shaped streaks on underparts. ◆ Legs greyish in race *lineata*. Both sexes of race *crawfurdii* of south-west Thailand have red legs; female has bolder white streaks on underparts than does female *lineata*. **Voice:** thin whistles and quiet, low muttering or grunting notes. **Habitat:** mixed deciduous, dry evergreen and hill evergreen forests from foothills to 1200 m. Uncommon to locally common resident.

119. Silver Pheasant *Lophura nycthemera* S: 51–120 ไก่ฟ้าหลังขาว

Distinguished from Kalij by red legs and by range (the only overlap is in the north-west of the country). **Male:** race *jonesi* (found throughout most of country) is silvery-whitish above, with fine black chevron markings and mainly whitish tail. **Female:** brown upperparts with dense pattern of fine whitish scales on breast. Curved black crest in both sexes. **Male:** (race *lewisi* of south-east Thailand) black above with white chevron markings. **Female:** upperparts reddish brown; underparts grey-brown, almost unmarked. Short, straight crest in both sexes. ◆ Sometimes associates with parties of Red Junglefowl. **Voice:** soft, thin, mewing whistles when feeding; a shriller whistle when alarmed. **Habitat:** evergreen forests from 700 m to 2000 m. Uncommon to locally common resident.

120. Crested Fireback *Lophura ignita* S: 69 ไก่ฟ้าหน้าเขียว

Facial skin blue; feet red. **Male:** glossy blackish blue plumage with a coppery-red patch on lower back and rump. White central tail feathers and flank streaks. **Female:** mainly chestnut-brown, with black and white scales on flanks and white breast streaks. **Habitat:** evergreen forest of the level lowlands and foothills, usually close to streams, rivers. Rare resident; probably endangered in Thailand due to lowland forest destruction.

121. Siamese Fireback *Lophura diardi* S: 60–82 ไก่ฟ้าพญาลอ

Slimmer and proportionately longer-legged than other gallopheasants. Facial skin red in both sexes. **Male:** dark grey upperparts, neck and breast; coppery-reddish rump and upper tail coverts; golden-yellow patch on lower back conspicuous in wing-whirring display. Tail blackish, glossed green. **Female:** easily distinguished from other female pheasants by broad, black and buff bars on wings and tail. Rufous-chestnut outer tail feathers and underparts. **Habitat:** evergreen forests, chiefly of the plains and foothills, though occasionally found up to 800 m. Uncommon to rare resident; now much reduced.

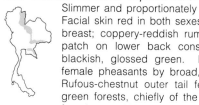

Plate 27 Pheasants, Junglefowl

♀

♂

.l. lineata

118 Kalij Pheasant

♀

♂

L.l. crawfurdii

♂

♀

L.n. jonesi

119 Silver Pheasant

♀

♂

L.n. lewisi

♂

♀

120 Crested Fireback

♂

♀

121 Siamese Fireback

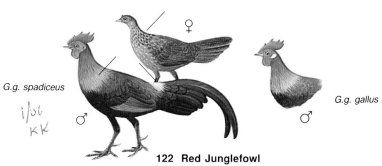

♀

G.g. spadiceus

♂

G.g. gallus

♂

122 Red Junglefowl

Mongkol

100

122. **Red Junglefowl** *Gallus gallus* S: 43–76 ไก่ป่า

The ancestor of the domestic chicken, from which distinguished usually by slate-grey legs and (male only) by prominent white patch at base of tail. **Male:** golden-bronze neck and upper back, reddish coppery lower back, glossy green wing coverts and tail. **Female:** dark brownish. From female pheasants by shorter, fan-shaped tail and golden neck hackles. ◆ Race *gallus* of eastern part of country has whitish ear spot. More inclined to fly when disturbed than other pheasants. Frequently perches in trees. **Voice:** gives the familiar *cock-a-doodle-do* of the domestic fowl, but slightly higher-pitched and ending more abruptly. Also typical chicken-like clucking notes. **Habitat:** evergreen and deciduous forests, secondary growth and scrub from plains up to 1800 m. Common resident, though much reduced due to hunting.

เหล่าไก่ฟ้าหางยาว

LONG-TAILED PHEASANTS: Genus *Syrmaticus*. Sexually dimorphic, the males having long, pointed tails.

123. **Hume's Pheasant** *Syrmaticus humiae* S: 60–90 ไก่ฟ้าหางลายขวาง

Male: long, pointed, pale grey tail, broadly barred with black and chestnut. Coppery mantle, white shoulder bar and two white wing bars; rump barred black and white; head, upper breast and upper back steely-blue. **Female:** shorter, blunt-ended, white-tipped tail with chestnut outer feathers. Buffy-brown body plumage, marked with black. **Voice:** a low grunting note and a muttering *buk buk buk* in alarm (Smythies). **Habitat:** open hill evergreen forest, secondary growth, clearings above 1200 m. Rare resident.

เหล่านกแว่นและนกยูง

PEACOCK-PHEASANTS and PEAFOWL: Genera *Polyplectron, Argusianus, Pavo.* Sexually dimorphic, the males having iridescent ocelli on the wing or tail feathers. Possess elaborate displays, and have loud vocalizations.

124. **Grey Peacock-Pheasant** *Polyplectron bicalcaratum* S: 56–76 นกแว่นสีเทา

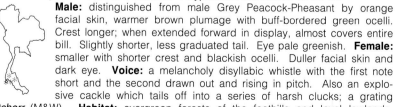

Male: facial skin pale yellow; crest short and bushy. Grey-brown body plumage with white-bordered, iridescent violet to greenish ocelli. Eye whitish. **Female:** smaller than male, with darker plumage and buff-bordered blackish ocelli; duller facial skin and dark eye. **Voice:** a loud whistled *trew-tree* at intervals. Also a harsh, rolling gargling which leads into a louder, excited *waak-waak-waak*, the full sequence lasting many minutes. All three calls are given by the male. **Habitat:** evergreen forest from foothills to 1800 m. Uncommon resident.

นกแว่นสีน้ำตาล

125. **Malaysian Peacock-Pheasant** *Polyplectron malacense* S: 56–76

Male: distinguished from male Grey Peacock-Pheasant by orange facial skin, warmer brown plumage with buff-bordered green ocelli. Crest longer; when extended forward in display, almost covers entire bill. Slightly shorter, less graduated tail. Eye pale greenish. **Female:** smaller with shorter crest and blackish ocelli. Duller facial skin and dark eye. **Voice:** a melancholy disyllabic whistle with the first note short and the second drawn out and rising in pitch. Also an explosive cackle which tails off into a series of harsh clucks; a grating *tchorr* (M&W). **Habitat:** evergreen forests of the foothills and level lowlands. Very rare resident; on the verge of extinction in Thailand due to lowland forest destruction.

Plate 28 Pheasants, Argus, Peafowl

123 Hume's Pheasant

124 Grey Peacock-Pheasant

125 Malaysian Peacock-Pheasant

126 Great Argus

127 Green Peafowl

Mongkol

126. Great Argus *Argusianus argus* S: 76–200   นกหว้า

Large; bare blue skin on head and neck. Plumage dark rusty-brown, intricately mottled black and buff. **Male:** greatly elongate secondaries which are marked with large, buffy-brown ocelli. Long, ribbon-like central tail feathers. Mainly solitary; a male clears a circular dancing ground, usually on a ridgetop. **Voice:** a loud, resonant *kwow-wow*, the second note being louder and longer than the first, given exclusively by males. Also a long series of up to 30 *wow* notes, of which the last few have an increasing upward inflection, given by both sexes. **Habitat:** evergreen forests of the hill slopes up to 900 m. Uncommon resident.

127. Green Peafowl *Pavo muticus* S: 102–245   นกยูง

Huge, with long legs and long neck. Brilliant green body plumage. In flight, wings show pale cinnamon primaries contrasting with blackish secondaries. Long erect crest; bright blue and yellow facial skin. **Male:** long train formed by elongate upper tail coverts, spread in an enormous fan during display. (Note that these are moulted out in April and May.) Triangular patch of dense black scale markings on upper back; black skin on lores. **Female:** slightly paler, bronze-green upperparts, with brown lores and black barring on outer webs of primaries and buffy barring on feathers of upper tail coverts. Lacks train. ◆ Often in small parties; roosts in tall trees. **Voice:** a loud braying; *toong-hoong* or *aow-aaw*, emphasis on second syllable, given by the male. The female has a more nasal *aa-ow* call with emphasis on the first syllable. Most frequently uttered in early morning and at dusk. **Habitat:** mixed deciduous woodland, secondary growth and clearings usually close to shallow streams or rivers with exposed sand bars. Mostly plains and foothills, but occasionally higher plateau areas. Rare resident; much reduced by human persecution.

เหล่านกกระทา

PARTRIDGES: Medium-sized, short-tailed birds; in most species, the sexes are similar or nearly so. *Francolinus* and *Bambusicola* have crowing or chattering calls and inhabit grasslands and scrub. *Rhizothera*, *Arborophila*, *Caloperdix and Rollulus* have more elaborate whistling calls and inhabit forests.

นกกระทาดงคอสีแสด

128. Rufous-throated Partridge *Arborophila rufogularis* S: 28

Orange-rufous throat and foreneck, with large black spots. Breast and belly grey, with prominent silver and rufous flank streaks. Shows pattern of broad black and buff bars across folded wing. Legs pinkish red. **Voice:** a long, clear, monotone whistle which leads into a series of whistled couplets, *hu-hu*, *hu-hu*.... ascending gradually in pitch. Duets, the other member simultaneously calling with a more rapid, continuous *kew-kew-kew*.... **Habitat:** evergreen forests from 1200 m to the highest summits. Uncommon resident; much reduced due to hunting.

129. Bar-backed Partridge *Arborophila brunneopectus* S: 28

Bold striped wing pattern like Rufous-throated, but distinguished by striking face pattern and prominent black and white spotting on flanks. Narrow black bars across mantle and dense gorget of black spots on throat and upper breast. Legs pinkish red. **Voice:** throaty, monotone, burring whistles which lead into see-sawing whistled couplets, *ti-hu, ti-hu, ti-hu...* of steady pitch and volume. Duets, the other member of the pair responding with a continuous *kew-kew-kew...* **Habitat:** evergreen forests from 500 m to 1300 m. Uncommon to locally common resident.

นกกระทาดงจันทบูรณ์

130. Chestnut-headed Partridge *Arborophila cambodiana* S: 29

Face pattern of endemic Thai race *diversa* (which may be a distinct species) resembles Bar-backed in having buffy cheek and a black eye-line. Back pattern and wing covert barring also similar but differs in having deep rufous breast band and even bolder black and white scaling on flanks, extending on to belly. **Voice:** of similar pattern to that of Bar-backed. **Habitat:** evergreen forests of the mountains, 700–1500 m. Local and uncommon resident; endemic to south-east Thailand and south-west Kampuchea.

131. Scaly-breasted Partridge *Arborophila chloropus* S: 29   นกกระทาดงแข้งเขียว

Upperparts mottled rufous-brownish, finely barred. From Bar-backed by more subdued facial pattern, and by lack of bold flank or wing markings. Finely barred, pale brownish breast band and rufous lower breast and belly. Legs greenish. **Voice:** a loud, whistling call which can be divided into three parts: a series of monotone notes, repeated at an increasing tempo; a series of shallow decending and ascending phrases; a series of wildly descending and ascending notes which ends abruptly. Duets. **Habitat:** evergreen and mixed deciduous forests, bamboo from plains to 1000 m. Common resident.

นกกระทาดงปักษ์ใต้

132. Chestnut-necklaced Partridge *Arborophila charltonii* S: 29

Formerly treated as conspecific with Scaly-breasted, but distinguished by dark chestnut breast band bordered on lower margin by bold black bars; yellowish legs and red orbital skin; reddish base to bill. **Voice:** similar to that of Scaly-breasted. **Habitat:** evergreen forests and bamboo of the level lowlands. Rare resident; probably on the verge of extinction.

133. Ferruginous Wood-Partridge *Caloperdix oculea* S: 26   นกกระทาสองเดือย

Deep rufous head and entire underparts, darker chestnut crown and black eye-line. Has black spots (not bars) on brown wings. Fine black and white scales on upper back and on flanks; lower back with black and rufous scales. Male has a leg spur (lacking in female). Legs greenish. **Voice:** an ascending and gradually accelerating trill which ends abruptly in two harsher notes *pi--pi-pi-pipipipipipi dit-duit dit-duit.* **Habitat:** evergreen forests of lowlands and hill slopes, up to 900 m. Uncommon or rare resident; very much reduced by hunting pressure

104

134. Crested Wood-Partridge *Rollulus rouloul* S: 26   ไก่จุก
Predominantly dark greenish plumage, with red legs, red orbital skin.
Male: distinctive maroon crest and white patch on crown. Glossy
plumage appears almost black; wings dark brown. **Female:** paler
green plumage with reddish brown wings; lacks crest. **Voice:** "a
melancholy, glissading whistle, *su-il*, repeated in a steady series and
uttered most frequently at daybreak" (M&W). **Habitat:** evergreen
forest of lowlands and lower hills. Rare resident, much reduced.

135. Long-billed Partridge *Rhizothera longirostris* S: 36   ไก่นวล
Heavy, curved bill. Unmarked rusty-brown throat and sides of head
contrast with darker brown crown and nape. Unmarked, rufous-buff
flanks and belly. **Male:** grey collar around neck and upper back.
Female: grey of neck collar replaced by rufous. **Voice:** a bell-like,
double whistle, given by duetting pairs, and resulting in a rising, 4
note sequence. Calls at dawn and dusk. **Habitat:** evergreen forests,
bamboo of plains and hill slopes. Rare resident; very much reduced.

136. Mountain Bamboo-Partridge *Bambusicola fytchii* S: 35   นกกระทาป่าไผ่
Longer tailed than other partridges, with long buffy-white supercilium
above dark eye-line and broad band of chestnut streaks across
upper breast and neck. Bold black spots on flanks and belly. **Male:**
heavier, blacker eye-line than female; spots and streaks on upperparts blacker. ◆ Has habit of fanning tail. **Voice:** a sudden, loud,
explosive chattering in which the same two notes are rapidly
repeated. **Habitat:** grassland, scrub and bamboo of deforested
areas above 1200 m. Uncommon resident, but possibly expanding
its range with increased deforestation.

137. Chinese Francolin *Francolinus pintadeanus* S: 33   นกกระทาทุ่ง
Male: distinctive face pattern, with white throat and cheeks, black
mask and moustache; bold black and white spotting and scaling on
both upperparts and underparts. Chestnut scapulars. **Female:** more
subdued facial pattern; duller brown plumage. Underparts buffy with
black bars. ◆ Often holds tail cocked while running; sometimes
perches in low trees when calling. **Voice:** harsh, grating *thi-tha-thaak-
tha-thaa*; carries long distances. **Habitat:** grassland, scrub country
from plains to 1500 m. Common resident.

เหล่านกคุ่ม

QUAILS: Genus *Coturnix*. Smaller than partridges, inhabiting open grasslands
and scrub.

138. Japanese Quail *Coturnix japonica* S: 19   นกคุ่มญี่ปุ่น
Distinguished from buttonquails by prominent buff streaks on mantle
and by lack of strong contrast on the upperwing in flight. **Male:**
breast buffy-rufous, usually unstreaked; throat ranges from rufous to
patterned black and white, similar to male Rain Quail. Flanks
streaked chestnut and whitish. **Female:** heavy streaks across upper
breast. Possibly indistinguishable from female Rain Quail. **Voice:**
probably silent. **Habitat:** grasslands, cultivated fields of lowlands.
Very rare winter visitor.

Plate 29 Partridges I

128 Rufous-throated Partridge

129 Bar-backed Partridge

130
Chestnut-headed Partridge

131
Scaly-breasted Partridge

132
Chestnut-necklaced Partridge

133 Ferruginous Wood-Partridge

134 Crested Wood Partridge

139. Rain Quail *Coturnix coromandelica* S: 18   นกคุ่มอกดำ

 Male: black patterning on white throat.   Large black patch on centre of breast, cinnamon patches on sides of breast and heavy black streaks on flanks.   **Female:** less distinctly spotted on breast than female Japanese Quail.   **Voice:** a sharp *whit-whit*, repeated at about one-second intervals.   **Habitat:** dry grasslands, croplands, paddy stubble and scrub country of plains.   Uncommon resident.

140. Blue-breasted Quail *Coturnix chinensis* S: 15   นกคุ่มสี

 From all except Small Buttonquail by tiny size.   **Male:** shows darker upperparts than other quail; black and white face pattern which contrasts with blue-grey sides of head and upper breast and rich chestnut belly and under tail coverts.   **Female:** buffy-brownish.   From other quail and buttonquail by buffy-rufous face with thin dark cheek bar and fine blackish barring across breast and flanks.   From Small Buttonquail by yellow legs.   **Voice:** a sweet double whistle, *ti-yu, ti-yu*.   **Habitat:** grasslands, scrub and cultivated country from plains to 1300 m.   Often favours slightly marshy areas.   Uncommon resident.

วงศ์นกคุ่มแท้

BUTTONQUAILS: Family *Turnicidae*.   Quail-like in appearance, but differ in lacking a hind toe; actually members of the Gruiformes, related to cranes, rails, etc.   Reversed sex roles; the females are more brightly-coloured than the males.   Have booming calls.   Inhabit grass, scrubland and cultivation and are usually much commoner in these habitats than the true quails.   World: 15 species.   Thailand: 3 species.

141. Small Buttonquail (Little Buttonquail) *Turnix sylvatica* S: 14   นกคุ่มอืดเล็ก

 In flight, all buttonquails distinguished from true quail by contrast between sandy-buff upperwing coverts and darker flight feathers.   Small Buttonquail is distinguished by tiny size and by chestnut spotting on sides of neck and wing coverts.   Buffy underparts.   Bill grey; feet fleshy to pale grey.   **Habitat:** grasslands, rice stubble of the plains.   Common resident.

142. Yellow-legged Buttonquail *Turnix tanki* S: 17   นกคุ่มอืดใหญ่

 Distinctive yellow legs are often visible in flight; upperwing contrast stronger than in other buttonquail.   At rest, folded wings appear pale sandy-buff with large black spots; centre of breast pinkish buff, unbarred.   Lower mandible usually yellow.   **Female:** shows more chestnut across upper back than male.   **Habitat:** grasslands, scrub country and rice stubble from plains to 2000 m.   Frequently in slightly marshy situations.   Common resident.

Plate 30 Partridges, Quail, Buttonquail

135 Long-billed Partridge

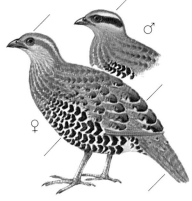

136 Mountain Bamboo-Partridge

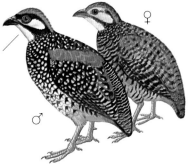

137 Chinese Francolin

138 Japanese Quail

139 Rain Quail

140 Blue-breasted Quail

141 Small Buttonquail

142 Yellow-legged Buttonquail

143 Barred Buttonquail

108

143. Barred Buttonquail *Turnix suscitator* S: 17 นกคุ่มอกลาย

Bill and feet grey. Prominent black bars on sides of breast. Flanks, belly and under tail coverts bright rufous-buff. **Female:** black throat and centre of upper breast. **Voice:** a long series of soft booming notes, roughly half a second apart, which gradually increase in volume and then cease abruptly. **Habitat:** dry grasslands, scrub country and cultivated fields, from plains to 1500 m. Very common resident.

วงศ์นกอัญชัน

RAILS: Family *Rallidae*. Terrestrial wading birds with long legs and toes. Walk with characteristic horizontal body posture, tail usually cocked or jerked upwards; most are capable of swimming. Inhabit dense vegetation of marshes, or waterside vegetation in both open country and wooded areas. Shy and difficult to observe except at dawn and dusk. Flight appears weak, on rounded wings with legs trailing, but many species are long-distance migrants. Calls are little known, but probably distinctive. Omnivorous. Build nests of reeds or grass in or near the water. Sexes similar in most. World: 139 species. Thailand: 15 species.

144. Water Rail *Rallus aquaticus* S: 30 นกอัญชันอกสีไพล

Long, reddish bill. Larger than Slaty-breasted Rail with black-streaked, brownish upperparts and greyish underparts with black and white bars on flanks and under tail coverts. **Juvenile:** browner underparts, usually lacking flank barring; some faint barring on upperwing coverts. **Voice:** while feeding, calls with a sharp *kik*. **Habitat:** marshes. Rare winter visitor.

145. Slaty-breasted Rail *Rallus striatus* S: 27 นกอัญชันอกเทา

Rather long bill and chestnut crown and hindneck. Profuse, thin, wavy white barring on entire upperparts. Grey breast with black and white bars on flanks and under tail coverts. **Juvenile:** has some dark streaking on crown and browner, less distinctly barred underparts. **Voice:** a sharp *cerrk*. **Habitat:** mangroves, marshes, streams and paddy margins; mainly in lowlands, but recorded up to 1300 m. Common resident.

146. Red-legged Crake *Rallina fasciata* S: 25 นกอัญชันป่าขาแดง

Heavy whitish barring on primaries, secondaries and wing coverts. Head, neck, throat and upper breast are bright chestnut-orange; broad black and white barring on lower breast and belly. Upperparts brighter, more reddish brown than in Band-bellied Crake. Legs bright red; broad red orbital ring and red eye. **Juvenile:** has chestnut replaced by brown and less distinct barring on coverts. **Habitat:** moist areas, streamsides in forest and secondary growth, mainly of the lowlands. **Voice:** a loud series of nasal *pek* calls, given at intervals of roughly 0.5 seconds, usually at dawn and dusk. Also a long descending trill, reminiscent of Ruddy-breasted Crake. Uncommon resident, passage migrant and winter visitor.

Plate 31 Rails I

144 Water Rail

145 Slaty-breasted Rail

146 Red-legged Crake

147 Slaty-legged Crake

148 Baillon's Crake

149 Spotted Crake

150 Ruddy-breasted Crake

151 Band-bellied Crake

Mongkol

110

147. Slaty-legged Crake *Rallina eurizonoides* S: 25   นกอัญชันป่าขาเทา

At rest, upperparts appear uniform dark brown; white barring on inner webs of flight feathers shows in flight only. From Red-legged by duller upperparts, lack of white barring on wing coverts, greenish to blackish grey legs and by dull, greyish pink orbital ring. Red eye. **Juvenile:** has chestnut areas on underparts replaced by dull olive-brownish. Eye dull brownish. **Habitat:** wet areas in forest and secondary growth; also marshes, gardens on passage, from plains to 1500 m. Uncommon or rare; probably breeds in the north. Passage migrant or winter visitor elsewhere.

148. Baillon's Crake *Porzana pusilla* S: 19   นกอัญชันเล็ก

The smallest crake, with a short greenish bill. Streaked brownish upperparts, with bold white flecking. Underparts greyish with finely barred black and white flanks and under tail coverts. **Juvenile:** less distinctly barred, browner underparts. ◆ In flight, shows prominent whitish leading edge to wing. Legs yellowish green. **Habitat:** marshes, ponds, ditches of open lowlands. Common winter visitor.

149. Spotted Crake *Porzana porzana* S: 22   นกอัญชันเล็กลายจุด

Resembles Baillon's Crake, but larger and more profusely speckled with white on both upperparts and underparts, and with unmarked buffy-whitish under tail coverts. Bill usually yellowish with red base. Shows whitish leading edge to wing in flight. **Habitat:** marshes. Very rare winter visitor.

150. Ruddy-breasted Crake *Porzana fusca* S: 22   นกกหนูแดง

Deep, dull chestnut underparts with narrow and inconspicuous black and white barring confined to hind flanks and under tail coverts. Unmarked, dark olive-brown upperparts. Legs reddish. Orbital ring red, but much thinner than in Red-legged and not easily seen. Eye red (adult) or brown (immature). **Voice:** a prolonged, 3–4 second burst of squeaky trilling, similar to the call of Little Grebe but descending slightly in pitch. **Habitat:** marshes and wet areas in open country. Common; both resident and migrant birds probably present.

151. Band-bellied Crake *Porzana paykullii* S: 23   นกอัญชันจีน

Distinguished from Slaty-legged and Red-legged Crakes by dark brownish crown and hindneck sharply demarcated from paler chestnut-rufous sides of head and breast. From Red-legged also by dull olive-brown upperparts. Shows whitish barring on wing coverts but not flight feathers. Legs red. Red orbital ring thinner and less obvious than in Red-legged. **Immature:** chestnut replaced by brown. **Habitat:** lowland swampy areas. Very rare winter visitor.

Plate 32 Rails II

152 Black-tailed Crake

153 White-browed Crake

154 White-breasted Waterhen

155 Watercock

♀ and non-breeding

♂ breeding

immature

ad. breeding

156 Common Moorhen

157 Purple Swamphen

152. Black-tailed Crake *Porzana bicolor* S: 25 นกอัญชันหางดำ

Bright rufous olive-brown back and wings; dark slaty grey head, neck, underparts and under tail coverts. Upper tail coverts blackish brown. Bill dull greenish and legs pinkish red. **Voice:** a prolonged trill, more obviously descending than in Ruddy-breasted Crake and usually preceded by quiet, harsh rasping notes. **Habitat:** marshy patches and streamsides of open secondary growth, above 1000 m. Rare resident, but may be much overlooked.

153. White-browed Crake *Porzana cinerea* S: 20 นกอัญชันคิ้วขาว

Distinctive facial pattern of black eye-line, white supercilium and cheek bar on otherwise grey head; grey breast. Upperparts brown, streaked blackish. Flanks buffy-brown and under tail coverts cinnamon-buff. Bill greenish yellow, with small area of red at base. **Juvenile:** brownish underparts and subdued face pattern; lacks red on bill. ◆ Legs pale green. **Habitat:** marshes, lakes. Favours dense mats of floating vegetation. Uncommon resident.

154. White-breasted Waterhen *Amaurornis phoenicurus* S: 33 นกกวัก

Diagnostic white face and underparts, cinnamon under tail coverts and blackish upperparts. Bill greenish yellow with red base. **Juvenile:** browner upperparts and sullied underparts. ◆ Usually keeps to water's edge, close to overhanging trees and bushes. **Voice:** demoniacal roaring noises and a long series of monotonous *kwaak* notes. Very common resident. **Habitat:** marshes, canals, paddyfields, mangrove edge.

155. Watercock *Gallicrex cinerea* S: 43 นกอีล้ำม

Identified by large size and slim, long-necked appearance. Shows whitish leading edge to wing in all plumages. **Breeding male:** blackish grey body plumage with yellow-tipped red bill and red frontal shield, red legs and buffy under tail coverts. **Female and non-breeding male:** buffy-brown with bold blackish streaking on upperparts. Bill dull greenish horn; legs olive-green. **Voice:** a deep, booming *toom*. **Habitat:** dense vegetation of marshes and paddy-field margins. Common resident and wet-season breeding visitor.

156. Common Moorhen *Gallinula chloropus* S: 33 นกอีล้ำ

Adult: blackish body with whitish streak along flank and white under tail coverts. Yellow-tipped red bill and red frontal shield. **Juvenile:** has brownish upperparts and whitish underparts with dull greenish bill. Frequently swims with tail cocked high, showing two large white oval patches on under tail coverts. **Voice:** a loud, harsh *prruk*. **Habitat:** marshy areas, ponds. Common resident; probably also partial migrant or winter visitor.

Plate 33 Coot, Finfoot, Jacanas

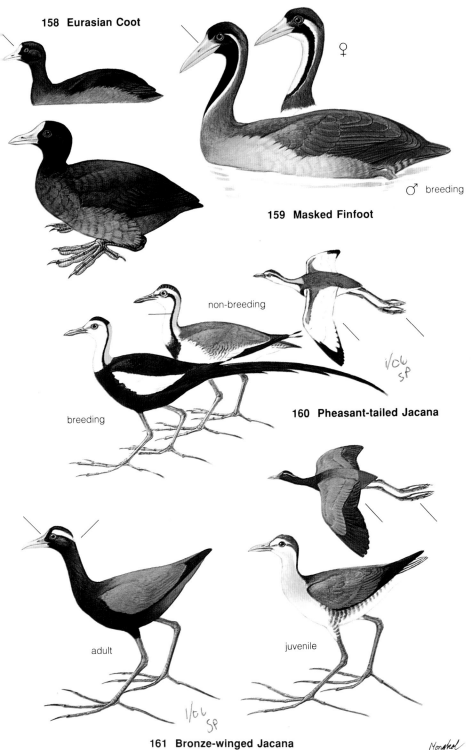

158 Eurasian Coot

159 Masked Finfoot

♀

♂ breeding

non-breeding

160 Pheasant-tailed Jacana

breeding

161 Bronze-winged Jacana

adult

juvenile

Mongkol

157. Purple Swamphen *Porphyrio porphyrio* S: 43 นกอีโก้ง

Easily recognised by large size and heavy build, large red bill and frontal shield, reddish legs and glossy, dark purplish blue plumage (somewhat paler on head). White under tail coverts. **Juvenile:** duller with blackish bill. **Voice:** harsh grunts and cackling. **Habitat:** marshes; often found in dense floating vegetation on lakes. Fairly common resident; numerous only in the larger, less disturbed wetlands.

158. Eurasian Coot (Common Coot) *Fulica atra* S: 41 นกคู้ท

A duck-like swimming bird with all black plumage; white bill and frontal shield. In flight, shows thin whitish trailing edge to wing. **Juvenile:** browner above and paler below. ◆ When taking off, patters along surface of water like a diving duck. Frequently dives. **Habitat:** open marshes, ponds and lakes. Uncommon winter visitor.

วงศ์นกฟินฟุท

FINFOOTS: Family *Heliornithidae*. Shy, aquatic birds with long necks and tapered bills. Dive well and swim partly submerged. World: 3 species: Thailand: one species.

159. Masked Finfoot *Heliopais personata* S: 53 นกฟินฟุท

Pointed yellow bill, green legs and feet. Olive brown upperparts with black face mask. **Male:** entirely black throat and front of neck, with narrow white border. Has a small knob above base of bill in breeding season. **Female:** whitish patch on centre of throat and foreneck. **Juvenile:** resembles female, but lacks black on crown. Shy, usually seen singly or in small groups. **Voice:** reputed to have a bubbling call (Smythies). **Habitat:** clear-water forest ponds and sluggish rivers; mangroves. Status uncertain; uncommon passage migrant and winter visitor; may perhaps also breed.

วงศ์นกพริก

JACANAS: Family *Jacanidae*. Noted for extremely long toes which allow the bird to walk across floating vegetation of lakes and ponds. Show reversed sex roles, the female often mating with more than one male, which she leaves to care for the eggs and young. World: 8 species. Thailand: 2 species.

160. Pheasant-tailed Jacana *Hydrophasianus chirurgus* S: 30 นกอีแจว

In flight, from Bronze-winged in all plumages by almost entirely white wings. Also by blackish line along side of neck. **Breeding:** mainly blackish brown body, white face and foreneck and yellowish hindneck. Greatly elongate tail. **Non-breeding:** brownish crown and hindneck and grey-brown upperparts. Shows yellow suffusion on sides of neck. **Juvenile:** similar but lacks any yellowish on neck. Nests on floating vegetation of the larger lakes. **Voice:** a peculiar nasal note *jaew*. **Habitat:** marshes, lakes and flooded fields. Common resident and winter visitor.

Plate 34 Lapwings, Plovers

underwing

upperwing

162 Northern Lapwing

163 Grey-headed Lapwing　**164 Red-wattled Lapwing**　**165 River Lapwing**

underwing

upperwing

non-breeding

breeding

166 Grey Plover

underwing

upperwing

non-breeding

breeding

Mongkol

167 Pacific Golden Plover

116

161. Bronze-winged Jacana *Metopidius indicus* S: 28   นกพริก

Adult: identified by glossy blackish body, bronze-olive back and wing coverts and striking white supercilium. **Juvenile:** whitish underparts with buffy neck and breast. In flight, blackish flight feathers contrast with bronze upperwing coverts. From Pheasant-tailed by lack of dark line on neck; lack of white in wing. **Voice:** musical piping notes and low, guttural notes. **Habitat:** marshes, ponds and canals. Common resident.

วงศ์นกกระแตและนกหัวโต

PLOVERS: Family *Charadriidae.* Small to medium-sized wading birds with large heads, short necks and short bills. Show a rather hesitant gait, typically running or walking a few steps then stopping to peck at food taken mostly from the ground surface. Often in drier situations than sandpipers. Nest in shallow, unlined depressions on the ground. Sexes usually similar. World: 65 species. Thailand: 12 species.

162. Northern Lapwing *Vanellus vanellus* S: 30   นกกระแตหงอน

Easily identified by long crest, dark glossy green upperparts, dark face mask and blackish breast band. In flight shows very broad, rounded, blackish wings with contrasting whitish primary tips and gleaming white underwing coverts. **Habitat:** marshes, paddies. Rare winter visitor.

163. Grey-headed Lapwing *Vanellus cinereus* S: 35   นกกระแตหัวเทา

Uniform grey head, neck and upper breast, grading into a blackish band of varying distinctness across lower breast. Yellow bill with black tip, yellow legs. In flight, shows all white secondaries and broad, black subterminal tail band. **Voice:** a sharp *kik*, usually uttered in flight. **Habitat:** rice stubbles, marshes. Chiefly found in the plains. Common winter visitor to the far north; less common further south.

164. Red-wattled Lapwing *Vanellus indicus* S: 33   นกกระแตแต้แว๊ด

Black head, neck, throat and upper breast with white patch behind eye, extending on to side of neck. Red bill, tipped black, and conspicuous red wattle. Legs yellow. In flight, shows much less white on secondaries than Grey-headed. From River Lapwing by white-tipped tail. **Voice:** a loud and penetrating *tae-tae-taewaet*, uttered mostly in flight. **Habitat:** dry bush country, cultivated fields, marshes, rivers. Very common resident.

165. River Lapwing *Vanellus duvaucelii* S: 30 นกกระแตหาด

Black cap and throat contrasts with grey-brown sides of head and breast. Black patch in centre of belly, black bill and black or greenish legs. No wattle. Flight pattern similar to Red-wattled, but lacks white tip to tail and has black patch on bend of wing. **Voice:** a shrill, high-pitched *keck*, frequently repeated. **Habitat:** sandy shores and sand bars of the larger streams and rivers. Uncommon resident.

166. Grey Plover *Pluvialis squatarola* S: 28 นกหัวโตสีเทา

The largest of the typical plovers. In flight, shows whitish underwing with diagnostic black axillaries; white wing bar, white rump and tail. **Non-breeding:** brownish grey upperparts and whitish underparts. From Pacific Golden Plover by larger size, heavier bill, and greyer appearance; flight pattern and call. **Breeding:** black face, breast and belly with broad white supercilium and sides of neck. Upperparts spangled black and white. Moulting birds with blotched white underparts are often seen, especially in spring. ◆ Often solitary. **Voice:** three slurred whistles, *tlee-u-ee*, rising on the final syllable. **Habitat:** mudflats and sandy shores; rarely inland. Common winter visitor.

นกหัวโตหลังจุดสีทอง

167. Pacific Golden Plover (Lesser Golden Plover) *Pluvialis fulva* S: 25

Proportions similar to Grey Plover, but has thinner bill and smaller head; wings extend beyond tail at rest. In flight, shows a slight white wing bar; rump and tail concolorous with rest of upperparts; underwing and axillaries mottled greyish. **Non-breeding:** upperparts appear mottled brownish but, at close range, are spangled with gold and buff. Pale, buffy whitish forehead and supercilium with a usually prominent dark spot on ear coverts. Neck and breast brownish buff, grading into white on belly. **Breeding:** black face, breast and belly, divided from black and gold-spangled upperparts by white forehead and supercilium which extends into broad line down sides of underparts. Under tail coverts mainly white. Moulting birds, with white-blotched underparts are frequently seen in spring and early autumn. **Voice:** a shrill *chew-eet*, the second syllable markedly higher. **Habitat:** mudflats, freshwater marshes, paddyfields and areas of short, dry grassland. Very common winter visitor.

168. Little Ringed Plover *Charadrius dubius* S: 18 นกหัวโตเล็กขาเหลือง

From other similar small plovers by yellowish to orange legs, lack of a wing bar in flight and by distinctive call. Upperparts uniform brownish with complete white neck collar. Black breast band, black mask and narrow white line above black on forehead. Prominent yellow orbital ring. **Immature and some non-breeding adults:** black parts replaced by brown and breast band sometimes broken. Orbital ring less distinct. **Voice:** a single, plaintive, falling tone whistle, *heu.* **Habitat:** mudflats, beaches, river flats, marshes and paddyfields. Common and widespread winter visitor; local and uncommon resident along the northern rivers.

118

169. **Kentish Plover** *Charadrius alexandrinus* S: 15 นกหัวโตขาดำ

From Little Ringed Plover by bold white wing bar in flight and (usually) greyish to black legs. From Lesser Sand-Plover by complete white neck collar and smaller size. See Malaysian Plover. **Breeding male:** rufous cap, black markings on sides of breast and black forecrown and mask. **Non-breeding male, female:** crown brown; black on head and breast replaced by brown. **Juvenile:** head and breast markings even paler than in adult female. **Voice:** a soft *tic*. **Habitat:** mainly coastal areas, mudflats and sandy beaches but also inland on paddyfields and freshwater marshes. Common winter visitor.

170. **Malaysian Plover** *Charadrius peronii* S: 15 นกหัวโตมลายู

Distinguished from Kentish Plover by sandier, distinctly mottled upperparts and usually paler, pinkish or greyish legs. Appears shorter-bodied than Kentish, with stubbier bill and longer legs. **Male:** broad black line across upper back. Black markings on sides of neck thinner than in Kentish, almost meeting across upper breast. Separate black loral and ear patches. Crown and nape bright sandy-rufous. **Female:** all black markings replaced by sandy-rufous. **Juvenile:** slightly duller than female; though still shows distinctly scaly upperparts and rufous breast patches. **Voice:** similar to Kentish Plover. **Habitat:** undisturbed sandy beaches; rarely on adjacent mudflats. Local and uncommon resident.

171. **Long-billed Plover** *Charadrius placidus* S: 21 นกหัวโตปากยาว

Markings similar to those of Little Ringed Plover, but is larger with a markedly longer bill; ear patch is brown in all plumages. Longer tail and legs. Shows a very narrow whitish wing bar in flight. Legs dull yellow. **Breeding:** black frontal bar and breast band. **Voice:** a loud, disyllabic or trisyllabic piping. **Habitat:** river flats, dry fields of plains. Rare winter visitor.

นกหัวโตทรายเล็ก

172. **Lesser Sand-Plover** (Mongolian Plover) *Charadrius mongolus* S: 23

Very similar to Greater Sand-Plover, but best distinguished by smaller bill with less noticeably tapering tip; smaller size when seen together and by shorter legs above the joint. Legs usually dark greyish. In flight, generally shows less white in outer tail feathers and, in some birds, legs do not project beyond the tail-tip. **Non-breeding:** dull greyish brown on head and upperparts with whitish forehead and supercilium. Underparts whitish with square, grey-brown patch at sides of breast. From Kentish Plover by larger size and lack of white collar across back of neck. **Breeding:** orange-rufous breast and sides of neck, front and sides of crown; black mask. Forehead becomes almost wholly black in *atrifrons* group of races, which predominate in Thailand. ◆ Often in mixed flocks with Greater Sand-Plover, which it always greatly outnumbers on mudflats. **Voice:** a short, rather hard trill; *chirrip* or *tittitip*. **Habitat:** coastal mudflats, shrimp ponds, beaches. Often roosts on offshore rocky islets. Very common winter visitor.

Plate 35 Plovers II

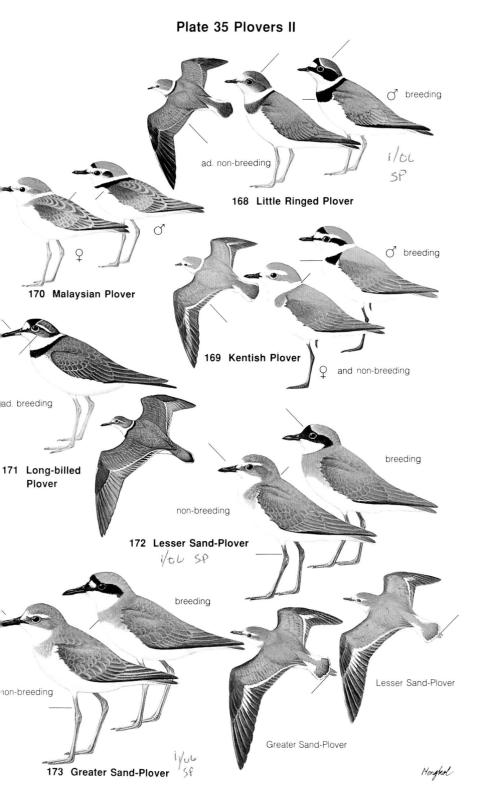

♂ breeding

ad. non-breeding

i/ᴄʟ SP

168 Little Ringed Plover

♀

♂

170 Malaysian Plover

♂ breeding

169 Kentish Plover

♀ and non-breeding

ad. breeding

171 Long-billed Plover

breeding

non-breeding

172 Lesser Sand-Plover

i/ᴄʟ SP

breeding

Lesser Sand-Plover

non-breeding

Greater Sand-Plover

173 Greater Sand-Plover

i/ᴄʟ SP

Mongkol

173. **Greater Sand-Plover** *Charadrius leschenaultii* S: 24   นกหัวโตทรายใหญ่
Distinguished from Lesser Sand-Plover by larger and heavier bill with more noticeably tapering tip; slightly larger size and longer legs when seen together. Legs usually paler, greenish grey. In flight, usually shows more white at sides of tail; subterminal band darker. Legs always project beyond the tail-tip. **Non breeding:** body plumage as Lesser Sand-Plover. **Breeding:** narrower orange-rufous breast band than Lesser, with more white on forehead. **Voice:** very similar to Lesser, but softer, more trilling. **Habitat:** open sandy shores and mudflats. (Often more abundant than Lesser Sand-Plover in the former situation.) Common winter visitor.

วงศ์นกอีก๋อย, นกชายเลนและนกปากซ่อม

CURLEWS, GODWITS, SANDPIPERS and SNIPES: Family *Scolopacidae*. Small to medium-sized, long-legged wading birds with long, slender bills which are used to probe in soft mud or water. Plumages often intricately mottled; juvenile and breeding plumages are usually brighter than the dull greys and browns of winter plumage. Identification is facilitated by distinctive field characters such as wing bars, tail pattern and flight calls, together with size and shape. Gregarious in the non-breeding season, when form large roosting and feeding flocks. Long distance migrants; no species breed in Thailand. Sexes usually similar. World: 88 species. Thailand: 39 species. (See under Additions, page 400.)

174. **Eastern Curlew** *Numenius madagascariensis* S: 59 นกอีก๋อยตะโพกสีน้ำตาล
Like Eurasian Curlew, but darker and browner, with more uniformly dark buff underparts. Bill often slightly longer. In flight, lower back and tail brownish, concolorous with mantle; underwing and axillaries barred brownish. **Habitat:** coastal mudflats, sandy beaches. Rare passage migrant.

175. **Eurasian Curlew** *Numenius arquata* S: 58   นกอีก๋อยใหญ่
Large, with very long, curved bill. In flight, shows white rump which extends part way up the back in a triangular patch. Underwing coverts and axillaries pure white. From Whimbrel by lack of bold head stripes, larger size and longer, more evenly curved bill. **Voice:** a loud, ringing *cour-li*, with rising inflection. **Habitat:** coastal mudflats, sandy beaches. Fairly common winter visitor.

176. **Whimbrel** *Numenius phaeopus* S: 43   นกอีก๋อยเล็ก
Smaller and stockier than Eurasian Curlew, with shorter, kinked (rather than evenly curved) bill. Bold blackish lateral crown stripes contrast sharply with pale buffy-brown central crown stripe. Race *N. p. phaeopus* has white rump like Eurasian Curlew; white much reduced in race *N. p. variegatus*. **Voice:** a clear, musical whinnying trill of about 7 notes; *ti-ti-ti-ti-ti-ti-ti*. **Habitat:** coastal mudflats, sandy beaches. At high tide, often roosts by perching in mangrove trees. Common winter visitor.

Plate 36 Curlews

174 Eastern Curlew

175 Eurasian Curlew

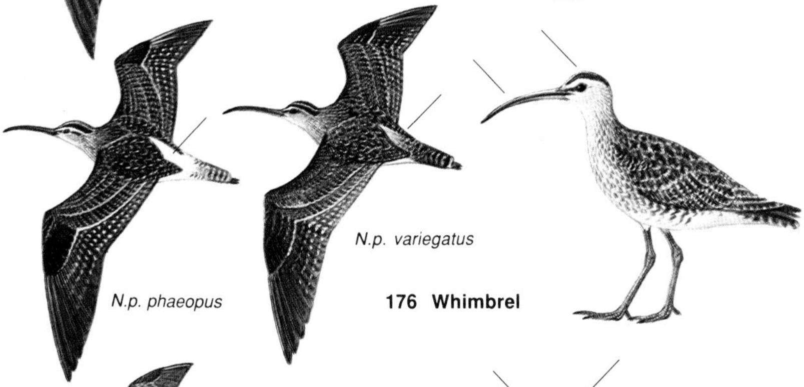

N.p. phaeopus

N.p. variegatus

176 Whimbrel

177 Little Curlew

Mongkol

122

177. Little Curlew *Numenius minutus* S: 30 นกอีก๋อยจิ๋ว

Like a small, fine-billed version of a Whimbrel; only slightly larger than Pacific Golden Plover. Shows Whimbrel-like head pattern of narrow whitish buff median crown stripe and broad blackish lateral crown stripes. Slightly broader, more strikingly pale buffy supercilium contrasts more with blackish eye-line than in Whimbrel. Underparts deeper buffy. In flight, shows uniformly brownish back, rump and tail; buffy brownish underwing coverts. **Voice:** flight call of 3–4 notes, *di-di-di*, ascending slightly, with somewhat Whimbrel-like quality. **Habitat:** fields of short grass; occasionally mudflats. Very rare passage migrant.

178. Black-tailed Godwit *Limosa limosa* S: 36–38 นกปากแอ่นหางดำ

Both godwits distinguished from Asian Dowitcher by bills which are flesh-coloured at base and which taper to a point. Size variable; females of both godwits are often larger than males. From Bar-tailed Godwit by broad white wing bar and by broad black terminal band on white tail. Bill straighter. **Non-breeding:** upperparts grey-brown, rather uniform; underparts whitish, washed brown on the breast. **Breeding:** neck and breast deep rufous, slightly brighter in male than female; belly and under tail coverts whitish. Broad dark bars on flanks, lower breast and belly. **Voice:** *wicka-wicka-wicka*, usually uttered in flight. **Habitat:** coastal mudflats, marshes. Fairly common winter visitor and passage migrant.

179. Bar-tailed Godwit *Limosa lapponica* S: 38–42 นกปากแอ่นหางลาย

In flight, from Black-tailed by lack of wing bar and barred tail. Usually shows distinctly upturned bill. Race *baueri* (less numerous than nominate race *lapponica*) shows barred brownish underwing coverts and reduced white on rump. **Non-breeding:** upperparts boldy streaked (uniform in non-breeding Black-tailed). **Breeding:** male shows deeper rufous underparts than male Black-tailed; lacks barring on flanks and belly. **Voice:** a loud *kaak, kaak, kaak*, uttered in flight. **Habitat:** sandy beaches, coastal mudflats. Fairly common winter visitor, usually outnumbered by Black-tailed Godwit except at one or two sites on the west coast.

180. Asian Dowitcher *Limnodromus semipalmatus* S: 35 นกซ่อมทะเลอกแดง

Distinguished from godwits by more compact, shorter-necked appearance and by straight, all black bill with slightly swollen tip. Bill almost always held angled downwards; shows distinctive 'stitching' feeding action. In flight, rump and tail whitish, finely and evenly barred brown, sometimes with a clear whitish spot at apex of rump patch. Shows diffuse whitish area at base of secondaries. **Non-breeding:** upperparts dull grey-brown, more boldly scaled than in godwits. Underparts pale grey-brown, less whitish than in godwits. **Breeding:** feathers of mantle and scapulars brownish black, with chestnut edges; breast deep chestnut. ◆ Shows extensive dark flank barring at all times of year. **Voice:** usually silent, but occasionally an airy *chaow*. **Habitat:** coastal mudflats. Uncommon passage migrant; a few birds may possibly overwinter in the Peninsula.

Plate 37 Godwits, Dowitchers

178 Black-tailed Godwit

¼06 SP

non-breeding   breeding

L.l. lapponica

L.l. baueri

non-breeding   breeding

179 Bar-tailed Godwit

non-breeding   breeding

180 Asian Dowitcher

non-breeding   breeding

181 Long-billed Dowitcher

Mongkol

124

181. Long-billed Dowitcher *Limnodromus scolopaceus* S: 30

Winter and breeding plumages similar to those of Asian, but distinguished by smaller size, shorter, paler, greenish grey legs (dark in Asian Dowitcher) and, in flight, by extensive white wedge on lower back and rump. Shows a fairly well-defined white trailing edge to the secondaries. **Voice:** a high, thin *keek*; sometimes a single note, but often repeated, recalling Wood Sandpiper. **Habitat:** marshes, coastal areas. Very rare winter visitor. (One record; description submitted did not fully rule out the less likely Short-billed Dowitcher *L. griseus*, which is best separated by its call, a mellow *tu-tu-tu*.)

182. Spotted Redshank *Tringa erythropus* S: 30   นกทะเลขาแดงลายจุด

Slim and long-legged. Red legs like Common Redshank, but bill is longer and proportionately finer, with brighter red base to lower mandible. In flight, lacks white patch on secondaries and legs project further beyond tail. Long wedge of white extends up the back. **Non-breeding:** upperparts usually greyer and paler than in Common Redshank and underparts whiter. Well-defined whitish supercilium. **Breeding:** plumage sooty-black, the upperparts finely spotted with white. **Voice:** an explosive *chew-it*, recalling Pacific Golden Plover; uttered both in flight and at rest. **Habitat:** freshwater marshes, flooded fields, coastal mudflats and fishponds. Fairly common winter visitor.

183. Common Redshank *Tringa totanus* S: 28   นกทะเลขาแดงธรรมดา

Red legs and base of bill. More compact with shorter bill and legs than Spotted Redshank. In flight, broad white patch on secondaries; wedge of white extends up the back. **Non-breeding:** upperparts grey-brown with less pronounced supercilium than Spotted Redshank. Underparts whitish, faintly streaked on neck and breast. **Breeding:** appearance similar, but darker and more heavily streaked, especially on underparts. **Voice:** usually 3 or 4 ringing notes, *teuuu*, *teu-heu-heu*, typically with a pause after the first note, which is slightly longer and higher-pitched. **Habitat:** coastal mudflats; occasionally freshwater marshes and flooded paddies. Very common winter visitor.

184. Common Greenshank *Tringa nebularia* S: 35   นกทะเลขาเขียว

Large, slim and long-legged. Greenish legs and slightly upturned bill, which basally rather thick and coloured pale greenish to greyish (often clearly demarcated from dark tip as in Nordmann's Greenshank). Striking contrast between dark greyish upperparts and whitish underparts. In flight, lacks a wing bar and has wedge of white extending up back; underwing and axillaries appear pale greyish. Feet project markedly beyond tail. **Non-breeding:** face and forehead whitish. Shows slight dark grey streaking across breast. **Breeding:** face and forehead darker; breast more boldly streaked blackish. Upperparts show some black markings. **Voice:** a loud, ringing *heu-heu-heu*; usually three notes, but may be from two to six. **Habitat:** coastal mudflats, freshwater marshes, paddyfields, rivers. Common winter visitor.

Plate 38 Redshanks, Greenshanks

182 Spotted Redshank

breeding

non-breeding

non-breeding

breeding

183 Common Redshank

non-breeding

breeding

184 Common Greenshank

breeding

non-breeding

non-breeding

185 Nordmann's Greenshank

Mongkol

126

185. Nordmann's Greenshank *Tringa guttifer* S: 32   นกทะเลขาเขียวลายจุด
Slightly smaller and stockier than Common Greenshank, with legs which are distinctly shorter above the joint and usually yellow-green. Noticeable yellow webs extend between bases of toes. Slightly upturned bill is proportionately thicker and broader-based than Common Greenshank when seen head-on. Basal half of bill markedly paler than distal half, but demarcation not usually sharp and contrast sometimes muted. Flight pattern similar to Common Greenshank but shows pure white underwing and axillaries; projection of feet beyond tail is shorter. **Non-breeding:** upperparts and head paler grey than in Common Greenshank and underparts whiter, unstreaked. **Breeding:** heavy blackish spotting on breast and flanks; dark upperparts. **Voice:** usually silent; occasionally gives a loud, hoarse *keyew*. **Habitat** mudflats, open sandy beaches. Annual but rare winter visitor; chiefly in the Peninsula.

186. Marsh Sandpiper *Tringa stagnatilis* S: 25   นกชายเลนบึง
Legs greenish; occasionally dull yellow. Resembles Common Greenshank, but distinguished by much lighter build, smaller size (close to Wood Sandpiper) and by straight, fine black bill. Legs project further beyond the tail-tip in flight. From Wood Sandpiper by longer, thinner bill and by white of rump extending far up back in a narrow wedge. Much paler upperparts in non-breeding plumage. **Non-breeding:** upperparts greyish, with white face, forehead and underparts. **Breeding:** loses pale appearance to head; upperparts finely spotted black. **Voice:** a single note, *teuk*, repeated at intervals, with piping quality very similar to that of Common Redshank. **Habitat:** coastal mudflats; freshwater marshes, paddyfields. Very common winter visitor.

187. Green Sandpiper *Tringa ochropus* S: 24   นกชายเลนเขียว
In flight, square white patch on rump and upper tail; lacks wing bar. From Wood Sandpiper by blackish underwing and by call. Dark greenish brown upperparts, with much less white spotting than in Wood Sandpiper; short, inconspicuous whitish supercilium; white eye-ring. Legs greenish. Dark upperparts and dark smudges on sides of breast recall Common Sandpiper; also bobs tail slightly when feeding, as in that species, but distinguished by folded wings and tail of approximately equal length. Usually solitary, or in small groups. **Voice:** a sharp, ringing *tlu-eet-weet-weet*. **Habitat:** mainly freshwater areas; ponds, ditches, puddles around paddy edges. Fairly common winter visitor.

188. Wood Sandpiper *Tringa glareola* S: 23   นกชายเลนน้ำจืด
In flight, square white rump patch; lacks wing bar. From Green Sandpiper by whitish basal part of underwing, more heavily barred tail (giving slightly smaller rump patch) and by call. At rest, upperparts browner, boldly freckled with white; long white supercilium gives dark-capped appearance to head. Yellowish legs. Often in large, scattered flocks. **Voice:** a high-pitched *chiff-chiff-chiff*. **Habitat:** freshwater marshes, paddyfields, coastal fish ponds, mangroves. Very common winter visitor; usually the most abundant wader in freshwater habitats.

Plate 39 Tringa Sandpipers

breeding

non-breeding

186 Marsh Sandpiper
VOC SP

187 Green Sandpiper

underwing

upperwing

underwing

upperwing

188 Wood Sandpiper
VOC SP

189 Common Sandpiper
VOC SP

Mongkol

128

189. Common Sandpiper *Actitis hypoleucos* S: 20 นกเด้าดิน

At rest, tail extends well beyond wing-tips. In flight, broad white wing bar, brownish rump and tail with white sides. Plain, brownish olive upperparts with slight whitish supercilium, white eye-ring; underparts white with brown smudges on sides of breast. Bobs tail constantly. Flies with shallow, flickering beats, alternating with short glides on downcurved wings. Usually solitary or in small groups. **Voice:** a shrill, high-pitched piping, *twee-wee-wee*. **Habitat:** ditches, marshes, paddyfields, rivers (including fast-flowing streams). Usually around the drier margins of extensive coastal mudflats. Very common winter visitor.

190. Terek Sandpiper *Xenus cinereus* S: 25 นกชายเลนปากแอ่น

Small, with long, upturned bill with yellow base and rather short, orange yellow legs. In flight, shows grey rump and tail, concolorous with back, and white trailing edge to secondaries. **Non-breeding:** pale, grey-brown upperparts, with blackish brown patch at bend of wing; thin whitish supercilia join across forehead. **Breeding:** blackish lines on mantle; loses pale forehead. A dashing and active feeder, which bobs its tail. **Voice:** a distinctive loud and ringing *kleet-kleet*, second note slightly lower pitched. **Habitat:** sandy beaches, mudflats. Fairly common winter visitor and passage migrant.

191. Grey-tailed Tattler *Heteroscelus brevipes* S: 25 นกตีนเหลือง

At rest, dark plumage and medium length, straight bill are suggestive of Common Redshank, but long wings give slender-bodied appearance; legs shorter, yellowish. At close range, plain, dark grey upperparts with whitish supercilia which meet across forehead. In flight, lacks wing bar; rump and tail appear concolorous with mantle. (Rump narrowly barred whitish, but bars difficult to discern.) Dusky underwing. **Non-breeding:** underparts unbarred, whitish, with grey wash on breast and flanks; forehead whitish. **Breeding:** breast and flanks narrowly barred grey; belly and under tail coverts whitish. ◆ Bobs tail. **Voice:** a sharp, ascending whistle, *tu-weet*; emphasis on last syllable. **Habitat:** around the drier edges of extensive coastal mudflats; also rocky coasts and sandy beaches. Rare passage migrant.

192. Ruddy Turnstone *Arenaria interpres* S: 23 นกพลิกหิน

Distinctive dark and white, boldly striped pattern in flight with white wing bar, white patch on wing coverts, white rump and black and white banded tail. At rest, rather short orange legs; stocky build. Short dark bill. **Non-breeding:** dark brown head, upperparts and breast band; white belly. **Breeding:** white head with black facial markings; black breast band and bright rufous upperparts. Feeds by flicking over pebbles, seaweed, etc. with bill, to expose small animals beneath. **Voice:** a hard, trilling *kiti-kiti-kiti-kiti-kit*. **Habitat:** rocky coasts, sandy beaches, mudflats. Common winter visitor.

Plate 40 Sandpipers, Turnstone, Phalarope

non-breeding

breeding

190 Terek Sandpiper

underwing

upperwing

breeding

non-breeding

191 Grey-tailed Tattler

breeding

non-breeding

192 Ruddy Turnstone

non-breeding

♀ breeding

193 Red-necked Phalarope

Mongkol

193. Red-necked Phalarope *Phalaropus lobatus* S: 19   นกลอยทะเลคอแดง

In flight, shows white wing bar and white lateral tail coverts. From *Calidris* waders by needle-like black bill and black eye patch or by diagnostic breeding plumage. Has lobed feet and frequently swims. **Non-breeding:** white forehead, black eye patch, crown and nape. Dark grey upperparts with long, whitish streaks; white underparts. **Breeding:** blackish head, white throat and orange-rufous patch on sides of neck. Female is markedly brighter than male. **Juvenile:** blacker upperparts than non-breeding, with some yellowish streaks. ◆ Flanks heavily streaked dark grey. Legs grey. **Habitat:** coastal mudflats, shrimp ponds. Rare winter visitor or passage migrant.

194. Rufous-necked Stint *Calidris ruficollis* S: 16   นกสติ๊นท์คอแดง

Very small size and short bills distinguish stints from other sandpipers. Rufous-necked distinguished from Temminck's and Long-toed by blackish legs and stocky, large-headed appearance. Bill-tip blunt, slightly swollen. In flight, shows white wing bar. **Non-breeding:** much paler grey-brown above than either Temminck's or Long-toed, the individual feathers showing dark shaft streaks and broad greyish fringes giving indistinctly scaled appearance. Whitish forehead and supercilium. Underparts whitish, almost unstreaked, with pale greyish lateral breast patches. **Breeding:** upper breast, face and neck bright rufous, but very variable; upperparts mottled dark brown and chestnut. **Juvenile:** darker above than non-breeding plumage with both rufous and white-edged scapular feathers. See also Little Stint (911) for distinctions from that species. **Voice:** a sharp *chit*. **Habitat:** mudflats, sandy beaches, coastal fish ponds. Usually the commonest stint in saline or brackish situations. Very common winter visitor.

195. Temminck's Stint *Calidris temminckii* S: 15   นกสติ๊นท์อกเทา

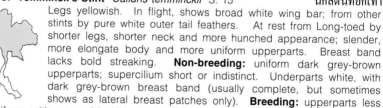

Legs yellowish. In flight, shows broad white wing bar; from other stints by pure white outer tail feathers. At rest from Long-toed by shorter legs, shorter neck and more hunched appearance; slender, more elongate body and more uniform upperparts. Breast band lacks bold streaking. **Non-breeding:** uniform dark grey-brown upperparts; supercilium short or indistinct. Underparts white, with dark grey-brown breast band (usually complete, but sometimes shows as lateral breast patches only). **Breeding:** upperparts less uniform with some blackish feathering; short whitish brow in front of eye. **Juvenile:** feathers of upperparts faintly scaled with warm brownish edges and black subterminal lines. **Voice:** a thin, high-pitched and metallic trilling *tirrr-r-r-r-*; very distinctive and quite unlike any other wader. **Habitat:** flooded paddyfields, marshes; usually keeps to the landward edge of extensive coastal fish ponds or mudflats. Often the commonest stint in freshwater situations. Common winter visitor.

Plate 41 Stints

194 Rufous-necked Stint
1/06 SP
non-breeding   breeding

195 Temminck's Stint
non-breeding   breeding

196 Long-toed Stint
1/06 SP
non-breeding   breeding

197 Spoon-billed Sandpiper
1/06 SP
non-breeding   breeding

Mongkol

198 Sanderling
non-breeding   breeding

132

196. Long-toed Stint *Calidris subminuta* S: 16   นกสติ๊นท์นิ้วยาว

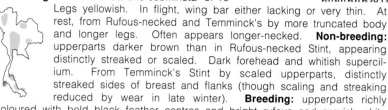

Legs yellowish. In flight, wing bar either lacking or very thin. At rest, from Rufous-necked and Temminck's by more truncated body and longer legs. Often appears longer-necked. **Non-breeding:** upperparts darker brown than in Rufous-necked Stint, appearing distinctly streaked or scaled. Dark forehead and whitish supercilium. From Temminck's Stint by scaled upperparts, distinctly streaked sides of breast and flanks (though scaling and streaking reduced by wear in late winter). **Breeding:** upperparts richly coloured with bold black feather centres and bright rufous and greyish white edgings. Breast and flank streaks bolder than in winter. **Juvenile:** brightly-patterned, resembling breeding plumage, but with bolder white lines on mantle. **Voice:** a trilling *trrrp*, lower-pitched and less metallic than the call of Temminck's Stint and somewhat recalling Curlew Sandpiper. **Habitat:** mainly freshwater marshes, muddy fish ponds. Avoids the open coastal mudflats. Common winter visitor.

นกชายเลนปากช้อน

197. Spoon-billed Sandpiper *Eurynorhynchus pygmaeus* S: 15

Both breeding and winter plumages closely resemble those of Rufous necked Stint. Best distinguished by diagnostic, spatulate tip to bill although this is difficult to observe in side views. (Beware also Rufous necked Stints with mud adhering to the tip of the bill.) Sometimes shows a distinctive, swishing, side-to-side feeding motion. **Non-breeding:** even whiter face and breast than Rufous-necked Stint. **Breeding:** chestnut-red face, neck and upper breast. All scapulars are black-centred with chestnut fringes. (Lower scapulars are greyish in Rufous-necked.) **Voice:** a quiet *preep*. **Habitat:** intertidal mudflats. Rare passage migrant and winter visitor.

198. Sanderling *Calidris alba* S: 20   นกคอสั้นตีนไว

Larger than the stints. In flight, shows a very broad white wing bar. Short, straight black bill and black legs. **Non-breeding:** upperparts very pale grey, with whitish face. Usually shows a blackish mark at bend of wing. **Breeding:** mottled rufous and black on upperparts; rufous upper breast. **Juvenile:** black centres to feathers of upperparts give more sharply contrasted appearance than in adult non-breeding. ◆ A very active feeder; runs quickly along the water's edge. **Voice:** a sharp, high-pitched *tik*. **Habitat:** primarily open sandy shores; occasionally mudflats. Fairly common winter visitor.

Plate 42 Calidris Sandpipers

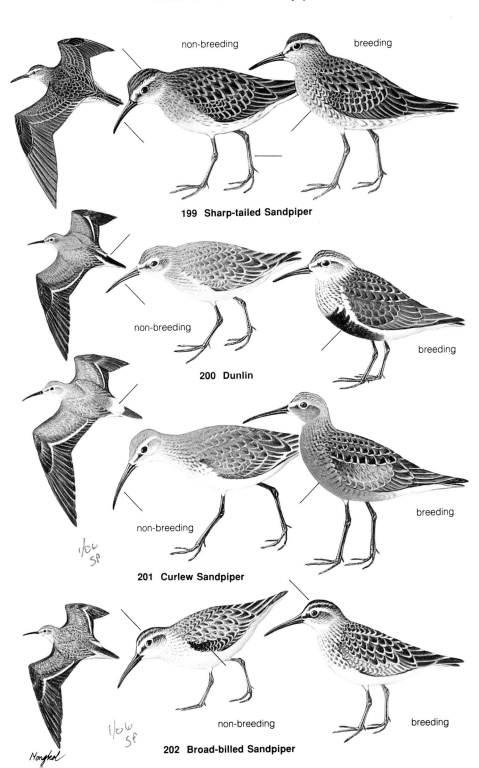

non-breeding

breeding

199 Sharp-tailed Sandpiper

non-breeding

breeding

200 Dunlin

non-breeding

breeding

201 Curlew Sandpiper

non-breeding

breeding

202 Broad-billed Sandpiper

Mongkol

134

199. Sharp-tailed Sandpiper *Calidris acuminata* S: 22   นกชายเลนกระหม่อมแดง
Legs and base of bill yellowish brown to greenish. Like a large version of a Long-toed Stint, appearing relatively short-billed. Heavily streaked brown and blackish upperparts, dark rufous cap and ear coverts contrasting with a long, whitish supercilium. In flight, shows a narrow white wing bar and a stint-like tail pattern. **Non-breeding:** slight streaking at sides of neck and breast; upperparts dull greybrown. **Breeding:** breast and neck washed with rufous-buff and heavily spotted with dark brown. Brown V-shaped markings on lower breast and flanks. Upperparts more strongly tinged rufous. **Juvenile:** much brighter than any other plumage with chestnut-fringed upperparts, bright rufous cap and ear coverts; rich orange-buff wash on breast. **Voice:** a soft, dry, *pleep* or *cheep*. **Habitat:** marshes, mudflats. Very rare winter visitor or passage migrant.

200. Dunlin *Calidris alpina* S: 19   นกชายเลนท้องดำ
Black legs and slightly decurved black bill. **Non-breeding:** greyish upperparts and whitish underparts. From Broad-billed Sandpiper by lack of bold head pattern. From Curlew Sandpiper by lack of white rump in flight; by slightly shorter legs and bill; and by smaller size when at rest. **Breeding:** bright chestnut-rufous on upperparts. Shows diagnostic belly patch. **Voice:** a thin, slightly harsh, reedy *kree*; higher pitched and more metallic than the call of Curlew Sandpiper. **Habitat:** coastal mudflats, marshes and riverine mud and sand bars. Rare winter visitor.

201. Curlew Sandpiper *Calidris ferruginea* S: 22   นกชายเลนปากโค้ง
In flight, from other small *Calidris* by white rump. **Non-breeding:** upperparts uniform greyish, with whitish supercilium; whitish underparts. From both Dunlin and Broad-billed Sandpiper by longer, more decurved bill, longer legs, larger size and less compact appearance. Lacks the bold head pattern of Broad-billed. **Breeding:** underparts deep chestnut, usually with some whitish around base of bill; lower belly and under tail coverts whitish. **Juvenile:** upperparts finely scaled; pinkish buff wash on breast. Upperparts dark brown, scaled with bright chestnut. **Voice:** a soft *chirrip*. **Habitat:** coastal mudflats; less frequently on freshwater areas. Very common winter visitor.

202. Broad-billed Sandpiper *Limicola falcinellus* S: 18   นกชายเลนปากกว้าง
Compact, stint-like appearance but distinguished by slightly longer bill, which is decurved at tip and by slightly larger size. Smaller and shorter legged than Dunlin and Curlew Sandpiper, with distinctly striped head pattern of black crown and ear coverts and whitish supercilium which forks behind eye. **Non-breeding:** head pattern less bold; upperparts dark greyish. Underparts white with breast lightly streaked grey. Blackish patch at bend of wing recalls Sanderling. **Breeding:** upperparts blackish, with feathers fringed pale chestnut to whitish. Converging white lines on coverts and scapulars, combined with head pattern, give a snipe-like appearance. Breast, sides of neck and flanks distinctly streaked. **Voice:** a distinctive, harsh and metallic *brzink*. **Habitat:** coastal mudflats. Fairly common winter visitor.

Plate 43 Knots, Ruff, Woodcock

non-breeding

breeding

203 Red Knot

breeding

non-breeding

204 Great Knot
1/06 SP

205 Ruff
1/06 SP

♀

♂ breeding

♂ non-breeding

206 Eurasian Woodcock

Mongkol

136

203. Red Knot *Calidris canutus* S: 25   นกน็อทเล็ก

Plump build, short greenish legs and straight black bill. Stint-like shape, but is very much larger. In flight, shows a narrow wing bar and a pale greyish-barred rump. **Non-breeding:** pale greyish upperparts, faintly scaled whitish. Underparts whitish with faint spotting on the breast. **Breeding:** darker, rufous-scaled upperparts; rufous breast and upper belly. **Juvenile:** whitish fringes and black subterminal lines on feathers of coverts and scapulars form a fine scaling on the upperparts. **Voice:** usually silent. **Habitat:** coastal mudflats, sandy beaches. Uncommon winter visitor and passage migrant, usually seen in groups of one to five individuals and often accompanying Great Knot.

204. Great Knot *Calidris tenuirostris* S: 30   นกน็อทใหญ่

Larger than Red Knot, with a conspicuously longer, tapering bill which is slightly decurved at the tip; longer blackish legs. In flight, shows a whiter rump and a less distinct wing bar than Red Knot. **Non-breeding:** blackish spotting on sides of breast is more prominent than in Red Knot. **Breeding:** brownish black upperparts with chestnut fringes to scapulars and sometimes tertials. Heavy blackish spotting and barring on throat, neck and breast. **Juvenile:** upperparts more strongly contrasted than in non-breeding plumage with black centres to scapulars and whitish fringes to coverts. **Voice:** usually silent. **Habitat:** coastal mudflats, sandy beaches. Uncommon; mainly passage migrant but may winter in the Peninsula. Occasionally seen in flocks of 20–300 birds, but more often in groups of less than ten.

205. Ruff *Philomachus pugnax* S: 30 (male); 23–28 (female)   นกรัฟ

In flight, shows narrow whitish wing bar and large white oval patches at base of tail which sometimes form a single U-shaped tail patch. Straight, or slightly decurved, medium length bill. Has a long-necked and small-headed appearance. **Non-breeding:** plumage variable; usually brownish, with scaled upperparts. Underparts buffy brown to whitish. Leg colour variable; usually yellowish to greenish, but often orange or reddish orange. **Breeding:** males may begin to show some black or cinnamon feathers on face or breast before spring departure. **Voice:** usually silent. **Habitat:** freshwater marshes, paddyfields. Uncommon winter visitor or passage migrant; usually seen singly.

เหล่านกปากซ่อม

SNIPES: Genera *Scolopax*, *Gallinago*, *Lymnocryptes*. Medium-sized waders, with extremely long bills, which have highly sensitive tips. Feed by probing deeply in soft mud. Noted for heavily streaked, cryptic plumage. Secretive when on the ground and usually seen when flushed from cover. Best identified in flight or in hand by the structure of the tail.

206. Eurasian Woodcock *Scolopax rusticola* S: 36   นกปากซ่อมดง

Much larger than any other snipe, with diagnostic black cross-bars on hindcrown and nape. In flight, wings broad and rounded; wingbeats heavy. Upperparts more softly mottled than in true snipes, lacking the clearly defined longitudinal pale stripes on the back. Usually silent when flushed. **Habitat:** moist areas in evergreen and deciduous forests, secondary growth and dense cover along streams, from plains up to the highest mountain summits. Uncommon winter visitor.

207. Wood Snipe *Gallinago nemoricola* S: 30 นกปากซ่อมพง

Unlike Eurasian Woodcock, all the snipes show prominent longitudinal stripes on upperparts. Wood Snipe is larger than other typical snipes, with broader, more rounded wings and a heavier, slower flight. Entire underparts and underwing barred dark brown; lacks pale trailing edge to the secondaries. In hand, has 18 tail feathers. **Voice:** a deep, guttural croak. **Habitat:** moist areas in evergreen forest, secondary growth of higher elevations. Very rare winter visitor.

208. Pintail Snipe *Gallinago stenura* S: 25 นกปากซ่อมหางเข็ม

In flight, from Common Snipe by paler, more sandy, lesser and median upperwing coverts which contrast more with blackish greater coverts and dark flight feathers; narrower, less distinct whitish trailing edge to secondaries; lack of white on underwing; more direct flight; toes which project slightly further beyond tail-tip and by call. At rest, shows narrow pale brown to whitish edgings to both outer and inner margins of scapulars. Tail projects only slightly beyond folded wings. Buffy supercilium is always broader than dark eyeline at base of bill. In hand, by narrow, pin-like 6–9 pairs of outer tail feathers. (Usually 24–28 feathers in the tail.) **Voice:** a short, rasping *squok*. **Habitat:** paddyfields; marshy areas of plains and hills to at least 1800 m. Often in drier areas than Common Snipe. Common winter visitor.

209. Swinhoe's Snipe *Gallinago megala* S: 28 นกปากซ่อมสวินโฮ

Very like Pintail Snipe and distinguished with difficulty by larger size and more lumbering flight and possibly by call; shares same upper and underwing pattern. In flight, projection of toes beyond tail-tip is shorter than in Pintail. Shows more white at corners of tail-tip than Pintail, but less than Common. At rest, may show obvious projection of primaries beyond tertials (tertials almost completely cover primaries in Pintail). In hand, tail usually has 20–22 feathers. Outer tail feathers narrow, but less so than in Pintail Snipe. **Voice:** possibly hoarser, more grating than Pintail Snipe. **Habitat:** marshy areas, paddyfield margins. Probably in less open, more wooded situations than Common and Pintail Snipes. Very rare visitor, but probably much overlooked.

210. Common Snipe *Gallinago gallinago* S: 28 นกปากซ่อมหางพัด

Distinguished from other snipes by conspicuous white trailing edge to secondaries and faster, more erratic flight. Toes project slightly beyond tail-tip in flight. Shows whitish base to underwing. At rest, striped head and back pattern. From Pintail Snipe by white only on outer edge of scapular feathers; dark eye-line broader than pale supercilium at base of bill; tail projects further beyond wing-tips. In hand, tail usually of 12–18 feathers. **Voice:** a rasping *scaap*; more drawn out than the call of Pintail Snipe. **Habitat:** open marshy areas, paddyfields. Usually commoner along the landward edge of the mangrove than Pintail. Very common winter visitor.

138

211. Jack Snipe *Lymnocryptes minimus* S: 20 นกปากซ่อมเล็ก

Much smaller and shorter-billed than other snipes, with an all brown, slightly wedge-shaped tail in flight. At rest, shows dark centre to crown. Often shows a peculiar bobbing motion when feeding. Difficult to flush and often not rising until almost underfoot, flying only a short distance before dropping back into cover. **Habitat:** open marshy areas and along sides of ditches. From plains up to at least 1300 m. Rare winter visitor.

วงศ์นกโป่งวิด

PAINTED-SNIPES: Family *Rostratulidae*. Show a superficial resemblance to true snipes, but have a slower flight on broader, more rounded wings; legs usually trailing. Secretive; most active at dawn and dusk. Have reversed sex roles; the female is larger and more brightly coloured while the male incubates the eggs and cares for the young. World: 2 species. Thailand: one species.

212. Greater Painted-snipe *Rostratula benghalensis* S: 25–28 นกโป่งวิด

In flight, shows buffy braces and partial neck collar on grey brown upperparts and white oval patches at sides of tail, due to overlapping flank feathers. At rest, broad whitish eye-ring and post-ocular stripe; pale buffy central crown stripe contrasting with blackish sides to crown. **Male:** large buff spots on wing coverts; neck and upper breast grey-brown. **Female:** darker, plainer upperparts; throat and neck maroon-chestnut. **Voice:** usually silent when flushed. A series of short *ooop* notes; like someone blowing repeatedly across the neck of a bottle in short bursts. Heard mainly at dusk and during the night. **Habitat:** marshy areas, paddyfields. Common resident.

วงศ์นกแอ่นทุ่ง

PRATINCOLES: Family *Glareolidae*. Small waders with very short bills and short legs. Have forked tails, very long, pointed wings and a buoyant, tern-like flight. Feed by hawking insects on the wing and are most active towards dusk. Nest in loose colonies. World: 17 species. Thailand: 2 species.

213. Oriental Pratincole *Glareola maldivarum* S: 25 นกแอ่นทุ่งใหญ่

Grey-brown upperparts with blackish primaries, white rump and black tipped, white tail. Lacks wing bar or white on trailing edge of wing. Underwing dark with reddish wing lining. Underparts warm buffy with a black necklet and creamy throat. Red base to the bill. **Juvenile:** all brownish; scaled above and mottled below, lacking the black necklace; bill all dark. **Voice:** a tern-like *kyeck*. **Habitat:** open country, marshes; nests on the hard-baked mud of dry paddies. Very common breeding visitor; scarce or absent during November to January.

214. Small Pratincole *Glareola lactea* S: 18 นกแอ่นทุ่งเล็ก

Much smaller and paler, greyer than Oriental Pratincole. Lacks dark necklace and shows a broad white wing bar in flight, visible on both upperwing and underwing; blackish wing-lining. **Juvenile:** shows a slight gorget of blackish streaks. **Habitat:** riverine sand-bars and dry mud of marshes and lake margins. Uncommon resident and winter visitor.

Plate 44 Snipes

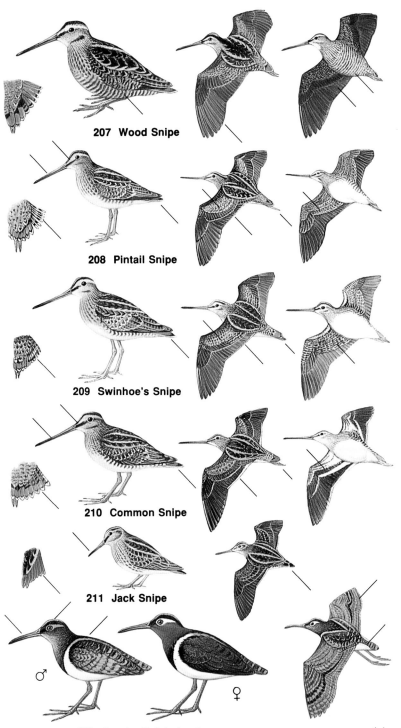

207 Wood Snipe

208 Pintail Snipe

209 Swinhoe's Snipe

210 Common Snipe

211 Jack Snipe

♂

♀

212 Greater Painted-snipe

Mongkol

140

STILTS: Family *Recurvirostridae*. Waders with very long legs and bills. Most have striking black and white plumage. World: 7 species. Thailand: one species.

215. Black-winged Stilt *Himantopus himantopus* S: 38   นกตีนเทียน

Black mantle, upper and underwings; white underparts and white rump which extends in a wedge up the back. Very long, reddish to pink legs which trail far beyond the tail in flight. Head may be all white, but both sexes may show some dusky or blackish on crown and hindneck. **Female:** brownish black upperparts. **Juvenile:** browner, with dull pinkish legs and a thin whitish band on trailing edge to the wing in flight. **Voice:** a shrill, high-pitched and anxiously repeated *keek*. **Habitat:** coastal areas and inland waters. Fairly common resident and winter visitor.

วงศ์นกหัวโตกินปู

CRAB PLOVER: Family *Dromadidae*. Plump-bodied with long legs and a huge, dagger-like bill. World: one species.

216. Crab Plover *Dromas ardeola* S: 38   นกหัวโตกินปู

Bill black; legs grey. White plumage with black mantle, primaries, secondaries and greater coverts. Dark streaking may be present on hindcrown and nape. **Immature:** mantle pale grey; crown and nape dark streaked. ◆ Flies with neck extended and legs trailing. Feeds by wading in shallow coastal waters. **Voice:** a harsh, tern-like call. **Habitat:** open, sandy shores. Rare, but annual non-breeding visitor in small numbers to only one site.

วงศ์นกกระแตผี

THICK-KNEES: Family *Burhinidae*. Long legs and compact bodies with large heads and bills and yellow eyes. Territorial and somewhat nocturnal; unusual wailing calls heard mostly after dark. World: 9 species. Thailand: 3 species.

217. Northern Thick-knee (Stone Curlew) *Burhinus oedicnemus* S: 40 นกกระแตผีเล็ก

Roughly lapwing-sized, with a shorter, thinner bill than other Thick-knees. At rest, back and upper breast streaked brownish. Whitish area around eye and black cheek bar give a spectacled appearance. In flight, shows pale speculum and a white patch in the outer primaries. **Voice:** a loud *cour-lee*. **Habitat:** dry, open areas; sand bars along rivers. Rare; status uncertain, perhaps only winter visitor.

218. Great Thick-knee *Esacus recurvirostris* S: 51   นกกระแตผีใหญ่

Long, heavy, yellow-based bill with straight culmen which is upturned at tip. Much bolder black and white facial pattern than Northen Thick-knee and more uniform, unstreaked body plumage. Narrow black border to pale greyish patch on folded wing. In flight, mainly black flight feathers with white patch on inner primaries contrasts with pale grey band on wing coverts. **Habitat:** riverine sand bars. Very rare resident; no recent records and possibly extirpated.

Plate 45 Pratincoles, Stilts, Thick-knees

juvenile

214 Small Pratincole

adult

213 Oriental Pratincole

215 Black-winged Stilt

Voi SP

juvenile

♂

216 Crab Plover

adult

♀

enile

219 Beach Thick-knee

218 Great Thick-knee

217 Northern Thick-knee

Mongkol

142

219. Beach Thick-knee *Esacus magnirostris* S: 51   นกกระแตผีชายหาด

 Very like preceding species, but distinguished by culmen which is downcurved towards tip; blackish forehead and narrower white supercilium. In flight, shows uniformly pale grey coverts and secondaries contrasting with mainly black outer primaries. **Habitat:** undisturbed sandy beaches of offshore islands. Local and rare resident.

วงศ์นกสกัว

SKUAS: Family *Stercorariidae*. Medium to large predatory seabirds of oceanic and coastal areas. Somewhat gull-like, but plumage mainly dark brown, with white wing flashes. Adults have diagnostic projecting tail feathers, though may take 4 years or more to acquire adult plumage. Chase other seabirds in order to steal the food which they regurgitate. Sexes similar. World: 7 species. Thailand: 3 species. (See under Additions, page 400.)

220. Pomarine Skua (Pomarine Jaeger) *Stercorarius pomarinus* S: 71   นกสกัว

 Larger, deeper-breasted and broader-winged than Arctic Skua. **Adult:** shows diagnostic spoon-shaped tail projections in breeding plumage. Light morph shows blackish brown upperparts, black cap and whitish under body with dark breast band. The less common dark morph is uniformly dark, with slightly paler yellowish cheeks. **Immature:** barred, dark brownish. From Arctic Skua by heavier build, more conspicuously barred upper and under tail coverts and by more heightened contrast between dark cap and pale dorsal neck collar. Tail shows small roundish projections. **Habitat:** coastal areas, oceans. Uncommon winter visitor.

นกสกัวขั้วโลกเหนือ

221. Arctic Skua (Parasitic Jaeger) *Stercorarius parasiticus* S: 57

 Smaller and more lightly built than Pomarine Skua. **Adult:** shows pointed tail streamers of varying length. Light morph usually shows paler breast band than Pomarine Skua, but very variable. **Immature:** less heavily barred than Pomarine Skua; paler, more rufous than adult Arctic or immature Pomarine. Shows pointed central tail feathers which project up to 2 cm. See also Long-tailed Skua (912). **Habitat:** coastal areas and oceans. Rare winter visitor.

วงศ์นกนางนวล

GULLS and TERNS: Family *Laridae*. Seabirds, mostly of coastal waters, and which generally have grey and white adult plumages. **Gulls** *Larus* spp. are large and robust with broad-based wings, usually rounded tails and slightly hooked bills. Feed mostly on fish and offal. The larger species take four years to reach maturity and immature plumages can be confusing. **Terns** are smaller and much slimmer with (usually) forked tails. **Sea Terns** (*Sterna* spp.) usually fish by plunge-diving while **Marsh Terns** (*Chlidonias* spp.) feed by picking small items off the water surface in a dipping flight. Most breed colonially; sexes similar. World: 88 species. Thailand: 23 species.

Plate 46 Skuas, Large Gulls

immature

dark morph breeding

pale morph breeding

220 Pomarine Skua

immature

dark morph breeding

pale morph breeding

221 Arctic Skua

first winter

first winter

ad. non-breeding

ad. breeding

222 Great Black-headed Gull

first winter

first winter

adult

adult

Mongkol

223 Herring Gull

222. Great Black-headed Gull *Larus ichthyaetus* S: 69   นกนางนวลหัวดำใหญ่

Large size; yellow (or pale) bill with a subterminal black band. All plumages (other than adult breeding) show a distinctive, broad black eye patch. **Adult:** grey upperwing with white leading edge and a subterminal black crescent across the primaries. Black hood and a red tip to the bill in breeding dress. **First winter:** black primaries and a broad black bar along secondaries, with a pale mid-wing panel. Usually grey mantle, contrasting with brownish upperwing coverts. From immature Herring Gull also by clear-cut black terminal band, contrasting with cleaner white upper tail coverts and tail. Takes 4 years to reach maturity. **Habitat:** open coastal areas, sandy beaches. Very rare winter visitor.

223. Herring Gull *Larus argentatus* S: 60   นกนางนวลแฮร์ริ่ง

Larger than all except Great Black-headed. **Adult:** mantle and upperwing grey with black outermost primaries and conspicuous white subterminal spots. Underwing whitish apart from black wing-tips. Head and neck streaked brownish in winter. Yellow bill with red spot on lower mandible. Legs pink or pale yellow. **First winter:** mottled brown upperparts, lacking white in outer primaries, but with a pale panel in inner primaries. Broad, blackish tail band which grades with brown bars and spots to whitish upper tail coverts and rump. Bill blackish, with pinkish base. Attains adult plumage in fourth year. **Habitat:** estuarine seacoasts; inland lakes. Uncommon or rare winter visitor.

224. Black-tailed Gull *Larus crassirostris* S: 47   นกนางนวลหางดำ

Intermediate in size between Herring and Brown-headed, with strikingly long bill and broad, sharply defined black on tail in all plumages. **Adult:** upperwing slaty-grey; primaries almost entirely black with only faint white tips. Tail mostly white with sharp-cut black terminal band. Crown and nape streaked grey in winter. Yellow bill with red tip and black subterminal band; yellow-green legs. **First winter:** mainly dusky grey-brown with uniformly blackish primaries; lacks any strong contrast on upperwing. Tail brownish black with whitish rump and upper tail coverts. Dusky flanks and sides of breast; when seen head-on, shows whitish forehead and broad white band down center of throat and breast. Bill pale flesh with dark tip; legs pinkish. **Habitat:** estuarine seacoasts. Very rare winter visitor.

225. Slender-billed Gull *Larus genei* S: 42   นกนางนวลปากเรียว

White wedge in outer primaries, like Common Black-headed Gull, but identified by diagnostic sloping crown and longer bill; clean white head in all plumages. **Adult:** secondaries and coverts of upperwing uniformly grey; tail white. Rosy flush on underparts often visible. Bill scarlet to dusky red; eye whitish. **Immature:** some brownish markings on coverts and secondaries. Bill pale orange, often dark-tipped. Eye may be brown. **Habitat:** estuarine seacoasts. Rare winter visitor.

Plate 47 Gulls II

first winter

adult

first winter

adult

224 Black-tailed Gull

immature

adult

immature

ad. breeding

225 Slender-billed Gull

immature

ad. non-breeding

ad. non-breeding

ad. breeding

226 Common Black-headed Gull

immature

ad. non-breeding

ad. non-breeding

ad. breeding

227 Brown-headed Gull

Nongkol

226. Common Black-headed Gull *Larus ridibundus* S: 40　นกนางนวลขอบปีกขาว

Distinguished from Brown-headed by white wedge in outer prima-ries; slightly smaller size and thinner bill. Eye dark in all plumages. **Adult:** secondaries and coverts of upperwing uniformly pale grey; tail all white. Dark ear spot and dark tip to red bill in winter plum-age; chocolate-brown hood and all dusky red bill in breeding dress. **Immature:** blackish secondaries and tail band and brown markings on upper wing coverts; bill dull orange, dark-tipped. **Habitat:** seacoasts, rivers. Fairly common winter visitor.

227. Brown-headed Gull *Larus brunnicephalus* S: 46　นกนางนวลธรรมดา

The commonest gull. Distinguished from Common Black-headed by black wing-tips, slightly larger size, heavier bill and thicker-necked appearance. **Adult:** single white mirror near leading edge of prima-ries; whitish eye and bright red bill. Chocolate-brown hood in breed-ing dress. **Immature:** dark brown secondaries, black tail band and brownish mottling on wing coverts; bill paler than adult. **Habitat:** estuarine and open seacoasts, rivers and lakes, occasionally well inland. Very common winter visitor.

228. Caspian Tern *Sterna caspia* S: 53　นกนางนวลแกลบแคสเปียน

Large, with massive red bill. Distinguished from gulls by forked tail and mainly black cap. Blackish underside to primaries. **Adult breeding:** all black cap. **Non-breeding:** forehead streaked whitish. **First winter:** slight dark carpal bar, dark tail-tip and dark secondar-ies with some brown scaling on coverts. **Habitat:** seacoasts and occasionally freshwater areas. Uncommon winter visitor.

229. Great Crested Tern *Sterna bergii* S: 46　นกนางนวลแกลบหงอนใหญ่

Distinguished from Caspian Tern by darker grey upperparts and yellow bill. Shows slight whitish collar. From Lesser Crested Tern by paler bill and darker upperparts. **Adult breeding:** narrow white band between black cap and base of bill. **Non-breeding:** white on crown extends to above eye. **First winter:** bill duller than adult, occasionally with dark tip; dark patterning on upperwing with pale mid-wing panel. **Voice:** a harsh *ke-eck*. **Habitat:** open seacoasts, sandy beaches and occasionally mudflats. Nests on offshore islets. Uncommon and local resident; possibly also non-breeding visitor.

230. Lesser Crested Tern *Sterna bengalensis* S: 40　นกนางนวลแกลบหงอนเล็ก

Smaller and slimmer than Great Crested with orange bill and paler grey upperparts. **Adult breeding:** black cap extends to base of bill. **Non-breeding:** black reduced to crescent around nape. **Immature:** dark primaries and bar across secondaries, but markings less con-trasted than in Great Crested. **Voice:** higher-pitched, less strident than Great Crested. **Habitat:** open seacoasts, islets. Rare winter visitor.

Plate 48 Terns I

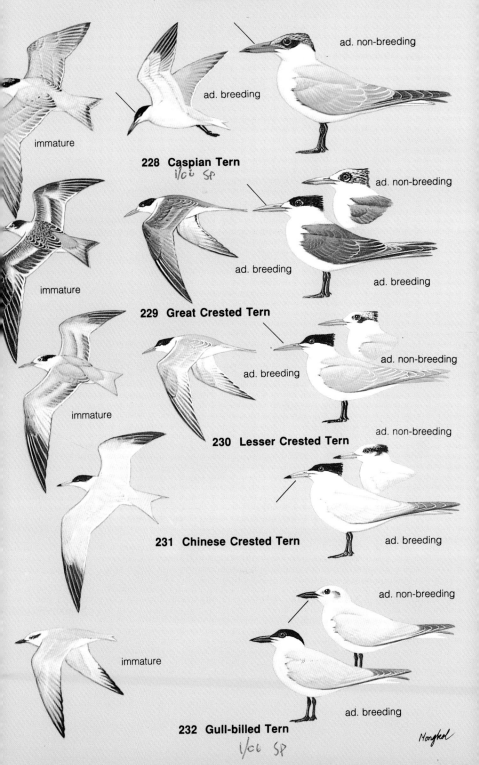

immature

ad. breeding

ad. non-breeding

228 Caspian Tern

l/ct SP

immature

ad. breeding

ad. non-breeding

ad. breeding

229 Great Crested Tern

immature

ad. breeding

ad. non-breeding

230 Lesser Crested Tern

ad. non-breeding

ad. breeding

231 Chinese Crested Tern

ad. non-breeding

ad. breeding

immature

232 Gull-billed Tern

l/ct SP

Mongkol

148

231. Chinese Crested Tern *Sterna bernsteini* S: 42   นกนางนวลแกลบจีน

Much whiter than either Great or Lesser Crested Terns, with a black-tipped yellow bill. Entirely black cap in breeding dress; white forecrown in winter. **Habitat:** seacoasts. Very rare and little known winter visitor, not seen for many years and may be extinct.

232. Gull-billed Tern *Gelochelidon nilotica* S: 38   นกนางนวลแกลบปากหนา

Larger than Whiskered or Common Terns, with heavy black bill and shallow forked tail. Upperwing, rump and tail pale silvery-grey. **Adult breeding:** entire cap black. **Non-breeding:** entire crown white; black on head reduced to a black spot or streak behind eye. **Juvenile:** from non-breeding adult by brownish mottling on coverts, darker grey primaries and dusky tail-tip. **Voice:** a soft *chew-ick*. **Habitat:** seacoasts, mudflats; occasionally inland over paddies. Fairly common winter visitor.

233. Common Tern *Sterna hirundo* S: 35   นกนางนวลแกลบธรรมดา

Mostly seen in non-breeding or immature plumage, when from Whiskered Tern by larger size, more deeply forked tail, longer bill, more extensive black on hindneck and whiter rump and tail, contrasting with grey back. From Roseate Tern by slightly darker grey upperparts. **Adult breeding:** complete black cap and long tail streamers. Breast and belly tinged greyish. Bill either red with a black tip or all black. **Non-breeding and immature:** whitish forecrown and bold dark carpal bar. Bill black. **Habitat:** seacoasts and mudflats; occasionally rivers and larger inland lakes. Very common winter visitor; some birds remain throughout the year.

234. Roseate Tern *Sterna dougallii* S: 39   นกนางนวลแกลบสีกุหลาบ

From Common Tern by whiter upperparts, shallower wingbeats and more buoyant flight. **Adult breeding:** pinkish flush on underparts, very noticeably long tail streamers and complete black cap. Bill colour variable, from completely black to completely orange-red, or bicoloured. Feet bright coral red. **Non-breeding:** forecrown white; underparts usually lacking pinkish cast; bill black, legs dull orange. **Juvenile:** sooty cap, with paler forecrown; boldly scaled saddle. Lacks tail streamers. **Voice:** a soft *chew-ick* and a harsh grating note. **Habitat:** open seacoasts. Breeds offshore, on small rocky islets; occasionally seen on mudflats. Uncommon resident.

235. Black-naped Tern *Sterna sumatrana* S: 31   นกนางนวลแกลบท้ายทอยดำ

Smaller and slimmer than Roseate Tern, with very strikingly white appearance and narrow black band around nape. Black bill. From winter plumage Whiskered by thinner wings, deeply forked tail and gleaming white appearance. **Juvenile:** bill dusky-yellow; tail rounded. Shows pronounced scaling on saddle and dark grey outer primaries. **Voice:** a sharp *kick*. **Habitat:** open seacoasts; breeds offshore, on rocky islets. Uncommon to locally common resident.

Plate 49 Terns II

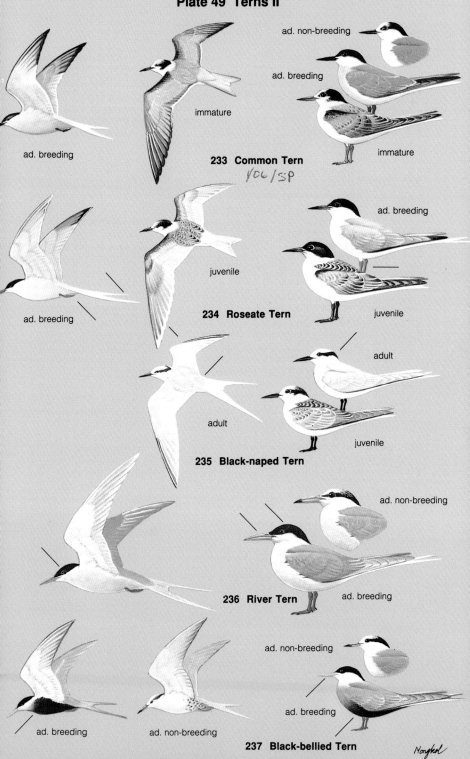

ad. breeding

immature

ad. non-breeding

ad. breeding

immature

233 Common Tern

yoc/sp

ad. breeding

ad. breeding

juvenile

ad. breeding

juvenile

234 Roseate Tern

adult

juvenile

adult

235 Black-naped Tern

ad. non-breeding

ad. breeding

236 River Tern

ad. breeding

ad. non-breeding

ad. non-breeding

ad. breeding

237 Black-bellied Tern

Mongkol

150

236. River Tern *Sterna aurantia* S: 41   นกนางนวลแกลบแม่น้ำ

Large, with stout yellow bill. From crested terns (229-231) by deeply forked tail, orange to red feet and lack of crest. Pale silvery grey 'windows' in primaries of otherwise deep grey upperwing. Underparts show greyish tinge. **Non-breeding:** whitish forecrown; dusky tip to bill. **Habitat:** mostly rivers, where breeds on sand bars; occasionally wanders to seacoasts. Very rare resident, possibly now extirpated.

237. Black-bellied Tern *Sterna acuticauda* S: 32   นกนางนวลแกลบท้องดำ

Adult breeding: black cap; whitish underwing contrasting with dark grey breast and belly. From Whiskered Tern by yellow bill. **Non-breeding:** forecrown white; underparts white, though often with black mottling on belly. Bill dull yellowish with dusky tip. Much smaller than River Tern. **Habitat:** rivers, lakes, ponds and marshes. Very rare resident, possibly now extirpated.

238. Little Tern *Sterna albifrons* S: 23   นกนางนวลแกลบเล็ก

Identified by small size, thin pointed wings and rapid wingbeats. Frequently hovers. See Saunders' Tern. **Adult breeding:** concave white area on forecrown and yellow bill with black tip. Upperparts pale grey, with outer 2–3 primaries and their coverts blackish; tail white. Feet yellow. **Non-breeding:** bill blackish and crown mostly white, with black streak extending from eye to nape. Feet dusky yellow. **Immature:** shows slight dark carpal bar. **Voice:** high-pitched, thin chattering notes *kik-ick, kik-ick.* **Habitat:** sandy beaches, mudflats, coastal fish ponds. Common resident.

239. Saunders' Tern *Sterna saundersi* S: 23   นกนางนวลแกลบน้ำเค็ม

Very like Little Tern, but shows more obvious blackish leading edge to wing (outer 3–6 primaries and their coverts are blackish), pale greyish tail and by straighter-cut white forecrown. **Habitat:** seacoasts, sandy beaches. Very rare winter visitor, though possibly much overlooked.

240. White-winged Tern *Chlidonias leucopterus* S: 23   นกนางนวลแกลบดำปีกขาว

Slightly smaller than Whiskered, with a stubbier bill. **Adult breeding:** easily identified by black head, body and underwing coverts contrasting with whitish upperwing coverts and rump. In all other plumages from Whiskered by darker upperwing, complete white neck collar and by contrast between whitish rump and pale grey tail. Shows dark, round spot on ear coverts which is almost distinct from black on nape. **Non-breeding:** often shows blackish scalloping along margins of underwing coverts. **Juvenile:** shows dark brown saddle. **Habitat:** coastal areas, rivers, marshes, flooded fields. Common winter visitor, though most numerous on spring and autumn passage.

Plate 50 Terns III

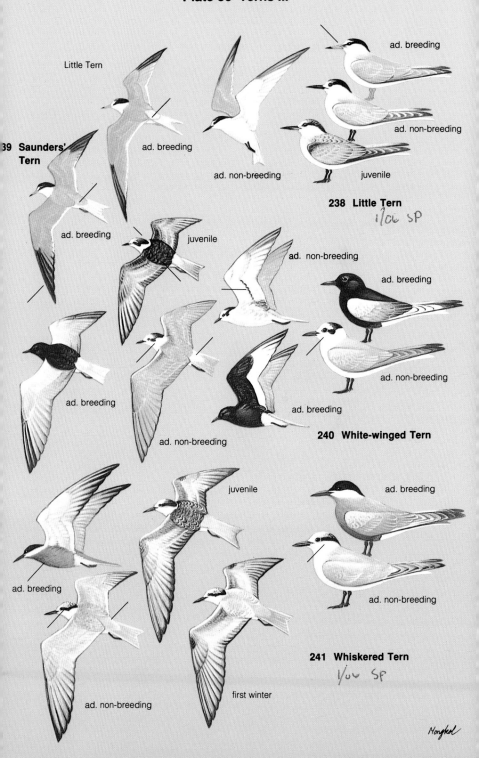

Little Tern

39 Saunders' Tern

ad. breeding

ad. breeding

ad. breeding

juvenile

ad. non-breeding

ad. non-breeding

ad. breeding

ad. non-breeding

juvenile

238 Little Tern

i/ce SP

ad. non-breeding

ad. breeding

ad. non-breeding

ad. breeding

240 White-winged Tern

juvenile

ad. breeding

ad. non-breeding

ad. breeding

ad. non-breeding

first winter

241 Whiskered Tern

i/uv Sp

Mongkol

241. Whiskered Tern *Chlidonias hybridus* S: 26   นกนางนวลแกลบเคราขาว
Shorter, proportionately broader wings than *Sterna* terns, with shallow forked tail and shorter bill. **Adult breeding:** black cap, white cheeks and dark grey underparts; silvery grey upperwing. From Black-bellied Tern by dull, dark red bill and white under tail coverts. **Non-breeding:** white underparts; whitish crown and narrow black streak behind eye, extending to nape. (Transitional plumaged birds can show almost as much black on nape as Common Tern.) **Immature:** like adult non-breeding, but shows pale mid-wing panel contrasting with darker secondaries and slight dark carpal bar. **Juvenile:** dark brown saddle; from White-winged Tern by lack of clear white dorsal neck collar. **Voice:** harsh *keck* notes. **Habitat:** coastal mudflats, shrimp ponds; rivers, freshwater swamps, lakes and flooded fields. Very common winter visitor.

242. Bridled Tern *Sterna anaethetus* S: 37   นกนางนวลแกลบคิ้วขาว
From all except Sooty Tern by dark brown upperparts and white underparts. White forehead extends in a narrow supercilium to behind eye. Black cap and slight greyish collar. **Juvenile:** pattern similar to adult but paler, brownish grey upperparts are slightly scaled. **Habitat:** open seacoasts; breeds offshore, on rocky islets. Uncommon resident, though may disperse outside breeding season.

243. Sooty Tern *Sterna fuscata* S: 44   นกนางนวลแกลบดำ
Distinguished from Bridled Tern by black upperparts. White patch on forehead is broader, but does not extend behind eye. Wings appear slightly shorter and broader than in Bridled. **Juvenile:** head, throat and breast dark brown; usually slight scaling on upperparts. From Brown Noddy by deeply forked tail, whitish underwing coverts. **Habitat:** seacoasts, oceans. Very rare visitor.

244. Brown Noddy *Anous stolidus* S: 42   นกน็อดดี้

Heavy, long, wedge-shaped tail, with slight fork at tip when fanned. Uniformly chocolate-brown plumage, with slightly paler areas on upperwing coverts and wing lining. Whitish crown. **Immature:** crown brown; usually shows a slight whitish eyebrow. **Habitat:** oceans, islets. Rare resident, possibly now extirpated; perhaps also non-breeding visitor.

Plate 51 Terns IV

adult

juvenile

ad. head pattern

242 Bridled Tern

juvenile

adult

ad. head pattern

243 Sooty Tern

adult

juvenile

adult

244 Brown Noddy

245 Indian Skimmer

Mongkol

154

SKIMMERS: Family *Rynchopidae*. Large, tern-like waterbirds with laterally compressed bills, the lower mandible being markedly longer than the upper. Feed in flight by skimming water surface, with lower mandible partly submerged. Sexes similar. World: 3 species. Thailand: one species.

245. Indian Skimmer *Rynchops albicollis* S: 43   นกกรีดน้ำ

Very distinctive; black back and upperwing, black cap with white forecrown, broad white collar and white trailing edge to wing. White underparts. Bill deep orange, tipped yellow. **Juvenile:** shows white feather edgings on upperparts; bill dusky yellow, tipped black. **Habitat:** coastal areas, lakes, rivers. Very rare visitor; only one record.

PIGEONS: Family *Columbidae*. Plump-bodied birds, with small heads, short bills and legs. Flight strong and direct. Most are gregarious, feeding on fruit, seeds and buds. Some species make seasonal or erratic movements in response to food supply. Most nest in trees, building flimsy, untidy, stick platforms. World: 305 species. Thailand: 28 species.

GREEN PIGEONS: Genus *Treron*. Though readily told from other pigeons by their predominantly green body, most are confusingly similar, particularly the females. Sexes differ, the males usually having colourful breast or shoulder markings. Feet are red in all but two species. Strictly arboreal and often difficult to observe in the forest canopy. Often found in large flocks in fruiting fig trees. Many species persistently pump their tails up and down. Have soft, musical whistling calls.

246. Pin-tailed Pigeon *Treron apicauda* S: 33   นกเปล้าหางเข็ม

Distinguished from other green pigeons by greatly elongate, pointed central tail feathers (shorter in female) and wedge-shaped, pale grey tail. Bright turquoise-blue base to bill. **Male:** indistinct orange suffusion on upper breast and cinnamon under tail coverts. **Female:** breast uniform greenish; under tail coverts whitish with dark streaks. **Voice:** duets, one bird giving low soft *cuc-coo*, the other a higher-pitched *huu*, repeated in an accelerating sequence. Also has a low growling. **Habitat:** usually evergreen forests from 600 m to 1800 m, though occasionally dispersing lower. Uncommon resident; possibly also winter visitor.

247. Yellow-vented Pigeon *Treron seimundi* S: 30   นกเปล้าหางเข็มหัวปีกแดง

Tail projection shorter than in Pin-tailed and difficult to detect. Also by darker green plumage, white centre to belly and bright yellow under tail coverts. Distinguished from both Pin-tailed and Wedge-tailed by bright cobalt blue bill, naked skin of lores and orbital ring. **Male:** maroon shoulder patch. **Female:** lacks shoulder patch; bold dark green streaks on yellow under tail coverts. **Habitat:** evergreen forests of the mountains, though has wandered to the open lowlands. Very rare; status uncertain.

Plate 52 Green Pigeons I

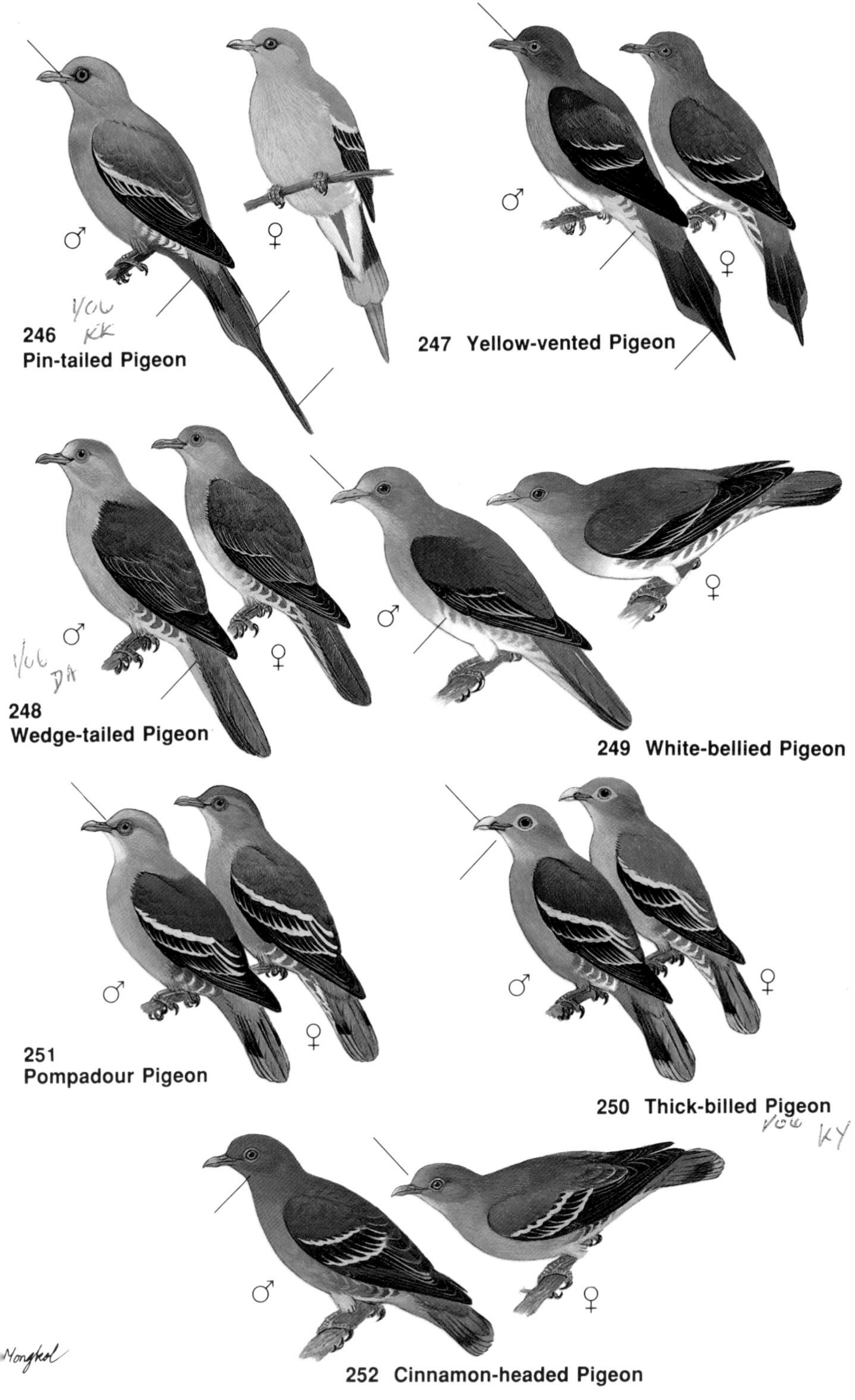

246 Pin-tailed Pigeon

247 Yellow-vented Pigeon

248 Wedge-tailed Pigeon

249 White-bellied Pigeon

251 Pompadour Pigeon

250 Thick-billed Pigeon

252 Cinnamon-headed Pigeon

Mongkol

156

248. Wedge-tailed Pigeon *Treron sphenura* S: 33   นกเปล้าหางพลั่ว

 Rather long, heavy, graduated (not pointed) tail and long under tail coverts almost reaching tail-tip. **Male:** maroon band on shoulders, which often extends across mantle; yellow-green underparts with a pale orange suffusion on upper breast and pale cinnamon-buff under tail coverts. **Female:** upperparts uniform green; lacks breast patch and has creamy buff under tail coverts with dark greenish central streaks. Base of bill blue-grey, less bright than Pin-tailed, Yellow-vented or White-bellied. Lores feathered. **Voice:** longer, slightly deeper notes, with a more hooting quality than those of Thick-billed. **Habitat:** evergreen forests, secondary growth from 600 m to the highest summits. Uncommon to locally common resident; usually the most numerous green pigeon of the higher hills.

249. White-bellied Pigeon *Treron sieboldii* S: 33   นกเปล้าท้องขาว

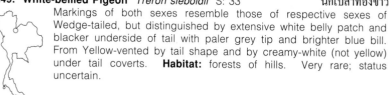 Markings of both sexes resemble those of respective sexes of Wedge-tailed, but distinguished by extensive white belly patch and blacker underside of tail with paler grey tip and brighter blue bill. From Yellow-vented by tail shape and by creamy-white (not yellow) under tail coverts. **Habitat:** forests of hills. Very rare; status uncertain.

250. Thick-billed Pigeon *Treron curvirostra* S: 27   นกเขาเปล้าธรรมดา

 Appears shorter-tailed and more compact than preceding species. Both sexes separated from other green pigeons by thick bill with deep, yellow-green tip and red base and by broad greenish orbital ring. Both sexes share greyish cap and blackish underside of tail with pale grey terminal band. **Male:** maroon mantle and cinnamon under tail coverts. **Female:** mantle green; under tail coverts creamy with olive-green bars; thighs dark green, scalloped whitish. **Habitat:** evergreen and mixed deciduous forests and secondary growth up to 1200 m; mangroves. Common resident; usually the commonest green pigeon of inland wooded habitats.

251. Pompadour Pigeon *Treron pompadora* S: 27   นกเปล้าหน้าเหลือง

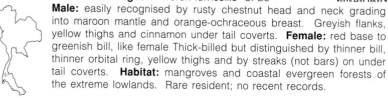 Both sexes similar to those of Thick-billed, but separated by thinner, entirely blue-grey bill and by lack of obvious orbital ring. **Male:** from Thick-billed by orange suffusion on breast. **Female:** separated by short streaks (not bars) on under tail coverts. **Habitat:** evergreen forests from plains up to 800 m (commonest in extreme lowlands). Uncommon or rare resident, now much reduced.

252. Cinnamon-headed Pigeon *Treron fulvicollis* S: 26   นกเปล้าแดง

Male: easily recognised by rusty chestnut head and neck grading into maroon mantle and orange-ochraceous breast. Greyish flanks, yellow thighs and cinnamon under tail coverts. **Female:** red base to greenish bill, like female Thick-billed but distinguished by thinner bill, thinner orbital ring, yellow thighs and by streaks (not bars) on under tail coverts. **Habitat:** mangroves and coastal evergreen forests of the extreme lowlands. Rare resident; no recent records.

Plate 53 Green Pigeons II

253 Little Green Pigeon

254 Pink-necked Pigeon

255 Orange-breasted Pigeon

256 Large Green Pigeon

257 Yellow-footed Pigeon

juvenile

258 Jambu Fruit-Dove

Mongkol

253. Little Green Pigeon *Treron olax* S: 20   นกเปล้าเล็กหัวเทา

Relatively small size and dark appearance. Tail dark slaty grey, with paler grey terminal band. **Male:** dark maroon mantle, dark grey head, throat and neck. Broad orange breast band and dark chestnut under tail coverts. **Female:** from female Orange-breasted by smaller size, darker, duller green underparts, lacking yellowish tinge; dark grey crown grades into green sides of head. When tail is folded, dark, dull green central feathers lie over the grey outer feathers, obscuring tail pattern. **Voice:** soft whistles, higher-pitched than other green pigeons. **Habitat:** evergreen forests of the level lowlands and foothills. Rare resident, much reduced.

254. Pink-necked Pigeon *Treron vernans* S: 25   นกเปล้าคอสีม่วง

Distinguished from Orange-breasted by pale grey tail, with broad blackish sub-terminal band. **Male:** also distinguished by grey head, grading into pinkish purple neck; orange band on lower breast and dark chestnut under tail coverts. Mantle grey-green. **Female:** head, neck and breast all greenish; buffy under tail coverts. From Orange-breasted by tail pattern. **Habitat:** secondary growth, mangroves, plantations and scrub, usually of coastal areas. Common resident, though much reduced.

255. Orange-breasted Pigeon *Treron bicincta* S: 26   นกเปล้าอกสีม่วงน้ำตาล

Distinguished from Pink-necked by blackish-appearing tail with broad, pale grey terminal band. (This character best seen in flight; pattern often obscured on folded tail.) **Male:** from Pink-necked by green head and throat with only thin band of pinkish purple above orange on breast; paler cinnamon under tail coverts. **Female:** from female Pink-necked by tail pattern, brighter yellowish green throat and breast and by grey patch on nape. ◆ Bill pale grey. **Habitat:** mixed deciduous woodland, secondary growth, deciduous and (rarely) evergreen forests, scrub up to 800 m. Also coastal areas. Uncommon resident.

256. Large Green Pigeon *Treron capellei* S: 37   นกเปล้าใหญ่

Much the largest green pigeon, with yellow feet and orbital ring and a heavy, pale yellow-green bill. **Male:** body plumage mainly pale green with conspicuous yellow wing bar. Yellow-orange breast band and chocolate under tail coverts. Underside of tail blackish with broad whitish terminal band. **Female:** fainter breast band; buffy under tail coverts, barred dark green. **Voice:** variable deep creaking and grunting notes; *oo-oo aah, oo-aah, aa-aa-aah.* **Habitat:** evergreen forest of the level lowlands, including peat swamp forest. Rare resident, now endangered.

257. Yellow-footed Pigeon *Treron phoenicoptera* S: 33   นกเปล้าขาเหลือง

Yellow feet and diagnostic bright yellow-olive band extending across breast and around back of neck. This contrasts sharply with grey hindcrown, pale grey-green mantle and grey underparts. Thighs yellow; under tail coverts chocolate, barred whitish. Sexes similar, though maroon shoulder patch is slightly more distinct in male. In flight, bright greenish upperside of tail contrasts sharply with broad, dark grey terminal band. **Habitat:** mixed deciduous woodlands, secondary growth, occasionally up to 800 m, but chiefly of the extreme lowlands. Uncommon resident, now much reduced.

เหล่านกเปล้าหน้าแดง

FRUIT-DOVES: Genus *Ptilinopus.* Mainly green plumage, but lack wing bars. Usually solitary and shy; rarely seen in groups.

258. Jambu Fruit-Dove *Ptilinopus jambu* S: 27   นกเปล้าหน้าแดง
Dark, glossy green upperparts; whitish orbital ring and bright orange bill. **Male:** crimson face, clean white underparts with pink patch on breast and chocolate under tail coverts. **Female:** purplish face and mainly green underparts with white limited to the centre of the belly. Under tail coverts cinnamon-buff. **Juvenile:** all green face. **Voice:** a soft *hooo* repeated at short intervals. Quality very similar to Emerald Dove but lacking the preliminary note. **Habitat:** evergreen forests from plains to 1200 m; mangroves. Uncommon resident.

เหล่านกลุมพู

IMPERIAL PIGEONS: Genus *Ducula.* Large, robust pigeons, with broad, rounded wings and slow wingbeats in flight. Sometimes seen in small groups, but much less gregarious than green pigeons. Fruit-eating; strictly arboreal and usually found in the high canopy. Deep, booming calls.

259. Green Imperial Pigeon *Ducula aenea* S: 43   นกลุมพู
Dull, bronze-green upperparts; green colour often difficult to detect except under extremely good lighting. Best distinguished from Mountain Imperial by lack of pale band in tail and by chestnut under tail coverts. Bill grey with crimson base; feet pinkish red. **Voice:** a deep *currr-hoo*, with emphasis on the *hoo*. Also bursts of deep, rhythmic purring. **Habitat:** evergreen and mixed deciduous forests of the plains and lower hills; forested limestone outcrops, mangroves and islands. Uncommon resident, much reduced by hunting pressure. Still fairly numerous at a few more remote sites.

260. Pied Imperial Pigeon *Ducula bicolor* S: 40   นกลุมพูขาว
Creamy white plumage with a black tail-tip and flight feathers of the wings. Bill and orbital ring grey-blue; feet pale purplish blue. **Immature:** white parts tinged grey. **Habitat:** mangrove and other coastal forests, principally on steep offshore islets. Locally common resident.

261. Mountain Imperial Pigeon *Ducula badia* S: 47   นกมูม
Pale grey head and underparts contrast with brownish maroon mantle and wings. From Green Imperial also by buffy under tail coverts which paler than grey breast and belly and by broad pale grey terminal band to dark tail, which conspicuous in flight. Bill reddish at base; feet pinkish red. **Voice:** a very deep, hooting *oomp-oomp*, the second syllable deeper and louder. **Habitat:** evergreen forests of the hill slopes up to the highest elevations. Occasionally disperses to the extreme lowlands. Common resident, though locally reduced due to hunting pressure.

160

WOOD-PIGEONS: Genus *Columba*. Moderately large and heavily-built, but smaller than imperial pigeons, with more pointed wings. Most feed arboreally on fruit.

262. Rock Pigeon *Columba livia* S: 33   นกพิราบป่า

Feral offspring of introduced stock. Broad-based, strongly pointed wings. Plumage highly variable, but usually dark grey with broad black wing bars and black tail-tip; underwing silvery whitish. Glossy greenish neck patch. Bill black; feet red. **Voice:** a soft, throaty *oo-roo-coo*. **Habitat:** cities, towns, villages, rocky cliffs, cultivated areas from lowlands to the higher mountains. Very common resident.

263. Speckled Wood-Pigeon *Columba hodgsonii* S: 38   นกพิราบป่าอกลาย

Dark maroon upperparts with diagnostic white speckling on wing coverts; tail and flight feathers blackish. Head, neck and breast ashy grey with dark striations on sides of neck. Belly and flanks dark maroon, flecked whitish; under tail coverts slaty grey. Bill black; feet dull greyish. **Habitat:** hill evergreen forests, secondary growth, above 1400 m. Uncommon or irregular winter visitor; occasionally in large flocks.

264. Ashy Wood-Pigeon *Columba pulchricollis* S: 39   นกพิราบเขาสูง

Striking pale buffy collar contrasts with dark slaty mantle and grey upper breast. Both upper back and breast glossed greenish; head pale grey. When seen from below, from Speckled by pale buffy belly and under tail coverts, red feet. **Voice:** a deep, single note; *ooop*. **Habitat:** hill evergreen forest, secondary growth above 1400 m. Local and uncommon resident; usually seen in groups of one to three birds.

265. Pale-capped Pigeon *Columba punicea* S: 39   นกกลุมพูแดง

Whitish cap contrasts with dark maroon-chestnut upperparts and paler vinous-brown underparts. Greenish gloss to sides of neck, upper back and to slaty rump. Blackish upper tail coverts and tail. **Juvenile:** lacks pale cap; body plumage duller. Red feet and base of bill. **Habitat:** evergreen forest from lowlands up to at least 800 m, especially on islands. In winter, also recorded from mangroves and scrub. Uncommon to rare; status uncertain; may be resident on islands. Probably also a passage migrant and winter visitor.

DOVES: Genera *Macropygia, Streptopelia, Geopelia, Chalcophaps*. Smaller than pigeons, with more pointed wings and (usually) longer tails. Wing and tail patterns are often diagnostic when seen in flight. Most are primarily ground-feeding.

Plate 54 Imperial Pigeons, Wood-Pigeons

259 Green Imperial Pigeon

260 Pied Imperial Pigeon

261 Mountain Imperial Pigeon

1/18 KK

262 Rock Pigeon

263 Speckled Wood-Pigeon

264 Ashy Wood-Pigeon

Mongkol

265 Pale-capped Pigeon

162

266. Barred Cuckoo-Dove *Macropygia unchall* S: 38   นกเขาลายใหญ่

In flight, from turtle-doves (268–270) by much longer, barred tail and more uniformly dark brown upperparts, lacking grey or white markings on wings, rump or tail-tip. At close range, upperparts narrowly barred black and rufous. Greenish gloss on neck; vinous underparts. **Male:** blackish bars on lower breast and belly broken and indistinct. **Female:** fine blackish bars on entire underparts. **Voice:** a deep *who-ooo*, with a falling intonation; uttered at approximately 1–2 second intervals. Louder than the similar call of Emerald Dove. **Habitat:** evergreen forests, forest edge and clearings from 500 m to 1800 m. Common resident.

267. Little Cuckoo-Dove *Macropygia ruficeps* S: 30   นกเขาลายเล็ก

Much smaller than preceding species, with orange-rufous crown and rufous-buff, unbarred underparts and a bright cinnamon-orange wing lining. Shows broader rufous scaling on upper wing coverts and an unbarred tail. **Male:** greenish gloss on neck and silvery-whitish scaling on upper breast. **Female:** some black mottling across upper breast. **Voice:** a series of soft, frog-like *wuck* notes, uttered at a rate of about two per second. **Habitat:** evergreen forest from 500 m to 1800 m; occasionally in adjacent deciduous habitats. Uncommon resident.

268. Oriental Turtle-Dove *Streptopelia orientalis* S: 32   นกเขาพม่า

Larger, but more compact than Spotted Dove, with a proportionately shorter tail and darker plumage. Broad rufous scaling on wing coverts and scapulars, blue-tinged slaty rump and a blue-grey panel on the greater coverts. Narrow pale greyish tips to outer tail feathers. Black patch with whitish bars on side of neck. **Voice:** a throaty, 4-note *croo*. **Habitat:** open forest, secondary growth and scrub, from foothills to 1800 m. Uncommon resident and winter visitor.

269. Red Turtle-Dove *Collared* *Streptopelia tranquebarica* S: 23   นกเขาไฟ

Small size and plump, short-tailed appearance. Narrow black collar around hindneck. Broad white tips to tail feathers form a nearly complete terminal band. **Male:** reddish body contrasts with blue-grey head and dark slaty rump and tail. **Female:** has dull brown instead of reddish body; grey parts duller than in male. **Voice:** distinctive, dry throaty call with rhythmic pattern, *croodle-oo-croo*, rapidly repeated. **Habitat:** dry open country, scrub and cultivated areas of the plains. Very common resident.

270. Spotted Dove *Streptopelia chinensis* S: 30   นกเขาใหญ่, นกเขาหลวง

In flight, shows rather long, wedge-shaped tail with broad, diffuse, whitish tips to the outer feathers. Pale greyish patch in greater coverts and contrasting blackish primaries. Upperparts much paler brown than Oriental Turtle-Dove, with blackish streaks. Breast and belly pale vinous. Broad hindneck collar of white spots on a black background. **Voice:** a soft cooing. Pattern variable, but usually 3 notes, *coo-crooo-crooo*, with emphasis on middle note. **Habitat:** cultivated fields, scrub, open country, open woodlands from plains up to 1800 m. Very common resident.

Plate 55 Turtle-Doves, Emerald Dove, Nicobar Pigeon

267 Little Cuckoo-Dove

66 Barred Cuckoo-Dove

268 Oriental Turtle-Dove

269 Red Turtle-Dove

270 Spotted Dove

271 Zebra Dove

272 Emerald Dove

273 Nicobar Pigeon

Mongkol

271. Zebra Dove (Peaceful Dove) *Geopelia striata* S: 21   นกเขาชวา

Very small, with a fairly long, graduated tail with white tips to the outer feathers. Upperparts brownish with broken black bars; dense black and white barring on sides of neck and breast. Forecrown and sides of head grey, contrasting with brown hindcrown. Broad blue-grey orbital ring. **Voice:** a high-pitched, soft trilling which leads into a series of short *coo* notes. Hollow and metallic, with a distinctive rhythmic pattern. **Habitat:** gardens, cultivation, scrub of lowlands. Common resident. Native to the Peninsula, but introduced elsewhere.

272. Emerald Dove (Green-winged Pigeon) *Chalcophaps indica* S: 25   นกเขาเขียว

Metallic, glossy green upperparts and reddish vinous face and underparts. Coral-red bill. Usually seen in flight, when striking combination of green upperparts and reddish chestnut wing lining is evident. **Male:** white forehead and supercilium; grey crown and nape. **Female:** slightly duller, with greyish supercilium and forehead and brownish crown and nape. **Voice:** a very soft *ti-hooo* (first note almost inaudible). Much quieter than call of Barred Cuckoo-Dove and repeated at intervals of about one second. **Habitat:** mixed deciduous and evergreen forests from plains up to 1500 m. Usually keeps to the deep shade. Common resident.

273. Nicobar Pigeon *Caloenas nicobarica* S: 41   นกชาปีไหน

Large, plump and short-tailed. Metallic dark green plumage with white tail and under tail coverts. Possesses a ruff of iridescent bronze neck hackles. **Immature:** lacks hackles. Largely terrestrial. **Habitat:** evergreen forests of the least disturbed offshore islands. Rare resident, threatened by human persecution.

วงศ์นกแก้ว

PARROTS: Family *Psittacidae*. Large heads and powerful, hooked bills. Have fast direct flight on pointed wings. The parakeets have elongate tails. Arboreal in habits and climb about in branches, often using the bill as an aid. Mainly frugivorous or granivorous, and manipulate food with their zygodactylous feet. Sometimes attack crops. Gregarious, often roosting or nesting in loose colonies. Hole-nesting. The larger species have been much reduced by the illegal bird trade. World: 271 species. Thailand: 7 species.

274. Alexandrine Parakeet *Psittacula eupatria* S: 51   นกแก้วโม่ง

Identified by large size, huge red bill and mainly green plumage with a maroon-red shoulder patch. Feet yellowish. **Male:** blackish necklet extends into a pinkish collar around the back of the neck. **Female:** greenish throat; lacks neck collar. **Juvenile:** like female, but both body plumage and bill duller. **Voice:** a loud, ringing *trrrieuw*, highest in the middle (JS). **Habitat:** lowland mixed deciduous forests, secondary growth. Rare resident, now very much reduced.

Plate 56 Parrots

274 Alexandrine Parakeet

275 Red-breasted Parakeet

juvenile

276 Blossom-headed Parakeet

277 Grey-headed Parakeet

juvenile

279 Vernal Hanging Parrot

278 Blue-rumped Parrot

280 Blue-crowned Hanging Parrot

Mongkol

166

275. Red-breasted Parakeet *Psittacula alexandri* S: 36   นกแขกเต้า

Identified by black bar across forehead, broad black moustache and by orange-pink breast. **Male:** red bill and violet-tinged breast. **Female:** black bill and more pinkish orange tinged breast. **Juvenile:** youngest stages have mainly green plumage, with dull greyish limited to sides of head, and faint facial markings. Older birds assume the adult face pattern but lack any pink on the breast. Bill mainly blackish. **Voice:** harsh, usually disyllabic or chattering screams. **Habitat:** deciduous woodlands, secondary growth and cultivated areas with relict tall trees; primarily in the plains but occasionally up to 1200 m. Uncommon to locally common resident.

276. Blossom-headed Parakeet *Psittacula roseata* S: 33   นกแก้วหัวแพร

Smaller than other parakeets: tail less elongate than in Grey-headed. Bill bicoloured, orange to yellowish, with the upper mandible darker than the lower. Reddish shoulder patch. **Male:** rosy-pink face; black throat and neck collar. Crown and nape violet. **Female:** duller, powdery blue-grey head lacking any black markings. **Juvenile:** all green with yellowish bill. From young juveniles of Grey-headed by smaller size and smaller bill. **Voice:** softer, less piercing than other parakeets. **Habitat:** deciduous forests, secondary growth, cultivation, up to 900 m. Uncommon resident.

277. Grey-headed Parakeet *Psittacula finschii* S: 41   นกกะลิง

Longer-tailed than other parakeets with a dark, slaty-grey head, black throat and red bill. **Female:** lacks the red shoulder patch of the male. **Juvenile:** lacks black on throat. Youngest stage has entirely greenish head and yellowish bill; in older juveniles, the head gradually becomes greyish (remaining paler than adult) and the bill more reddish. **Voice:** a loud, whistled *sweet* with an upward inflection. **Habitat:** mainly deciduous woodlands, secondary growth from plains up to 1300 m. Uncommon to locally common resident.

278. Blue-rumped Parrot *Psittinus cyanurus* S: 19   นกหกใหญ่

Short-tailed, stocky appearance. From hanging parrots by larger size and by blackish underwing with red wing lining. **Male:** blackish back, red shoulder patch, blue-grey head, neck, lower back and rump. Red bill. **Female:** brownish head and dull brown bill. Only slight blue tinge on back. **Voice:** a loud, discordant jangling, reminiscent of Black-collared Starling (830). **Habitat:** evergreen forests of the level lowlands; occasionally cultivated areas where these are close to forest. Rare resident; much reduced.

279. Vernal Hanging Parrot *Loriculus vernalis* S: 14   นกหกเล็กปากแดง

Very small and short-tailed. Green plumage with red bill, red rump and upper tail coverts and yellowish feet. Underside of wings turquoise. Frequently hangs upside down. **Male:** blue-tinged throat. **Voice:** a squeaky, rattling *pe-zeez-eet* (sometimes rendered as *tsee-sip*), uttered in flight. **Habitat:** deciduous and evergreen forests, secondary growth, up to 1500 m. Common resident.

280. Blue-crowned Hanging Parrot *Loriculus galgulus* S: 14　นกหกเล็กปากดำ

Distinguished from Vernal Hanging Parrot by black bill and by grey-green feet. **Male:** red breast patch, blue crown patch; golden-yellow patch on mantle and yellow band above rump. **Female:** like female Vernal apart from bill and feet colour. **Juvenile:** shows dull yellowish feet and bill. **Voice:** a shrill *dzii* ; slightly higher pitched than call of Vernal and usually monosyllabic. **Habitat:** evergreen forest, forest edge, secondary growth from lowlands up to 1200 m. Locally common resident.

วงศ์นกคัคคู

CUCKOOS: Family *Cuculidae*. Characterised by slender bodies and long graduated tails. Bills are slightly decurved and feet zygodactylous, with 2 toes pointing forward and 2 back. A highly varied family; most are insectivorous. (Malkohas and Coral-billed Ground-Cuckoo, 298–304, and coucals, 305–306, are now usually placed in separate families, *Coccyzidae* and *Centropodidae* respectively.) World: 134 species. Thailand: 26 species.

เหล่านกคัคคูแท้

PARASITIC CUCKOOS: Genera *Clamator, Cuculus, Cacomantis, Chrysococcyx, Surniculus, Eudynamys.* Brood parasites which lay their eggs in the nests of other species. Generally solitary; arboreal, often keeping to the canopy where they are difficult to observe. Loud, monotonously-repeated calls are invaluable for identification since many species share similar plumages. Sexes usually similar, though reddish brown (hepatic morph) females, which resemble juveniles, are found in some species.

281. Chestnut-winged Cuckoo *Clamator coromandus* S: 46　นกคัคคูหงอน

Diagnostic black crest and rufous wings contrasting with black back and tail. (Coucals, 305–306, have both back and wings chestnut.) White nuchal collar. Underparts whitish, with rufous-buff wash on throat and upper breast. Thighs dark greyish; under tail coverts black. **Juvenile:** shows rufous scaling on back. **Voice:** raucous screams and a harsh whistle. **Habitat:** open bush country and bamboo thickets of lowlands and hills up to 1300 m. Occurs in mangroves in winter and on passage. Uncommon; movements poorly understood but probably wet-season breeding visitor and passage migrant throughout continental Thailand, wintering in the Peninsula.

282. Large Hawk-Cuckoo *Cuculus sparverioides* S: 44　นกคัคคูเหยี่ยวใหญ่

Broad-based, slightly rounded wings and boldly barred tail give superficial similarity to the *Accipiter* hawks (74–80). From other hawk-cuckoos by size and call. Tail narrowly tipped whitish, with a broader rufous subterminal band. Head, cheeks and nape dark grey; rest of upperparts somewhat browner. Black chin; breast rufous, boldly streaked dark grey brown. Belly whitish, barred dark brown. **Juvenile:** entire underparts streaked; upperparts barred rufous-brown. Head browner than in adult, often with a slight suggestion of a darker moustache. **Voice:** a shrill, 3-note whistle *pipeeah* (sometimes rendered as *brain-fe-ver*), with emphasis on the middle syllable. Repeated in a long sequence, at diminishing intervals, becoming progressively higher-pitched. **Habitat:** deciduous and evergreen woodlands from foothills to 2500 m. Migrant and wintering individuals occur to the plains, often in gardens and in mangroves. Common resident and winter visitor.

168

283. Common Hawk-Cuckoo *Cuculus varius* S: 35   นกคัคคูเหยี่ยวพันธุ์อินเดีย

Very similar to Large Hawk-Cuckoo; distinguished with difficulty by smaller size and by less distinct breast streaking and belly barring; less black on chin. Slightly paler, ashy-grey upperparts. **Juvenile:** tail tipped rufous (whitish or whitish rufous in Large). **Voice:** slightly more shrill than that of Large; *wee-piwhit*, repeated in a similar fashion. **Habitat:** deciduous woodland, secondary growth of the plains. Very rare visitor; only one record.

284. Moustached Hawk-Cuckoo *Cuculus vagans* S: 30   นกคัคคูเหยี่ยวเล็ก

Distinguished from other hawk-cuckoos by dark grey moustachial stripe contrasting with paler cheeks and throat. Upperparts brownish with white-tipped tail. Underparts whitish with dark brown streaks. **Adult:** crown and nape slaty. **Juvenile:** crown and nape brownish. **Voice:** a double note, *kaen-ko*, repeated on a monotone for long periods. Also has a rapidly ascending series of double whistles, which rises to a crescendo and ceases abruptly. **Habitat:** evergreen forest from plains to 900 m. Uncommon resident.

285. Hodgson's Hawk-Cuckoo *Cuculus fugax* S: 29   นกคัคคูเหยี่ยวอกแดง

Distinguished from Moustached Hawk-Cuckoo in all plumages by lack of moustache and by narrow rufous tail-tip. **Adult:** slaty grey upperparts. Breast rufous with no more than vague, blurred streaking (race *C. f. nisicolor* of continental Thailand) or white with dark rufous brown streaks (race *C. f. fugax*, resident in Peninsula). **Juvenile:** underparts whitish with dark brown streaks; brownish barred upperparts. From Moustached by lack of moustache; largely rufous tail-tip with only narrow whitish terminal band. **Voice:** a dry, tuneless *eez-wheet* (sometimes rendered as *gee-whiz*) in a series, increasing gradually in volume and rising in pitch. Also has a breathless, bubbling call which rises to a crescendo and then tails off. **Habitat:** evergreen and mixed deciduous forests from plains to 1100 m. Uncommon resident and winter visitor.

286. Indian Cuckoo *Cuculus micropterus* S: 33   นกคัคคูพันธุ์อินเดีย

Adult: from hawk-cuckoos by pointed wings, grey upper breast and throat. From following three species by broad, dark subterminal band on upperside of tail and by brown-tinged tail, wings and back, which contrast slightly with grey head. Orbital ring dull yellowish to grey-green. **Juvenile:** from immatures and hepatic morph of other cuckoos by broad buffy bars on head and upper back. **Voice:** a 4-note whistle, *ko-ko-to-ko* (sometimes rendered as *one more bot-tle*) the third note highest. **Habitat:** evergreen and deciduous forests, secondary growth from plains to 1800 m. Fairly common resident and winter visitor.

Plate 57 Cuckoos I

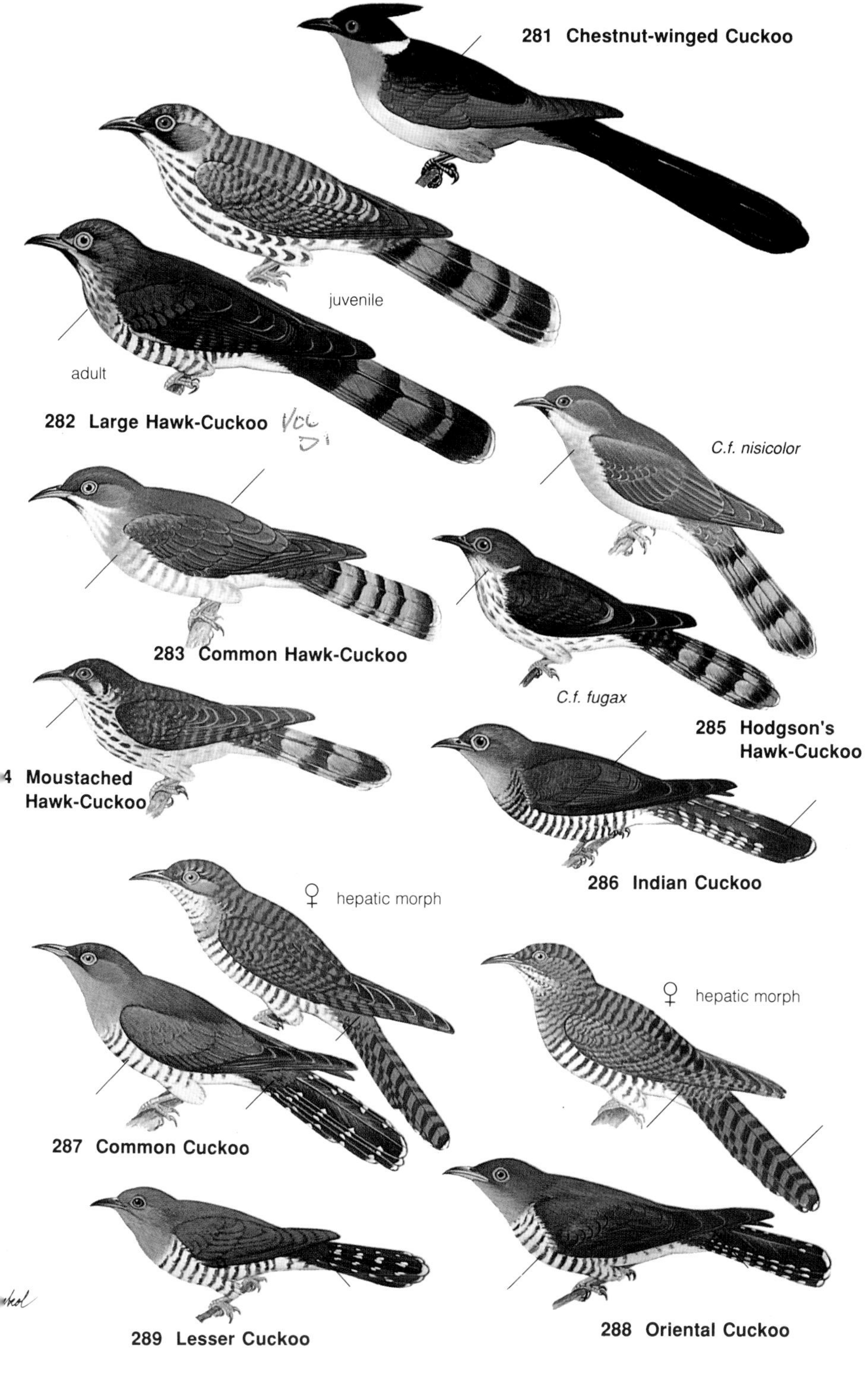

281 Chestnut-winged Cuckoo

juvenile

adult

282 Large Hawk-Cuckoo

C.f. nisicolor

283 Common Hawk-Cuckoo

C.f. fugax

285 Hodgson's Hawk-Cuckoo

4 Moustached Hawk-Cuckoo

286 Indian Cuckoo

♀ hepatic morph

287 Common Cuckoo

♀ hepatic morph

289 Lesser Cuckoo

288 Oriental Cuckoo

287. Common Cuckoo *Cuculus canorus* S: 33 นกคัคคุพันธุ์ยุโรป

Difficult to distinguish from Oriental Cuckoo except by call, though barring on underparts is marginally narrower. Also tends to be paler grey on upperparts. In hand, white patch at bend of wing has grey barring. **Hepatic morph female:** black bars of upperparts usually narrower than intervening rufous bars. Black barring on upper tail coverts is very noticeably less heavy than in Oriental Cuckoo. **Juvenile:** from hepatic female by white patch on nape. ◆ Orbital ring yellow. **Voice:** male sings with the familiar, mellow *cuc-koo*, the second note lower in pitch, repeated at roughly one-second intervals. The female gives a bubbling trill. **Habitat:** open woodland, secondary growth of the mountains. Status uncertain; may be resident. Rare.

288. Oriental Cuckoo *Cuculus saturatus* S: 33 นกคัคคุพันธุ์หิมาลัย

Grey morph adult: blackish tail contrasts with grey upperparts, rump and upper tail coverts. Closely resembles Common Cuckoo but blackish barring on underparts broader and darker; usually darker grey above. Small individuals may be confused with Lesser Cuckoo. In hand, shows unbarred white patch at bend of wing. **Hepatic morph and immature:** from similar plumage of Common Cuckoo by black bars on upper tail coverts broader than intervening rufous bars. ◆ Orbital ring yellow. **Voice:** three or four dull hooting or booming monotone notes, similar in quality to call of Hoopoe. **Habitat:** open wooded country and secondary growth of lowlands and hills. Uncommon; chiefly passage migrant, most often seen in spring.

289. Lesser Cuckoo *Cuculus poliocephalus* S: 28 นกคัคคุเล็ก

Difficult to distinguish on plumage from small individuals of Oriental Cuckoo, but rump and upper tail coverts darker and not contrasting with blackish tail; black barring on usually buffier underparts often wider spaced and bolder. **Voice:** a shrill, cackling whistle of six notes with stress on prolonged third syllable; *that's your choky pepper.* **Habitat:** deciduous forests and secondary growth of lower hills. Very rare; status uncertain and only known in Thailand from three specimens collected in Chiang Mai province in May.

290. Banded Bay Cuckoo *Cacomantis sonneratii* S: 23 นกคัคคูลาย

Distinguished from immature or hepatic morph of Plaintive Cuckoo by longer bill, broad whitish supercilium and striking dark eye patch. Entire underparts whitish with fine dark bars; upperparts dark rufous brown, finely barred blackish. Often perches erect. **Voice:** diagnostic call is of four shrill whistled notes, the first two same pitch, and last two descending; *pi-pi-pew-pew.* Also an ascending series of notes somewhat similar to those of Plaintive Cuckoo but introduced by a preliminary two or three note sequence. **Habitat:** deciduous and evergreen forests, secondary growth, up to 1500 m. Uncommon resident.

Plate 58 Cuckoos II

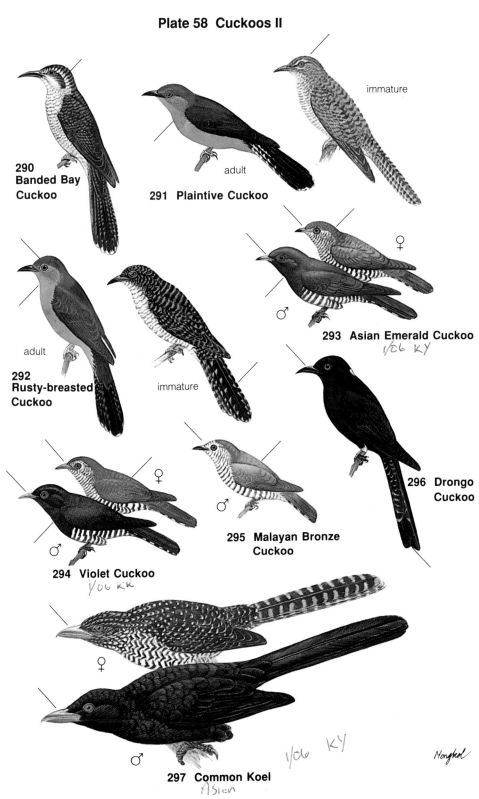

290 Banded Bay Cuckoo

291 Plaintive Cuckoo

adult

immature

292 Rusty-breasted Cuckoo

adult

immature

293 Asian Emerald Cuckoo

♀

♂

1/06 KY

296 Drongo Cuckoo

294 Violet Cuckoo

♀

♂

1/06 KK

295 Malayan Bronze Cuckoo

♀

♂

297 Common Koel

♀

♂

1/06 KY

Asian

Mongkol

172

291. Plaintive Cuckoo *Cacomantis merulinus* S: 22 นกอีวาบตั๊กแตน

Head, throat and upper breast pale grey; mantle and wings darker, grey brown. Lower breast and belly rufous-buff, showing a fairly sharp demarcation from throat and upper breast. From Rusty-breasted Cuckoo by lack of contrasting orbital ring. **Juvenile and hepatic morph:** from Banded Bay Cuckoo by mottled brownish head and upper breast, lacking sharply contrasted eye patch and supercilium. **Voice:** usually three monotone whistles followed by a series of shorter slurred notes descending in pitch. Also a hurriedly repeated, 3 note ascending sequence. **Habitat:** secondary growth, gardens (including those in towns and cities) and cultivated areas from plains up to 1800 m. Very common resident.

นกคัคคูหางแพน
292. Rusty-breasted Cuckoo (Brush Cuckoo) *Cacomantis sepulcralis* S: 24

Similar to Plaintive Cuckoo, but rufous-buff of underparts extends on to throat and grades into greyish cheeks. Head usually dark as back; orbital ring yellow. **Juvenile:** from juvenile Plaintive Cuckoo by more extensive black on central tail feathers with rufous limited to small lateral notches. Has little or no rufous-buff on black-barred white underparts. **Voice:** 10–15 melancholy, upward-inflected whistles, *chu-ii, chu-ii....*, uttered at about one per second on a gradually descending scale. Other notes distinguished with difficulty from those of Plaintive Cuckoo. **Habitat:** mangroves, evergreen forest and secondary growth up to about 600 m. Uncommon resident.

293. Asian Emerald Cuckoo *Chrysococcyx maculatus* S: 18 นกคัคคูมรกต

Adult male: iridescent, dark bronze-green upperparts, head and upper breast, with broad whitish bars on belly, under tail coverts and wing lining. Bill orange-yellow, usually dark-tipped; orbital ring orange. **Subadult male:** entire underparts barred. **Female:** paler, coppery green upperparts and diagnostic light chestnut crown and nape. Underparts entirely barred. **Immature:** may show a mixture of dull bronze-green and rufous-barred feathers on upperparts, with some whitish feathering on forecrown. Entire underparts whitish, dark-barred. Bill mainly dark. From juvenile Violet Cuckoo by duller, less rufous appearance and, in flight, by broader white band on underwing. **Voice:** a sharp *chweek*, uttered in flight. **Habitat:** evergreen forest and secondary growth of the higher hills up to at least 1800 m. Occurs to the plains in gardens, orchards on passage and in winter. Uncommon resident and winter visitor.

294. Violet Cuckoo *Chrysococcyx xanthorhynchus* S: 17 นกคัคคูสีม่วง

Male: metallic violet upperparts, head, upper breast, with white bars on belly, under tail coverts and wing lining. Bright orange bill with red base. **Female:** differs from Asian Emerald in having uniform reddish bronze upperparts with only slight greenish tinge; sometimes shows slight whitish speckling on forehead. Barring on underparts narrower. Outer tail feathers rufous. Bill usually red at base, but overall less bright than in male. Orbital ring reddish in both sexes. **Juvenile:** rufous, dark-barred upperparts with slight greenish gloss. Lacks red on bill. From juvenile Asian Emerald Cuckoo by lack of white band on underside of wing. **Voice:** a loud, distinctly disyllabic *che-wick*, uttered in flight. Also an accelerating trill (JS). **Habitat:** deciduous and evergreen forests, usually below 600 m. Occasionally in gardens in winter or on passage, and wandering as high as 1100 m. Uncommon resident and winter visitor.

295. Malayan Bronze Cuckoo *Chrysococcyx minutillus* S: 16 นกคัคคูสีทองแดง

Sexes similar. From female Violet Cuckoo by more extensive white speckling on forehead, more greenish upperparts and lack of rufous in outer tail feathers. Bill blackish; eye red. Orbital ring red in male, green in female. **Voice:** a tremulous descending whistled call of three to five notes, *teu, teu, teu*. **Habitat:** mangrove, forest edge, gardens and scrub of lowlands and lower hills. Uncommon resident.

296. Drongo Cuckoo *Surniculus lugubris* S: 25 นกคัคคูแซงแซว

Glossy black plumage; narrow white transverse bands on under tail coverts and on short, outermost tail feathers. Small whitish nuchal patch and white thighs are difficult to see in the field. From drongos (546–552) by thinner, slightly decurved bill and unforked tail. **Voice:** 4–6 whistled notes, ascending the scale. **Habitat:** forest and secondary growth up to 1200 m. Occasionally in gardens and mangroves (perhaps on migration). Uncommon resident, passage migrant and winter visitor.

297. Common Koel *Eudynamys scolopacea* S: 43 นกกาเหว่า

Large size; long, broad-ended tail, red eye and heavy, greenish bill. **Male:** glossy black plumage. **Female:** dark brown, boldly spotted and barred with buff. Often difficult to see, usually calls from thick cover. **Voice:** a loud *ko-el*, with stress on the second note, often repeated, successive calls becoming progressively louder. Also a loud ascending bubbling *kwow kwow-kwow-kwow*. **Habitat:** open woodland and scrub, cultivation and gardens of lowlands. Usually close to human habitations. Common resident.

เหล่านกบั้งรอก

MALKOHAS: Genus *Phaenicophaeus*. Large, extremely long tailed and arboreal. Non-parasitic, building their own cup-shaped nests in thick foliage. Favour thick vegetation in middle storey of forest. Often in pairs. Rather silent; feed on insects and small vertebrates.

298. Black-bellied Malkoha *Phaenicophaeus diardi* S: 37 นกบั้งรอกเล็กท้องเทา

Resembles Green-billed, but smaller with proportionately shorter tail and darker underparts (lower belly blackish). Lacks whitish margin to red eye patch and white tips to tail feathers are narrower. **Voice:** a single, soft falling tone *taup*. **Habitat:** evergreen forest of lowlands and lower hills. Common resident.

นกบั้งรอกเล็กท้องแดง

299. Chestnut-bellied Malkoha *Phaenicophaeus sumatranus* S: 40

Distinguished from Black-bellied by chestnut lower belly and under tail coverts (though not always easily seen), heavier bill and by bright pinkish orange (rather than crimson-red) eye patch. **Habitat:** mangroves, lowland evergreen forest and secondary growth. Uncommon resident.

174

300. Green-billed Malkoha *Phaenicophaeus tristis* S: 56   นกบั้งรอกใหญ่

Very long, prominently white-tipped tail and grey plumage. Underparts paler than Black-bellied Malkoha. Usually shows a whitish feathered margin around bright red eye patch. The only malkoha over most of the country. **Voice:** deep guttural grunting or croaking notes; a soft, falling tone *poouw*. **Habitat:** deciduous and evergreen forests, secondary growth and scrub up to 1500 m. Very common resident.

301. Raffles' Malkoha *Phaenicophaeus chlorophaeus* S: 33   นกบั้งรอกแดง
The smallest malkoha, sexually dimorphic in plumage. Sexes share chestnut mantle and wings and broad white tips to tail feathers. **Male:** blackish tail and buffy-rufous throat and upper breast. **Female:** grey head, neck, throat and breast. Tail chestnut with black subterminal band on each feather. **Voice:** 3–4 querulous reedy notes, *kiau, kiau, kiau*, on a descending scale. Call has a trogon-like quality. **Habitat:** evergreen forest and forest edge up to 900 m. Common resident.

302. Red-billed Malkoha *Phaenicophaeus javanicus* S: 45   นกบั้งรอกปากแดง
Distinguished from all other malkohas by red bill. Upperparts greyish, with steely gloss; throat and upper breast pale cinnamon; belly and under tail coverts chestnut with lower breast pale grey. **Voice:** a quiet, deep *kuk*. **Habitat:** secondary growth and evergreen forest up to 1000 m. Common resident.

นกบั้งรอกเขียวอกแดง
303. Chestnut-breasted Malkoha *Phaenicophaeus curvirostris* S: 46
Upperparts, including basal two-thirds of tail, dark glossy green. No white tips to tail feathers; distal third of tail and entire underparts dark chestnut. Very thick green bill and red facial skin. **Habitat:** forest and secondary growth up to 900 m. Common resident.

เหล่านกโกโรโกโส
GROUND-CUCKOOS: Genus *Carpococcyx*. Large, terrestrial forest birds with a running gait. Shy and difficult to see. Nest and often roost in trees. Non-parasitic.

304. Coral-billed Ground-Cuckoo *Carpococcyx renauldi* S: 69   นกโกโรโกโส

Glossy black head, neck, upper breast and black tail contrast with grey back and wings, greyish white underparts. Coral-red bill and legs, violet facial skin and yellow-straw iris. **Voice:** a hoarse, deep, rolling whistle. Can also duet; one bird giving a peculiar 3 note phrase, *whup, whoo-up*, the other giving a rolling gargle. **Habitat:** evergreen forest, from plains to 900 m. Uncommon resident.

Plate 59 Malkohas, Coucals, Ground-Cuckoo

298 Black-bellied Malkoha

299 Chestnut-bellied Malkoha

300 Green-billed Malkoha
1/06
KK

301 Raffles' Malkoha
♂ ♀

302 Red-billed Malkoha

304 Coral-billed Ground-Cuckoo

303 Chestnut-breasted Malkoha 1/06 KK

juv. or non-breeding

breeding

juvenile

306 Lesser Coucal
1/06 KY

adult

305 Greater Coucal

176

เหล่านกกระปูด

COUCALS: Genus *Centropus*. Terrestrial birds of grass and scrub, with walking gait. Feed on small terrestrial vertebrates and insects. Build round or globular nests of grass with side entrance, placed in low bushes.

305. Greater Coucal *Centropus sinensis* S: 53 นกกระปูดใหญ่

Identified by large size, glossy black head, neck, underparts and tail; uniform chestnut back and wings, black underwing coverts. Much larger and heavier-billed than Lesser Coucal. Eyes red; bill and legs black. **Juvenile:** black barring on chestnut areas and fine greyish spotting or barring on black parts. **Voice:** a series of deep hooting notes, *poop, poop, poop, poop*..... in a long series, at first descending in pitch, then rising in pitch again towards end. Also has a popping call *tok tok tok*.... and a harsh, rasping *skaaah*. **Habitat:** scrub, grassland and secondary growth from plains to at least 1500 m. mangroves. Very common resident.

306. Lesser Coucal *Centropus bengalensis* S: 38 นกกระปูดเล็ก

Much smaller than preceding species, with chestnut underwing coverts. **Breeding adult:** like Greater, (though often showing dark brown primary tips which conspicuous in flight). **Juvenile and non-breeding adult:** dark brown head, neck and mantle with prominent long buff streaks; upper tail coverts finely barred black and rufous-buff; green-glossed blackish tail. Underparts buffy with paler streaks on throat and breast, fine dark barring on flanks. Intermediate plumage stages occur. **Voice:** starts off with 4 or 5 *whoop* notes which lead into a short series of higher-pitched, ringing *kotok* notes. **Habitat:** long grass, scrub from plains to 1800 m. Often favours marshy areas. Common resident.

วงศ์นกเค้า

OWLS: *Order Strigiformes.* Nocturnal birds of prey which possess large heads with large, forward-directed eyes and a feathered facial disc which is an adaptation to focus sound in order to locate prey in the dark. Fly noiselessly on broad, rounded wings. Usually spend the daylight hours roosting in thick cover. Difficult to observe but distinctive calls are very useful for identification. Lay round, white eggs, most species nesting in tree cavities, taking over the old stick nests of other birds or, in a few larger species, nesting on bird's-nest ferns, *Asplenium*. A few species nest in crevices in buildings. Sexes similar. World: 162 species. Thailand: 19 species.

307. Barn Owl *Tyto alba* S: 34 นกแสก

Identified by white or buffy underparts and by pale, grey and golden-buff upperparts which lack any strong markings; narrow dark tail bars. Has a heart-shaped facial disc. Eyes dark brown. **Voice:** a drawn out rasping or hissing sound. **Habitat:** open areas, cultivation, marshes, towns and cities, up to 1200 m. Often nests or roosts in buildings. Common resident.

308. Bay Owl *Phodilus badius* S: 29 นกแสกแดง

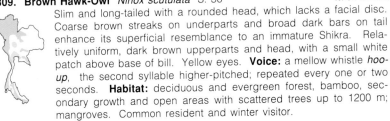

Smaller than Barn Owl with darker reddish chestnut upperparts; breast and belly tinged vinous, and marked with small round spots. Facial disc separated from breast by a thin, waxy-looking, gleaming white necklace. Shows dark smudges below eyes and rudimentary ear tufts. Eyes dark brown. Often perches one foot above the other on vertical or steeply sloping branches and vines in forest understorey. **Voice:** a series of eerie, musical, upward-inflected whistles. **Habitat:** evergreen and mixed deciduous forests from lowlands up to 2200 m. Uncommon resident.

309. Brown Hawk-Owl *Ninox scutulata* S: 30 นกเค้าเหยี่ยว

Slim and long-tailed with a rounded head, which lacks a facial disc. Coarse brown streaks on underparts and broad dark bars on tail enhance its superficial resemblance to an immature Shikra. Relatively uniform, dark brown upperparts and head, with a small white patch above base of bill. Yellow eyes. **Voice:** a mellow whistle *hoo-up*, the second syllable higher-pitched; repeated every one or two seconds. **Habitat:** deciduous and evergreen forest, bamboo, secondary growth and open areas with scattered trees up to 1200 m; mangroves. Common resident and winter visitor.

310. White-fronted Scops-Owl *Otus sagittatus* S: 27 นกเค้าหน้าผากขาว

Shape very like Collared Scops-Owl, but larger, with a slightly longer tail. Distinguished by white forehead and eyebrows, whitish bill and by chestnut-bay upperparts. Lacks any nuchal collar. Eyes brown. **Voice:** a hollow, whistled, monotone *hoooo*, like the call of Reddish Scops-Owl but each individual note both starts and finishes more abruptly (BK). **Habitat:** evergreen forest of the level lowlands. Rare resident, probably threatened by habitat destruction.

311. Reddish Scops-Owl *Otus rufescens* S: 19 นกเค้าแดง

Rather uniform rufescent plumage like Mountain Scops-Owl, but white spots on back are tipped with black arrowhead markings. Eyes usually brown but occasionally yellow. Best identified by call, habitat and range. **Voice:** a hollow, whistled *hoooo*, lacking any inflection and dying off; usually uttered at intervals of 7–11 seconds. **Habitat:** evergreen forests of the extreme lowlands. Rare resident, threatened by habitat destruction.

312. Mountain Scops-Owl *Otus spilocephalus* S: 20 นกเค้าภูเขา

Rufescent plumage which lacks any bold markings other than white spots on scapulars. Eyes yellow. **Voice:** two high-pitched, uninflected bell-like notes, *plew-plew*, with only a slight pause between them. Some individual variation in the pitch of notes uttered. **Habitat:** evergreen forest from foothills to 2200 m. Common resident.

178

313. Oriental Scops-Owl (Common Scops-Owl) *Otus sunia* S: 19   นกเค้าหูยาวเล็ก
Distinguished from other scops-owls by bolder blackish streaks on underparts and yellow eyes. Dimorphic; plumage usually greyish, though some birds are rufous. Often perches on the larger boughs of trees, in more open situations than other scops-owls. **Voice:** calls with a measured, tuneless *toik, toik-ta-toik* (the same tempo as *Here comes the bride*). Birds of wintering race *O. s. stictonotus* are mainly silent but occasionally give a purring 3-note call, *toik-to-toik*.
Habitat: mixed deciduous forest and the more open evergreen forests of lowlands to 1000 m. Wintering birds occur in a variety of habitats, including gardens, from plains to 2000 m. Uncommon resident and winter visitor.

314. Collared Scops-Owl *Otus lempiji* S: 23   นกฮูก, นกเค้ากู่
Dull brownish plumage with diagnostic pale buff nuchal collar. Shows a sharp contrast between the dark brown forehead and buffy whitish eyebrows. Markings on underparts are indistinct. Ear tufts very prominent when excited or alarmed. Eyes usually dark brown. Bill can appear pale, sometimes causing confusion with White-fronted Scops-Owl. **Voice:** a mellow, falling tone *bouu* repeated at approximately 12 second intervals. Considerable individual variation in pitch. Occasionally calls with a strident series of notes, *kuuk-kuuk-kuuk*. **Habitat:** evergreen and deciduous forests, secondary growth, open areas with scattered trees and gardens of town and villages, from plains up to 2200 m. Very common resident.

315. Collared Owlet *Glaucidium brodiei* S: 16   นกเค้าแคระ
Very small, with round head and a diagnostic buff and black imitation facial pattern on nape and hindneck. Otherwise markings recall Asian Barred Owlet but face darker, less contrasted. Eyes yellow. **Voice:** series of 4 hollow whistles in a distinctive rhythm; *poop, poo-poop poop.* Often calls during the day. **Habitat:** evergreen forests, usually above 600 m. Common resident.

316. Asian Barred Owlet *Glaucidium cuculoides* S: 23   นกเค้าโมง, นกเค้าแมว
Upperparts, including tail, dark brown, finely barred buff; whitish eyebrows. Underparts barred dark brown on upper breast; broadly streaked rufous brown on belly and flanks. Rounder head and longer tail than Spotted Owlet, with less contrasting face pattern. Eye yellow. **Voice:** a variety of calls. A long trill which descends in pitch and increases in volume. Also a long series of two-note squawks, uttered at increasing pitch and volume and preceded by widely-spaced, mellow *poop* notes, like one of the calls of Green-eared Barbet. **Habitat:** deciduous and the more open evergreen forests, secondary growth and open country with scattered trees. From plains up to 1800 m. Very common resident.

Plate 60 Owls I (Barn Owls, Scops-Owls, Owlets)

07 Barn Owl

308 Bay Owl

309 Brown Hawk-Owl

311 Reddish Scops-Owl

312 Mountain Scops-Owl

10 White-fronted Scops-Owl

grey morph

fous morph

313 Oriental Scops-Owl

314 Collared Scops-Owl

eye-spot pattern on back of head

315 Collared Owlet

316 Asian Barred Owlet

317 Spotted Owlet

Nongkol

180

317. Spotted Owlet *Athene brama* S: 20 นกเค้าจุด

Upperparts grey-brown, spotted with white. Shorter tail and flatter head than Asian Barred Owlet, with more prominent white eyebrows. Broad, broken bars on underparts. **Voice:** an assortment of high-pitched screeches and chuckles. **Habitat:** cultivated areas, scrub and open country of the drier lowlands. Often in towns, villages, frequently nesting in buildings. Common resident.

318. Spot-bellied Eagle-Owl *Bubo nipalensis* S: 61 นกเค้าใหญ่พันธุ์เนปาล

Very large. Eagle-owls may be distinguished from fish-owls by feathered tarsi and by conspicuous pale yellowish bills, generally more erect ear-tufts. Spot-bellied Eagle-Owl easily distinguished by large, blackish brown spots on underparts. Eyes brown. **Voice:** a deep, double hoot, *hoo*, *hoo*, with usually about 2 seconds between the notes and uttered about once every 1–2 minutes. Also a mournful scream, first rising, then falling in tone. Both calls carry a great distance. **Habitat:** deciduous and evergreen forests from 400 m to high elevation. Uncommon resident.

319. Barred Eagle-Owl *Bubo sumatranus* S: 48 นกเค้าใหญ่พันธุ์สุมาตรา

Smaller than preceding species with narrow buffy barring on upperparts. Underparts have broad, scaly bars, not spots. Eyes brown. **Voice:** two deep hoots, *hu hu*. Also has a loud, quacking *gagagago gogo*, suggestive of a huge gecko (DRW) and a mournful hooting scream, like Spot-bellied. **Habitat:** evergreen forest from lowlands up to 600 m. Uncommon resident.

320. Dusky Eagle-Owl *Bubo coromandus* S: 53 นกเค้าใหญ่สีคล้ำ

Very large. Greyer plumage than other large owls; underparts pale grey brown with narrow black streaks. Eyes yellow; from fish-owls by feathered legs. **Voice:** a series of hollow notes repeated at diminishing intervals, like a ping-pong ball bouncing to a halt; *kok*, *kok kok-kok-kokaloo*. **Habitat:** open wooded areas of level lowlands, usually near water. Very rare; status uncertain.

321. Brown Fish-Owl *Ketupa zeylonensis* S: 53 นกทึดทือพันธุ์เหนือ

Very large. Fish-owls are distinguished from eagle-owls by their unfeathered tarsi and by narrower, buffy bars on mainly dark tails in flight. Also from Spot-bellied and Barred Eagle-Owls by darker, grey-green (not yellow) bills and yellow eyes. Brown Fish-Owl has paler, sandier-brown upperparts than Buffy Fish-Owl with narrower black shaft streaks on feathers of mantle, scapulars and upperwing coverts. Shows pattern of indistinct cross-bars on streaked underparts and lacks any white above base of bill. **Voice:** a soft, rapid, deep *hup-hup-hu*; usually only the first two notes are audible. Also a succession of deep mutterings rising to a maniacal laugh; *hu-hu-hu-hu-hu....hu ha*. Has a mournful scream, somewhat like Spot-bellied Eagle-Owl, but hoarser. **Habitat:** deciduous and open evergreen woodlands; open areas with scattered trees. Usually near streamsides or other open water, from plains up to 800 m. Uncommon resident.

Plate 61 Owls II (Larger Owls)

319 Barred Eagle-Owl

320 Dusky Eagle-Owl

318 Spot-bellied Eagle-Owl

321 Brown Fish-Owl

322 Buffy Fish-Owl

323 Brown Wood-Owl

324 Spotted Wood-Owl

325 Short-eared Owl

Mongkol

322. Buffy Fish-Owl *Ketupa ketupu* S: 50 นกทึดทือมลายู
Large. Underparts deeper, warmer buff than in Brown Fish-Owl, lacking cross-bars. Upperparts darker brown with much thicker black streaks on feathers of mantle, scapulars and upperwing coverts. Shows a whitish patch above base of bill. **Habitat:** near streams in evergreen forest, parks, wooded gardens; mangroves. From plains to 800 m. Uncommon resident.

323. Brown Wood-Owl *Strix leptogrammica* S: 55 นกเค้าป่าสีน้ำตาล
Very large. Distinguished from Spotted Wood-Owl by much finer dark barring on underparts. Facial pattern is more contrasted than in Spotted Wood-Owl, with whiter facial disc and broad dark circles around eyes. Forecrown is unmarked dark brown. Eyes usually brown. **Voice:** a deep, soft and rapidly uttered hooting phrase; *koh-koh-kaloo.* **Habitat:** evergreen and mixed deciduous forests from plains up to the highest summits. Uncommon resident.

324. Spotted Wood-Owl *Strix seloputo* S: 48 นกเค้าป่าหลังจุด
Large. Distinguished from Brown Wood-Owl by bolder dark brown bars on buffy underparts; white spotting on dark brown upperparts and on forecrown and by uniformly pale, rufous facial disc. Eyes brown. **Voice:** usually a deep, powerful and explosive *who*, uttered at intervals (DRW). **Habitat:** lowland open woodlands, secondary growth, mangroves and plantations. Uncommon resident.

325. Short-eared Owl *Asio flammeus* S: 38 นกเค้าแมวหูสั้น

Rich, tawny-brown upperparts, streaked darker. Underparts buffy with a band of dark breast streaks. Facial disc whitish; ear tufts usually indiscernible. In flight, longer-winged than Barn Owl; tawny-rufous bases of primaries contrast boldly with black carpal patch. Bold, dark tail bars. Often flies during daylight. At rest, perches more horizontally than other owls. Eyes yellow with dark-feathered surrounds. **Habitat:** marshes, open grasslands of both plains and mountains. Very rare winter visitor.

วงศ์นกปากกบ

ASIAN FROGMOUTHS: Family *Batrachostomidae.* Delicately mottled plumage; differ from nightjars in having heavy, broad bills and shorter, more rounded wings. Nocturnal and feed by gleaning insects from among foliage. Usually inhabit the lower middle storey of the forest, perching upright on thin horizontal branches. Very difficult to observe and, under usual viewing conditions, plumage features difficult to discern. Best located by listening for calls at night. The three smaller species have a confusing range of soft whistles (which may be contact notes), wheezy croaks and laughter (probably territorial calls). Build small, pad-shaped nests which are placed in tree forks or on horizontal limbs. World: 9 species. Thailand: 4 species.

Plate 62 Frogmouths, Eared Nightjars

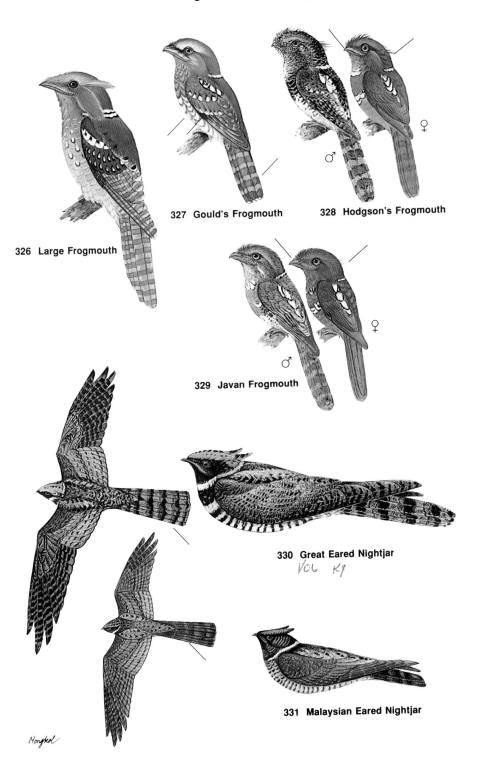

326 Large Frogmouth

327 Gould's Frogmouth

328 Hodgson's Frogmouth
♂ ♀

329 Javan Frogmouth
♂ ♀

330 Great Eared Nightjar
VOC KY

331 Malaysian Eared Nightjar

Mongkol

184

326. Large Frogmouth *Batrachostomus auritus* S: 41   นกปากกบยักษ์

 Much larger than other frogmouths. Chestnut upperparts with white collar around hindneck and white spots on the wing coverts. Throat and breast rather uniform rufous-brown, with slight white spotting, and grading into buffy belly. Sexes similar. **Voice:** a deep, hollow-sounding tremolo; *ooerrrrrr*, which may be repeated up to 8 times (JS). **Habitat:** evergreen forest, especially secondary forest, of the level lowlands. Very rare resident.

327. Gould's Frogmouth *Batrachostomus stellatus* S: 25   นกปากกบปักษ์ใต้

 Both sexes from female Javan by whiter underparts with even, tawny-brown scaling on breast (can appear streaked in the field); white spots on wing coverts by smaller and less conspicuous whiskers on head. Tail is much more conspicuously barred than in female Javan. Sexes similar, but females are a slightly deeper rufous than males. Eye may be either yellow or brown. **Voice:** usual call is a distinctive *oooh-wheeow*, the first note markedly aspirated and the second note falling in tone. Also gives falling tone whistles and *tu-lick* notes similar to Javan. **Habitat:** evergreen forest of lowlands and extreme lower hill slopes, below 200 m. Rare resident.

328. Hodgson's Frogmouth *Batrachostomus hodgsoni* S: 25   นกปากกบลายดำ

 Male: plumage boldly mottled grey-brown, black and white. Prominent blackish markings on upper breast; belly and under tail coverts mainly whitish. **Female:** from female Javan by smaller, shallower bill and more prominent white spots on throat. Eye never yellow; usually light brown to mottled yellow and brown. **Voice:** usual call is a series of soft, burring *gwaaa* notes with rising inflection. Also has quiet, falling tone whistles. **Habitat:** evergreen forest of hill slopes, occasionally as low as 300 m but usually from 900 m to 1900 m. Uncommon resident.

329. Javan Frogmouth *Batrachostomus javensis* S: 25   นกปากกบพันธุ์ชวา

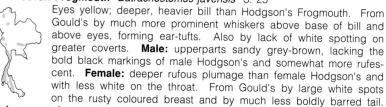 Eyes yellow; deeper, heavier bill than Hodgson's Frogmouth. From Gould's by much more prominent whiskers above base of bill and above eyes, forming ear-tufts. Also by lack of white spotting on greater coverts. **Male:** upperparts sandy grey-brown, lacking the bold black markings of male Hodgson's and somewhat more rufescent. **Female:** deeper rufous plumage than female Hodgson's and with less white on the throat. From Gould's by large white spots on the rusty coloured breast and by much less boldly barred tail. **Voice:** most frequently heard calls are a wavering, ascending whistle, *tee-loo-eee*; a maniacal descending laugh, *kerrr-ker-ker* and falling tone *gwaa* notes. Also have soft, falling tone whistles, *tu-lick* notes and quiet frog-like croaks. **Habitat:** evergreen and mixed deciduous forest from plains to 800 m, though most abundant at the lower elevations. Uncommon resident.

Plate 63 Nightjars

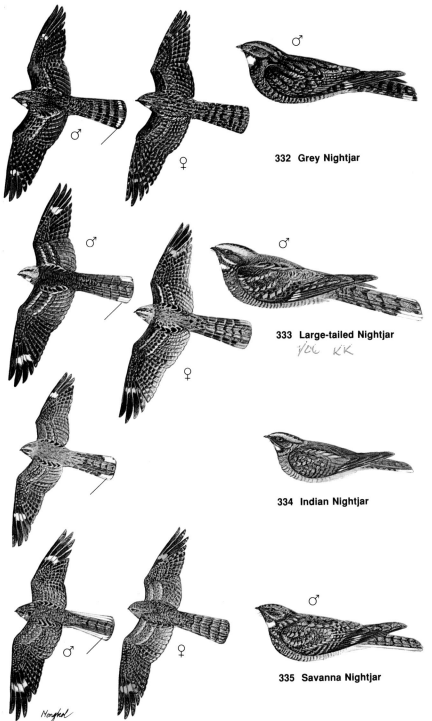

♂

♀

♂

332 Grey Nightjar

♂

♀

♂

333 Large-tailed Nightjar

√oc KK

334 Indian Nightjar

♂

♀

♂

335 Savanna Nightjar

Mongkol

วงศ์นกตบยุง

NIGHTJARS: Family *Caprimulgidae.* Soft, beautifully mottled plumage, long tails and long, relatively narrow wings. Large eyes and tiny bills which open to reveal enormous gapes. Nocturnal, catching insects on the wing and spending the day perched either on the ground or lengthwise along horizontal branches. Usually solitary, though sometimes feeding concentrations may be noted around lights at night. Nest directly on the ground. Best identified by diagnostic calls, heard throughout dry season. The Eared Nightjars *Eurostopodus* spp. are now sometimes placed in a separate family, *Eurostopodidae.* World: 78 species. Thailand: 6 species.

330. Great Eared Nightjar *Eurostopodus macrotis* S: 41   นกตบยุงยักษ์

Distinguished from other nightjars by large size and much slower, more buoyant wingbeats and by lack of white in wings and tail. Broad, dark bands on tail often visible. Feeds much higher in the air than all but Malaysian Eared. At rest, erect ear tufts sometimes visible. **Voice:** one sharp note, followed by two long, airy whistles; *pit, pee-wheeoow.* Distinct pause after first note (which is not always audible) and second and third notes more drawn out than in Malaysian Eared. Calls in flight and, occasionally, while at rest. **Habitat:** evergreen and deciduous forests, forest edge and clearings up to 1200 m. Common resident.

331. Malaysian Eared Nightjar *Eurostopodus temminckii* S: 27 นกตบยุงพันธุ์มลายู

Distinguished from Great Eared by smaller size, more rapid and erratic flight, less distinctly banded tail, and by call. At rest, primaries appear dark with irregular pale markings. **Voice:** call, given in flight, is similar to Great Eared, but first note is louder and always audible, and second note shorter with less of a pause between notes. **Habitat:** lowland evergreen forest, forest edge. Local and uncommon resident.

332. Grey Nightjar *Caprimulgus indicus* S: 28   นกตบยุงภูเขา

Much darker, greyer plumage tones than other nightjars; lacks rusty nuchal collar. **Male:** white wing patches. From all other nightjars by white subterminal spots on outer four pairs of tail feathers. **Female:** like male, but wing patch buff; tail patches dusky, often invisible in the field. **Voice:** a long series of notes *chook-chook-chook-chook....,* uttered rapidly at the rate of about four notes per second. **Habitat:** evergreen forest, clearings and secondary growth, chiefly of hills above 600 m. Occasionally found in open lowlands, gardens on passage. Fairly common winter visitor. Local and uncommon breeder on higher summits of northern and western hills.

333. Large-tailed Nightjar *Caprimulgus macrurus* S: 30   นกตบยุงหางยาว

Much browner plumage than Grey Nightjar: shows bold black streaking on scapulars and a rusty nuchal collar. **Male:** obvious white wing patches and large white corners to the tail. **Female:** wing and tail patches buffy, much less distinct. **Voice:** a loud, resonant *chonk* uttered at roughly one second intervals while at rest. **Habitat:** forest edge, open wooded areas, scrub, cultivation from plains up to 2000 m. Common resident.

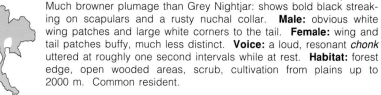

187

334. Indian Nightjar *Caprimulgus asiaticus* S: 23 นกตบยุงเล็ก

Sexes similar. Like a compact miniature of Large-tailed Nightjar, with obvious white wing patches and corners to the tail. Rufous nuchal collar more conspicuous. **Voice:** a series of knocking sounds which speeds up progressively, like a ping-pong ball dropping on to a table-top; *chook, chook chook-chookeruk.* A soft, clucking *pook* when flushed in daytime. **Habitat:** dry open plains country, scrub and cultivation. Common resident.

335. Savanna Nightjar *Caprimulgus affinis* S: 25 นกตบยุงป่าโคก

Upperparts pale grey-brown, more finely mottled than in Large-tailed Nightjar and lacking any bold black markings. **Male:** distinguished from all other nightjars by almost wholly white outer tail feathers. **Female:** from females of Grey and Large-tailed by lack of paler tips to tail feathers. **Voice:** a harsh, rasping *chaweez* uttered at intervals, both at rest and in flight. **Habitat:** open dry dipterocarp, pine and hill evergreen forests, dry scrub from plains up to 900 m. Uncommon to locally common resident.

วงศ์นกขุนแผน

TROGONS: Family *Trogonidae.* Characterised by long, square-ended tails, short, rounded wings and stubby, broad bills. Short legs; rest on branches with an upright posture, usually in the middle storey of forest. Feed primarily on insects, often caught on short flights from perch. Shy; usually in pairs. Scoop out nest cavities in rotten tree stumps. Sexually dimorphic; the males have brighter plumage than the females. Wavy barring on wing coverts is whitish grey in males and buffy in females. In addition to diagnostic territorial calls, all species have similar dry whirring notes, which may be given by both sexes. World: 37 species. Thailand: 6 species.

336. Red-naped Trogon *Harpactes kasumba* S: 32 นกขุนแผนท้ายทอยแดง

Male: similar to male Diard's, but distinguished by deep blue (not purple) orbital skin; bold white crescent across breast, bright red nuchal patch and by brighter red underparts. Also shows boldly contrasting black and white under tail pattern. **Female:** dark brownish grey throat and breast, sharply demarcated from tawny brownish belly. Larger than female Cinnamon-rumped. **Voice:** a series of up to 6 widely spaced notes on an even pitch; *taup, taup, taup, taup.* Given by both sexes, but call of female slightly higher pitched and more reedy. Call of male is slower, deeper. **Habitat:** evergreen forest of lowlands and lower hills; also peat swamp forest. Rare resident.

337. Diard's Trogon *Harpactes diardii* S: 30 นกขุนแผนหัวดำ

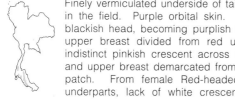
Finely vermiculated underside of tail appears uniformly greyish white in the field. Purple orbital skin. **Male:** pinkish red nuchal patch; blackish head, becoming purplish on hindcrown. Black throat and upper breast divided from red underparts by no more than an indistinct pinkish crescent across breast. **Female:** brownish head and upper breast demarcated from pinkish red belly. Lacks nuchal patch. From female Red-headed by slightly paler pinkish red underparts, lack of white crescent on belly; tail pattern and by habitat. **Voice:** a series of 10–12 *kau* notes in descending sequence. Slightly higher-pitched, more strident and more rapidly uttered than the notes of Red-naped. **Habitat:** evergreen forest of lowlands and extreme lower hill slopes, rarely up to 600 m. Uncommon resident.

นกขุนแผนตะโพกสีน้ำตาล

338. Cinnamon-rumped Trogon *Harpactes orrhophaeus* S: 25
Small size. **Male:** black of head and throat does not extend down to breast. Small patch of pale blue orbital skin above and in front of eye. From male Scarlet-rumped Trogon by cinnamon rump, concolorous with back. **Female:** lacks any red in plumage; breast and belly uniform rusty-buff. From female Red-naped by small size and lack of contrast between breast and belly. From juvenile Scarlet-rumped by bright rusty-buff area around eye. ◆ Often perches lower in foliage than other trogons. **Voice:** usually 3 or 4 weak falling tone notes in descending sequence; *taup, taup, taup.* **Habitat:** evergreen forests, below 200 m. Rare resident.

339. Scarlet-rumped Trogon *Harpactes duvaucelii* S: 25　นกขุนแผนตะโพกแดง
Small size. Striking pale-blue orbital skin above and in front of eye in both sexes. **Male:** from male Cinnamon-rumped by bright red rump and upper tail coverts. **Female:** shows both red and rufescent brown feathers mixed on rump and upper tail coverts. Head brownish; rusty upper breast fades gradually into pinkish red belly and under tail coverts. **Juvenile:** like female, but lacks red on rump and underparts. **Voice:** highly distinctive. An accelerating, descending cadence of about 12 notes; *teuk, teuk teuk-euk-euk-euk....* **Habitat:** evergreen forests of lowlands and lower hill slopes; occasionally as high as 400 m. Uncommon resident.

340. Orange-breasted Trogon *Harpactes oreskios* S: 30　นกขุนแผนอกสีส้ม
From all other trogons by orange-yellow underparts. **Male:** underparts brighter, tinged more deeply orange than in female. Head and breast tinged greenish olive. **Female:** paler, yellower underparts; head and upper breast tinged greyish. **Voice:** a rapidly uttered series of 3–5 notes on an even pitch; *teu teu teu.* Call of male is higher-pitched and more rapid than that of female. **Habitat:** both evergreen and mixed deciduous forests from plains up to 1100 m. Common resident. By far the most abundant trogon in the Peninsula.

341. Red-headed Trogon *Harpactes erythrocephalus* S: 34　นกขุนแผนหัวแดง
Male: has diagnostic dull red head and brighter red underparts. **Female:** brownish cinnamon head and upper breast, red belly and under tail coverts. ◆ Both sexes show a conspicuous whitish crescent across the breast. **Voice:** a series of 5 or more widely spaced notes, uttered in a descending sequence; *tiaup, tiaup, tiaup.....* **Habitat:** evergreen forests from foothills to 2000 m. Common resident.

วงศ์นกกะเต็น

KINGFISHERS: Family *Alcedinidae.* Long, dagger-like bills, large heads and compact bodies with short legs and tails. Most have brilliant plumage. Typically perch upright in exposed situations; many species hunt on water bodies, catching fish and other aquatic animals by plunge-diving. Others feed on insects and terrestrial animals, often far from water. Many are forest birds. Flight rapid and direct; some species hover. Usually solitary or in pairs, but are often noisy with harsh or piercing calls. Most nest in horizontal tunnels, dug into steep earth banks and some utilise tree holes or termitaria. World: 86 species. Thailand: 15 species.

Plate 64 Trogons

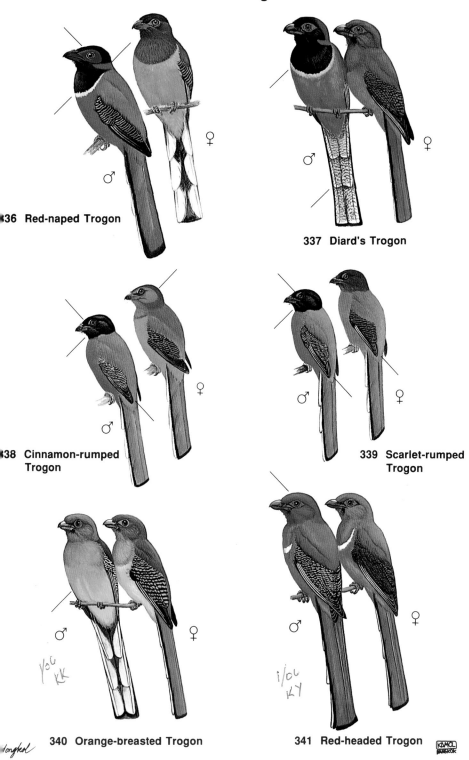

336 Red-naped Trogon ♂

337 Diard's Trogon ♂ ♀

338 Cinnamon-rumped Trogon ♂ ♀

339 Scarlet-rumped Trogon ♂ ♀

340 Orange-breasted Trogon ♂ ♀

341 Red-headed Trogon ♂ ♀

190

342. Crested Kingfisher *Megaceryle lugubris* S: 43   นกกะเต็นขาวดำใหญ่

Much larger than Pied Kingfisher, with a conspicuous full crest and a complete white neck collar. Upperparts blackish, finely barred and spotted with white. (In flight, appear uniformly grey, contrasting markedly with black cap.) Blackish breast band sometimes admixed with rufous. **Male:** white underwing coverts. **Female:** cinnamon underwing coverts. **Voice:** flight call is a squeaky *aick*. **Habitat:** favours larger streams and rivers with steep, forested banks in lowlands and lower hills, occasionally up to 1200 m. Rare resident.

343. Pied Kingfisher *Ceryle rudis* S: 30   นกกะเต็นปักหลัก

Strikingly variegated black and white plumage with a broad white supercilium and a short crest. In flight, shows broad white wing panels. **Male:** two breast bands, the lower one narrow. **Female:** only one broad band, usually broken in the middle. ◆ Frequently hovers. **Voice:** a shrill whistle, somewhat reminiscent of the call of Green Sandpiper (187). **Habitat:** the larger rivers, canals, lakes and occasionally flooded fields. Usually near steep earth banks in which it nests. Fairly common but local resident.

344. Blyth's Kingfisher *Alcedo hercules* S: 23   นกกะเต็นเฮอคิวลิส

Larger than Common Kingfisher, with a longer, heavier bill. Lacks chestnut on ear coverts. Upperparts darker, the mantle appearing blackish brown with small blue spots; bluish scales on the head. In flight, shows a bright blue stripe down the back as do other *Alcedo*. **Habitat:** forested streams of lower elevations. Very rare winter visitor.

345. Common Kingfisher *Alcedo atthis* S: 17   นกกะเต็นน้อยธรรมดา

Blue-green upperparts with a brilliant turquoise-blue back and rump, conspicuous in flight. Ear coverts rufous. Underparts are orange-rufous. **Juvenile:** underparts paler, sometimes almost whitish, with a slight dusky gorget. ◆ Bill black, with lower mandible often reddish at the base. **Voice:** a shrill, high-pitched piping of usually two or three notes. **Habitat:** streams of open and forested areas, canals, marshes, mangroves and open coastal areas, (chiefly lowlands but occasionally up to 1800 m). Resident birds may be mainly confined to wooded streams, but little data exists. Very common winter visitor; apparently rare resident.

346. Blue-eared Kingfisher *Alcedo meninting* S: 16   นกกะเต็นน้อยหลังสีน้ำเงิน

Distinguished from Common Kingfisher by lack of rufous behind eye and by much deeper, more vivid blue on crown, back, wings and rump. Underparts deeper orange-rufous. (Beware confusion with bright-plumaged Common Kingfishers on forest streams.) Bill usually all black. **Voice:** higher-pitched and shorter than Common Kingfisher, usually giving only one note. **Habitat:** pools and streams in evergreen and mixed deciduous forests up to 900 m. Uncommon resident.

Plate 65 Kingfishers I

342 Crested Kingfisher

343 Pied Kingfisher
Ital SP

344 Blyth's Kingfisher

5 Common Kingfisher
Ici SP

346 Blue-eared Kingfisher

347 Blue-banded Kingfisher
♂ ♀

ack-backed"

348 Oriental Dwarf Kingfisher

"Red-backed"

349 Banded Kingfisher
♂ ♀

347. **Blue-banded Kingfisher** *Alcedo euryzona* S: 20   นกกะเต็นน้อยแถบอกดำ
Blackish blue upperparts with fine blue speckling on wing coverts and a very pale, silvery-blue band down back and rump, conspicuous in flight. Rufous lower border to white neck spot. **Male:** scaly blue breast band on otherwise whitish underparts. **Female:** pale rufous underparts, usually with some indistinct dark scaling at sides of breast. **Voice:** less shrill than that of Common Kingfisher. **Habitat:** streams of evergreen forest, from lowlands up to 800 m. Uncommon resident.

348. **Oriental Dwarf Kingfisher** *Ceyx erithacus* S: 14   นกกะเต็นน้อยสามนิ้ว
Tiny size, bright coral-red bill and yellowish underparts distinctive. Violet-rufous crown and lilac rump and upper tail coverts. The 'Black-backed Kingfisher' (resident and passage migrant/winter visitor throughout Thailand) has a dark blue spot on the ear coverts and on the forehead and a blue-black mantle. The 'Red-backed Kingfisher', resident in peninsular Thailand and sometimes treated as a separate species, *C. rufidorsus*, lacks the dark ear coverts and forehead patches and has a dark rufous mantle and coverts. Mixed breeding pairs have been seen and many intermediates occur. **Juvenile:** underparts whitish, with a ginger breast band. **Voice:** sharp, metallic piping is weaker and higher-pitched than similar calls of Blue-eared Kingfisher. **Habitat:** evergreen forests of lowlands up to 900 m (resident birds may be mainly restricted to the level lowlands and foothills). Usually close to streams or pools. Occurs in gardens, mangroves on passage. Uncommon resident and winter visitor.

349. **Banded Kingfisher** *Lacedo pulchella* S: 23   นกกะเต็นลาย
Comparatively long tail, barred plumage and short, broad red bill. **Male:** chestnut forehead, sides of head and blue crown. Rest of upperparts intricately barred blue, black and white. Whitish underparts with rufous-buff suffusion across breast and on flanks. **Female:** entire upperparts barred black and rufous; underparts whitish with short, fine black bars on sides of breast and flanks. ◆ Often sits motionless in middle storey, puffing out crown feathers, and allowing close approach. **Voice:** a long, whistled cadence of up to 15 *chi-wiu* notes. As song progresses, there is increasing emphasis on the first syllable, until the sound dies gradually away. Calls most frequently in the early morning and around dusk, usually from a high perch. **Habitat:** evergreen and mixed deciduous forests and bamboo, up to 1100 m. Fairly common resident.

นกกะเต็นใหญ่ปีกสีน้ำตาล
350. **Brown-winged Kingfisher** *Halcyon amauroptera* S: 36
Large size, huge red bill and chocolate-brown wings, mantle and tail; rump turquoise. Head and underparts bright ginger. **Voice:** tremulous, descending whistles; usually *tree treew-treew* with slight pause after first note. Also a dry cackling like Stork-billed. **Habitat:** mangroves, especially in areas where larger trees remain. Uncommon resident.

Plate 66 Kingfishers II

350 Brown-winged Kingfisher

351 Stork-billed Kingfisher

352 Ruddy Kingfisher

353 White-throated Kingfisher

355 Collared Kingfisher

354 Black-capped Kingfisher

356 Rufous-collared Kingfisher

Mongkol

351. Stork-billed Kingfisher *Halcyon capensis* S: 37   นกกะเต็นใหญ่ธรรมดา

Size and proportions as preceding species, but wings, mantle and tail dull blue green and has pale brown cap. Underparts ginger. In flight, from other red-billed *Halcyon* kingfishers of freshwater areas by lack of white wing patches. **Voice:** a two-note whistle, *tree-trew*, the second note lower. Occasionally a quavering whistle similar to call of Brown-winged, and a dry cackling *kek-ek-ek-ek*. **Habitat:** bodies of fresh water with scattered trees. Also streamsides in mixed deciduous and evergreen forests, up to at least 800 m. Occasionally mangroves. Uncommon to fairly common resident.

352. Ruddy Kingfisher *Halcyon coromanda* S: 25   นกกะเต็นแดง

Entire body bright rufous; slightly darker rufous, tinged violet on upperparts. In flight, shows narrow bluish white patch on rump. Bill bright red. **Voice:** 4 or 5 loud, mournful whistles in descending sequence. Also a tremulous *quirrr-r-r-r*. **Habitat:** resident in mangroves, island forests and along streams and rivers in lowland forests of the plains. In winter or on migration in forests, secondary growth up to 900 m. Uncommon resident, passage migrant and winter visitor.

353. White-throated Kingfisher *Halcyon smyrnensis* S: 28   นกกะเต็นอกขาว

Dark chestnut head and abdomen contrast with white throat and upper breast. Brilliant turquoise mantle, wings and tail. In flight, shows white patch at base of primaries and a black band on wing coverts. Bill dusky reddish. **Voice:** a shrill, staccato, descending laugh. Also a whinnying call. **Habitat:** open country, including cultivated areas, secondary growth and open woodland up to 1500 m. Very common resident.

354. Black-capped Kingfisher *Halcyon pileata* S: 30   นกกะเต็นหัวดำ

Black cap, separated from deep blue upperparts by narrow white collar. Throat and upper breast whitish, grading into rufous-buff belly. In flight, white wing patches like White-throated Kingfisher but upperparts deeper, more vivid blue, with more extensive black on wing coverts. Bill brighter red. **Voice:** a whinnying laugh and other calls very similar to those of White-throated. **Habitat:** mangroves, swamps and paddyfields; occasionally gardens, close to fresh water. Mainly lowlands, but up to 900 m on passage. Common winter visitor and passage migrant.

355. Collared Kingfisher *Halcyon chloris* S: 24   นกกินเปี้ยว

Blue-green upperparts with a prominent white collar and all white underparts. In flight, unmarked blue-green wings. Bill blackish, with flesh-coloured lower mandible. **Voice:** a shrill, staccato laugh, *krerk krerk krerk krerk.....*, slightly descending and ending in characteristic *jee-jaw* disyllables (DRW). **Habitat:** mangroves, tidal areas. Also gardens and cultivated areas close to the coast and occasionally inland along the larger rivers and in swamps. Very common resident.

นกกะเต็นสร้อยคอสีน้ำตาล

356. Rufous-collared Kingfisher *Actenoides concretus* S: 24

Green crown, distinctive facial pattern, rufous collar and underparts. Turquoise-blue rump patch shows in flight. Bill yellowish, with dark culmen. **Male:** dark blue wings and upper back. **Female:** wing coverts and upper back dull green with large buff spots. ◆ Feeds to a great extent on large insects. **Voice:** a long series of airy, rising whistles, *kwi-i, kwi-i...*, repeated at the rate of about one note per second. Also calls with softer, more tremulous notes, *kwi-irr, kwi-irr, kwi-irr*. **Habitat:** evergreen forest of lowlands and lower hills. Rare resident, probably much reduced due to habitat destruction.

วงศ์นกจาบคา

BEE-EATERS: Family *Meropidae*. Have long, curved, narrow bills, slender bodies and long, pointed wings. Plumages are usually predominantly green, though show a coppery underwing in flight. Feed on bees and other insects, caught in flight by hawking from an exposed perch. Excavate nest burrows in steep earth banks or low hummocks in the ground. Sexes similar or nearly so. *Merops* species are usually gregarious and are active and graceful fliers, inhabiting mostly open country. They have soft burring calls. *Nyctyornis* are found solitarily or in pairs, are larger and more sluggish, inhabiting forests, and call with deep guttural croaks. World: 24 species. Thailand: 6 species.

357. Chestnut-headed Bee-eater *Merops leschenaulti* S: 23   นกจาบคาหัวสีส้ม

Creamy-yellow throat, with dark gorget and light chestnut crown, nape and upper back. Lacks elongate central tail feathers. In flight, shows very pale, iridescent bluish white rump and upper tail coverts, like Blue-throated. **Juvenile:** duller, with greenish crown, concolorous with mantle. **Voice:** a soft, burring *prruuip, prruuip*. **Habitat:** open wooded country, secondary growth, From plains up to 1800 m. Common resident.

358. Blue-tailed Bee-eater *Merops philippinus* S: 30   นกจาบคาหัวเขียว

Greenish crown and upper back. Yellowish upper throat and brownish lower throat with a conspicuous whitish blue streak below the black eye-line. In flight shows concolorous blue upper tail coverts and tail with elongate central tail feathers. Nests in colonies, favouring riverbanks. **Habitat:** open country, usually near fresh water, marshes, mangroves. Mainly plains, but often up to 800 m. Common resident, passage migrant and winter visitor.

359. Green Bee-eater *Merops orientalis* S: 20   นกจาบคาเล็ก

Green plumage with coppery brown crown and nape and a green throat with a black gorget. Elongate central tail feathers. **Juvenile:** dull yellowish throat; lacks elongate central tail feathers, superficially resembling Chestnut-headed. ◆ Often excavates burrows in more or less level ground. **Voice:** a higher-pitched and more metallic trilling than other bee-eaters. **Habitat:** dry open country from plains up to 1500 m. Very common resident.

196

360. Blue-throated Bee-eater *Merops viridis* S: 28   นกจาบคาคอสีฟ้า

Blue throat, lacking gorget; dark chestnut crown, nape and upper back. In flight, shows striking bluish white rump and upper tail coverts and darker blue tail with elongate central tail feathers. **Juvenile:** crown and upper back green, concolorous with mantle; lacks elongate central tail feathers. **Habitat:** open forest, secondary growth, coastal scrub and mangroves, from plains up to at least 800 m. Fairly common passage migrant and winter visitor; uncommon resident.

361. Red-bearded Bee-eater *Nyctyornis amictus* S: 32   นกจาบคาเคราแดง

Large size. Mainly green plumage with shaggy red throat and breast patch, lilac forecrown. Underside of tail pale orange-yellow with a broad blackish terminal band. **Female:** red extends to a small patch above base of bill. **Juvenile:** plumage, including underside of tail, entirely greenish. **Voice:** a deep, guttural croaking *aark* and a squirrel-like chatter *kakakakakakow*, descending slightly. **Habitat:** evergreen forest from plains up to 1500 m. Fairly common resident.

362. Blue-bearded Bee-eater *Nyctyornis athertoni* S: 35   นกจาบคาเคราน้ำเงิน

Mainly green plumage with shaggy blue patch on throat and breast. Belly straw-coloured, with coarse greenish streaks. Underside of tail lacks dark terminal band. **Voice:** various deep, guttural croaking noises. Also an even-pitched, rolling *kirrr-r-r-r.* **Habitat:** both evergreen and mixed deciduous forests, up to 2200 m. In the small area of geographical overlap with Red-bearded, the Blue-bearded inhabits the drier, more deciduous forests of the foothills with the Red-bearded on the moister, evergreen, submontane slopes. Fairly common resident.

วงศ์นกตะขาบ

ROLLERS: Family *Coraciidae.* Have large heads, stout bills and bulky bodies, with dark purplish or bluish plumage. Typically hunt large insects, lizards and other small animals from exposed perches, either by dropping to the ground or by making aerial sorties. Usually solitary or in pairs. Strong fliers and are noted for acrobatic, rolling display flights. Nest in tree hollows or rock crevices. World: 11 species. Thailand: 2 species.

363. Indian Roller *Coracias benghalensis* S: 33   นกตะขาบทุ่ง

When perched, appears very dark with black bill, turquoise crown and rump and purplish brown underparts. Brilliant blue in wings and tail is evident in flight. Feeds chiefly by dropping to the ground to seize large insects, reptiles, etc. but occasionally makes aerial sallies. **Voice:** a harsh *kyak* and other croaking notes. **Habitat:** open country, especially drier areas, up to 1500 m. Very common resident.

Plate 67 Bee-eaters, Rollers, Hoopoe

357 Chestnut-headed Bee-eater
1/06 KK

358 Blue-tailed Bee-eater

359 Green Bee-eater
Ya SP

360 Blue-throated Bee-eater

362 Blue-bearded Bee-eater
1/06 KY

363 Indian Roller
Ya KK

361 Red-bearded Bee-eater

365 Hoopoe

364 Dollarbird
1/06 KK

Mongkol

364. Dollarbird *Eurystomus orientalis* S: 30 นกตะขาบดง

At rest, appears blackish, with red bill. At close range, body glossy, dark blue-green. In flight, shows broad silvery patch at base of primaries. **Immature:** dull, fleshy bill. ◆ Is mainly an aerial feeder, taking winged insects. See Dusky Broadbill (428). **Voice:** harsh croaks. **Habitat:** deciduous woodlands, secondary growth, edge and clearings in evergreen forest, from plains up to at least 1000 m. Fairly common resident and winter visitor.

วงศ์นกกะรางหัวขวาน

HOOPOE: Family *Upupidae.* Erectile crest and long, slightly decurved bill. Flight undulating on broad, rounded wings. Feeds by probing in soft ground, largely taking insect grubs and pupae. Cavity-nesting, using holes in trees and in earth banks. World: one species.

365. Hoopoe *Upupa epops* S: 30 นกกะรางหัวขวาน

Easily recognised by pinkish body plumage and boldly black and white-barred wings and tail; long crest which usually held flat while feeding. Feeds on the ground, probing into soft turf, animal dung, etc. **Voice:** a soft, mellow two or three note hooting, *hoop-hoop-hoop*, reminiscent of one of the calls of White-browed Scimitar-Babbler. **Habitat:** scrubby open country, including the more open mixed deciduous and hill evergreen forests, cultivated areas from plains up to 1500 m. Common resident.

วงศ์นกเงือก

HORNBILLS: Family *Bucerotidae.* Large, broad-winged forest birds with long tails and huge bills, often bearing a casque. Plumage mostly black and white, the white parts sometimes stained yellowish by preen oil. Take several years to reach maturity, during which time the casque enlarges gradually to the adult form. Strong, slow flight, the wingbeats of the larger species producing a loud swishing noise. Mainly frugivorous, but also take some small animals such as snakes, lizards and the nestlings of other birds. Outside the breeding season, some species roost communally in large numbers. Nest in tree holes, mud and droppings being used as plaster to reduce the size of the nest entrance. The female remains sealed inside the nest and is dependent upon food brought in by the male or by the social group for part of the breeding cycle. Populations of all species have been reduced due to forest destruction and hunting. World: 46 species. Thailand: 12 species.

366. White-crowned Hornbill *Berenicornis comatus* S: 90 นกเงือกหัวหงอก

Bushy white crest and blackish bill with small casque. In flight, combination of all white tail and white trailing edge to wing is diagnostic. **Male:** neck and underparts white. **Female:** neck and underparts black. **Immature:** resembles female, but plumage browner; bill yellowish horn, with patches of dark colour. ◆ Occasionally feeds on the forest floor. **Voice:** a deep, resonant hooting phrase with an owl or pigeon-like quality. The lowest first note is usually followed, after a brief pause, by rapid, 3–4 note sequences; *hoo..hu-hu-hu, hu-hu-hu..* **Habitat:** evergreen forests from foothills to 1000 m or occasionally higher. Uncommon resident.

Plate 68 Hornbills I

♀

♂

♀ underwing

366 White-crowned Hornbill

♂ *P.t. austeni*

♀

i/cc KK

367 Brown Hornbill

♀ (some)

typical

368 Bushy-crested Hornbill

♀

♂

♀ underwing

369 Rufous-necked Hornbill

♀

♂

♀ underwing

71 Wreathed Hornbill

1/00 KK

♀

♂

♀ underwing

370 Wrinkled Hornbill

♂

♀

372 Plain-pouched Hornbill

♀

♂

♂

373 Black Hornbill

Mongkol

367. Brown Hornbill *Ptilolaemus tickelli* S: 74   นกเงือกสีน้ำตาล

Relatively small size and brownish plumage, with bluish orbital skin and usually dull yellowish bill. Casque small. In flight, shows white-tipped primaries and white tips to outer feathers of otherwise dark brown tail. **Male:** throat and upper breast whitish; lower breast and belly brownish rufous (race *austeni*, illustrated) or entire underparts, including throat, bright brownish rufous (race *tickelli*). **Female:** plumage uniformly dark brown. Female *P. t. tickelli* has blackish bill. ◆ Shy, generally keeping within canopy foliage. Almost always in small groups. **Voice:** airy, piercing screams or yelps, generally upward inflected; *klee-ah.* **Habitat:** evergreen forests of the hill slopes up to 1500 m. Occasionally in mixed deciduous forest where adjacent to evergreen. Uncommon resident

368. Bushy-crested Hornbill *Anorrhinus galeritus* S: 89   นกเงือกปากดำ

Mainly blackish plumage with small casque, thick, drooping crest and pale bluish gular and orbital skin. In flight, all black wings with basal two-thirds of tail grey and distal one-third black. Bill usually black but in some females, may be mainly dull yellowish. Usually in groups. Sometimes feeds on the forest floor. **Voice:** excited, yelping notes *klee-ah* and *klee-klee-klee*, somewhat like Brown Hornbill, but noisier, the members of the group usually calling together and the notes building up into a crescendo. **Habitat:** evergreen forests from plains to 1200 m. Fairly common resident.

369. Rufous-necked Hornbill *Aceros nipalensis* S: 117   นกเงือกคอแดง

Identified by combination of bright blue orbital skin and bright orange-red gular pouch. Yellowish ivory bill lacks casque. In flight, combination of white primary tips and black basal half of tail is diagnostic. **Male:** bright orange-rufous head, neck and underparts. **Female:** head, neck and underparts black. **Voice:** a soft, barking *kup*, given by both sexes. Not as deep as similar note of Great Hornbill. **Habitat:** evergreen and hill evergreen forests from 600 m to 1800 m. Rare resident.

370. Wrinkled Hornbill *Rhyticeros corrugatus* S: 81   นกเงือกปากย่น

All black wings. Distinguished from Wreathed Hornbill by smaller size, black basal half of tail, larger reddish casque and blue orbital skin. Distal half of tail frequently stained yellowish. **Male:** whitish gular pouch, white head and neck. **Female:** blue gular pouch, black head and neck. **Voice:** a short, barking *kak-kak*, a little reminiscent of the call of a Tockay Gecko. **Habitat:** evergreen forests of the level lowlands. Rare; either already extinct or on the verge of extinction in Thailand, due to habitat destruction.

371. Wreathed Hornbill *Rhyticeros undulatus* S: 100 นกเงือกกรามช้าง

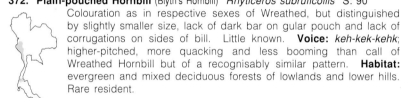

Shows all black wings and an entirely white tail; black bar on gular pouch. Small, wrinkled casque and diagnostic corrugations on sides of both upper and lower mandibles. Red orbital skin. **Male:** chestnut crown and crest, white neck and yellow gular pouch. **Female:** black head and neck, blue gular pouch. **Immature:** both sexes resemble adult male in having white neck and yellow gular pouch. Younger juveniles lack casque and lateral corrugations on bill; gular bar is fainter (greyish rather than black). ◆ Outside the breeding season, may be found in large roosting flocks. **Voice:** a harsh *kuk-kwehk*, with emphasis on higher second note. Not as deep as calls of Great Hornbill. **Habitat:** evergreen and mixed deciduous forests from plains to 1800 m. Occasionally seen flying over deforested country. Also found on islands. Uncommon to locally common resident.

นกเงือกกรามช้างปากเรียบ

372. Plain-pouched Hornbill (Blyth's Hornbill) *Rhyticeros subruficollis* S: 90

Colouration as in respective sexes of Wreathed, but distinguished by slightly smaller size, lack of dark bar on gular pouch and lack of corrugations on sides of bill. Little known. **Voice:** *keh-kek-kehk*; higher-pitched, more quacking and less booming than call of Wreathed Hornbill but of a recognisably similar pattern. **Habitat:** evergreen and mixed deciduous forests of lowlands and lower hills. Rare resident.

373. Black Hornbill *Anthracoceros malayanus* S: 76 นกเงือกดำ

Small; size and shape approaches Oriental Pied Hornbill. All black plumage, with white tips to outer tail feathers. Some individuals show broad white supercilia behind eyes which meet on the nape. Large casque. **Male:** bill yellowish white; orbital skin blackish. **Female:** bill blackish; pinkish red orbital skin. **Juvenile:** bill and casque whitish in both sexes. **Voice:** a distinctive deep growling or retching sound. **Habitat:** evergreen forests, frequently along streamsides, of plains and foothills. Rare resident.

นกแก๊ก, นกแกง

374. Oriental Pied Hornbill (Indian Pied Hornbill) *Anthracoceros albirostris* S: 70

Identified by small size, whitish face patches and white lower breast and belly. In flight, shows white trailing edge to wing; bursts of rapid wingbeats are interspersed with short glides. Bill and casque ivory-coloured, marked with black. (Casque larger in males but more heavily marked blackish in females.) Race *A. a. albirostris*, found in most of country, has black tail with white tips to all but central feathers. 'Southern Pied Hornbill' *A. a. convexus* of the extreme southern Peninsula has the outer pair of tail feathers mainly white, though often asymmetrically marked with black. ◆ Roosts communally. **Voice:** loud, high-pitched yelping laughter; *gak-gak-gak-gak-gak*. **Habitat:** evergreen and mixed deciduous forests, secondary growth from plains to 1400 m. (In the Peninsula is confined to the level lowlands, usually along rivers, and on islands.) Fairly common resident.

202

375. Rhinoceros Hornbill *Buceros rhinoceros* S: 122   นกเงือกหัวแรด
Very large. Mainly black with white belly and white tail with broad black transverse band. Wings all black in flight. Large upturned casque is suffused reddish. Casque of immature develops slowly over several years to attain adult shape. Bill yellowish. **Male:** red eye. **Female:** white eye. **Voice:** members of pair duet; follows similar pattern to Great Hornbill, but is not quite as low pitched. Flight call *ger-ok* (DRW). **Habitat:** evergreen forest, from lowlands up to 1200 m. Rare resident in the extreme south.

376. Great Hornbill *Buceros bicornis* S: 122   นกกก, นกกาฮัง
Very large. Easily recognised by golden-stained, white wing bar, white trailing edge to wing and by white tail with transverse band. At rest, mainly yellow bill and casque, black face and golden-stained head and neck. **Male:** red eye. **Female:** white eye; less black on casque than male. ◆ Usually in pairs, but sometimes in small flocks outside the breeding season. **Voice:** duets. A series of deep *gok* notes, given by both members of the pair, leads into loud roaring or barking notes. Flight call *ger-ok*. **Habitat:** evergreen and mixed deciduous forests, from plains up to 1500 m. Also found on some larger islands. Uncommon to locally common resident.

377. Helmeted Hornbill *Rhinoplax vigil* S: 127   นกชนหิน
Large, with elongate central tail feathers up to a further 50 cm. In flight, combination of white trailing edge to dark wings and black bar on tail is diagnostic. At rest, appears blackish brown with a white belly. Short conical bill and rounded casque are reddish, tipped yellow. Bare red skin on neck. Female slightly smaller than male. Solitary or in pairs. **Voice:** a long series of calls which may last many minutes. Widely spaced, resonant *poop* notes give way to disyllabic *ke-hoop* notes leading into a maniacal laugh. Can also give a series of staccato barking or quacking notes, usually in flight. **Habitat:** evergreen forests from plains up to 1200 m. Uncommon to rare resident.

วงศ์นกโพระดก

ASIAN BARBETS: Family *Megalaimidae*. Heavy-bodied birds, with large heads and stout bills. Body plumage usually green, but have distinctive coloured facial patches. Slow-moving; mainly frequent the canopy and can often be difficult to see. Chiefly frugivorous; hole-nesting. Most species have confusingly similar bubbling or trilling calls in addition to their diagnostic territorial songs. Sexes usually similar. World: 27 species. Thailand: 13 species.

378. Great Barbet *Megalaima virens* S: 32   นกตั้งล้อ
Large size, with long, yellowish white bill, dark blue-green head and red under tail coverts. Mantle dark greenish brown and breast dark brown. Lower breast and belly streaked yellowish. **Voice:** a high-pitched, ringing *kay-oh*, repeated at the rate of about one note per second. Often duets; one bird calling as described, the other uttering a more rapid and continuous *piou-piou-piou...* Feeding or contact call is a grating *keeah*. **Habitat:** evergreen and occasionally deciduous forests, from 600 m to the highest summits. Common resident.

Plate 69 Hornbills II

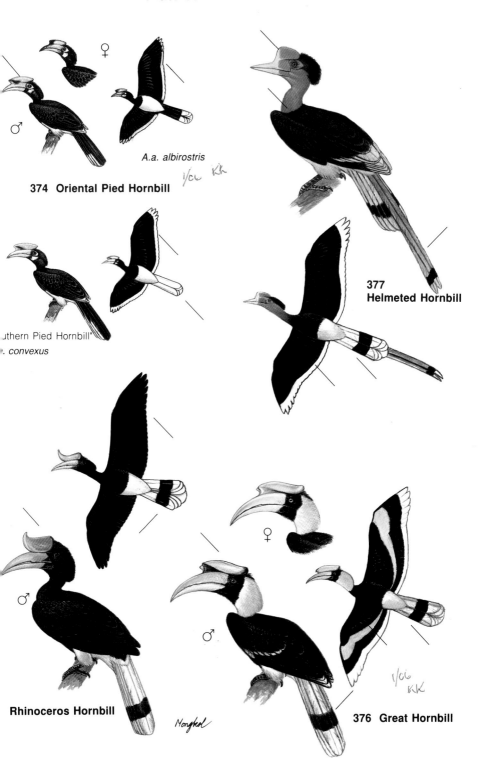

♀

♂

A.a. albirostris

1/06 KK

374 Oriental Pied Hornbill

uthern Pied Hornbill"
. *convexus*

**377
Helmeted Hornbill**

Rhinoceros Hornbill

Mongkol

♂

♀

♂

1/06
KK

376 Great Hornbill

204

379. Lineated Barbet *Megalaima lineata* S: 29   นกโพระดกธรรมดา

Easily identified by straw-coloured head and upper breast, with dark brown streaks. Prominent yellowish bill and orbital skin; dark eye stands out on otherwise pale head. **Voice:** a mellow, fluty *poo-poh*, the second note higher; also a rapid *koh-koh-koh* and other dry bubbling calls. **Habitat:** deciduous forests, open areas with scattered trees. Often in cultivated areas, from plains up to 800 m. Common resident.

380. Green-eared Barbet *Megalaima faiostricta* S: 24   นกโพระดกหูเขียว

Distinguished from Lineated Barbet by green ear patch, darker, more densely streaked head and blackish bill. Has a small red patch on side of neck. **Voice:** a throaty *per-roo-roo-rook*; also a mellow, fluty *pooouk*, with a rising inflection. **Habitat:** evergreen and mixed deciduous forests, chiefly of the lowlands, up to 900 m. Common resident.

381. Gold-whiskered Barbet *Megalaima chrysopogon* S: 30 นกโพระดกเคราเหลือง

Large size, bright yellow cheek patch and grey throat. Red patch at base of upper mandible, greyish forecrown, dark grey-brown eye patch and reddish hindcrown, mixed with blue. **Voice:** a deep, continuous *kootook-ootook-ootook....* uttered at a rate of about 2 complete disyllables per second. **Habitat:** evergreen forest from plains to 1000 m. Fairly common resident.

382. Red-crowned Barbet *Megalaima rafflesii* S: 27   นกโพระดกหลากสี

Easily identified by fairly large size, red crown, blue throat and round yellow cheek patch. Also shows a broad black eye-line and a blue eyebrow. **Voice:** a distinctive pattern of one or two notes, *took*, followed by a more rapid series of up to about 20 shorter notes *tuk-tuk-tuk-tuk*..., uttered at a rate of about 3 per second. Deep and resonant. **Habitat:** evergreen forests of the level lowlands. Rare resident, threatened by forest destruction.

383. Red-throated Barbet *Megalaima mystacophanos* S: 23   นกโพระดกคางแดง

A medium sized barbet with a disproportionately large blackish bill. **Male:** the only barbet with a red throat. Has à yellow forehead and red hindcrown. **Female:** throat and head mainly greenish. Small reddish patches on lores and hindcrown. **Voice:** a slow series of deep, alternating single and double notes, *chok... chok-chok... chok...* Sometimes, a series of single notes at a rate of about one per second. **Habitat:** evergreen forest, from lowlands to about 750 m. Common resident.

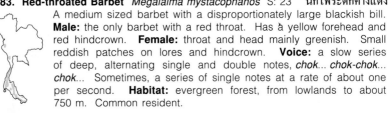

Plate 70 Barbets

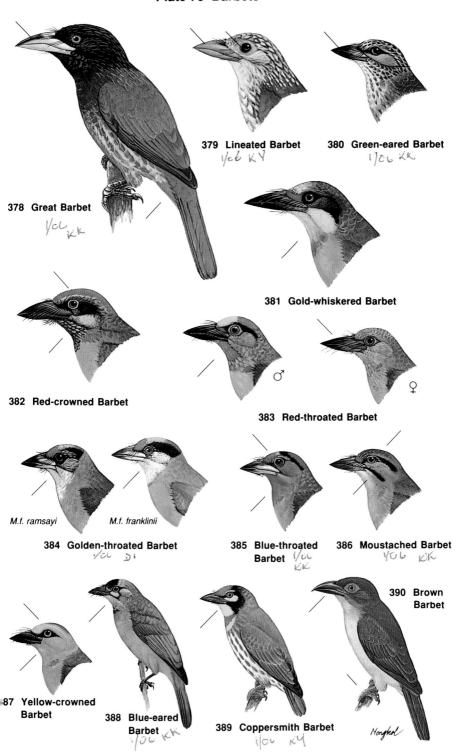

379 Lineated Barbet

380 Green-eared Barbet

378 Great Barbet

381 Gold-whiskered Barbet

382 Red-crowned Barbet

383 Red-throated Barbet

M.f. ramsayi   M.f. franklinii

384 Golden-throated Barbet

385 Blue-throated Barbet

386 Moustached Barbet

390 Brown Barbet

87 Yellow-crowned Barbet

388 Blue-eared Barbet

389 Coppersmith Barbet

Mongkol

206

384. Golden-throated Barbet *Megalaima franklinii* S: 23 นกโพระดกคางเหลือง

 Identified by yellowish upper throat and greyish lower throat; red forecrown and nape and by yellow hindcrown. Sides of head grey, streaked with black around eye. Race **M. f.** *franklinii* of Nan Province and the mountains of the North-east has a continuous, broad black eye-line. **Voice:** a ringing *ki-ti-yook*. **Habitat:** hill evergreen forests; usually replaces Blue-throated Barbet above 1500 m, though occasionally found as low as 900 m. Common resident.

385. Blue-throated Barbet *Megalaima asiatica* S: 23 นกโพระดกคอสีฟ้า

 Identified by unmarked, turquoise-blue sides of head and throat. Also shows red forecrown, hindcrown and nape and a black eyebrow which extends across midcrown. **Voice:** a hurried, repeated *took-arook*. **Habitat:** evergreen forest, secondary growth, usually from 600 m to 1800 m. Common resident.

386. Moustached Barbet *Megalaima incognita* S: 23 นกโพระดกคอสีฟ้าเคราดำ

 Distinguished by broad black cheek bar; turquoise-green sides of head and throat. Short black eyebrow and mainly green crown with small area of red above base of bill and on nape. **Voice:** *took-a-rook*, closely similar to that of Blue-throated but notes more widely spaced and deliberate. **Habitat:** evergreen forest of hill slopes from 600 m to 1700 m. Where overlaps with Blue-throated Barbet, is usually found at a lower elevation than that species. Common resident.

387. Yellow-crowned Barbet *Megalaima henricii* S: 21 นกโพระดกหัวเหลือง

Distinguished by yellow forecrown and eyebrow combined with blue throat and hindcrown. Sides of head greenish, with black lores and eye-ring. **Voice:** a highly distinctive short trill, followed by usually four to six clucks; *trrok, tok-tok-tok-tok...trrok, tok-tok-tok-to...* **Habitat:** evergreen forests from plains to 800 m. Uncommon resident.

388. Blue-eared Barbet *Megalaima australis* S: 17 นกโพระดกหน้าผากดำ

 Much smaller than Blue-throated, with a conspicuous yellowish mark below eye. Blackish forehead, blue crown and short black moustache which becomes red on the sides of the neck. Red patch behind and above eye. **Juvenile:** head all dull greenish. **Voice:** a monotonous *ko-tek, ko-tek*, higher-pitched than calls of preceding species. Also a whistled *pleow, pleow...* at approximately one second intervals. **Habitat:** evergreen and mixed deciduous forests, secondary growth, from plains to 1500 m. Common resident; often seen in large flocks in fruiting trees.

389. Coppersmith Barbet *Megalaima haemacephala* S: 16 นกตีทอง

Striking black and yellow face pattern, red breast band and fore-crown. Upperparts dark green; underparts yellowish with broad, dark streaks. **Juvenile:** lacks red markings; face pattern duller. **Voice:** a long series of resonant *tonk* notes, supposedly reminiscent of a coppersmith hammering on metal, uttered at varying rates (usually once to twice per second). **Habitat:** deciduous woodlands and forest edge, open country with scattered trees, mangroves, gardens (including those in towns and cities) from plains up to at least 800 m. Very common resident.

390. Brown Barbet *Calorhamphus fuliginosus* S: 18 นกจอกป่าหัวโต

Upperparts dull, dark brown; underparts dusky whitish. Large brownish bill and pinkish orange feet. Lacks the strong rictal bristles of the other barbets. **Voice:** a thin, high-pitched screaming *pseeoo* and similar notes. **Habitat:** evergreen forests, clearings, secondary growth with tall relict trees from plains to 1000 m. Fairly common resident.

วงศ์นกพรานผึ้ง

HONEYGUIDES: Family *Indicatoridae*. Long, pointed wings and short, stubby bills. Have zygodactylous toes like woodpeckers, but otherwise superficially resemble bulbuls. Some African species lead man and other mammals to stores of honey. Feed both on insects and on beeswax. Most are nest parasites, laying their eggs in the nests of other birds. World: 16 species. Thailand: one species.

391. Malaysian Honeyguide *Indicator archipelagicus* S: 18 นกพรานผึ้ง

Upperparts dark olive-brown and underparts whitish, with greyish wash on breast and dark streaks on flanks. Bill much heavier and stubbier than any bulbul. Whitish inner webs to outer 3 pairs of tail feathers difficult to see in the field. Eye red (brown in immature). **Male:** lemon-yellow shoulder patch. **Voice:** a mewing note, followed by an ascending, nasal, grinding rattle. **Habitat:** evergreen forests, up to 800 m. Rare resident.

วงศ์นกหัวขวาน

WOODPECKERS: Family *Picidae*. Arboreal birds which usually cling to tree trunks, using the stiff feathers of the tail as a brace. Have long, straight, chisel-tipped bills with which they excavate insects from under bark and from both living and dead wood. Many species eat ants, sometimes taken from the ground. Undulating flight with the wings usually closed during short glides. Usually territorial and sedentary, having loud calls and showing distinctive drumming behaviour. Nest in cavities, usually excavated in trees. World: 200 species. Thailand: 36 species.

392. Eurasian Wryneck *Jynx torquilla* S: 19 นกคอพัน

Slender body with mottled and barred, greyish upperparts and tail. Wings finely barred black and rufous. Distinctive broad blackish line down back and dark eye-line. Underparts buffy, finely dark-barred. Feeds mainly on the ground. **Habitat:** open secondary growth, scrub, grassland, cultivation from plains to 2000 m. Fairly common winter visitor.

208

393. Speckled Piculet *Picumnus innominatus* S: 10   นกหัวขวานจิ๋วท้องลาย
Very small and short-tailed, with bold black spots on creamy white underparts and black and white striped face and tail. Upperparts bright olive-green. **Male:** brighter orange forecrown than female. ◆ Often found in bird waves and frequently detected by loud tapping noise made while feeding. **Voice:** a sharp *tsick*; also drums loudly. **Habitat:** evergreen and mixed deciduous forests, bamboo, from foothills up to 1800 m. Common resident.

394. White-browed Piculet *Sasia ochracea* S: 9   นกหัวขวานจิ๋วคิ้วขาว
Very small and short-tailed. Bright olive-green upperparts and orange-rufous underparts with thin white brow extending behind eye. Broad, red orbital ring (blackish in race *hasbroucki* of the Peninsula). **Male:** yellow forehead. **Female:** rufous forehead. **Voice:** a high-pitched, staccato trill, *ti-i-i-i-i-i*. Drums loudly. **Habitat:** evergreen and mixed deciduous forest, bamboo from plains up to 1800 m. Fairly common resident.

395. Rufous Piculet *Sasia abnormis* S: 9   นกหัวขวานจิ๋วอกแดง
Similar to preceding species, with pinkish red orbital ring, but lacks eyebrow. **Male:** yellow forehead. **Female:** rufous forehead. **Voice:** a high-pitched, loud and insistent *kik-ik-ik-ik-ik-ik*; drums loudly in bursts of 1.5 to 2 seconds. **Habitat:** evergreen forests, secondary growth, especially in association with bamboo, from plains to 1300 m. Fairly common resident.

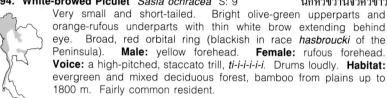

นกหัวขวานหลังสีส้ม
396. Orange-backed Woodpecker *Reinwardtipicus validus* S: 30
Blackish brown upperparts contrast sharply with a broad pale band down back and rump. Broad rufous bars in flight feathers of wings. **Male:** back and rump yellowish orange; crown and underparts red. **Female:** back and rump whitish; dull grey-brown crown and underparts. **Voice:** drums weakly in very short bursts. Calls with a squeaky, high-pitched and anxious-sounding *kit kit kit kit kit-it*, which rises sharply on the last note. Also has a very rapid trilling, *ki-i-i-i-i-i-ik*. **Habitat:** evergreen forests up to 700 m, but mainly lowlands and lower hill slopes. Uncommon resident.

นกหัวขวานสี่นิ้วหลังทอง
397. Greater Flameback (Greater Goldenback) *Chrysocolaptes lucidus* S: 33
Golden upperparts with red rump and black flight feathers of wings and tail. Underparts scaled black and white. Distinguished from Common Flameback by longer, heavier bill and by thin, double, black moustachial stripes separated by a white patch. Has shaggy, rather than neatly pointed, crest and yellow eye; 4 toes. **Male:** red crest. **Female:** black crest, spotted with white. **Voice:** drums loudly and frequently; some bursts may be 2 seconds long. Usual call is a sharp, metallic, monotone *di-di-di-di-di-di-di...*, sounding like a giant cicada. A lower pitched, more rapid *di-i-i-i-i-it* in flight. **Habitat:** deciduous and evergreen forest below 1200 m; mangroves. Common resident.

Plate 71 Honeyguide, Woodpeckers

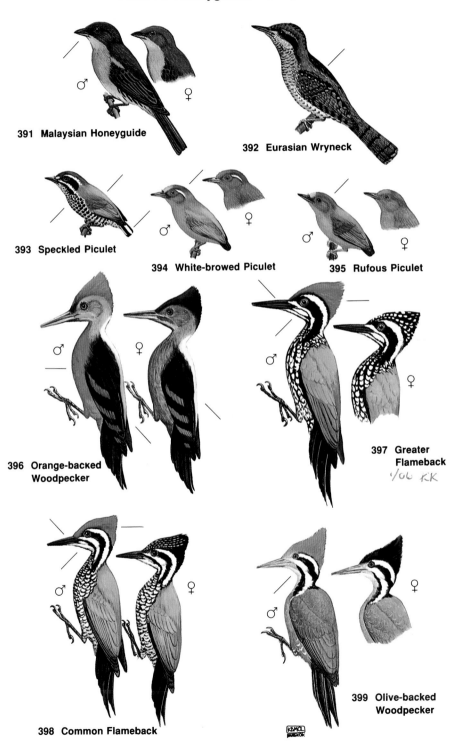

391 Malaysian Honeyguide ♂ ♀

392 Eurasian Wryneck

393 Speckled Piculet

394 White-browed Piculet ♂ ♀

395 Rufous Piculet ♂ ♀

396 Orange-backed Woodpecker ♂ ♀

397 Greater Flameback ♂ ♀

398 Common Flameback ♂ ♀

399 Olive-backed Woodpecker ♂ ♀

210

นกหัวขวานสามนิ้วหลังทอง

398. Common Flameback (Common Goldenback) *Dinopium javanense* S: 30

From Greater Flameback by much shorter bill and by single broad black moustachial stripe. Has only 3 toes; chestnut eye. **Male:** red crest. **Female:** black crest with white streaks. **Voice:** drums more softly than does Greater, and has a faster, less metallic, trilling call, a little reminiscent of the trilling of some crakes *Porzana* spp. Flight call similar to Greater Flameback. **Habitat:** open deciduous woodland, scrub, gardens of lower elevations. Also mangroves. Common resident.

นกหัวขวานสามนิ้วหลังสีไพล

399. Olive-backed Woodpecker *Dinopium rafflesii* S: 28

From the Flamebacks by darker, olive-green mantle and by lack of red on rump. From other green-backed woodpeckers by bold black and white striped face pattern. **Male:** red crown and crest. **Female:** black crown and crest. **Voice:** not known to drum. A soft, even trilling *ti-i-i-i-i*; also a squeaky *tiririt.* **Habitat:** dense, wet evergreen forests of the lowlands. Rare resident.

400. Pale-headed Woodpecker *Gecinulus grantia* S: 28   นกหัวขวานหัวเหลือง

Differs from Bamboo Woodpecker (with which sometimes considered conspecific), by bright, maroon-chestnut upperparts. **Male:** differs additionally from male Bamboo in having the red on head restricted to a patch on the forecrown. **Habitat:** lowland evergreen forests, bamboo. Very rare resident, known only from the banks of the Mekong River in the far north. Possibly now extinct in Thailand due to deforestation.

401. Bamboo Woodpecker *Gecinulus viridis* S: 28   นกหัวขวานป่าไผ่

Distinguished from other green-backed woodpeckers by plain, brownish buff, yellow-tinged sides of head, and whitish bill. Shows red mottling on rump; underparts uniform dark brownish. **Male:** red crown. ◆ Usually makes nest hole in the stems of the larger bamboos. **Voice:** drums in loud bursts of about one second. A shrill series of monotone *kyeek kyeek kyeek kyeek* notes, uttered at the rate of about 3 notes per second. Also a dry, undulating cackle similar to Bay Woodpecker. **Habitat:** bamboo clumps in both evergreen and deciduous forests from plains up to 1400 m. Uncommon resident.

402. Laced Woodpecker *Picus vittatus* S: 30   นกหัวขวานเขียวป่าไผ่

Upperparts green and sides of head grey with a blackish moustache which slightly speckled whitish. From Grey-headed Woodpecker by bold scaling on lower breast and belly which contrasts with unmarked, yellow-green upper breast and throat. Yellowish rump and darker green upper tail coverts. **Male:** red crown. **Female:** black crown. **Voice:** drums. Most often gives an explosive, shrill, falling tone *kweep.* **Habitat:** deciduous and evergreen forests, secondary growth, scrub and gardens up to 1500 m. In west and south-west Thailand, where overlaps with Streak-breasted, is mainly restricted to mangroves, dryer deciduous woodlands and coastal scrub. Common resident.

Plate 72 Woodpeckers II

400 Pale-headed Woodpecker

401 Bamboo Woodpecker

402 Laced Woodpecker

403 Streak-breasted Woodpecker

404 Streak-throated Woodpecker

405 Grey-headed Woodpecker

406 Black-headed Woodpecker

212

403. Streak-breasted Woodpecker *Picus viridanus* S: 30 นกหัวขวานเขียวคอเขียว

Resembles respective sexes of Laced Woodpecker (with which sometimes considered conspecific) but is distinguished by greener throat which is often streaked; greener breast with bold whitish scaling. Black moustache is usually less bold than in Laced; upper tail coverts olive-green. Note range. **Voice:** gives at least one note, an explosive *kirrr* (recalling Banded Pitta), which not known in Laced though other vocalizations similar. **Habitat:** in west and south-west Thailand, where overlaps with Laced, is restricted to moist evergreen forests of the lower hills. In the Peninsula, inhabits both inland forests and secondary growth, together with mangroves and coastal scrub. Uncommon resident.

นกหัวขวานเขียวท้องลาย

404. Streak-throated Woodpecker *Picus xanthopygaeus* S: 30

Very like preceding species, but black moustache lacking or very much less distinct, and has brighter yellowish rump and upper tail coverts (though difficult to see when perched as usually covered by folded wings). Eye whitish or pale pinkish (dark reddish in Laced and Streak-breasted). Entire underparts are whiter than in preceding species, with bolder black scaling. **Habitat:** deciduous forests of lowlands and lower hills. Uncommon or rare resident.

405. Grey-headed Woodpecker *Picus canus* S: 33 นกหัวขวานเขียวหัวดำ

Distinguished from Laced Woodpecker by unmarked olive-green underparts, more uniform grey sides to head and pure black moustache. **Male:** red confined to forecrown. **Female:** entire crown black. **Voice:** drums; calls with a descending sequence of usually 3 or 4 mournful notes; *kiu, kiu, kiu....* **Habitat:** evergreen and deciduous forests, pines, from foothills up to 1800 m. Uncommon resident.

นกหัวขวานเขียวตะโพกแดง

406. Black-headed Woodpecker *Picus erythropygius* S: 33

Black head contrasts with yellow throat and upper breast; bright greenish upperparts. Whitish eye. In flight, shows bright red rump and white patches at base of primaries. **Male:** red patch on centre of forecrown. **Voice:** distinctive, undulating, yelping laughter; *ka-tek-a-tek-a-tek-a-tek.......* **Habitat:** deciduous forests up to 900 m. Uncommon resident.

407. Greater Yellownape *Picus flavinucha* S: 34 นกหัวขวานใหญ่หงอนเหลือง

Bright, uniformly green upperparts, with conspicuous orange-yellow crest. From Lesser Yellownape by lack of white cheek bar, unbarred underparts and by bold black barring on rufous flight feathers of wings. Sides of crown rufous-brown, not red. **Male:** creamy yellow throat and malar area. **Female:** throat streaked dark; malar region brownish. **Voice:** drums infrequently. The usual call is a loud *kiyaep.* **Habitat:** evergreen and deciduous forests, pines, from lowlands up to 2000 m. Common resident.

Plate 73 Woodpeckers III

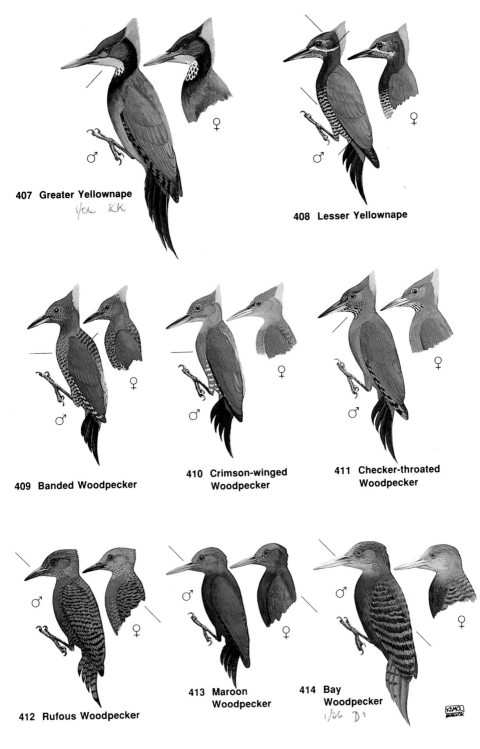

407 Greater Yellownape

You ïïck

♂   ♀

408 Lesser Yellownape

♂   ♀

409 Banded Woodpecker

♂   ♀

410 Crimson-winged Woodpecker

♂   ♀

411 Checker-throated Woodpecker

♂   ♀

♂   ♀

412 Rufous Woodpecker

♂   ♀

413 Maroon Woodpecker

♂   ♀

414 Bay Woodpecker

i/ᴜᴜ D⁴

KAMOL BANGKOK

214

408. Lesser Yellownape *Picus chlorolophus* S: 27 นกหัวขวานเล็กหงอนเหลือง

Separated from Greater Yellownape by long, thin white cheek bar and by bright red sides to crown. Barred underparts; throat olive, concolorous with upper breast. Flight feathers of wings rufous, unbarred. **Male:** red moustache; red on head extends to forecrown. **Female:** red restricted to hindcrown. **Voice:** drums. Usually calls with a mournful descending *peee-uu*, with emphasis on first syllable. Also a shrill, slightly descending series of notes; *kee kee kee kee kee*. **Habitat:** evergreen and deciduous forests from foothills to 1800 m. Common resident.

409. Banded Woodpecker *Picus miniaceus* S: 25 นกหัวขวานแดงลาย

Yellow-tipped red crest and red wings, like Crimson-winged Woodpecker, but distinguished by pale barring on mantle and by bolder, much more extensive whitish barring on underparts. Dull rufous throat and upper breast. **Male:** reddish sides to head. **Voice:** not known to drum. Usually calls with a mournful, falling tone *peew*, uttered at intervals. **Habitat:** evergreen forest, secondary growth and plantations, usually below 900 m. Uncommon resident.

410. Crimson-winged Woodpecker *Picus puniceus* S: 25 นกหัวขวานปีกแดง

Distinguished from Banded Woodpecker by greener body and sides of head, which sharply demarcated from crown; unbarred mantle. Also by barring on underparts usually restricted to flanks and pale grey-green orbital skin. **Male:** red malar stripe. **Juvenile:** lacks red on head and has more extensive barring on underparts. **Voice:** drums rather weakly. Usually calls with a very distinctive *pee-bee*, the second syllable being lower. Sometimes gives a descending series *pee-hee-hee-hee* and occasionally a single, falling tone *pi-eew* like Banded, but more strident and less mournful. **Habitat:** evergreen forest, secondary growth and plantations below 600 m. Common resident.

411. Checker-throated Woodpecker *Picus mentalis* S: 28 นกหัวขวานคอลาย

Yellow nuchal crest, green crown, chestnut collar and streaked black and white throat. Reddish wings. **Male:** malar area streaked, as throat. **Female:** malar area chestnut. **Voice:** drums in very short bursts. Calls with a series of upward inflected notes; *kiyee kiyee kiyee* (emphasis on the first syllable of each note). **Habitat:** evergreen forests below 1000 m. Uncommon resident.

412. Rufous Woodpecker *Celeus brachyurus* S: 25 นกหัวขวานสีตาล

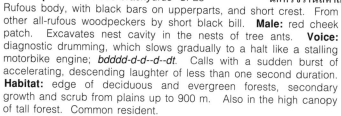

Rufous body, with black bars on upperparts, and short crest. From other all-rufous woodpeckers by short black bill. **Male:** red cheek patch. Excavates nest cavity in the nests of tree ants. **Voice:** diagnostic drumming, which slows gradually to a halt like a stalling motorbike engine; *bdddd-d-d--d--dt*. Calls with a sudden burst of accelerating, descending laughter of less than one second duration. **Habitat:** edge of deciduous and evergreen forests, secondary growth and scrub from plains up to 900 m. Also in the high canopy of tall forest. Common resident.

413. Maroon Woodpecker *Blythipicus rubiginosus* S: 23 นกหัวขวานแดง

Pale yellowish bill and chestnut-maroon, unbarred upperparts. Underparts dark brown. Indistinct pale bars on flight feathers of wings and tail. **Male:** crimson on sides of neck and nape. **Voice:** not known to drum. Usual call is a high-pitched, anxious, constantly repeated *kik....kik..* at frequent intervals; sometimes *kik-ik....kik-ik*, the second syllable with marked upward inflection. Also a shrill descending sequence; *keek-eek-eek-eek-eek-eek*. **Habitat:** evergreen forest up to 900 m. Common resident.

414. Bay Woodpecker *Blythipicus pyrrhotis* S: 30 นกหัวขวานแดงหลังลาย

Large size and pale yellowish bill. Upperparts dark rufous with bold black bars. **Male:** crimson patch on sides of neck. **Voice:** not known to drum. Loud descending laughter; *keek, keek-keek-keek-keek-keek*. Also an undulating, dry cackle. **Habitat:** evergreen forests, usually from 600 m to 2200 m, but occasionally in mixed deciduous forest down to the foothills. Uncommon resident.

นกหัวขวานใหญ่สีเทา

415. Great Slaty Woodpecker *Muelleripicus pulverulentus* S: 50

The largest Old World woodpecker. Diagnostic uniform grey plumage and buffy throat. **Male:** red moustache. **Voice:** not known to drum. Gives a loud bray or whinny of 4 or 5 notes; also a soft *whu-ick*, given both at rest and in flight. **Habitat:** deciduous and evergreen forests. Most frequent in the lowlands and lower hills, but found up to 1000 m. Also mangroves. Uncommon resident.

416. White-bellied Woodpecker *Dryocopus javensis* S: 43 นกหัวขวานใหญ่สีดำ

Easily identified by large size and black plumage with white belly. Rump white in race *feddeni* of continental Thailand; black in race *javensis* of Peninsula. **Male:** red moustache and entire crown and crest. **Female:** forecrown black. ◆ In flight shows white wing lining and white patch at base of primaries. **Voice:** drums. Usually calls with a loud single, falling tone note, *keer* (race *feddeni*) or *kiauk* (race *javensis*). A high-pitched, staccato *kek-ek-ek-ek-ek* in flight. **Habitat:** mainly deciduous forests, below 600 m. Race *javensis* inhabits evergreen forests and forest edge of the level lowlands, and mangroves. Uncommon resident. Race *javensis* now rare due to habitat destruction.

นกหัวขวานลายตะโพกเหลือง

417. Buff-rumped Woodpecker *Meiglyptes tristis* S: 19

Has a more prominent crest than does Buff-necked and broader whitish or buffy bars on both upperparts and underparts. Whitish rump. **Male:** red moustache. **Voice:** drums. A very rapid, uninflected trill; *ki-i-i-i-i-i-i*. In flight, gives a single note, *chit*. **Habitat:** evergreen forest, especially around forest edge and in clearings, up to 600 m. Common resident.

216

418. Buff-necked Woodpecker *Meiglyptes tukki* S: 22 นกหัวขวานลายคอแถบขาว

Dark brown plumage with narrow buffy bars on upperparts and underparts; buff neck patch and dark rump. Has only a short crest so that head appears somewhat rounded. Short, blackish bill. **Male:** red moustache. **Voice:** drums. Calls with a monotone high-pitched trill; *ki-ti-ki-ti-ki-ti-ki-ti.* **Habitat:** evergreen forests, below 600 m. Uncommon resident.

นกหัวขวานด่างท้องดำ

419. Black-and-Buff Woodpecker *Meiglyptes jugularis* S: 19

Closely resembles Heart-spotted Woodpecker from which distinguished by large white patch on sides and rear of neck and by fine buff bars on flight feathers of wings. Blackish throat and head, finely barred buff. Tail longer, extending beyond the folded wings. **Male:** shows red moustache. ◆ Often hangs upside down on small leafy twigs and branches in understorey. **Voice:** calls similar to those of Heart-spotted. A nasal *ki-yew* and a sequence of *keek-eek-eek* notes. **Habitat:** evergreen forests, below 900 m. Uncommon resident.

นกหัวขวานแคระจุดรูปหัวใจ

420. Heart-spotted Woodpecker *Hemicircus canente* S: 15

Black upperparts with large white wing patches and white rump. From Black-and-Buff Woodpecker by tail shorter than wings at rest; black sides and rear of neck and by white throat. Flight feathers of wings black, unbarred. **Male:** crown black, with only indistinct whitish speckling on forecrown. **Female:** white forecrown. ◆ Favours higher dead branches. **Voice:** drums weakly and infrequently. Usually gives a nasal *ki-yew*, with emphasis on the second syllable. Also an uninflected high-pitched *kee-kee-kee-kee.* In flight, a squeaky *chirrick*. **Habitat:** deciduous and evergreen forests, forest edge, from plains up to 900 m. Fairly common resident.

นกหัวขวานแคระอกเทา

421. Grey-and-Buff Woodpecker *Hemicircus concretus* S: 13

Very small size. Very short-tailed, with prominent crest like Heart-spotted. Blackish upperparts with even white scaling; white rump. Face and underparts dark grey. **Male:** red crown. **Female:** crown concolorous with sides of head. **Juvenile:** dull orange-yellowish crown in both sexes and broader white scaling above. **Voice:** drums weakly. Calls with a *ki-yow* note, higher-pitched than that of Heart-spotted. **Habitat:** evergreen forests below 900 m. Uncommon resident.

นกหัวขวานอกแดง

422. Crimson-breasted Woodpecker *Picoides cathpharius* S: 18

Distinguished from other similarly-marked woodpeckers by large white shoulder patch and by black malar stripes which extend to form a black band across lower breast. Crimson breast patch and red under tail coverts. **Male:** hindcrown and nape red. **Female:** lacks red on head. **Juvenile:** entire crown red in both sexes, but lacks red on breast; paler, less extensive red on abdomen. **Voice:** an explosive *tchick*; a shrill *kee-kee-kee.* **Habitat:** hill evergreen forests above 1400 m. Local and uncommon resident.

Plate 74 Woodpeckers IV

415 Great Slaty Woodpecker

416 White-bellied Woodpecker

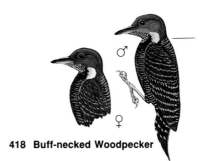

417 Buff-rumped Woodpecker

418 Buff-necked Woodpecker

419 Black-and-Buff Woodpecker

420 Heart-spotted Woodpecker

218

นกหัวขวานด่างท้องน้ำตาลแดง

423. Rufous-bellied Woodpecker *Picoides hyperythrus* S: 23

Diagnostic combination of black and white barred upperparts and deep rufous underparts with red under tail coverts. **Male:** red crown. **Female:** black crown. ◆ Feeds partly by sucking the sap of deciduous oak trees. **Voice:** a staccato *ki-i-i-i-i-i-i* trill; reminiscent of Greater Flameback, but weaker. **Habitat:** open woodlands of oaks, pines and dry dipterocarp trees between 600 and 1200 m. Uncommon resident.

นกหัวขวานด่างหัวแดงอกลาย

424. Stripe-breasted Woodpecker *Picoides atratus* S: 22

Barred black and white upperparts; underparts buffy, with black streaks and red lower abdomen. From Fulvous-breasted Woodpecker by mainly black tail, with white barring confined to the short, outer 2 or 3 pairs of tail feathers. **Male:** red crown. **Female:** black crown. **Juvenile:** both sexes show red on crown. **Voice:** probably drums. Calls with an explosive *tchick*, typical of the genus. **Habitat:** hill evergreen forest from 800 to 2200 m. Fairly common resident.

นกหัวขวานด่างอกลายจุด

425. Fulvous-breasted Woodpecker *Picoides macei* S: 18

Distinguished from Stripe-breasted Woodpecker by bold white bars across entire tail and by whiter underparts with sparse, round spots on upper breast. From Grey-capped by larger size, whiter face and reddish-pink lower abdomen. **Male:** red crown. **Female:** black crown. **Voice:** drums weakly. Calls with an explosive *tchick* and a soft chatter, *chik-a-chik-a-chit.* **Habitat:** open deciduous woodlands, gardens and open country with scattered trees, of plains and lower hills. Uncommon resident.

นกหัวขวานด่างหน้าผากเหลือง

426. Yellow-crowned Woodpecker *Picoides mahrattensis* S: 19

Entire upperparts profusely barred and spotted with white; rump mainly white. Sides of head whitish, tinged brown and underparts streaked brown. Forecrown yellowish. **Male:** red hindcrown. **Female:** brownish hindcrown. ◆ Drums. **Habitat:** deciduous woodland of plains; scrub and open country with scattered trees. Very rare resident.

427. Grey-capped Woodpecker *Picoides canicapillus* S: 15 นกหัวขวานด่างแคระ

Distinguished from the preceding four species by very small size, grey crown and by lack of red on underparts. Broad dark patch on ear coverts. Lacks any malar streak. **Male:** small red streak on sides of hindcrown. **Voice:** drums very softly. Usually calls with a characteristic rapid trill or chatter; *chik-it-chik-it-chik-it.* Flight call is a single shrill *pic*, repeated in unison with flight dips (DRW). **Habitat:** deciduous and open evergreen woodlands, secondary growth and scrub country from plains up to 1800 m; coastal scrub. Common resident.

Plate 75 Woodpeckers V

421 Grey-and-Buff Woodpecker

422 Crimson-breasted Woodpecker

423 Rufous-bellied Woodpecker

424 Stripe-breasted Woodpecker

425 Fulvous-breasted Woodpecker

426 Yellow-crowned Woodpecker

427 Grey-capped Woodpecker

220

BROADBILLS: Family *Eurylaimidae*. Medium–sized, thickset, arboreal forest birds with broad bills, large heads. Most are brightly coloured. Feed on insects and other small animals; some species take fruit. Social and usually encountered in family parties. Loud, diagnostic calls. Build hanging, purse-shaped nests, usually positioned over forest streams. World: 14 species. Thailand: 7 species.

428. Dusky Broadbill *Corydon sumatranus* S: 28 นกพญาปากกว้างสีดำ

Ungainly appearance. Blackish body with reddish pink bill and orbital skin. Buffy throat patch, white wing patch and white tips to tail feathers. Orange streak on back is usually difficult to see. Broad white wing bar in flight. **Juvenile:** bill paler, pinkish; throat dark, lacks back patch. ◆ Becomes conspicuously active in late afternoon, evening. **Voice:** a series of shrill, thin screams with rising inflection; *ky-ee ky-ee ky-ee ky-ee*. Also a falling tone *pseeoo* of similar quality. **Habitat:** evergreen forest (and mixed deciduous forest when close to water) from plains up to 1000 m. Uncommon resident.

นกพญาปากกว้างท้องแดง

429. Black-and-Red Broadbill *Cymbirhynchus macrorhynchos* S: 25

Blackish upperparts with white wing stripe. Crimson-maroon rump and underparts, with narrow black breast band. Upper mandible turquoise-blue, lower mandible yellowish. **Juvenile:** throat and breast grey-brown. From juvenile Banded by lack of yellow on upperparts. **Voice:** short, grating, cicada-like notes. Also has a rising trill, like that of Black-and-Yellow, but softer and briefer. **Habitat:** evergreen forest and wooded secondary growth along the larger streams and rivers, below 300 m. Also enters the landward edge of mangroves. Rare resident; much reduced due to lowland deforestation and now the scarcest broadbill in Thailand.

430. Banded Broadbill *Eurylaimus javanicus* S: 23 นกพญาปากกว้างลายเหลือง

Distinguished from Black-and-Yellow Broadbill by larger size and lack of white neck collar. From Black-and-Red Broadbill by yellow spotting on wings and upperparts; paler vinous red underparts; entirely turquoise-blue bill. **Male:** narrow black band across upper breast. **Juvenile:** duller brownish head and speckled greyish white underparts. ◆ Inhabits middle storey and canopy. **Voice:** a loud, rising, bubbling trill, 5–6 seconds long, introduced by a preliminary *wheeoo* (falling tone) note, followed by a short pause. Often duets, one bird starting its trill shortly after the other. Also a falling tone *kyeeoo* (like one of the notes of Blue or Blue-winged Pitta); a throaty, rolling *keowrr* and a yelping *keek-eek-eek*. **Habitat:** evergreen forest (and also mixed deciduous forest in the vicinity of streams) from plains up to 900 m. Uncommon to fairly common resident.

Plate 76 Broadbills, Pittas

430 Banded Broadbill

juvenile

♀

428 Dusky Broadbill

429 Black-and-Red Broadbill

♂

433 Long-tailed Broadbill

VOL
KK

♂

♀

431 Black-and-Yellow Broadbill

♂

♀

432 Silver-breasted Broadbill

♂

♀

434 Green Broadbill

♂

♀

435 Rusty-naped Pitta

♀

♂

436 Blue-rumped Pitta

437 Giant Pitta

♂

♀

Mongkol

222

431. Black-and-Yellow Broadbill *Eurylaimus ochromalus* S: 17

Relatively small. From Banded Broadbill by much smaller size; black head separated from black of back by white collar and by paler pinkish underparts. Pale lemon yellow lower belly and under tail coverts. **Male:** complete black band across upper breast. **Female:** black band usually broken. **Juvenile:** greyish white underparts and pale yellow eyebrow. **Voice:** a rising, bubbling trill of about 8–11 seconds duration; similar to Banded but accelerates gradually and lacks the introductory note. Also possesses a throaty *keowrr* and squeaky *kyeeow* like Banded. Duets. **Habitat:** evergreen forests, forest edge and secondary growth up to 700 m. Fairly common resident.

432. Silver-breasted Broadbill *Serilophus lunatus* S: 18 นกพญาปากกว้างอกสีเงิน

Subdued, pale greyish colouration. Broad black eyebrow contrasts with pale crown. Striking blue, black and rufous markings in wing; chestnut rump and upper tail coverts, black tail with white-tipped outer feathers. Thin yellow orbital ring. In flight, shows broad white band at bases of flight feathers of wing. **Female:** thin silver necklace across upper breast. ◆ Inhabits middle storey. **Voice:** a melancholy *ki-uu* (second syllable lower) like a rusted hinge. Also a short, thin and grating high-pitched trill, *kitikitikit*, in flight. **Habitat:** evergreen forests and occasionally mixed deciduous forests and bamboo, between 300–1800 m. Fairly common resident.

433. Long-tailed Broadbill *Psarisomus dalhousiae* S: 28 นกพญาปากกว้างหางยาว

Green body plumage, striking black and yellow head pattern and long, blue tail. In flight, shows white patch at base of primaries. Frequently jerks tail sharply upwards while perched. Inhabits middle storey and canopy. After the breeding season, occasionally seen in large flocks of 40 or more birds. **Voice:** a series of five to eight loud, shrill, falling tone screams, uttered at constant pitch; *pseew pseew pseew....* Occasionally a short, rasping *psweep.* **Habitat:** evergreen forests from foothills to 2000 m. Fairly common resident.

434. Green Broadbill *Calyptomena viridis* S: 18　　　นกเขียวปากงุ้ม

Plump and short-tailed, with bright green plumage. **Male:** bill almost completely covered by feathering. Black ear patch and wing bars. **Female:** duller green, unmarked plumage. ◆ In flight, has peculiar shape, with short tail and broad-based, pointed wings. Unlike other broadbills, feeds largely on fruit. **Voice:** a soft, accelerating, bubbling trill *toi, toi-oi-oi-oi-oick.* When feeding, groups of birds also give a soft mournful whistling, recalling notes of green pigeons, *Treron* spp. **Habitat:** evergreen forest below 800 m. Fairly common resident.

วงศ์นกแต้วแล้ว

PITTAS: Family *Pittidae*. Terrestrial forest birds with plump bodies, stout bills and long legs. Have an erect carriage and a characteristic bounding gait. Many are brilliantly-coloured but all are usually secretive and difficult to observe and are best detected by diagnostic calls. Wings make a noisy whirring in flight. Some species smash snails, using stones or exposed tree roots as anvils. Build domed nests of sticks, leaves and grass, placed either on the ground or in understorey trees or palms. World: 29 species. Thailand: 12 species.

435. Rusty-naped Pitta *Pitta oatesi* S: 25   นกแต้วแล้วใหญ่หัวสีน้ำตาล

Identified by rusty crown and nape. Black line behind eye and dull green upperparts; rump sometimes tinged bluish. Underparts warm fulvous. **Female:** green upperparts sometimes tinged rusty; underparts duller than in male. **Juvenile:** upperparts dark brown with white spotting on wing coverts. Underparts whitish with dark spotting and streaking. From juvenile Blue Pitta by large orange-flesh bill. **Voice:** a sharp, breathless *chow-whit*, recalling Blue Pitta but with the first syllable more truncated. Also a liquid, falling tone *poouw*. Juvenile heard to give an explosive, almost woodpecker-like, *tchick* in alarm. **Habitat:** evergreen forests and wooded secondary growth from 800 m to the highest summits. Uncommon resident.

436. Blue-rumped Pitta *Pitta soror* S: 25   นกแต้วแล้วใหญ่หัวสีน้ำเงิน

Similar to Rusty-naped Pitta, but lower back and rump distinctly blue. **Male:** blue crown and nape. **Female:** green crown and nape. **Juvenile:** like Rusty-naped. ◆ Note range. **Voice:** a sharp, breathless *tew* (like first syllable of Rusty-naped Pitta call) and also a longer, mellow, falling tone *tiu*. Calls rather infrequently. **Habitat:** evergreen forests above 900 m. Uncommon and local resident.

437. Giant Pitta *Pitta caerulea* S: 29   นกแต้วแล้วยักษ์, นกซุ้มหมู

Large size with a massive bill; grey-brown underparts with a black necklace diagnostic. Sides of head pale greyish, with black eye-line. **Male:** entirely blue upperparts; black hindcrown and nape. **Female:** rufous brown back, pale blue rump and tail. Crown greyish, as sides of head, with black scaling. **Juvenile:** dark unspotted upperparts; pale grey cheeks with black eye-line; bright orange-flesh bill. ◆ Takes large snails and occasionally small frogs. **Voice:** a soft *wheer*, lacking the explosive quality of most other pitta calls and often uttered in a long series, suggesting call of Rufous-collared Kingfisher. **Habitat:** evergreen forests of the lowlands, but apparently once recorded at 800 m. Rare resident, probably endangered by lowland deforestation.

438. Blue-winged Pitta *Pitta moluccensis* S: 20   นกแต้วแล้วธรรมดา, นกกอหลอ

Sexes similar. From Mangrove Pitta by smaller bill and by pale buffy-brown lateral coronal bands which contrast with prominent black centre to crown. Bright glossy-blue wing coverts; duller greenish mantle and scapulars. Black mask, whitish throat and cinnamon-buff breast and belly with a crimson patch extending up from under tail coverts. Shows large, round, white wing patches in flight, recalling Black-capped Kingfisher. **Juvenile:** bright red base to bill, duller upperparts and lacks crimson belly patch. ◆ Frequently perches in low trees, bamboos, especially when calling. **Voice:** a loud, fluty, *taew-laew*, *taew-laew*, with emphasis on second syllable and usually uttered in couplets. A harsh *skyeew*, in alarm. **Habitat:** mixed deciduous and the more open evergreen forests, bamboos, secondary growth from plains to 800 m. Occurs in gardens, mangroves on passage. Common wet season breeding visitor, passage migrant. Very few birds remain in the dry season, most migrating to Malaysia and Indonesia.

439. Mangrove Pitta *Pitta megarhyncha* S: 20   นกแต้วแล้วป่าโกงกาง

Sexes similar. Very like Blue-winged Pitta, but distinguished by disproportionately long bill and more uniform, darker brown crown. Believed to feed largely on crabs. When calling, frequently perches high up in mangrove trees. **Voice:** *tae-laew tae-laew*, similar to Blue-winged but more slurred in delivery and with a shorter interval between notes. A similar *skyeew*, usually in alarm. **Habitat:** restricted to mangroves. Uncommon to locally common resident.

440. Garnet Pitta *Pitta granatina* S: 18   นกแต้วแล้วแดงมลายู

Sexes similar. Blackish forecrown and throat with red hindcrown and nape and an iridescent pale bluish eyebrow. Dark purple-blue upperparts with pale, iridescent blue wing coverts; crimson belly and under tail coverts. (Plumage appears mainly dark under usual forest lighting.) Lacks white in wing. **Juvenile:** brownish with rufescent crown and underparts; blackish sides to head. **Voice:** a ventriloquial, drawn-out monotone whistle of about one and a half seconds. From similar whistle of Malaysian Rail-babbler by almost imperceptible terminal upward inflection. **Habitat:** moist areas in evergreen forest of the extreme lowlands. Very rare resident; probably endangered due to lowland deforestation.

441. Hooded Pitta *Pitta sordida* S: 19   นกแต้วแล้วอกเขียว

Sexes similar. Black face and throat, green underparts with red under tail coverts and lower belly. Upperparts green, with small area of turquoise-blue on wing coverts. In flight, shows large, round, white wing patches. Crown dark brown in *P. s. cucullata*. (One bird with an all black crown from the far south has been assigned to the race *P. s. muelleri*.) **Voice:** a fluty *raew-raew*, similar in quality to Blue-winged and also uttered in couplets, but each note monosyllabic. A *skyew* in alarm; shorter and squeakier than Blue-winged. **Habitat:** evergreen and occasionally moist mixed deciduous woodlands, secondary growth. Principally lowlands, but occasionally up to 750 m. Uncommon to locally common wet season breeding visitor, wintering mainly in the Peninsula or further to the south.

Plate 77 Pittas II

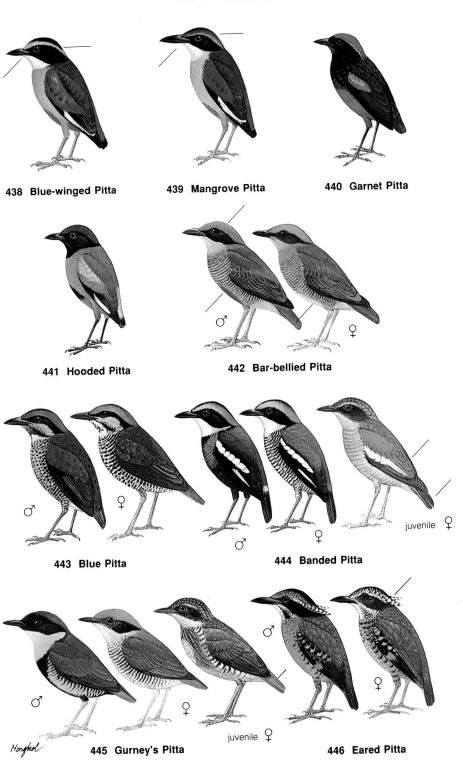

438 Blue-winged Pitta

439 Mangrove Pitta

440 Garnet Pitta

441 Hooded Pitta

442 Bar-bellied Pitta
♂ ♀

443 Blue Pitta
♂ ♀

444 Banded Pitta
♂ ♀ juvenile ♀

445 Gurney's Pitta
♂ ♀ juvenile ♀

446 Eared Pitta
♂ ♀

Nongkol

226

442. Bar-bellied Pitta *Pitta ellioti* S: 23 นกแต้วแล้วเขียวเขมร

Both sexes show green upperparts, narrow black mask and black and yellow bars on lower breast and flanks; tail blue. No white in wing. **Male:** blue-green crown and pale blue throat; dark blue patch in centre of belly. **Female:** dull ochraceous-buff head, throat and upper breast. Yellowish center to belly. **Voice:** a trisyllabic note, *tu-wi-whil.* Also gives a whining *skyew* note in alarm. **Habitat:** evergreen forests of lowlands and lower hills to at least 400 m. Very rare resident. Endangered due to forest destruction.

443. Blue Pitta *Pitta cyanea* S: 24 นกแต้วแล้วสีน้ำเงิน

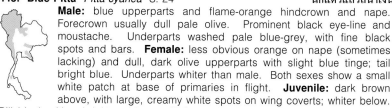

Male: blue upperparts and flame-orange hindcrown and nape. Forecrown usually dull pale olive. Prominent black eye-line and moustache. Underparts washed pale blue-grey, with fine black spots and bars. **Female:** less obvious orange on nape (sometimes lacking) and dull, dark olive upperparts with slight blue tinge; tail bright blue. Underparts whiter than male. Both sexes show a small white patch at base of primaries in flight. **Juvenile:** dark brown above, with large, creamy white spots on wing coverts; whiter below. Bill black with a bright red base. **Voice:** a liquid *pleoow-whit*, more drawn-out than similar call of Rusty-naped Pitta, the first note having a sliding quality, the last note sharp. Sometimes gives a more truncated version, *priaw-pit.* Also a rasping, squeaky *skyeew* in alarm. **Habitat:** evergreen forest, bamboo and the moister mixed deciduous forests from plains to 1500 m. Fairly common resident.

444. Banded Pitta *Pitta guajana* S: 23 นกแต้วแล้วลาย

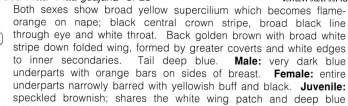

Both sexes show broad yellow supercilium which becomes flame-orange on nape; black central crown stripe, broad black line through eye and white throat. Back golden brown with broad white stripe down folded wing, formed by greater coverts and white edges to inner secondaries. Tail deep blue. **Male:** very dark blue underparts with orange bars on sides of breast. **Female:** entire underparts narrowly barred with yellowish buff and black. **Juvenile:** speckled brownish; shares the white wing patch and deep blue tail of adult. **Voice:** a falling tone *pouw* and a short, whirring *kirrr.* Both calls have an explosive quality, but are deceptively soft so that bird often seems to be more distant than it is. **Habitat:** evergreen forest from plains to 600 m. Uncommon resident.

445. Gurney's Pitta *Pitta gurneyi* S: 22 นกแต้วแล้วท้องดำ

Back and wings golden-brown in both sexes; no visible white in wing; tail paler, more turquoise-blue than Banded Pitta. **Male:** very striking. Black face, forecrown and sides of head; deep, iridescent blue hindcrown and nape. Black belly, bright yellow gorget and barred black and yellow flanks. **Female:** entire crown dull ochraceous-yellow; blackish brown eye patch. Breast and belly finely barred yellow-buff and black. **Juvenile:** speckled brownish with blackish mask. From juvenile Banded by lack of white in wing and paler turquoise-blue tail. **Voice:** the male territorial call is a short, explosive *lilip.* Usual contact and alarm note is a falling tone *skyeew*, given by both sexes. (Less squeaky than similar notes of Blue-winged and Hooded Pittas and with a distinctly tremulous quality.) **Habitat:** evergreen forest and moist, older secondary growth of the extreme lowlands. Rare resident; endemic to Thailand and the extreme southern tip of Burma. Endangered due to lowland forest destruction.

446. Eared Pitta *Pitta phayrei* S: 23   นกแต้วแล้วหูยาว

Warm golden-brown upperparts, broad buffy whitish supercilia or lateral head stripes, finely scaled blackish and sometimes protruding behind head like ears. Bold, black and rufous speckling on wing coverts. **Male:** black central crown and nape; broad black eye-line and malar stripe. Underparts deep rufous-buff with sparse black speckling on sides. **Female:** black of head replaced by dark brown. Underparts paler brown, profusely spotted black. ◆ Fans tail when excited. Feeds by smashing snails and by probing in rotten wood of fallen tree trunks. **Voice:** an airy whistle, *wheeow-whit*, with the first note much more drawn out than in Blue Pitta. Calls mainly at dusk. Also gives a distinctive, short, dog-like whine in alarm. **Habitat:** evergreen and mixed deciduous forests, bamboo, and wooded secondary growth, usually below 900 m but occasionally up to 1500 m. Generally prefers drier areas than Blue Pitta. Uncommon to fairly common resident.

วงศ์นกแอ่นบินเร็ว

SWIFTS: Family *Apodidae*. Superficially resemble swallows, but have longer, thinner, usually crescent-shaped wings. Fly with rapid wingbeats, interspersed with long glides. Many species have screaming calls. Aerial insectivores, they never perch on trees or wires like swallows but with their short claws can only hang from vertical surfaces. Spend much of their time on the wing: grooming, copulating, and, in some species, apparently even sleeping in flight. Sensitive to weather conditions, large numbers often moving ahead of rainstorms to take advantage of feeding opportunities. Best identified when forced by bad weather to descend low or when drinking or bathing, skimming low over water surface. The large species are among the fastest flying birds in the world. Gregarious. Sexes similar. World: 80 species. Thailand: 12 species.

เหล่านกแอ่นขนาดเล็ก

SWIFTLETS: Genera *Aerodramus*, *Collocalia*. Small size and rather fluttering flight on bowed wings; tail only slightly notched rather than forked and appearing almost square-ended. Wings more rounded, not so slender as Asian Palm-Swift. Nest in huge numbers in caves or sometimes buildings. Build cup nests incorporating hardened saliva which, in some species, provides material for birds' nest soup. Echolocation, audible to human ears, has been demonstrated in the *Aerodramus* species. (The similar-sized Asian Palm-Swift and Silver-rumped Swift are placed out of proper sequence at the end of the swiftlets for ease of comparison.)

447. Edible-nest Swiftlet *Aerodramus fuciphagus* S: 13   นกแอ่นกินรัง

Difficult to distinguish from Black-nest and Himalayan Swiftlets. Upperparts blackish brown; underparts slightly paler; rump ranges from whitish in *A. f. germani* (the most widespread race in Thailand) to as dark as back in birds from the extreme south, *A. f. amechana*. In hand, shows unfeathered tarsus. Nest edible and white, consisting wholly of hardened saliva. **Habitat:** nests mainly around the coast and offshore islets, though birds forage widely inland over forest and open country. Common resident.

228

448. Black-nest Swiftlet *Aerodramus maximus* S: 14   นกแอ่นหางสี่เหลี่ยม

Probably indistinguishable in field from Himalayan, though slightly more heavily built than Edible-nest and rump usually darker, greyish to as dark as back. Tail notch less pronounced than in Edible-nest or Himalayan. In hand, from both species by feathered tarsus. Nest blackish, containing some feathers. **Habitat:** as Edible-nest Swiftlet. Common resident.

449. Himalayan Swiftlet *Aerodramus brevirostris* S: 14   นกแอ่นพันธุ์หิมาลัย

Rump greyish to as dark as back. In hand, unfeathered or slightly-feathered tarsus. Tail notch slightly deeper than in Black-nest. Incorporates moss in nest. **Habitat:** limestone hills up to 2200 m; frequently feeding low over open country, rice paddies, etc. Common resident in northern and western Thailand but probably only a winter visitor elsewhere.

450. White-bellied Swiftlet *Collocalia esculenta* S: 10   นกแอ่นท้องขาว

Very small. Glossy blackish upperparts, whitish belly. Throat and breast dark grey. Does not use echolocation. **Habitat:** nests in cave mouths, under bridges and culverts. Feeds over both forested hills and open country. Uncommon or rare resident.

451. Asian Palm-Swift *Cypsiurus balasiensis* S: 13   นกแอ่นตาล

Entirely dark brown plumage, small size and slender, sharply pointed wings. From swiftlets by longer, slender tail (appears pointed when closed; deeply forked when spread). From treeswifts (459–461) by much smaller size, darker colouration and shorter tail. Nests and roosts in palms. **Voice:** shrill screaming, best described as a rapidly repeated *deedle-ee-dee*. **Habitat:** open country, often near towns, villages and close to palms. Also often feeds over forested hills. Very common resident.

นกแอ่นเล็กหางหนามตะโพกขาว
452. Silver-rumped Swift *Rhaphidura leucopygialis* S: 11
Closely related to the needletails and like them shows elongate spine-like shafts to the tail feathers (not usually discernible in the field). Much smaller than other needletails; distinctive, bat-like shape with peculiar truncated appearance to tail. Entirely blackish underparts; large, square white patch on rump and upper tail coverts. Usually feeds low over the forest canopy with a somewhat fluttering flight. **Habitat:** evergreen forests and forest clearings. Common resident.

Plate 78 Swifts

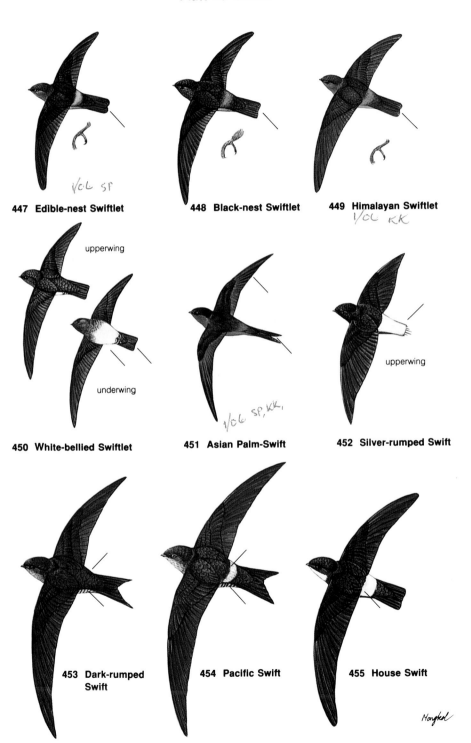

447 Edible-nest Swiftlet

448 Black-nest Swiftlet

449 Himalayan Swiftlet

upperwing

underwing

450 White-bellied Swiftlet

451 Asian Palm-Swift

452 Silver-rumped Swift

453 Dark-rumped Swift

454 Pacific Swift

455 House Swift

Mongkol

เหล่านกแอ่นขนาดกลาง

TYPICAL SWIFTS: Genus *Apus.* Medium-sized. Fly with fast beats of long, tapered wings.

453. Dark-rumped Swift *Apus acuticauda* S: 18   นกแอ่นท้องลาย
Resembles Pacific Swift but slightly smaller and lacking white on rump. Has similar whitish barring on breast and belly. **Habitat:** forests and secondary growth of higher mountains. Very rare winter visitor; little known.

454. Pacific Swift (Fork-tailed Swift) *Apus pacificus* S: 19   นกแอ่นตะโพกขาวหางแฉก
Larger and longer winged than House Swift, with more deeply-forked tail (fork still visible when tail fanned). Narrow, curved band of white across rump varies in distinctness; being broader in wintering race *pacificus* and narrower (sometimes difficult to see) in resident race *cooki.* Whitish throat and narrow whitish scaling and barring on breast and belly is only visible at close range. **Habitat:** forests, secondary growth of hills from lowlands up to the highest elevations. Fairly common winter visitor; uncommon resident.

455. House Swift *Apus affinis* S: 15   นกแอ่นบ้าน
Thicker-bodied and proportionately thicker-winged than other typical swifts. Tail only slightly notched, appearing square-ended at a distance; slightly rounded when fanned. Large, square white rump patch and whitish throat, plumage otherwise blackish. **Voice:** staccato screaming. **Habitat:** nests on cliffs, under bridges and often under ledges of buildings in the middle of cities. Feeds mainly over open areas. Common resident.

เหล่านกแอ่นขนาดใหญ่

NEEDLETAILS: Genus *Hirundapus.* Large, heavily-built swifts with broad, paddle-shaped wings and short, squarish tails with needle-like projections. Nest in tree hollows.

456. White-throated Needletail *Hirundapus caudacutus* S: 20 นกแอ่นใหญ่คอขาว
This and the remaining needletails are very powerful fliers, and all share dark brown underparts with a white, horseshoe-shaped patch on vent and flanks. Heavy-bodied with broad-based wings and short tail. White-throated Needletail shows a silvery whitish back like White-vented Needletail, but is distinguished by strikingly clean white throat and by small white patch on tertials. **Habitat:** feeds over forest and open areas. Rare passage migrant and possibly also winter visitor. Probably much overlooked.

Plate 79 Needletails, Treeswifts

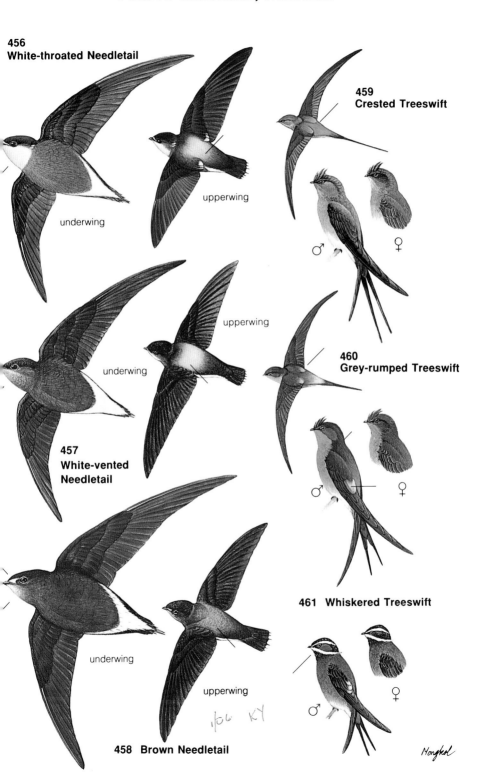

456
White-throated Needletail

underwing

upperwing

459
Crested Treeswift

♂   ♀

457
White-vented Needletail

upperwing

underwing

460
Grey-rumped Treeswift

♂   ♀

461 Whiskered Treeswift

underwing

upperwing

♂   ♀

1/06 KY

458 Brown Needletail

Mongkol

232

457. White-vented Needletail *Hirundapus cochinchinensis* S: 20

Distinguished from Brown Needletail by silvery white saddle on otherwise blackish upperparts, and by slightly smaller size when seen together. Never shows any white on lores. From White-throated by greyish throat and lack of white on tertials. **Habitat:** feeds over forest and secondary growth. Uncommon; status uncertain but probably winter visitor.

458. Brown Needletail *Hirundapus giganteus* S: 25   นกแอ่นใหญ่หัวตาขาว

Distinguished from White-vented Needletail by pale buffy brown saddle. Also noticeably larger when seen at close range and tail, when fanned, appears somewhat rounded. Has conspicuous whitish on lores (lacking in race *H. g. giganteus*, resident in the Peninsula). **Habitat:** feeds mainly over forest, secondary growth, up to at least 1800 m. Common resident; probably also passage migrant and winter visitor.

วงศ์นกแอ่นฟ้า

TREESWIFTS: Family *Hemiprocnidae*. Closely related to the true swifts, but have more colourful plumage and are less strictly aerial in habits, often hawking insects from a perch. In flight, have slender, crescentic wing shape like swifts, but much longer tails. Elongate, slender appearance when perched, the wing tips crossing. Fly with rapid wingbeats interspersed with glides. Build very small, shallow, cup-shaped nests attached with saliva to the upper surface of a branch. Sexes differ slightly. World: 4 species. Thailand: 3 species.

459. Crested Treeswift *Hemiprocne coronata* S: 23   นกแอ่นฟ้าหงอน

Upperparts blue-grey with darker, glossy wings. Whitish lower abdomen and under tail coverts. Wing lining greyish, concolorous with flight feathers. Wing-tips fall short of tail-tip at rest. Tall, pointed crest on forehead. **Male:** has chestnut cheek patch. **Juvenile:** has scaly body plumage and white spots on scapulars and tertials. **Voice:** a distinctive, disyllabic *kee-kyew*, second note lower, uttered in flight. **Habitat:** secondary growth, cultivated areas and open deciduous and hill evergreen woodlands up to 1400 m. Common resident.

นกแอ่นฟ้าตะโพกสีเทา

460. Grey-rumped Treeswift *Hemiprocne longipennis* S: 21

Similar to Crested, but crown, nape and mantle dark green, contrasting with powdery grey rump. Conspicuous pale grey pattern on tertials, and underwing coverts dark green, contrasting with grey-brown flight feathers. At rest, wings extend beyond tail. **Male:** chestnut ear coverts. ◆ Makes longer feeding flights than does Whiskered Treeswift. Gregarious, roosting and foraging communally outside the breeding season. **Voice:** a staccato chatter, *chi-chi-chi-chew*. **Habitat:** forest edge, secondary growth and open country. Common resident.

461. Whiskered Treeswift *Hemiprocne comata* S: 15   นกแอ่นฟ้าเคราขาว

Smaller and more compact than other treeswifts with darker bronzy plumage and two bold white facial stripes. **Male:** chestnut ear coverts. ◆ Usually feeds by making short aerial sallies from an exposed perch. **Habitat:** evergreen forest edge, up to 800 m. Common resident.

วงศ์นกนางแอ่น

SWALLOWS: Family *Hirundinidae*. Aerial feeding insectivores, like swifts, but quite unrelated and distinguished by shorter, broader wings and more fluttering flight. Frequently perch on branches or wires. Gregarious, and often roost communally in large numbers outside the breeding season. Either nest in natural hollows or excavate their own burrows or build mud-nests under cliff ledges, buildings, etc. Most species are winter visitors to Thailand. Sexes usually similar. World: 74 species. Thailand: 11 species.

นกเจ้าฟ้าหญิงสิรินธร

462. White-eyed River-Martin *Pseudochelidon sirintarae* S: 15

Plump-bodied appearance. Broad, rather triangular wings and rounded tail in flight may recall Ashy Wood-swallow (820). Blackish plumage with white band across rump, broad white orbital ring and eye and stout yellow bill. **Adult:** bears elongate wire-like streamers from central tail feathers (difficult to discern in flight). **Immature:** head and underparts slightly browner than in adult; lacks tail streamers. ◆ Endemic to Thailand; so far known only in winter from Bung Boraphet, where a few birds roost in reedbeds with congregations of wintering Barn Swallows. Thought to nest in burrows on riverine sand bars though breeding area unknown. Very rare; not seen for many years and possibly on the verge of extinction.

463. Plain Martin *Riparia paludicola* S: 11   นกนางแอ่นทรายสีน้ำตาล

Brownish upperparts, like Sand Martin, but lacks brown breast band. Throat and upper breast pale grey-brown, grading into whitish lower breast and belly. **Voice:** a buzzing chatter, like Sand Martin but slightly harsher. **Habitat:** open country, especially near larger rivers, marshes. Nests in colonies, excavating nest burrows in riverbanks. Local and uncommon resident.

464. Sand Martin *Riparia riparia* S: 13   นกนางแอ่นทรายสร้อยคอดำ

Identified by brown upperparts and by narrow, sharply-defined brown breast band on otherwise white underparts. Slightly smaller than Barn Swallow, and usually seen singly among large numbers of that species. **Habitat:** open country, usually near marshy areas and lakes but also occasionally in the hills to at least 800 m. Fairly common winter visitor.

234

465. Dusky Crag-Martin *Hirundo concolor* S: 14 นกนางแอ่นผาสีคล้ำ

Dark brown plumage with white subterminal spots to tail feathers. From swifts by more stocky appearance with shorter, broader wings and broader, square-cut tail. Relatively small; usually forages by flying back and forth across cliff faces. **Habitat:** nests on steep, rocky (usually limestone) crags; disperses outside breeding season to all manner of hilly country, from foothills to high summits. Locally common resident.

466. Barn Swallow *Hirundo rustica* S: 15 นกนางแอ่นบ้าน

Adult: glossy blue-black upperparts and breast band with chestnut forehead, throat and gorget. Rest of underparts vary in colour from pinkish red (race *H. r. tytleri*) to pure white. Tail deeply forked, with elongate outer tail feathers extending up to a further 2 cm. **Moulting adults, juvenile:** duller, dark brown upperparts; frequently with small whitish patches on back. Breast band browner, less clear-cut, grading into rufous-brown gorget. Lack elongate tail streamers. From Pacific Swallow by paler, pinkish to whitish flanks and under tail coverts. **Habitat:** open country from plains to over 2000 m, though most abundant in well-watered lowlands. Roosts in reedbeds and even on electric wires in some major towns and cities. Very common winter visitor; apparently breeds locally on a few high mountains.

467. Pacific Swallow *Hirundo tahitica* S: 14 นกนางแอ่นแปซิฟิค

Distinguished from Barn Swallow by dusky flanks and uniformly dusky underwing; dark brown under tail coverts with white scalloping. Shows more chestnut on forehead and lacks dark breast band. **Juvenile:** browner upperparts with less chestnut on forehead and paler throat. **Habitat:** sea coasts, open country, towns and villages. Common resident.

468. Wire-tailed Swallow *Hirundo smithii* S: 13 นกนางแอ่นหางลวด

From Barn Swallow by pure white underparts, including throat; gleaming white underwing coverts which contrast more with black undersides of flight feathers. Square tail; has greatly elongate, wire-like projections from outer tail feathers (though very difficult to discern in the field). Crown chestnut. **Habitat:** open riverine floodplains. Has been recorded nesting under roadside culverts. Local and uncommon resident.

469. Red-rumped Swallow *Hirundo daurica* S: 18 นกนางแอ่นตะโพกแดง

(Elongate tail streamers extend up to a further 2 cm.) From other swallows by square, pale rufous-buff to chestnut rump and by black under tail coverts; lacks any white in tail. Underparts whitish with dark streaks of variable boldness. Race *H. d. badia*, resident in the Peninsula, has deep chestnut underparts. (This, and the heavily streaked, short distance migrant and resident races *mayri*, *stanfordi* and *vernayi* are sometimes treated as a separate species: Striated Swallow *H. striolata*.) Broader wings than Barn Swallow. **Voice:** a loud, metallic *cheenk*. **Habitat:** both open and wooded country, crags, from plains to the highest elevations. Common winter visitor; locally common resident.

Plate 80 Swallows

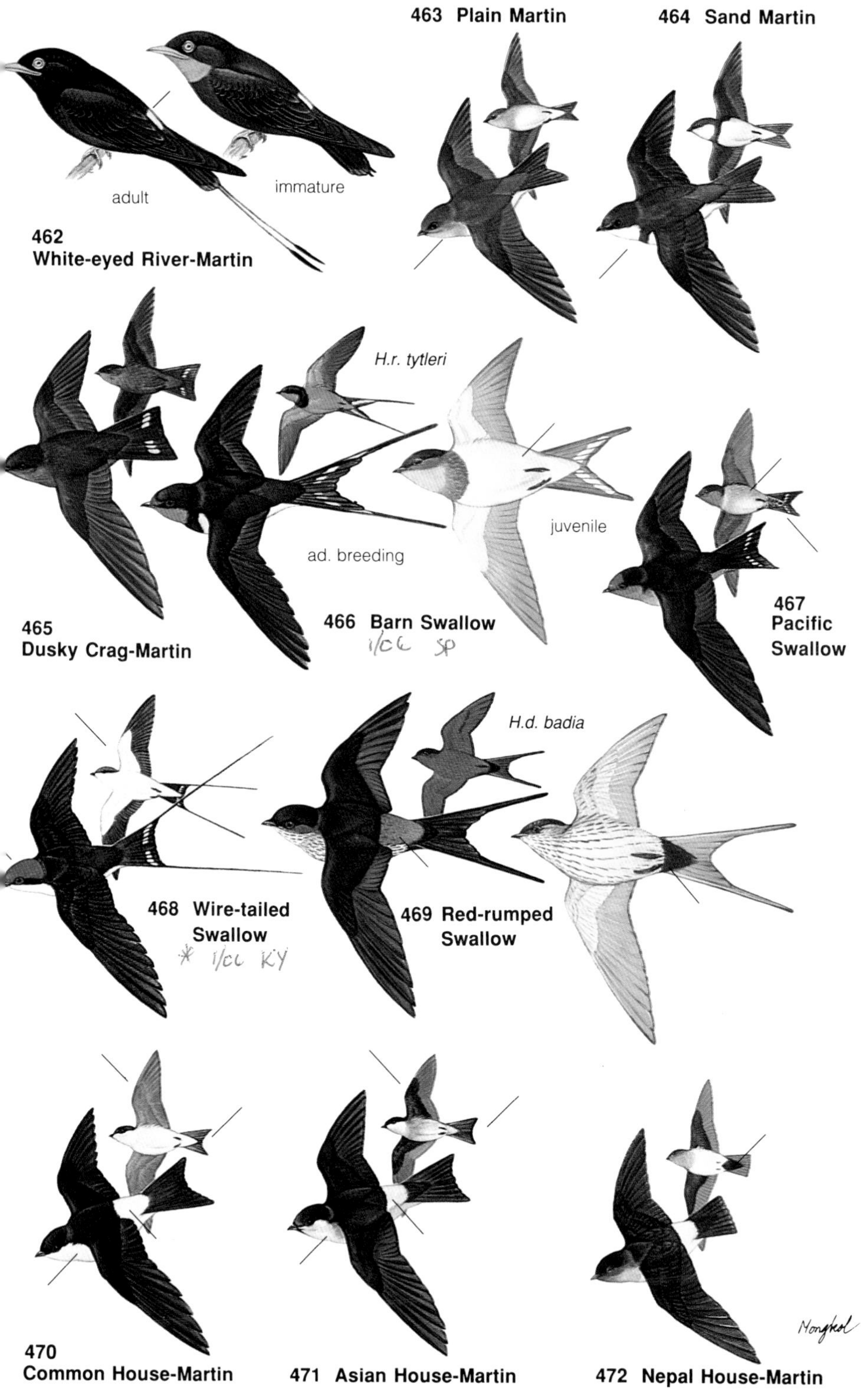

463 Plain Martin

464 Sand Martin

adult   immature

462
White-eyed River-Martin

H.r. tytleri

465
Dusky Crag-Martin

ad. breeding

juvenile

466 Barn Swallow
i/cc sp

467
Pacific
Swallow

468 Wire-tailed
Swallow
* i/cc KY

H.d. badia

469 Red-rumped
Swallow

Mongkol

470
Common House-Martin

471 Asian House-Martin

472 Nepal House-Martin

470. Common House-Martin *Delichon urbica* S: 14 นกนางแอ่นมาตินพันธุ์ไซบีเรีย

Distinguished from Asian House-Martin by larger white patch on rump and upper tail coverts, by uniform greyish underwing and by purer white underparts. Tail more deeply forked. **Habitat:** occurs over forests and open country, chiefly in hilly or mountainous areas, up to the highest summits. Rare winter visitor.

471. Asian House-Martin *Delichon dasypus* S: 13 นกนางแอ่นมาตินพันธุ์เอเซียใต้

Distinguished from Common House-Martin by smaller white rump patch, by slight dusky wash on breast and by contrast between sooty black underwing coverts and greyish flight feathers. Tail only slightly forked. **Habitat:** over forests and open wooded country, from plains to the highest summits. Fairly common winter visitor.

472. Nepal House-Martin *Delichon nipalensis* S: 12 นกนางแอ่นมาตินพันธุ์เนปาล

Distinguished from Asian House-Martin by black throat and under tail coverts; square tail. **Habitat:** rugged forested country, crags. Very rare winter visitor; only one sight record.

วงศ์นกจาบฝน

LARKS: Family *Alaudidae*. Terrestrial birds of open country, usually frequenting drier areas. Resemble pipits in their streaked, brownish plumage but have stouter bodies, heavier bills and shorter tails. Flight undulating, like pipits, but generally weaker, with more fluttering flight on broader wings. Some have beautiful and elaborate songs, often uttered in flight. Feed on both seeds and insects. Nest on the ground in small depressions with a loose lining of grass. World: 80 species. Thailand: 3 species.

473. Singing Bushlark *Mirafra javanica* S: 15 นกจาบฝนเสียงใส

Distinguished from Oriental Skylark by thick, stubby bill, brighter rufous wing patches and lack of any pale trailing edge to the wing in flight. From Rufous-winged Bushlark by slimmer build, slightly longer tail with white outer feathers (though these may be difficult to see when in worn plumage) and by much finer breast streaking. Ear coverts appear relatively uniform brownish. In flight, has a weaver-like shape, though flight is weak, with jerky wingbeats. Shy and unobtrusive; when flushed, does not usually call but flies only a short distance before dropping again to the ground. **Voice:** song is chat-like, with short, melodic whistled phrases; delivered either while perched on the ground or in a high, towering song flight on winnowing or flickering wings. **Habitat:** dry margins to marshy areas and paddy stubble. Local and uncommon resident.

237

474. Rufous-winged Bushlark *Mirafra assamica* S: 16   นกจาบฝนปีกแดง

Bill thicker than Oriental Skylark, but longer than that of Singing Bushlark. Orange-rufous edges to primaries and secondaries are conspicuous both at rest and in flight; lacks white in tail. Has coarse, spot-like streaks on breast. Ear coverts have pale centre and dark margins. Buffy white supercilia frequently appear to be joined across the nape by a narrow whitish line. Plumper-bodied and shorter-tailed than other larks. **Voice:** a loud *sweety-sweeow*, *sweety-sweeow*... uttered either from a low perch or on the ground, or in short upward flight and vertical descent to perch. Often sings from telegraph wires and never in soaring or towering flight like other species. Also has a long, drawn-out metallic trill. **Habitat:** cultivated areas, open scrublands of plains and lower hills. Usually in more wooded areas than other larks. Common resident.

475. Oriental Skylark *Alauda gulgula* S: 18   นกจาบฝนเสียงสวรรค์

Distinguished from bushlarks by noticeably thinner bill, more prominent crest which, though short, is often raised. In fresh plumage, shows rufous edges to primaries and secondaries though these are usually less prominent than in the bushlarks. Breast band of fine, dense streaks; broad buffy white supercilium. In flight, shows whitish sandy outer tail feathers and an indistinct, narrow buffy trailing edge to the wing. Flight strong. **Voice:** a sweet, high-pitched, incessant song, uttered in a high, soaring song flight. Call-note is a dry, twanging *chizz*. **Habitat:** nearly treeless open plains, including the dry margins of paddies and marshes and coastal flats. Uncommon resident; possibly also winter visitor.

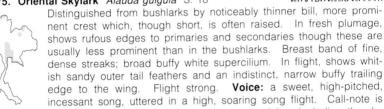

วงศ์นกเด้าดินและนกเด้าลม

PIPITS AND WAGTAILS: Family *Motacillidae*. Small to medium, slender terrestrial birds of (usually) open country. Thin bills. Rather long legs and tails which have white outer feathers. Mostly gregarious. Feed on insects usually caught from the ground, but also occasionally snatched from the air. World: 56 species. Thailand: 9 species.

เหล่านกเด้าดิน

PIPITS: Genus *Anthus*. Streaked brownish plumage; voice important in assisting identification. Longer-tailed, slimmer and thinner-billed than larks. Sexes usually similar.

476. Olive-backed Pipit (Olive Tree-Pipit) *Anthus hodgsoni* S:16   นกเด้าดินสวน

Identified by unstreaked or faintly-streaked olive upperparts, rump and upper tail coverts and by coarse black spotting on buffy upper breast; finer streaking usually extends to flanks. Shows distinctive head pattern of white spot on ear coverts below and behind creamy white supercilium and just above a blackish spot on hind lower margin of ear coverts. Often flies up to perch in trees when flushed. Shows constant, gentle up-and-down pumping of tail both when feeding and when perched. **Voice:** a hoarse *teez* in flight. Also a short, almost inaudible *tsi....tsi....* when at rest. **Habitat:** mostly in open forest, secondary growth and wooded cultivation from plains to the highest summits. Sometimes also in moist paddies, favouring shady areas. Common winter visitor.

238

477. Richard's Pipit *Anthus novaeseelandiae* S: 16–20   นกเด้าดินทุ่ง

Distinctive erect posture when alert; much longer legged than other pipits with a markedly long hind claw. General colour tawny-brown with upperparts streaked distinctly, but not heavily; unstreaked rump and upper tail coverts. Streaking on underparts is usually confined to upper breast; flanks tawny, unstreaked; long, broad, buffy-white supercilium and usually a bold dark margin to pale-centred ear coverts. Colouration varies somewhat; worn adults may be paler, almost creamy; juveniles more heavily streaked with brighter rusty or tawny suffusion on flanks. Migrant race *A. n. richardi* is much larger than any other pipit and shows heavier breast streaking than smaller resident races, *A. n. rufulus* and *A. n. malayensis*, which are sometimes treated as a separate species, the Paddyfield Pipit. **Voice:** resident races sing with *chew-ii, chew-ii* notes, delivered in undulating songflight, and call with an explosive *chip*. Migrant race *richardi* calls with a very loud, harsh and ringing *schree-ep*. **Habitat:** grasslands, paddyfields and open cultivated areas from plains to 1800 m. Very common resident and winter visitor.

478. Red-throated Pipit *Anthus cervinus* S: 16   นกเด้าดินอกแดง

Distinguished from other pipits by boldly streaked rump and upper tail coverts; relatively short-tailed appearance in flight and by distinctive call. Upperparts buffy-brown, closely and boldly dark-streaked; usually shows two buffy-white lines on mantle. **Adult:** rufous pink suffusion on face and breast. Dark malar stripe usually weak or lacking in males and streaking chiefly confined to flanks. Bolder, more extensive breast streaking in females (a few may lack any reddish colour and be as boldly streaked as immatures). **Immature:** buffy white underparts and supercilium; bold black malar stripe and ventral streaking. Usually lacks any reddish tinge. **Voice:** a highly distinctive, high-pitched and piercing *pseeoo*. **Habitat:** open areas, drier paddyfields and coastal flats; chiefly in the plains. Very common winter visitor.

479. Rosy Pipit *Anthus roseatus* S: 18   นกเด้าดินอกสีชมพู

Non-breeding: from other pipits by combination of bold, spot-like streaks on breast and flanks, recalling Olive-backed, together with coarse black streaking on greyish olive upperparts. Rump and upper tail coverts unstreaked or nearly so. Shows long whitish supercilium and submoustachial stripe which almost meet behind uniform greyish ear coverts. Sometimes shows a pale spot near hind margin of ear coverts and frequently a faint vinous-pink tinge on throat and breast. **Breeding:** throat, supercilium and upper breast vinous-pink, unstreaked. ◆ At all times from Red-throated Pipit by more coarsely-streaked upperparts which are greyish-tinged rather than brown-tinged, unstreaked rump and upper tail coverts and larger, longer-tailed appearance. **Voice:** flight call is a thin *tsip, tsip, tsip*, very similar to the call of the Meadow Pipit *A. pratensis* of Europe. **Habitat:** marshy areas, paddyfields, from plains to 1000 m. Local and uncommon winter visitor.

Plate 81 Larks, Pipits

73 Singing Bushlark

474 Rufous-winged Bushlark

75 Oriental Skylark

476 Olive-backed Pipit

A.n. rufulus

A.n. richardi

477 Richard's Pipit

♂

♀

immature

478 Red-throated Pipit

non-breeding

breeding

479 Rosy Pipit

240

เหล่านกเด้าลม

WAGTAILS: Genera *Motacilla, Dendronanthus*. Unstreaked, with brighter plumage and bolder markings than pipits. Long tails are wagged constantly; strongly undulating flight. Sexes usually differ.

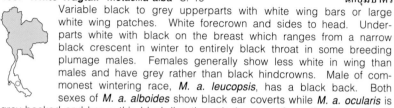

480. White Wagtail *Motacilla alba* S: 19 นกอุ้มบาตร
Variable black to grey upperparts with white wing bars or large white wing patches. White forecrown and sides to head. Underparts white with black on the breast which ranges from a narrow black crescent in winter to entirely black throat in some breeding plumage males. Females generally show less white in wing than males and have grey rather than black hindcrowns. Male of commonest wintering race, *M. a. leucopsis*, has a black back. Both sexes of *M. a. alboides* show black ear coverts while *M. a. ocularis* is grey-backed and has a thin black line through the eye. **Juvenile:** thinner black gorget and creamier underparts. **Voice:** a harsh, clearly disyllabic *chizzick*. **Habitat:** open country, grasslands, riverine sand bars, from plains to 2000 m. Common winter visitor.

481. Grey Wagtail *Motacilla cinerea* S: 19 นกเด้าลมหลังเทา
Distinguished from Yellow Wagtail by longer tail and by contrast between bright yellow-olive upper tail coverts and grey back. In flight, shows white wing bar along bases of flight feathers. Underparts vary from all bright yellow to creamy-whitish, but always shows bright yellow under tail coverts. **Male breeding:** black throat. **Voice:** a disyllabic *zittick*; sharper and more metallic than in White Wagtail. **Habitat:** open country and forested areas from plains to the highest summits. Prefers shady areas close to water, especially flowing streams. Very common winter visitor; usually the first autumn migrant to return in July.

482. Yellow Wagtail *Motacilla flava* S: 18 นกเด้าลมเหลือง
Distinguished from Grey Wagtail by slightly shorter tail, by call, concolorous greenish olive to brownish back and upper tail coverts and by lack of a white wing bar in flight. From pipits by unstreaked upperparts. **Adult male:** yellow underparts. Head dull bluish slaty, with darker ear coverts. Commonest wintering race, *M. f. angarensis*, has a thin white supercilium which is lacking in *M. f. macronyx*. Race *M. f. taivana* has a greenish crown and a usually yellow supercilium. **Female and immature:** mainly or entirely whitish below and dark olive to olive-brown above, with a white supercilium. All plumages show buffy-whitish to yellow-white wing bars (broader in immatures than adults) and narrow whitish edges to tertials. **Voice:** a harsh, monosyllabic but drawn-out, *chrzeep*. **Habitat:** grassy plains, cultivated fields, often near water. Also around the edges of mangroves and on dry coastal flats. Large numbers roost communally in mangroves and in reedbeds. Very common winter visitor.

Plate 82 Wagtails

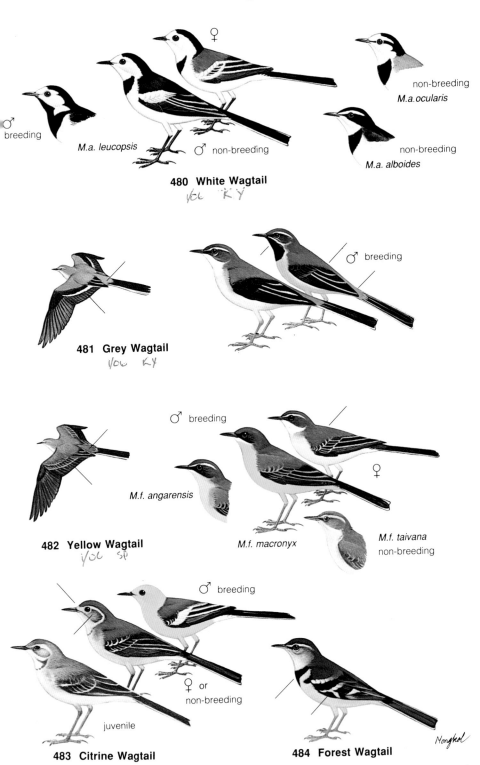

♀

non-breeding
M.a.oculars

♂ breeding

M.a. leucopsis

♂ non-breeding

non-breeding
M.a. alboides

480 White Wagtail
Voc KY

481 Grey Wagtail
Voc KY

♂ breeding

♂ breeding

M.f. angarensis

♀

482 Yellow Wagtail
Voc sp

M.f. macronyx

M.f. taivana
non-breeding

♂ breeding

♀ or
non-breeding

juvenile

483 Citrine Wagtail

484 Forest Wagtail

Mongkol

242

483. Citrine Wagtail (Yellow-hooded Wagtail) *Motacilla citreola* S: 19   นกเด้าลมหัวเหลือง

Non-breeding adults, breeding female: from Yellow Wagtail by yellow forehead and by yellow or pale-centred ear coverts. Supercilium appears to curve around hind margin of ear coverts on to side of neck. Upperparts greyish, usually with broad white wing bars and tertial edges (though these may be reduced by wear in late winter). **Immatures:** tend to have whiter underparts than non-breeding adults, contrasting with yellow face.   **Breeding male:** either grey or black mantle, with large white patch in wing and bright yellow head and underparts.   **Juvenile:** lacks yellow in plumage and shows dark patch on side of breast. Forehead may be dark or with only a slight buffy patch but still shows pale (whitish) centre to ear coverts and curving supercilium. ◆ Longer-legged and heavier-breasted than Yellow Wagtail.   **Voice:** a harsh *dzeep*, very similar to call of Yellow Wagtail. Also, less often, a diagnostic higher-pitched and less rasping *pzeeoow*.   **Habitat:** marshes, wet paddyfields, lake margins and riverine sandbars. Generally favours wetter conditions than Yellow Wagtail. Uncommon to locally common winter visitor.

484. Forest Wagtail *Dendronanthus indicus* S: 18   นกเด้าลมดง

Distinctive pattern of broad black and creamy-white stripes on folded wing and broad black breast bands on creamy-white underparts. Upperparts grey-brown with white supercilium and white outer tail feathers. Unlike other wagtails, sways from side to side and does not wag tail up and down. Frequently perches in trees.   **Voice:** a metallic *pink*.   **Habitat:** evergreen and deciduous forest, gardens, wooded cultivation and mangroves. From plains to 1500 m. Often roosts communally in large numbers in mangroves, together with Yellow Wagtail. Common winter visitor, especially in the south. Also passage migrant.

วงศ์นกเฉี่ยวและนกพญาไฟ

CUCKOO-SHRIKES, MINIVETS: Family *Campephagidae*. Arboreal birds with medium to long, rather pointed wings and longish, somewhat graduated tails: strong bills and short legs. Feed chiefly on insects and build shallow, cup-shaped nests often in forks of exposed branches of trees. **Cuckoo-shrikes** have greyish or black and white plumage, which differs only slightly between the sexes. **Minivets** are mainly bright-coloured, the males being chiefly red and the females yellow. World: ca. 79 species. Thailand: 18 species.

485. Pied Triller *Lalage nigra* S: 18   นกเขนน้อยคิ้วขาว

Shows white supercilium, black eye-line, grey rump and upper tail coverts and white tail-tip.   **Male:** black crown and back; unbarred white underparts.   **Female:** dark brownish grey crown and back; underparts finely barred grey.   **Juvenile:** resembles female, but upperparts browner, scaled with buff.   **Voice:** a disyllabic whistle, the second note lower. Also a descending series of nasal *chack* notes. **Habitat:** coastal scrub, plantations and gardens of lowlands and lower hills. Favours stands of *Casuarina* trees. Uncommon resident.

486. Bar-winged Flycatcher-shrike *Hemipus picatus* S: 15　นกเขนน้อยปีกแถบขาว
Male: black head, lacking supercilium; black or dark brown upperparts with white wing patch, white rump and tips to outer tail feathers. Underparts dusky white with vinous wash on upper breast. **Female:** duller, browner than male. ◆ See Little Pied Flycatcher (783). Slender and active, catching insects on the wing and by foliage-gleaning. Frequently found in bird-waves. **Voice:** a short, musical trill. **Habitat:** deciduous and evergreen forests, bamboo, secondary growth from plains to 1800 m. Very common resident.

487. Black-winged Flycatcher-shrike *Hemipus hirundinaceus* S: 15 นกเขนน้อยปีกดำ
Similar to respective sexes of Bar-winged Flycatcher-shrike, but lacks white in wings or tail. Male always has black back. **Voice:** similar to Bar-winged, but calls are generally shorter, harsher. **Habitat:** evergreen forest, including tall swamp forest, of the plains; mangroves. Local and uncommon resident.

488. Large Wood-shrike *Tephrodornis virgatus* S: 23　　นกเฉี่ยวดงหางสีน้ำตาล
Identified by relatively large size, thickset appearance and heavy black bill; shows black eye patch and white rump. From Common Wood-shrike also by lack of pale supercilium or white in tail. **Male:** upperparts greyish; underparts whitish. **Female:** upperparts browner than in male and mask slightly smaller, browner. **Juvenile:** upperparts scaled. ◆ Usually frequents canopy; commonly in small parties. **Voice:** a loud, ringing *pi-pi-pi-pi-pi*; rather more airy, less sharply whistled, and with a shorter interval between notes than similar whistling calls of Black-naped Monarch (809) and Asian Paradise-flycatcher (813). Also harsh scolding notes; *chreek, chreek, chreek.* **Habitat:** deciduous and evergreen forests, secondary growth from plains to 1400 m. Common resident.

489. Common Wood-shrike *Tephrodornis pondicerianus* S: 18　　นกเฉี่ยวดงธรรมดา
Smaller than preceding species, with proportionately longer tail and less heavy bill. Also differs in having broad, greyish white supercilium, white outer tail feathers and smaller, less distinct rump patch. Bears superficial resemblance to female Grey Bushchat (748). Usually in small parties among low trees. **Voice:** an accelerating trill; *pi-pi-i-i-i-i-i.* Similar in quality to song of Large Wood-shrike, but more rapid. **Habitat:** dry dipterocarp and mixed deciduous woodlands; open country with scattered trees, usually in plains and foothills but occasionally up to 1100 m. Fairly common resident.

490. Large Cuckoo-shrike *Coracina macei* S: 30　　　　　นกขี้เถ้าใหญ่
Large size and broad rounded wings in flight. Mainly grey plumage, the grey of the breast grading into whitish lower belly and under tail coverts. Diffuse blackish mask. Conspicuous pale greyish white edges to blackish flight feathers of wings. **Female:** usually shows some faint barring on lower breast and belly. ◆ Distinctive habit of flicking up each wing alternately after landing on perch. **Voice:** a loud, ringing *kle-eep*, uttered both from perch and while in flight. Also a chuckling note. **Habitat:** deciduous and the more open evergreen woodlands, pines; open areas with scattered trees. From plains to at least 1800 m. Fairly common resident.

491. Bar-bellied Cuckoo-shrike *Coracina striata* S: 30   นกขี้เถ้าลายขวาง

Male: very like Large Cuckoo-shrike, but less distinct mask and whitish or pale lemon eye. Rarely shows slight barring on upper tail coverts. Note range. **Female:** lower breast to under tail coverts distinctly barred black and white. Also has bars on rump and upper tail coverts. **Voice:** in flight, gives a series of clear whistles with a whinnying quality; *kliu-kliu-kliu-kliu* (M&W). **Habitat:** evergreen forest, including swamp forests and mangroves, secondary growth of the level lowlands. Rare resident. Probably much reduced due to lowland deforestation.

492. Indochinese Cuckoo-shrike *Coracina polioptera* S: 23   นกเฉี่ยวบุ้งกลาง

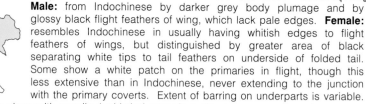

Distinguished from Large Cuckoo-shrike by smaller size, thinner bill and by broad white tips to tail feathers. From female and immature Black-winged by (usually) larger white patch in primaries, visible in flight and extending usually to the base of primary coverts. Both sexes show narrow whitish edges to primaries on folded wing. Additionally from Black-winged at rest by more extensive white tips to tail feathers, appearing barely separated by black and merging to form an almost solid white patch on the underside of folded tail; upperside of tail shows greyer central tail feathers than Black-winged. **Male:** body plumage unbarred. **Female:** thin white eye-ring. Shows fine barring on underparts and ear coverts. **Juvenile:** from female by barred rump and upper tail coverts. ◆ A sluggish feeder, usually moving with slow, deliberate actions through crowns and middle storey of trees. **Voice:** whistled song of 6–7 notes in a descending sequence. More rapidly uttered and more slurred than song of Black-winged. **Habitat:** deciduous woodlands from the plains to 1000 m. Fairly common resident.

493. Black-winged Cuckoo-shrike *Coracina melaschista* S: 24   นกเฉี่ยวบุ้งใหญ่

Male: from Indochinese by darker grey body plumage and by glossy black flight feathers of wing, which lack pale edges. **Female:** resembles Indochinese in usually having whitish edges to flight feathers of wings, but distinguished by greater area of black separating white tips to tail feathers on underside of folded tail. Some show a white patch on the primaries in flight, though this less extensive than in Indochinese, never extending to the junction with the primary coverts. Extent of barring on underparts is variable. **Voice:** sings with usually 4 whistled notes in a slower, more measured sequence than Indochinese; *wii wii jeeow jeeow*. **Habitat:** resident in evergreen forests from foothills to 1700 m. Wintering birds occur down to the plains in gardens and open areas with scattered trees. Common resident and winter visitor.

494. Lesser Cuckoo-shrike *Coracina fimbriata* S: 20   นกเฉี่ยวบุ้งเล็ก

Male: uniform dark grey body and black wings, resembling male Black-winged, but is smaller with smaller white tips to tail feathers. **Female:** distinct barring on underparts and ear coverts, like female Indochinese. Usually lacks a white wing patch in flight. **Voice:** a clear, whistled descending sequence. Delivery slow and measured, recalling song of Black-winged but up to 7 or 8 notes; *whip-whip, whip, wait, wait, wait, wait, wait* (M&W). **Habitat:** evergreen forests, plantations and secondary growth from plains to 900 m. Common resident.

Plate 83 Cuckoo-shrikes

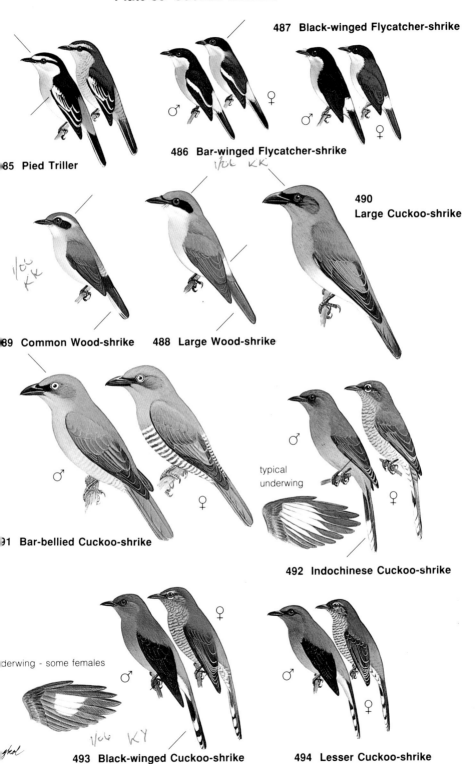

487 Black-winged Flycatcher-shrike

486 Bar-winged Flycatcher-shrike

1/oc KK

85 Pied Triller

490
Large Cuckoo-shrike

1/oc
KK

89 Common Wood-shrike   488 Large Wood-shrike

♂

typical
underwing

♀

91 Bar-bellied Cuckoo-shrike

492 Indochinese Cuckoo-shrike

♀

derwing - some females

♂

1/oc KY

493 Black-winged Cuckoo-shrike   494 Lesser Cuckoo-shrike

246

495. Ashy Minivet *Pericrocotus divaricatus* S: 20 นกพญาไฟสีเทา

Slimmer and much longer-tailed than any cuckoo-shrike. Rump and upper tail coverts are concolorous with mantle. Clean grey upperparts and white underparts; shows white wing bar in flight. **Male:** identified by conspicuous white forecrown and black hindcrown and nape. **Female:** crown and nape grey, with narrow white band on forehead and above lores. Difficult to separate from *cantonensis* race of Rosy Minivet. ◆ Often in flocks. **Voice:** a jingling trill. **Habitat:** evergreen and mixed deciduous forests, wooded gardens, mangroves and coastal vegetation. From plains to at least 1000 m. Passage birds sometimes occur even in towns. Fairly common winter visitor and passage migrant.

496. Rosy Minivet *Pericrocotus roseus* S: 20 นกพญาไฟสีกุหลาบ

Male: identified by grey crown and mantle, pinkish underparts and bright red wing and tail patches. **Female:** from other female minivets by pale, washed-out yellow underparts and greyish white throat. ◆ Both sexes of grey race *P. r. cantonensis* (sometimes treated as a separate species) resemble female Ashy Minivet but are distinguished by pale, buffy brown-tinged rump and upper tail coverts which contrast slightly with darker grey-brown mantle. Never shows black on hindcrown and nape; wing bar is usually slightly yellow-tinged. **Voice:** a trill like that of Ashy Minivet. **Habitat:** deciduous and evergreen forests from foothills to at least 1500 m. Fairly common winter visitor; often in large flocks.

497. Small Minivet *Pericrocotus cinnamomeus* S: 16 นกพญาไฟเล็ก

Small. **Male:** from male Grey-chinned Minivet by darker grey throat and by contrast between flame-orange upper breast, rump, upper tail coverts, wing and tail patches and yellower belly and under tail coverts. **Female:** grey forecrown. Flame-orange rump and upper tail coverts contrasts with washed-out, dusky yellowish belly. Throat and upper breast greyish white; wing and tail patches orange-yellow. **Voice:** a thin, drawn-out whistle, *tswee-eet*. **Habitat:** deciduous woodlands, open areas with scattered trees, gardens, from plains to 1000 m. Also in coastal scrub. Common resident.

498. Fiery Minivet *Pericrocotus igneus* S: 15 นกพญาไฟเล็กคอดำ

Small. **Male:** like a small version of male Scarlet Minivet, but distinguished by orange-yellow wing bar and by simple wing pattern, lacking a separate red patch on the secondaries. **Female:** identified by flame-orange rump and upper tail coverts and bright yellow underparts, throat and forecrown. Shows orange-yellow wing patch and outer tail feathers. **Voice:** *swee-eet* with rising inflection. Not as thin as call of Small Minivet and somewhat similar to call of Scarlet. **Habitat:** evergreen forest of the level lowlands. Uncommon resident.

Plate 84 Minivets

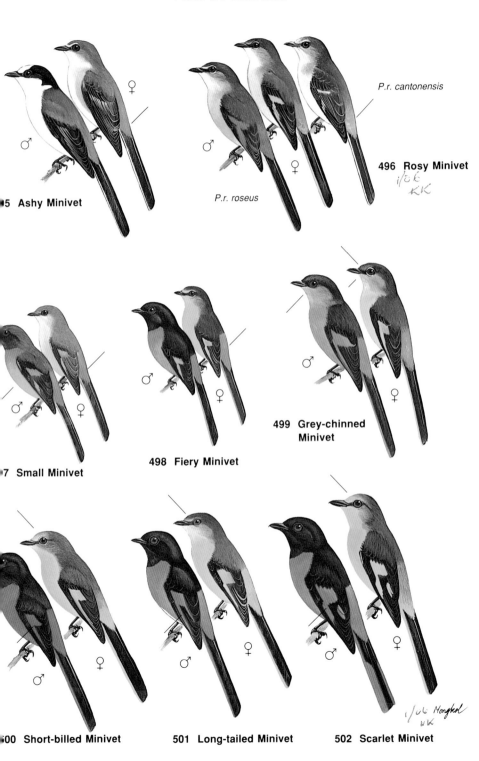

♀ **♂**

5 Ashy Minivet

P.r. roseus

♂ **♀**

P.r. cantonensis

496 Rosy Minivet
i/úb
KK

♂ **♀**

7 Small Minivet

♂ **♀**

498 Fiery Minivet

♂ **♀**

499 Grey-chinned
Minivet

♂ **♀**

00 Short-billed Minivet

♂ **♀**

501 Long-tailed Minivet

♂ **♀**

502 Scarlet Minivet

1/úb Mongkol
vK

248

499. Grey-chinned Minivet *Pericrocotus solaris* S: 18   นกพญาไฟคอเทา
Male: pale grey throat, often suffused orange. Underparts, rump and wing patches flame-orange. **Female:** lacks any yellow on forecrown; throat whitish and rest of underparts bright yellow. From female Long-tailed by call. ◆ Usually in pairs. **Voice:** a diagnostic *tsee-sip*, with a slightly rasping quality, somewhat recalling note of Vernal Hanging Parrot (279). **Habitat:** hill evergreen forests, secondary growth, from 1000 to 1800 m. Common resident.

500. Short-billed Minivet *Pericrocotus brevirostris* S: 19   นกพญาไฟแม่สะเรียง
Plumage of both sexes very bright, recalling Scarlet Minivet, but smaller, slimmer and proportionately longer-tailed with simple wing patch, lacking any markings on inner secondaries. **Male:** a more saturated red on underparts than male Long-tailed, with a single slash of red in the wing. **Female:** from females of Grey-chinned and Long-tailed by bright yellow on forecrown. ◆ Usually found in pairs. **Voice:** a loud, sweet monosyllabic whistle. **Habitat:** hill evergreen forests from 1000 to 2000 m. Common resident.

501. Long-tailed Minivet *Pericrocotus ethologus* S: 20   นกพญาไฟพันธุ์เหนือ
Male: from male Short-billed by wing patch like inverted 'U' and by less saturated, more pinkish red of underparts. More liable to show a longitudinal white patch between the legs than other minivets (though all species may show this). **Female:** difficult to distinguish from female Grey-chinned except at close range by indistinct dull yellowish suffusion above base of bill. ◆ Often found in flocks. **Voice:** a diagnostic, sweet double whistle, *pi-ru*, the second note markedly lower than the first. **Habitat:** hill evergreen forest, pines, secondary growth from 900 to 1800 m. Usually in drier, more open areas than Short-billed Minivet. Common resident; probably also winter visitor or partial migrant.

502. Scarlet Minivet *Pericrocotus flammeus* S: 20-22   นกพญาไฟใหญ่
Stouter and proportionately shorter-tailed than other minivets (though form in Peninsula slightly smaller than continental birds). Both sexes possess a complex wing pattern with a second, roundish patch on the inner secondaries of the closed wing. **Male:** black head, throat, upperparts and upper breast; scarlet underparts, rump and wing patches. **Female:** bright yellow forecrown and entire underparts including throat; bright yellow rump and wing patches. (These parts bright orange-yellow in subadult male.) ◆ Seen in pairs or small parties. **Voice:** loud, piercing, whistled *sweeep-sweeep* notes. **Habitat:** evergreen and deciduous forests, secondary growth, from plains to 1700 m. Common resident.

วงศ์นกขมิ้นน้อยและนกเขียวก้านตอง
IORAS and LEAFBIRDS: Family *Chloropseidae*. Small, arboreal birds with mostly green plumage. (A recent taxonomic revision places leafbirds with fairy-bluebirds (559) in the Family *Irenidae* and separates Ioras as a subfamily of the crows, *Corvidae*.) World: 12 species. Thailand: 8 species.

IORAS: Genus *Aegithina*. Larger and slower-moving than warblers with heavier bills which have blue-grey lower mandible. Long, silky-white flank feathers are frequently puffed out over the base of the tail, giving a white-rumped appearance. Glean insects from foliage. Usually seen singly or in pairs. Build shallow and compact cup nests.

503. Green Iora *Aegithina viridissima* S: 14　　　นกขมิ้นน้อยสีเขียว

Male: dark olive-green plumage with yellow patch above and below eye forming a spectacle. Two broad white wing bars and black wings and tail. **Female:** similar to Common Iora, but plumage slightly more green tinged, with both wing bars yellowish. Shows slight yellow spectacle. **Voice:** chattering *tit-teeer* notes. **Habitat:** evergreen forest, forest edge below 800 m. Uncommon resident.

504. Common Iora *Aegithina tiphia* S: 15　　　นกขมิ้นน้อยธรรมดา

Bright yellow underparts and two white wing bars. Usually has white-rumped appearance (see above). **Male:** black wings and tail; frequently black back and hindcrown in the breeding season. **Female:** black of upperparts replaced by bright olive-green; underparts duller. Greater coverts wing bar tinged yellowish. **Voice:** highly variable. A long, drawn out whistle which slides abruptly down to a similarly long whistle an octave lower; *wheee-teooo*. Various other whistling and chattering notes. **Habitat:** mangroves, secondary growth, open woodland, gardens up to 1500 m. Very common resident.

505. Great Iora *Aegithina lafresnayei* S: 17　　　นกขมิ้นน้อยปีกสีเรียบ

From Common Iora by larger size and by lack of wing bars. From leafbirds by yellow underparts and blue-grey lower mandible. **Male:** upperparts variable from olive-green (as female) to blackish. **Voice:** sings with a rapid *chew chew chew*... **Habitat:** evergreen and mixed deciduous forests from plains up to 900 m. Common resident.

เหล่านกเขียวก้านตอง

LEAFBIRDS: Genus *Chloropsis*. Bright green plumage; some species are confusingly similar. Often take nectar and fruits, as well as gleaning the foliage for insects and sometimes accompany bird waves. Build loose cup nests, suspended hammock-like from twigs and outer branches. Have loud, drongo-like or bulbul-like chattering songs; often highly mimetic.

506. Lesser Green Leafbird *Chloropsis cyanopogon* S: 18　　นกเขียวก้านตองเล็ก

Lacks turquoise-blue in wing. From Greater Green Leafbird by noticeably smaller size. **Male:** from male Greater by narrow yellow border to black throat. **Female:** all green head, body and wings. From female Greater by lack of yellow eye-ring and no more than faint yellow suffusion on throat. Shows a thin blue moustache. **Habitat:** evergreen forest, forest edge from plains to 700 m. Common resident.

250

507. Greater Green Leafbird *Chloropsis sonnerati* S: 21   นกเขียวก้านตองใหญ่

Never shows more than a small blue shoulder patch at most. From Lesser Green Leafbird by larger size and much heavier bill. **Male:** from males of Lesser Green and Blue-winged by lack of yellowish border around black face and throat patch. **Female:** all green with fairly conspicuous and sharply defined yellow throat and eye-ring; slight blue moustache. **Habitat:** evergreen forest from plains to 900 m; mangroves. Common resident.

นกเขียวก้านตองหน้าผากสีทอง

508. Golden-fronted Leafbird *Chloropsis aurifrons* S: 20

Adult: bright orange forecrown and blue central throat patch, turquoise shoulder patch. **Juvenile:** plumage uniform green, lacking face markings and with no more than diffuse yellowish patch on forecrown. Bill slightly decurved. **Habitat:** dry dipterocarp and mixed deciduous forests, secondary growth, principally of the lowlands and lower hills. Only occasionally in evergreen, up to 1200 m. Very common resident.

นกเขียวก้านตองปีกสีฟ้า

509. Blue-winged Leafbird *Chloropsis cochinchinensis* S: 19

Turquoise-blue on flight feathers of wings and tail diagnostic. **Male:** black throat patch with yellow border; diffuse yellowish bronze tint on head and upper breast. **Female:** entirely green head and body; throat sometimes tinged turquoise-blue. Thin blue moustache. Turquoise-blue in flight feathers duller than in male. **Habitat:** evergreen and mixed deciduous forests, secondary growth from plains to 1200 m. Very common resident.

นกเขียวก้านตองท้องสีส้ม

510. Orange-bellied Leafbird *Chloropsis hardwickii* S: 20

Diagnostic orange belly and under tail coverts in both sexes. **Male:** black face, throat and upper breast; deep blue in wings and tail. Orange of underparts brighter and more extensive than in female. **Female:** green head and breast. Orange restricted to belly. **Juvenile:** entirely green, lacking belly patch. **Habitat:** evergreen forests from 600 – 2000 m. Fairly common resident.

วงศ์นกปรอด

BULBULS: Family *Pycnonotidae*. Medium-sized arboreal birds with soft plumage; frequently crested. Very vocal; most have pleasant songs and harsher calls. Gregarious and not usually shy. Feed to a great extent upon fruit and several species can often be found together in fruiting trees. Sexes usually similar; build flimsy, shallow, cup-shaped nests of grass and leaves, placed in bushes or low trees. World: 125 species. Thailand: 36 species. (See also under Additions, page 400).

Plate 85 Ioras, Leafbirds

♀
♂

503 Green Iora

♀
♂

504 Common Iora

♀
♂

505 Great Iora

♀
♂

506 Lesser Green Leafbird

♀
♂

507 Greater Green Leafbird

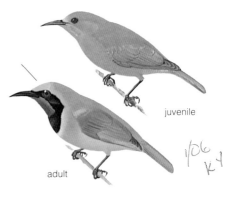

juvenile

adult

508 Golden-fronted Leafbird

♀
♂

509 Blue-winged Leafbird

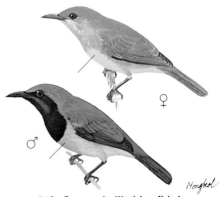

♀
♂

510 Orange-bellied Leafbird

Mongkol

252

Genera *Spizixos, Pycnonotus.* Typically birds of forest edge and secondary growth and many species· even enter ·gardens, cultivation. Most have bright plumage.

511. Crested Finchbill *Spizixos canifrons* S: 22   นกปรอดหงอนปากหนา
Short and heavy yellowish bill; grey head with distinctive forward-pointing crest and bright yellow-green body plumage. Tail shows a broad blackish terminal band. **Voice:** calls with a long, dry, bubbling trill. **Habitat:** scrub and secondary growth of mountains, above 1200 m. Locally common resident.

นกปรอดแม่พะ, นกปรอดแม่ทะ

512. Straw-headed Bulbul *Pycnonotus zeylanicus* S: 29

Our largest bulbul. Yellowish head with black eye-line and moustache. Wings and tail olive-green; shows greyish white streaks on brownish breast and back. **Juvenile:** duller, brownish head. **Voice:** a rich, bubbling song with a melodious, almost oriole-like, quality; sometimes duets or sings in chorus. **Habitat:** evergreen forest and partly cleared country along the banks of larger streams and rivers, below 250 m. Rare resident; possibly now almost extirpated, due to a combination of habitat destruction and illegal capture for the cagebird trade.

513. Striated Bulbul *Pycnonotus striatus* S: 23   นกปรอดลาย
Easily identified by prominent crest, boldly streaked breast and belly, lemon yellow throat and under tail coverts. Upperparts bright olive-green with thin whitish streaks on crown and mantle. **Voice:** a distinctive, repeated disyllabic call, *chi-chirp.* **Habitat:** forest edge, secondary growth from 1200 m to the highest summits. Fairly common resident.

514. Black-headed Bulbul *Pycnonotus atriceps* S: 18   นกปรอดทอง
Diagnostic yellow terminal band and blackish subterminal band to tail. Head rounded, lacking crest. Body plumage yellow-olive, brighter on underparts, and contrasting with blackish brown primaries and primary coverts. Eye blue. A rare colour morph shows a slaty grey breast, upper belly and neck collar. **Voice:** a hesitant series of short, tuneless whistles; calls with a ringing, metallic *chewp.* **Habitat:** mixed deciduous and evergreen forests, forest edge and secondary growth from plains to (rarely) 1600 m. Common resident.

515. Black-crested Bulbul *Pycnonotus melanicterus* S: 19   นกปรอดเหลืองหัวจุก

Tall black crest, black head, with olive upperparts and bright yellow underparts. Tail unmarked. Eye white. Throat red in race *P. m. johnsoni* of the eastern provinces. **Voice:** a cheery, slurred whistling; *whit-whaet-ti-whaet.* **Habitat:** evergreen and mixed deciduous forests from plains to the highest summits. Very common resident.

Plate 86 Bulbuls I

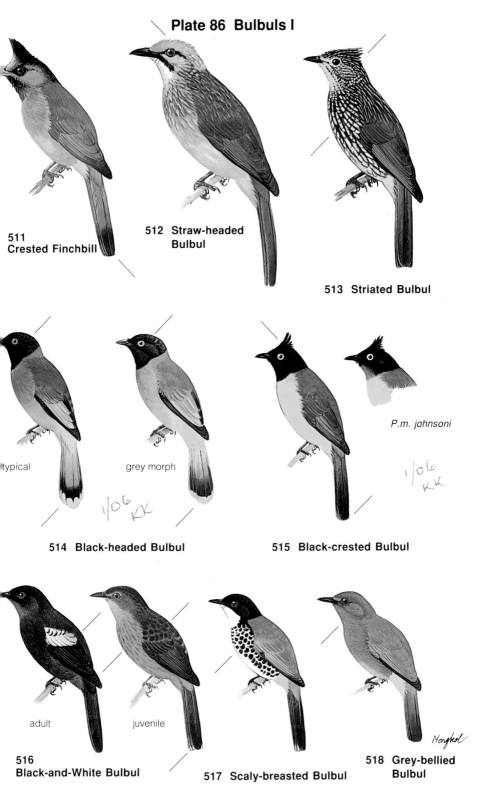

511
Crested Finchbill

512 Straw-headed
Bulbul

513 Striated Bulbul

typical

grey morph

P.m. johnsoni

514 Black-headed Bulbul

515 Black-crested Bulbul

adult

juvenile

516
Black-and-White Bulbul

517 Scaly-breasted Bulbul

518 Grey-bellied
Bulbul

Mongkol

254

516. Black-and-White Bulbul *Pycnonotus melanoleucos* S: 18 นกปรอดดำปีกขาว
Adult: easily identified by black plumage, large white wing patch and white wing lining. **Juvenile:** dark brown above, and paler grey brown on underparts, which are indistinctly mottled and streaked. Lacks wing patch. ◆ Rather little known; apparently forages over very wide areas, usually frequenting canopy. **Voice:** an unobtrusive, tuneless disyllable, *pet-it.* **Habitat:** evergreen forests from plains to 1800 m. Uncommon or rare resident.

517. Scaly-breasted Bulbul *Pycnonotus squamatus* S: 16 นกปรอดอกลายเกล็ด
Black head, which sharply contrasts with white throat. Blackish breast and flanks are prominently white-scaled; yellow under tail coverts. Has yellowish upper tail coverts and black tail with broad white tips to outer feathers. Blackish outer primaries contrast with bright yellow-olive of wings. Usually frequents canopy. **Voice:** calls with a series of sharp *wit* notes. **Habitat:** evergreen forests of the hill slopes, up to 1000 m. Fairly common resident.

518. Grey-bellied Bulbul *Pycnonotus cyaniventris* S: 16 นกปรอดท้องสีเทา
Grey head, breast and belly, blackish lores and yellow vent. Blackish outer primaries contrast with bright yellow-olive of rest of upperparts. No more than faint, narrow, whitish tips to outer tail feathers. Frequents canopy. **Voice:** a bubbling or trilling whistle, which descends slightly in tone; *pi-pi-pi-pi-pi-pi-pi.* **Habitat:** evergreen forest, forest edge from plains to 1000 m. Common resident.

519. Red-whiskered Bulbul *Pycnonotus jocosus* S: 20 นกปรอดหัวโขน
Tall, erect black crest and thin black malar stripe joining blackish partial necklace. Small red spot below eye is difficult to discern. White cheeks and underparts, red under tail coverts. Upperparts uniform brownish, with white-tipped outer tail feathers. **Juvenile:** lacks red whiskers; under tail coverts paler, pinkish. **Voice:** a varied, musical whistled phrase; *wit-ti-waet.* Also a musical *prroop* call, recalling notes of some bee-eaters. **Habitat:** open country, scrub, clearings, cultivation from plains to at least 1800 m. Shuns the driest areas. Very common resident.

นกปรอดหัวโขนก้นเหลือง
520. Brown-breasted Bulbul *Pycnonotus xanthorrhous* S: 20
Diagnostic brown breast band, contrasting with clear white throat; whitish lower breast and belly and yellow under tail coverts. Short black crest, black lores and moustache and brown cheeks. From Sooty-headed Bulbul by uniform brown upperparts and lack of white in tail. **Voice:** a harsh *brzzp.* **Habitat:** scrub, secondary growth and clearings, above 1200 m. Locally common resident.

Plate 87 Bulbuls II

519
Red-whiskered
Bulbul 1/06
KY

520 Brown-breasted
Bulbul

521 Sooty-headed Bulbul
1/06 KY

522
Puff-backed Bulbul

523 Stripe-throated Bulbul
Voc KK

524 Flavescent Bulbul
1/06 KK

525
Yellow-vented Bulbul

Mongkol

526 Olive-winged Bulbul

527 Streak-eared Bulbul
1/06 SP

256

521. Sooty-headed Bulbul *Pycnonotus aurigaster* S: 20   นกปรอดหัวสีเขม่า

Short black crest, black facial mask contrasting with whitish grey cheeks. Upperparts grey-brown with whitish patch on upper tail coverts; tail broadly white-tipped. Underparts greyish white. Dimorphic; under tail coverts may be either red or yellow. **Voice:** mellow chuckles and harsh rasping notes. **Habitat:** dry scrub, gardens, cultivation and open woodlands, from plains to at least 1800 m. Very common resident.

522. Puff-backed Bulbul *Pycnonotus eutilotus* S: 23   นกปรอดหงอนหลังลาย

Distinguished from other crested, brown-backed bulbuls by more rufescent wings and tail and by clean white underparts, with slight greyish wash on upper breast. Narrow white or buff tips to outer tail feathers (occasionally absent). Eyes usually red, sometimes brown. Usually frequents middle storey. **Voice:** a loud, cheerful, whistling; *tju-li-lip, tju-lip.* **Habitat:** evergreen forest, forest edge of plains and foothills. Uncommon resident.

523. Stripe-throated Bulbul *Pycnonotus finlaysoni* S: 19   นกปรอดคอลาย

Diagnostic yellow streaks on forecrown, face and throat. Breast and belly pale greyish and under tail coverts yellow. Crown and back greyish olive; wings and tail brighter, greenish olive. **Voice:** a musical squawking, *whic-ic, whic-ic.* **Habitat:** mixed deciduous and evergreen forests, forest edge, secondary growth, clearings, from plains to 900 m. Common resident.

524. Flavescent Bulbul *Pycnonotus flavescens* S: 22   นกปรอดหัวตาขาว
Greyish head and throat, with blackish lores and short white supercilium in front of eye; short crest. Body dull yellowish olive, brighter on underparts; yellow under tail coverts. **Juvenile:** head yellower, with less conspicuous supercilium. **Voice:** harsh, buzzing *tcherrp* notes. **Habitat:** scrub, clearings, grassland, from 900 m to the highest summits. Common resident.

525. Yellow-vented Bulbul *Pycnonotus goiavier* S: 20   นกปรอดหน้านวล
Distinctive head pattern of broad white supercilium, whitish throat and sides of head, contrasting with black lores and blackish brown centre to crown. Upperparts dark brown; underparts whitish with yellow under tail coverts. **Voice:** a sweet musical chuckle; also a harsh, sharp *chwich-chwich* call. **Habitat:** cultivated areas, scrub, palm groves and secondary growth, chiefly in well-watered or coastal sites. Common resident.

526. Olive-winged Bulbul *Pycnonotus plumosus* S: 20   นกปรอดสีไพลใหญ่

Upperparts slightly darker than those of Streak-eared Bulbul, with obvious olive-green edges to feathers of wings and tail, and a greyish tinged crown. Streaks on ear coverts are slightly less pronounced than in Streak-eared and under tail coverts are buffy brown. Eye reddish (brown in juvenile). **Voice:** squeaky chattering notes which are more musical and less dry and rasping than those of Streak-eared, recalling Stripe-throated Bulbul. **Habitat:** lowland secondary growth and coastal scrub, islands. Common resident.

527. Streak-eared Bulbul *Pycnonotus blanfordi* S: 20   นกปรอดสวน

Rather nondescript, brownish, apart from greyish white streaks on ear coverts and yellow-tinged under tail coverts. Paler and browner than Olive-winged Bulbul. Eye grey in male, duller grey-brown in females and juveniles. **Voice:** a harsh, rasping *which-which-which*. Also gives an unobtrusive, quiet, squeaky warbling subsong. **Habitat:** mixed deciduous forests, scrub, gardens, cultivated areas including those of towns and cities. Chiefly lowlands. Very common resident.

528. Cream-vented Bulbul *Pycnonotus simplex* S: 18   นกปรอดสีน้ำตาลตาขาว

Rather nondescript. From Red-eyed Bulbul by white eye (dull yellow-orange in juvenile) and by paler underparts with buffy or creamy throat, under tail coverts and centre of belly. **Voice:** a subdued, dry, unmusical chattering. **Habitat:** evergreen forest and forest edge, secondary growth from plains to 700 m. Uncommon to locally common resident.

529. Red-eyed Bulbul *Pycnonotus brunneus* S: 19   นกปรอดสีน้ำตาลตาแดง

Shows staring red eye (brownish in juvenile) but lacks any orbital ring. Shows less contrast between upperparts and more uniformly brownish buff underparts than Cream-vented. May show a slight olive cast to wings and tail, recalling Olive-winged. **Voice:** high-pitched bubbling or trilling, with sharply rising terminal notes; *pri-pri-pri-pri-pri-pit-pit*. Also calls with a strident, short *chi-chirrp*. **Habitat:** evergreen forest, forest edge and secondary growth from plains to 900 m. Common resident.

530. Spectacled Bulbul *Pycnonotus erythropthalmos* S: 16   นกปรอดเล็กท้องเทา

Noticeably smaller, with a thinner bill and a smaller, more rounded head than either of preceding two species. Distinctive thin orange orbital ring and dark red eye (brown in juvenile). Sides of head tinged greyish; white of throat and breast suffused greyish; belly and under tail coverts creamy-buff. **Voice:** a distinctive, high-pitched, metallic tinkling. **Habitat:** evergreen forest, forest edge and secondary growth from plains to 800 m. Common resident.

258

Genus *Criniger.* Have thicker bills than preceding group and are mostly drab-coloured. Throat feathers are often held puffed-out. Inhabit forest undergrowth and middle storey.

531. White-throated Bulbul *Criniger flaveolus* S: 22   นกปรอดโอ่งหน้าผากเทา

Tall, shaggy crest, white throat and bright yellow underparts. Much paler ashy, almost whitish, sides of head than either Puff-throated or Ochraceous Bulbuls, and more rufescent olive on upperparts. Whitish lores. Note restricted range. **Voice:** chacking calls are similar to Puff-throated but are sharper, higher-pitched and more metallic, *chi-chack chi-chack chi-chack.* Also has a nasal *cheer* note, recalling Grey-eyed Bulbul (539) but monosyllabic, lacking upward inflection. **Habitat:** evergreen forests from foothills to 1400 m. Uncommon to locally common resident.

532. Puff-throated Bulbul *Criniger pallidus* S: 24   นกปรอดโอ่งเมืองเหนือ

Brightness of yellow suffusion on underparts varies, but is never as bright as White-throated. Some birds with very faint yellow tinge are difficult to distinguish from Ochraceous Bulbul except by voice and range. **Voice:** a variety of harsh, squawking notes; *churrk, churrk, churrk* or *chick-it, chick-it.* Not known to give any whistled song. **Habitat:** evergreen forests, from foothills to 1200 m. Common resident.

533. Ochraceous Bulbul *Criniger ochraceus* S: 23   นกปรอดโอ่งท้องสีน้ำตาล

Distinguished from Puff-throated Bulbul by duller brown upperparts, lacking an olive tinge and by buffy brown underparts which lack any yellowish suffusion. Under tail coverts have a slight tawny hue. **Voice:** usually 2–3 weak, fluty whistles, *chiri, chiru,* followed by harsh chacking notes like those of Puff-throated. **Habitat:** evergreen forest from plains to 900 m. Common resident.

534. Grey-cheeked Bulbul *Criniger bres* S: 22   นกปรอดโอ่งแก้มเทา

Tones of plumage closely resemble those of Puff-throated, though is smaller, with a much shorter crest and a yellower belly, and does not overlap in range. Easily separated from Ochraceous by yellowish underparts and short crest. **Voice:** short whistles of similar quality to those of Ochraceous, but richer, more varied, with a rippling quality; *chiri, chiriu, chiru,* followed by harsh chacking notes. **Habitat:** evergreen forests, chiefly of the lowlands. Uncommon resident.

Plate 88 Bulbuls III

528
Cream-vented Bulbul

529 Red-eyed Bulbul

530 Spectacled Bulbul

531
White-throated Bulbul

532 Puff-throated Bulbul
1/06 KY

533 Ochraceous Bulbul
1/06 KK

534
Grey-cheeked Bulbul

535 Yellow-bellied Bulbul

536 Finsch's Bulbul

537 Hairy-backed
Bulbul

Mongkol

535. Yellow-bellied Bulbul *Criniger phaeocephalus* S: 20   นกปรอดโอ่งไร้หงอน
Lacks crest. Grey head with whitish lores, white throat, and bright yellow underparts diagnostic. Stubby, blackish bill. **Voice:** harsh, grating *scree*, *scree* notes; somewhat reminiscent of Blue Whistling Thrush (752). **Habitat:** evergreen forest from plains to 900 m. Fairly common resident.

536. Finsch's Bulbul *Criniger finschii* S: 17   นกปรอดสีคล้ำใต้คอเหลือง
Recognized by bright yellow throat, yellow centre to belly and under tail coverts, contrasting with dark olive upper breast. From Hairy-backed Bulbul by uniform dark olive sides of head; dark olive (not rufescent) tail. **Habitat:** evergreen forests from foothills to 600 m. Confined to the extreme southern provinces. Uncommon resident.

เหล่านกปรอดดง
Genus *Hypsipetes*. Have longer, more slender bills than other bulbuls. Most favour forest canopy, rarely descending to the low undergrowth. Often in large flocks at flowering or fruiting trees.

537. Hairy-backed Bulbul *Hypsipetes criniger* S: 17   นกปรอดหลังฟู
Shows diffuse yellowish area around eye and on sides of head which contrasts with olive-brown crown. Mottled, greyish white throat and upper breast grades into yellow belly and under tail coverts. Rufescent wings and tail. Frequents understorey. **Voice:** a scratchy warbling, and a long, clear ascending whistle. **Habitat:** evergreen forests from plains to 900 m. Fairly common resident.

538. Olive Bulbul *Hypsipetes viridescens* S: 19   นกปรอดเล็กสีไพลตาแดง
Very similar to Grey-eyed Bulbul, but distinguished by voice, slightly yellower breast and belly and by dark reddish to brown eyes. Tawny under tail coverts. Note restricted range; often occurs alongside White-throated Bulbul (531). **Voice:** a disyllabic musical *whe-ic*, very like Buff-vented Bulbul; less nasal than Grey-eyed. **Habitat:** evergreen and occasionally mixed deciduous forests, from foothills to at least 900 m. Locally common resident.

Plate 89 Bulbuls IV

538 Olive Bulbul

539 Grey-eyed Bulbul

540 Buff-vented Bulbul

541 Mountain Bulbul

542 Streaked Bulbul

H.f. cinereus

543 Ashy Bulbul

544 Black Bulbul

H.m. leucothorax

H.m. stresemanni

545 White-headed Bulbul

262

539. Grey-eyed Bulbul *Hypsipetes propinquus* S: 19   นกปรอดเล็กตาขาว

Distinctive whitish grey eyes, like Buff-vented Bulbul, though can often be difficult to discern.   Best distinguished by voice and by tawny under tail coverts.   Dull yellowish on breast and belly, short, indistinct, yellowish grey supercilium and slight crest.   **Voice:** distinctive, nasal, mewing *cheer-y* cry.   Race *H. p. cinnamomeoventris* of the Peninsula gives a much less nasal *prrrit*; flatter and less musical than call of Buff-vented.   **Habitat:** evergreen forests, secondary growth from plains to 1100 m.   Very common resident; race in Peninsula is uncommon.

540. Buff-vented Bulbul *Hypsipetes charlottae* S: 20   นกปรอดหงอนตาขาว

Distinguished from Grey-eyed by duller, greyer breast and belly with at most only a faint yellowish tinge on the midline of the lower belly and by creamy-buff under tail coverts which lack any tawny suffusion.   From Olive Bulbul by range; greyish white eyes.   **Voice:** a musical *whe-ic*, very like call of Olive Bulbul and much less nasal than Grey-eyed.   **Habitat:** evergreen forests, secondary growth, from plains to 750 m.   Common resident.

541. Mountain Bulbul *Hypsipetes mcclellandii* S: 24   นกปรอดภูเขา

Narrow whitish streaks, both on grey throat and on shaggy, brownish crown.   Back, wings and tail bright yellow-olive; sides of head and neck and upper breast rufous-brown; lower breast and belly whitish and under tail coverts yellow.   Throat feathers often puffed-out.   Frequents canopy.   **Voice:** a metallic, ringing or squawking *tsiuc, tsiuc*.   **Habitat:** evergreen forests from 800 m to the highest summits.   Common resident.

542. Streaked Bulbul *Hypsipetes malaccensis* S: 23   นกปรอดหลังเขียวอกลาย

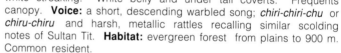

Dull olive upperparts and ashy grey throat and breast with narrow white streaking.   White belly and under tail coverts.   Frequents canopy.   **Voice:** a short, descending warbled song; *chiri-chiri-chu* or *chiru-chiru* and harsh, metallic rattles recalling similar scolding notes of Sultan Tit.   **Habitat:** evergreen forest from plains to 900 m.   Common resident.

543. Ashy Bulbul *Hypsipetes flavala* S: 20   นกปรอดสีขี้เถ้า

Blackish crest and face mask, with slaty grey upperparts and large, yellow-green patch in the wing.   Lower breast and belly strikingly white; greyish suffusion on upper breast.   Race *H. f. cinereus* from the Peninsula has uniformly grey wings.   Frequents upper middle storey and canopy.   **Voice:** a loud, ringing call of 4–5 notes, the second or third highest and the last two in descending sequence.   **Habitat:** evergreen forests of hill slopes, occurring as low as 200 m in the Peninsula, up to 2100 m.   Common resident.

544. Black Bulbul *Hypsipetes madagascariensis* S: 25 นกปรอดดำ

Blackish plumage, bright red bill and legs. Tail broadens terminally but is not deeply forked like a drongo. Shaggy head and throat feathers. Subspecies *H. m. stresemanni* (which has a white head) and *H. m. leucothorax* (white head and upper breast) occur only as migrant visitors. Often found in flocks. **Voice:** a four note sequence, similar to that of Ashy Bulbul, with second note highest; also a falling tone mewing, and metallic squawking notes. **Habitat:** evergreen and mixed deciduous forests, secondary growth, from 500 m to the highest summits; occasionally dispersing to lower elevations. Common resident and winter visitor.

545. White-headed Bulbul *Hypsipetes thompsoni* S: 20 นกปรอดเทาหัวขาว

Distinguished from white-headed forms of Black Bulbul by chestnut under tail coverts, greyer body plumage, more compact appearance and shorter bill. Shows black lores. **Voice:** calls are harsher, more buzzing than Black Bulbul. Sings with varied, short, scratchy or squeaky phrases, including a distinctive, rhythmic, *chit-chiriu, chit-chiriu.* **Habitat:** edge of evergreen forests, secondary growth, scrub and clearings, from 900 to 2000 m (occasionally descending to foothills). Uncommon resident; numbers may possibly be augmented by some winter visitors.

วงศ์นกแซงแซว

DRONGOS: Family *Dicruridae.* Usually black plumage; usually diagnostic tail shapes, but beware of moulting birds. Eyes often red in adults. Arboreal and conspicuous, usually hunting from exposed perches and catching insects on the wing. Found mostly in pairs when territorial, but sometimes in flocks in winter or when on migration. Noisy; harsh scolding notes alternate with varied, musical whistles. Frequently mimic the calls of other species. Build shallow cup nests placed in the forks of trees. World: 22 species. Thailand: 7 species.

546. Black Drongo *Dicrurus macrocercus* S: 28 นกแซงแซวหางปลา

Black, slightly glossy plumage and long, deeply forked tail with slight upturn. **Juvenile:** whitish scaling on abdomen and under wing coverts. ◆ The only drongo likely to be found in open country, often feeding in association with domestic cattle and taking the insects which they disturb. Often roosts communally in large numbers. **Habitat:** open scrub country, paddyfields and other cultivation, marshes, towns. Mostly plains but found up to 1200 m on passage. Common resident; very common winter visitor and passage migrant.

547. Ashy Drongo *Dicrurus leucophaeus* S: 29 นกแซงแซวสีเทา

Shape and proportions very like Black Drongo. Plumage variable, depending on subspecies, but never as black as in Black Drongo. Upperparts with slight gloss, always darker than more matt underparts which never show any iridescence. The resident races and some migrant races are dark, steely-grey. Migrant race *leucogenis* is pale ashy grey all over with whitish patch on side of head. **Voice:** often gives a characteristic mewing, Shikra-like call. **Habitat:** deciduous and evergreen forests, forest edge, clearings and secondary growth from the lowlands up to the highest elevations. In the Peninsula, resident birds are confined to mangroves, beach scrub. Common resident and winter visitor.

264

548. Crow-billed Drongo *Dicrurus annectans* S: 28   นกแซงแซวปากกา
Glossy black plumage. From Black Drongo by much heavier bill, slightly shorter and proportionately broader tail which widely splayed, though less deeply forked at tip. **Juvenile:** underparts boldly scaled whitish. ◆ Usually seen singly. **Voice:** loud musical whistles and churrs and a characteristic descending series of harp-like notes (M&W). **Habitat:** evergreen and mixed deciduous forests, mangroves and coastal vegetation, usually below 800 m but occasionally higher on passage. Fairly common winter visitor, principally in south; passage migrant. Possibly also local and uncommon breeder in lowland deciduous woodlands of the West.

549. Bronzed Drongo *Dicrurus aeneus* S: 23   นกแซงแซวเล็กเหลือบ
Noticeably smaller than other drongos, with a very glossy, metallic blue-green sheen on upperparts and across upper breast. Deeply forked tail. See Drongo Cuckoo (296). **Habitat:** edge and clearings of deciduous and evergreen forests, secondary growth from plains up to 2000 m. Common resident.

นกแซงแซวหางบ่วงเล็ก

550. Lesser Racket-tailed Drongo *Dicrurus remifer* S: 25
(Has elongate tail of a further 35 to 40 cm.) Glossy, metallic blue-green sheen on upperparts and upper breast. Flat tuft of feathers covering base of bill give a distinctive flat-headed appearance. Tail square-ended with very long naked shaft to outer feathers, terminating in elongate racket at tip. (Elongate feathers frequently missing, however.) See Large Niltava (792), Maroon-breasted Flycatcher (811). Commonly found in bird waves. **Habitat:** evergreen forests, usually above 800 m, up to the highest summits. Common resident.

นกแซงแซวหงอนขน

551. Hair-crested Drongo (Spangled Drongo) *Dicrurus hottentottus* S: 32
Identified by broad-ended tail, only slightly forked but with very pronounced upturn at tip. Long, tapering, slightly decurved bill and glossy metallic green sheen on upperparts and upper breast. Long, hair-like crest difficult to see in the field. Frequently found in flocks, feeding on nectar in flowering trees. **Habitat:** deciduous and evergreen forests, secondary growth, usually below 1000 m though up to 2000 m on passage. Sometimes in wooded gardens in winter. Common resident and winter visitor.

นกแซงแซวหางบ่วงใหญ่

552. Greater Racket-tailed Drongo *Dicrurus paradiseus* S: 32
(Has elongate tail of a further 30 cm.) From Lesser Racket-tailed by larger size and heavier bill with prominent crest at base. Shorter elongate tail feathers with twisted rackets. **Juvenile:** shorter crest and lacks rackets. From Lesser Racket-tailed by slightly forked tail. **Voice:** very loud and harsh whistles. A frequent call is of 4–5 whistles in ascending sequence. A prodigious mimic; frequently imitates calls of Blue-winged Pitta and Green Magpie. **Habitat:** deciduous and evergreen forests, orchards, plantations, usually of lower elevations though rarely up to 1700 m. Common resident.

Plate 90 Drongos

Ashy Drongo
migrant race
D.l. leucogenis

546 Black Drongo

Voc
SP

547 Ashy Drongo

1/06 KK

550 Lesser Racket-tailed Drongo

1/06
KK

48 Crow-billed Drongo

549 Bronzed Drongo

1/06
KK

552 Greater Racket-tailed Drongo

adult

1/06
KK

juvenile

Hair-crested Drongo

1/06
KK

Mongkol

วงศ์นกขมิ้น

ORIOLES: Family *Oriolidae*. Robust arboreal birds with colourful plumage. Swift, slightly undulating flight. Usually seen singly or in pairs. All species have similar, mellow and fluty songs, the phrases of which are highly variable. Call notes harsher, with nasal, mewing quality. Feed on fruit and insects and build cup-shaped nests placed in high trees, usually slightly below a forked branch. World: 29 species. Thailand: 6 species.

553. Dark-throated Oriole *Oriolus xanthonotus* S: 20   นกขมิ้นหัวดำเล็ก

Smaller than other orioles. In all plumages, shows white belly with broad black streaks and yellow under tail coverts. **Male:** black head, throat and upper breast. Yellow mantle and rump. **Female and immature:** upperparts uniform bright olive-green; throat, breast and belly whitish, streaked black. From immature Black-naped by smaller size, lack of dark eye-line and lack of yellow tinge on underparts. **Voice:** in addition to fluty whistling song, has a high-pitched piping *kyew* call, less nasal and rasping than calls of other orioles. **Habitat:** evergreen forest and wooded secondary growth of extreme lowlands up to 300 m. Uncommon resident; much reduced due to lowland forest destruction.

554. Black-naped Oriole *Oriolus chinensis* S: 27   นกขมิ้นท้ายทอยดำ

Distinguished from Slender-billed Oriole by heavier bill and, in adult male, by brighter plumage. Otherwise distinguished by broader black on nape; rump and upper tail coverts which slightly brighter, more yellowish than mantle. **Adult male:** mantle, rump and upperwing coverts bright golden-yellow as underparts. **Subadult male and female:** mantle and coverts duller, olive-yellow. **Immature:** dull yellowish olive upperparts and yellowish white underparts with bold black streaks; yellow under tail coverts. All but youngest stages usually show slight dark eye patch. ◆ Bill pinkish (blackish in juvenile). **Voice:** calls with a long, rasping and nasal *kyehhr*. Also gives fluty whistles. **Habitat:** evergreen and deciduous forests, mangroves, gardens and open country with scattered trees, from plains up to 1500 m. Common winter visitor; may possibly breed.

555. Slender-billed Oriole *Oriolus tenuirostris* S: 27   นกขมิ้นปากเรียว

Adult and immature plumages resemble Black-naped Oriole, with which sometimes considered conspecific, but distinguished by thinner bill and by narrower black patch across nape and by voice. Some birds may be inseparable from Black-naped, though never shows bright golden-yellow upperparts. **Voice:** a diagnostic, high-pitched, woodpecker-like *kick* (UT). **Habitat:** hill evergreen forest and secondary growth, up to 1500 m. Fairly common winter visitor; may over-summer and possibly breed in the hills of the extreme north-west.

556. Black-hooded Oriole *Oriolus xanthornus* S: 25   นกขมิ้นหัวดำใหญ่

Adult: yellow body plumage with black head and throat; black and yellow wings and tail. **Immature:** distribution of colour similar to adult, but eye-ring and forehead yellowish; throat whitish, densely streaked black. ◆ Bill pinkish-red in adult; blackish in juvenile. **Voice:** call-note is less harsh and rasping than in Black-naped. **Habitat:** dry dipterocarp and mixed deciduous woodlands and open, secondary evergreen forest, from plains up to 900 m. Occurs in mangroves in the Peninsula. Common resident.

Plate 91 Orioles, Fairy-bluebird

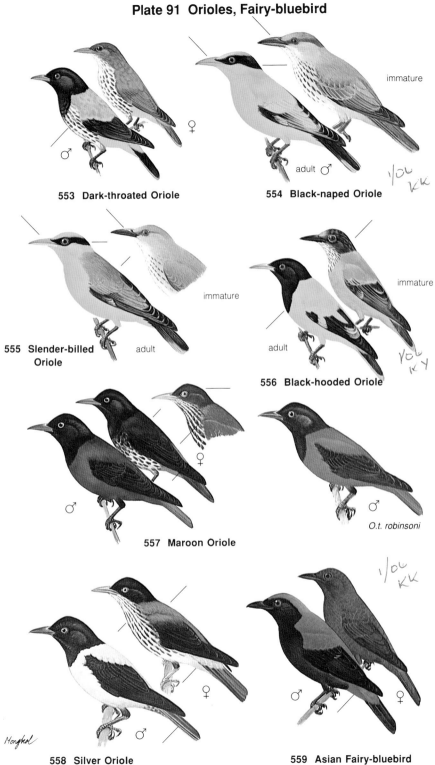

immature

♀

553 Dark-throated Oriole

adult ♂

554 Black-naped Oriole

immature

555 Slender-billed Oriole

adult

immature

adult

556 Black-hooded Oriole

♀

♂

557 Maroon Oriole

♂

O.t. robinsoni

Mongkol

♀

♂

558 Silver Oriole

♂

♀

559 Asian Fairy-bluebird

557. Maroon Oriole *Oriolus traillii* S: 27   นกขมิ้นแดง

Mainly dark plumage with pale blue-grey bill and straw-coloured iris: reddish maroon tail. **Male:** glossy black head, throat and wings; dark maroon body. Race *robinsoni* (a winter visitor) shows brighter reddish body plumage. **Female:** breast and belly whitish with coarse blackish streaks. Upper and under tail coverts maroon, blackish brown upperparts are not distinctly demarcated from black hood. May show either whitish or blackish throat. ◆ In silhouette, the long slender bill and habit of puffing out the crown feathers give a superficial resemblance to Black Bulbul. Often accompanies bird waves. **Voice:** a rich, fluty, *pi-lo-i-lo* song. The drawn-out, nasal squawking call-note is much less harsh than call of Black-naped. **Habitat:** evergreen forests above 800 m, though may disperse to lower elevation, deciduous woodlands during wet season; passage or wintering birds can also occur in extreme lowlands. Common resident; uncommon winter visitor.

558. Silver Oriole *Oriolus mellianus* S: 28   นกขมิ้นขาว

Male: silvery white body plumage with black head, throat and wings; maroon tail. **Female:** from female Maroon Oriole by underparts which whiter, and more finely streaked black, and by whitish to pinkish under tail coverts. Blackish head more sharply demarcated from greyer mantle and sides of breast. ◆ Sometimes considered conspecific with Maroon Oriole. **Habitat:** evergreen forests up to at least 800 m. Rare winter visitor.

วงศ์นกเขียวคราม

FAIRY-BLUEBIRDS: Family *Irenidae*. Actually related to leafbirds (506-510) but here placed with orioles for reasons of similarity of size and build. World: 2 species. Thailand: one species.

559. Asian Fairy-bluebird *Irena puella* S: 25   นกเขียวคราม

Male: Shows distinctive shining blue upperparts and under tail coverts. Rest of underparts, wings and tail black. **Female:** uniform, drab, dark turquoise-blue with blackish flight feathers. Red eye. See drongos, Maroon-breasted Flycatcher. ◆ Sometimes in flocks, feeding in fruiting or flowering trees. **Voice:** a liquid *tu-lip wae-waet-oo*; also various shorter liquid notes. **Habitat:** evergreen forests up to 1500 m. Also mixed deciduous forests, where scarcer. Common resident.

วงศ์กา

CROWS, JAYS and MAGPIES: Family *Corvidae*. Large perching birds with fairly long tails. Noisy and gregarious. Crows are black and frequent open areas and human habitation while jays and magpies are usually more brightly coloured, shyer and inhabit mostly wooded country. Omnivorous. Many species rob the nests of other birds. Most build flimsy, untidy, cup-shaped nests, usually placed in trees. Sexes similar. World: 110 species. Thailand: 11 species.

269

560. Crested Jay *Platylophus galericulatus* S: 33   นกกาน้อยหงอนยาว

Black plumage with white patch on side of neck and very long crest. **Juvenile:** browner with rusty spotting on wing coverts; dark grey underparts. ◆ Usually in small parties. **Voice:** a highly distinctive, harsh, grating rattle, *dat-at-at-at-at-at*. **Habitat:** evergreen forest from plains up to 750 m. Uncommon resident.

561. Eurasian Jay *Garrulus glandarius* S: 33   นกปีกลายสก๊อท

Striking white face with bold black moustache, black hindcrown and nape. In flight, shows white rump, black tail and blue patches in mainly black wings. Body plumage pinkish brown. Almost always in parties. Usually in treetops, but often drops to the ground to feed. **Voice:** a loud, rasping, drawn-out *shaak, shaak*. Often mimics other birds, giving a great variety of notes. **Habitat:** open evergreen, pine, and deciduous forests from plains up to 1800 m. Common resident.

นกสาลิกาเขียวหางสั้น

562. Eastern Green Magpie (Short-tailed Magpie) *Cissa hypoleuca* S: 35

Distinguished from Green Magpie by shorter tail and by lack of black and white tips to inner secondaries. Breast yellowish to yellowish green, paler than upperparts. **Voice:** a loud, screaming *keek-a-wee*. **Habitat:** evergreen forests from foothills up to 1500 m. Uncommon resident.

563. Green Magpie *Cissa chinensis* S: 38   นกสาลิกาเขียว

Distinguished from Eastern Green Magpie by black and white markings on tips of inner secondaries and by longer tail. Bright apple-green plumage, with striking chestnut-red in wings. Red bill and orbital ring and black eye patch. Often associates with bird waves, and particularly with mixed flocks of laughingthrushes. Shy. **Voice:** a loud, shrill *keek* ; a harsh rattle *kak-ak-ak-ak.....* **Habitat:** evergreen and mixed deciduous forests up to 1800 m. Common resident.

564. Blue Magpie *Urocissa erythrorhyncha* S: 66   นกขุนแผน

Very long, white-tipped tail, bright red bill, black head and throat and blue upperparts. Shows a whitish streak on the nape. Flies with short bursts of wingbeats, interspersed with short glides on outstretched wings. See Green-billed Malkoha (300). **Voice:** an airy scream; more drawn-out than call of Green Magpie. Very harsh, staccato notes, *cha-chak, cha-chak*. **Habitat:** deciduous woodlands; occasionally secondary growth, scrub and open evergreen woodlands, up to 1500 m (mostly lowlands). Uncommon to locally common resident.

270

565. Rufous Treepie *Dendrocitta vagabunda* S: 43 นกกะลิงเขียด

Light rufous-brown body plumage and sooty-grey head, neck and upper breast. From Grey Treepie by large pale grey wing patch and pale grey tail with sharply contrasting black tip. **Voice:** rattling, chacking and squawking notes. **Habitat:** dry dipterocarp and mixed deciduous woodlands, secondary growth of plains and lower hills. Uncommon to locally common resident.

566. Grey Treepie *Dendrocitta formosae* S: 38 นกกะลิงเขียดสีเทา

Distinguished from Rufous Treepie by small white patch at base of primaries, greyish underparts and greyish hindcrown and nape contrasting with black facial mask. Greyish instead of rufous rump and mainly blackish tail. **Voice:** a distinctive, ringing *kokil-ko-ko* and similar notes. **Habitat:** hill evergreen forests, secondary growth above 800 m. Common resident.

567. Racket-tailed Treepie *Crypsirina temia* S: 33 นกกาแวน

Smaller than other treepies. From drongos by proportionately longer, spatulate-ended tail and by thicker bill. Velvety-black face patch shows slight contrast with bronze-sheened body plumage. Blue eye. Does not usually flycatch like drongos and usually perches inside foliage rather than on exposed branches. **Voice:** a short nasal mewing call and a harsh *chraak-chraak*. **Habitat:** mangroves, scrub, secondary growth, bamboo and mixed deciduous woodlands, up to 900 m. Common resident.

568. Black Magpie *Platysmurus leucopterus* S: 41 นกกาน้อยแถบปีกขาว

Black plumage with white bar on wing coverts and secondaries. Short crest over base of bill and fairly long, heavy tail. Red eye. Inhabits upper and middle storey. **Voice:** a loud, discordant, metallic *keh-eh-eh-eh-eh* and a bell-like *tel-ope*. **Habitat:** lowland evergreen forest and forest edge below 200 m. Uncommon resident.

569. Large-billed Crow *Corvus macrorhynchos* S: 51 อีกา

Large, all black, with a massive bill. See cormorants, birds of prey. Direct flight, with slow regular wingbeats. Uses communal roosts. **Voice:** a low, harsh *kaak*. **Habitat:** open country and wooded areas, mangroves, towns and cities. From plains up to high mountains. Common resident.

Plate 92 Crows

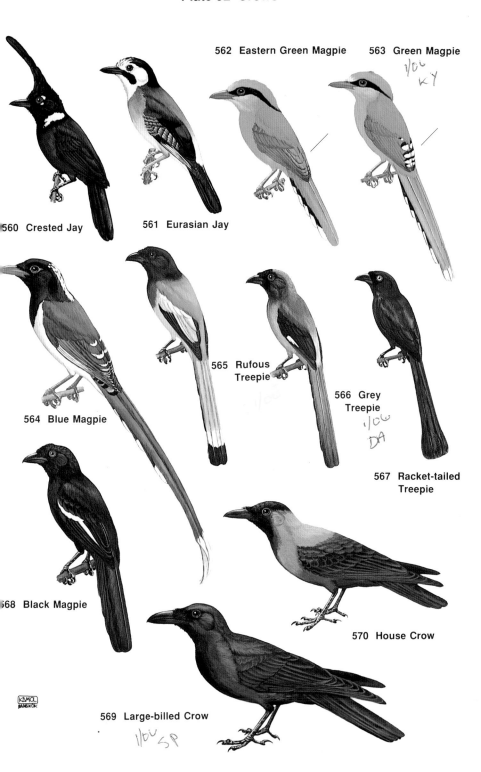

562 Eastern Green Magpie

563 Green Magpie

1/00 KY

560 Crested Jay

561 Eurasian Jay

564 Blue Magpie

565 Rufous Treepie

566 Grey Treepie

1/00 DA

567 Racket-tailed Treepie

568 Black Magpie

570 House Crow

569 Large-billed Crow

1/00 SP

272

570. House Crow *Corvus splendens* S: 43   อีแก

From Large-billed Crow by less massive bill and by greyish neck, breast and upper back. **Voice:** higher pitched than that of Large-billed Crow. **Habitat:** open plains, towns, coastal areas. Probably extirpated from Thailand; formerly known only from the vicinity of Phetchaburi, but not seen for many years.

วงศ์นกติ๊ด

TITS: Family *Aegithalidae*. Long-tailed Tits. World: 8 species. Thailand: one species, *Aegithalos*.

วงศ์นกติ๊ดแท้

TITS: Family *Paridae*. Penduline Tits and typical Tits. World: 58 species. Thailand: 5 species. Genera *Cephalopyrus, Sylviparus, Parus, Melanochlora*.

Small, plump bodies and short, conical bills. Noted for acrobatic postures, often clinging upside down to leaves or twigs. Flit actively through trees and undergrowth, occasionally feeding on ground. Usually in small flocks, often mixed with warblers, etc. Noisy; omnivorous. Cavity nesters, except for Aegithalidae and some Penduline Tits.

571. Black-throated Tit *Aegithalos concinnus* S: 10   นกติ๊ดหัวแดง

Tiny, with chestnut crown, black mask and round black patch on white throat. Chestnut flanks and narrow breast band; belly whitish. Mantle, wings and tail grey. Bears a superficial resemblance to Black-throated Parrotbill (655). Sometimes in large, single-species flocks outside the breeding season; otherwise usually in pairs. **Voice:** calls with a quiet *tup* and has other squeaky buzzing and chattering notes. **Habitat:** evergreen forest, above 1500 m. Locally common resident on Doi Pha Hom Pok.

572. Fire-capped Tit *Cephalopyrus flammiceps* S: 10   นกติ๊ดหน้าแดง

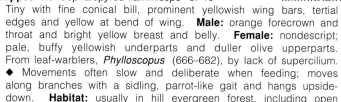

Tiny with fine conical bill, prominent yellowish wing bars, tertial edges and yellow at bend of wing. **Male:** orange forecrown and throat and bright yellow breast and belly. **Female:** nondescript; pale, buffy yellowish underparts and duller olive upperparts. From leaf-warblers, *Phylloscopus* (666–682), by lack of supercilium. ◆ Movements often slow and deliberate when feeding; moves along branches with a sidling, parrot-like gait and hangs upside-down. **Habitat:** usually in hill evergreen forest, including open forest, above 1400 m. Once recorded in riverine scrub of the plains. Rare winter visitor.

573. Yellow-browed Tit *Sylviparus modestus* S: 10   นกติ๊ดคิ้วเหลือง

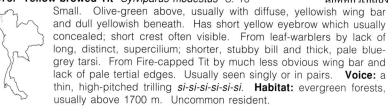

Small. Olive-green above, usually with diffuse, yellowish wing bar and dull yellowish beneath. Has short yellow eyebrow which usually concealed; short crest often visible. From leaf-warblers by lack of long, distinct, supercilium; shorter, stubby bill and thick, pale blue-grey tarsi. From Fire-capped Tit by much less obvious wing bar and lack of pale tertial edges. Usually seen singly or in pairs. **Voice:** a thin, high-pitched trilling *si-si-si-si-si-si*. **Habitat:** evergreen forests, usually above 1700 m. Uncommon resident.

574. Great Tit *Parus major* S: 13   นกติ๊ดใหญ่

White cheeks contrast with black head and throat. Whitish underparts with a bold black line down the center of the breast and belly. Greyish upperparts, tinged green on the mantle. **Voice:** calls with a metallic, explosive *pi-chi-chew.* **Habitat:** pines of hill evergreen and dry dipterocarp forests, usually above 800 m. Also inhabits mangroves and coastal woodland in the Peninsula.

575. Yellow-cheeked Tit *Parus spilonotus* S: 14   นกติ๊ดแก้มเหลือง

Easily recognised by yellow cheeks and forecrown and erect black crest. Greyish upperparts with bold white spots on wings. **Male:** yellow flanks; black throat extends into a broad band down center of breast and belly. **Female:** paler yellow flanks and dull greyish yellow throat and center of breast. **Voice:** sings with a loud, ringing *tee-cher, tee-cher.* **Habitat:** hill evergreen forests, above 900 m. Common resident.

576. Sultan Tit *Melanochlora sultanea* S: 20   นกติ๊ดสุลต่าน

Large size; shaggy yellow crest, yellow belly and under tail coverts. **Male:** black upperparts, face and upper breast. **Female and juvenile:** black of upperparts tinged olive; throat and breast slightly duller than in male. ◆ Usually keeps to canopy and upper branches of large trees. **Voice:** a loud, rapidly uttered, squeaky whistle *tcheery-tcheery-tcheery*; also a rattling, metallic *tji-jup.* Song is a series of up to about 5 loud, ringing *chew* notes. **Habitat:** evergreen and mixed deciduous forest; principally in lowlands, though found up to 1000 m. Uncommon to locally common resident.

วงศ์นกไต่ไม้

NUTHATCHES: Family *Sittidae.* Compact bodies, with short tails and sharply pointed bills, which they use both to probe into crevices for insects and their larvae and, in some species, to chisel open hard nuts and seeds. Often move head-first down tree trunks. Undulating flight. Build nests in natural tree holes or crevices. World: 23 species. Thailand: 5 species. (See also Additions, page 401.)

นกไต่ไม้ใต้โคนหางสีน้ำตาล

577. Chestnut-vented Nuthatch *Sitta nagaensis* S: 13

Blue-grey upperparts with black line through eye and small white subterminal tail spots. From Chestnut-bellied Nuthatch by contrast between pale greyish buff underparts and chestnut flanks and chestnut, white-scalloped, under tail coverts. Often found in bird waves, together with tits, babblers and warblers. **Voice:** a mellow, vibrating trill *duiduiduiduidui...* of about one second duration (JS). Gives a nasal mewing note in alarm. **Habitat:** hill evergreen forests above 1300 m. Fairly common resident.

274

578. Chestnut-bellied Nuthatch *Sitta castanea* S: 13   นกไต่ไม้ท้องสีเม็ดมะขาม

From Chestnut-vented Nuthatch by relatively uniform chestnut to pinkish buffy underparts with flanks same colour as centre of breast and belly. Under tail coverts grey or blackish with bold white tips. **Male:** shows contrast between whitish cheeks and chestnut underparts. **Female and juvenile:** paler, pinkish chestnut to vinous underparts showing much less contrast with whitish cheeks. Both sexes of the race *tonkinensis* of the extreme north are correspondingly darker. **Voice:** short trills, *prrt, prrt* ; like the 'telephone ringing tone' call of Dark-necked Tailorbird (702), but louder, more strident. **Habitat:** dry dipterocarp woodlands of the plains and lower hills. Uncommon to fairly common resident.

579. Velvet-fronted Nuthatch *Sitta frontalis* S: 12   นกไต่ไม้หน้าผากกำมะหยี่

Lacks white in tail; violet-blue upperparts with red bill and black patch on forehead. Whitish throat and vinous underparts. **Male:** thin black eyebrow. **Juvenile:** black bill. ◆ Often accompanies bird waves. **Voice:** a thin ringing *tsit-tsit-tsit.* **Habitat:** deciduous and evergreen forests from plains up to 1800 m. Very common resident.

580. Giant Nuthatch *Sitta magna* S: 20   นกไต่ไม้ใหญ่

Much larger than Chestnut-vented Nuthatch with pale grey central crown and broad black lateral head stripes. Underparts pale greyish with white-scalloped, chestnut under tail coverts. **Voice:** a short, repeated harsh chatter or cackle, *get-it-up.* Also a repeated single-note, clear, piping whistle. **Habitat:** open hill evergreen forests, usually in close association with pines, 1200 – 1800 m. Local and uncommon resident.

วงศ์นกไต่เปลือกไม้

NORTHERN TREECREEPERS: Family *Certhiidae.* Small birds with slender, curved bills and moderately long, graduated, stiff tails, which are used for support when climbing vertical trunks. Cryptically mottled upperparts, with a pale band at the base of primaries which is conspicuous in flight. When feeding, typically move upwards around tree trunks in a spiral and, after reaching upper branches, fly down to the base of an adjacent tree to begin climbing again. Feed on insects. Nest in tree holes or crevices. Sexes similar. World: 6 species. Thailand: one species.

581. Brown-throated Treecreeper *Certhia discolor* S: 16   นกไต่เปลือกไม้

Intricately mottled brownish upperparts with uniform rufous rump, upper tail coverts and tail and buffy supercilium. In the field, underparts appear whitish, with a light brownish wash on throat, flanks and under tail coverts. (In the hand, the underparts are revealed as being uniformly dark grey-brown.) See Rufous-winged Fulvetta (631). Favours areas with huge trees. **Voice:** sings with a series of explosive *tchi-chip* notes. **Habitat:** denser, moister, hill evergreen forests above 1400 m. Uncommon resident.

Plate 93 Tits, Nuthatches, Treecreeper, Dipper

572 **Fire-capped Tit**
♂ ♀

574 **Great Tit**

571 **Black-throated Tit**

♀
♂

575 **Yellow-cheeked Tit**

♂ ♀
576 **Sultan Tit**

showing
eyebrow

573 **Yellow-browed Tit**

577
**Chestnut-vented
Nuthatch**

♀
♂
S.c. tonkinensis

S.c. delacouri
♀
♂

578 **Chestnut-bellied Nuthatch**

♀
♂
579
Velvet-fronted Nuthatch

580 **Giant Nuthatch**

581 **Brown-throated Treecreeper**

582 **Brown Dipper**

Mongkol

276

วงศ์นกมุดน้ำ

DIPPERS: Family *Cinclidae.* Medium-sized, with plump, compact bodies and short tails. Inhabit swift-flowing streams, where they feed on aquatic insects caught while wading or swimming, using their wings to propel themselves under water. Rapid, direct flight. Sharp, shrill calls. Build dome-shaped nests placed in crevices or under overhangs. Sexes similar. World: 5 species. Thailand: one species.

582. Brown Dipper *Cinclus pallasii* S: 22 นกมุดน้ำ

Uniformly chocolate brown plumage with white eye-ring (and white nictitating membrane covering eye when blinking). Tail usually cocked. **Voice:** a shrill *zzit, zzit.* **Habitat:** rushing streams of forested hills from foothills up to 1000 m. Rare; status uncertain but possibly only a non-breeding visitor.

วงศ์นกกินแมลงโลกเก่า

BABBLERS: Family *Timaliidae.* A highly varied grouping of mainly insectivorous birds with strong feet, soft plumage, and short, rounded wings. Noisy and gregarious. Most have rather stereotyped, easily-imitated whistling songs and a variety of chattering notes. Many species duet. Mainly sedentary. Build cup-shaped or domed nests. Sexes usually similar and juveniles unspotted. (Very closely related to warblers and now usually placed in the same family, *Sylviidae.*) World: 253 species. Thailand: 70 species.

เหล่านกกินแมลงป่า

JUNGLE BABBLERS: Relatively plain-coloured birds. *Pellorneum* and *Trichastoma* are found in low undergrowth or on the ground. *Malacopteron* species are longer-tailed, more arboreal and have sweeter, much more complex songs.

583. Puff-throated Babbler *Pellorneum ruficeps* S: 17 นกจาบดินอกลาย

Recognised by rufous cap, whitish supercilium, bold face pattern and by streaked underparts. Upperparts unmarked. Throat feathers are often puffed out. Usually feeds on the ground and may adopt either a walking or hopping gait. **Voice:** the song is a continuous, undulating whistling; *sweety-swee-sweeow, sweety-swee-sweeow, sweety-swee-sweeow......* Calls with a diagnostic *pre-tee-sweet*; the first note often inaudible, the middle note highest, and the last falling in tone. Also makes harsh churring notes. **Habitat:** scrub, forest undergrowth and bamboo from plains up to 1800 m. Very common resident.

584. Black-capped Babbler *Pellorneum capistratum* S: 18 นกจาบดินหัวดำ

Black cap and moustache contrasting with grey cheeks and whitish supercilium, bright orange-rufous underparts and white throat. Feeds on the ground, usually with walking gait. **Voice:** usual call is a plaintive ringing *pi-uu*, falling in tone. Also gives an explosive, decending 3–4 note song, *pretty-too*, followed by squeaky chattering. **Habitat:** evergreen forest, from plains to 750 m. Common resident.

Plate 94 Jungle Babblers I

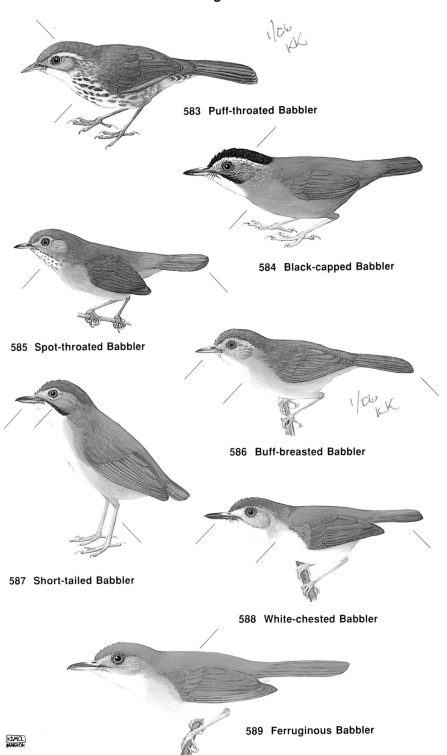

583 Puff-throated Babbler

584 Black-capped Babbler

585 Spot-throated Babbler

586 Buff-breasted Babbler

587 Short-tailed Babbler

588 White-chested Babbler

589 Ferruginous Babbler

278

585. **Spot-throated Babbler** *Pellorneum albiventre* S: 14 นกจาบดินสีน้ำตาลคอลาย
From Buff-breasted Babbler and from fulvettas by more strongly
rounded tail. Uniformly deep rufous-buff to rufous-brown underparts
and diagnostic whitish throat with fine, dark chevron-like spots (often
not easily discernible). Greyish sides to head. Keeps on or near
the ground; very highly skulking. **Voice:** a rich, warbling thrush-like
song, with the phrases varied, but repeated. Much less stereotyped
than other babbler songs. Also a sharp *pwit* and a plaintive piping
or mewing. **Habitat:** grassland, clearings, scrub and bamboo,
1100 – 2100 m. Uncommon resident.

586. **Buff-breasted Babbler** *Trichastoma tickelli* S: 15 นกกินแมลงป่าอกสีน้ำตาล
Rather nondescript; uniform warm, buffy underparts and buffy-brown
sides of head with chestnut eye. Smaller than Abbott's Babbler with
a proportionately longer tail and a finer bill. Pink feet. Frequents
understorey and low herbage. From Spot-throated Babbler by more
square-ended tail. See Brown-cheeked Fulvetta. **Voice:** a diagnostic
pi-chew, with emphasis on the lower second syllable. Also a wheezy
descending trill (often given in a duet) and a metallic churring.
Habitat: evergreen and occasionally mixed deciduous forests,
secondary growth, from plains to 1500 m. Common resident.

587. **Short-tailed Babbler** *Trichastoma malaccense* S: 15 นกกินแมลงป่าหางสั้น
Very short tail. From Horsfield's Babbler by pinkish feet, thinner bill
and by black moustache which contrasts with grey sides of head.
Clean white throat and breast with warm tawny-buff sides, flanks
and under tail coverts. Feeds on the ground. **Voice:** a dry trill
which leads into 6 or 7 loud, descending pitch whistles, *pi-pi-pi-pi-pi
pew, pew, pew, pew, pew, pew*. Rich and sibilant. **Habitat:** evergreen forests, secondary growth from plains to 900 m. Fairly
common resident.

588. **White-chested Babbler** *Trichastoma rostratum* S: 15 นกกินแมลงป่าโกงกาง
Identified by strikingly long, thin bill, moderately short tail and by
gleaming white underparts. Slight greyish wash on sides of breast.
Upperparts uniform dark brownish. Inhabits low bushes of streamsides and damp valley bottoms. **Voice:** a distinctive, slurred, 3 or 4
note whistle; *chiri-biri-bee* or *chiri-biri-bee-riu*. Also a harsh scolding
chatter. **Habitat:** evergreen forest, secondary growth below 200 m;
also mangroves, peat swamp forest. Uncommon resident; now
much reduced due to habitat destruction.

589. **Ferruginous Babbler** *Trichastoma bicolor* S: 18 นกกินแมลงป่าสีน้ำตาลแดง
Identified by bright orange-rufous crown, mantle, wings and tail.
Sides of head slightly duller brownish. Clean buffy-whitish underparts. Longer-tailed than most other *Trichastoma*. Usually in middle
and lower storey. **Voice:** a diagnostic, loud *huit*; a plaintive, ringing
piu and a soft trilling scold. The song, seldom heard, is a series of
whistles recalling Short-tailed Babbler. **Habitat:** evergreen forests,
below 200 m. Uncommon resident.

590. Horsfield's Babbler *Trichastoma sepiarium* S: 15 นกกินแมลงปากหนา

Like Abbott's Babbler, but much shorter-tailed; flanks and under tail coverts duller brownish. From Short-tailed Babbler by drabber plumage, lack of moustache and by much heavier bill. Greyish feet. Often near streams. **Voice:** usually three spaced whistles: *chip, chop, tiu* ; the middle note lowest and the last note stressed. **Habitat:** evergreen forest from foothills to 700 m. Rare resident.

591. Abbott's Babbler *Trichastoma abbotti* S: 17 นกกินแมลงป่าฝน

Heavy bill and moderately short tail; much plumper appearance than Buff-breasted Babbler. Olive brown upperparts with greyish sides to head and supercilium. Throat whitish; breast and belly warm brownish buff, shading to bright rusty on flanks and under tail coverts. Greyish feet. Favours rattans and similar undergrowth. **Voice:** 3–4 whistled notes, usually rendered as *three cheers for me*, with the last note highest, though some variation in dialect in different parts of the country. Sometimes duets, the mate often giving one or two *peep* notes. Also a short, buzzing and a plaintive piping or mewing. **Habitat:** evergreen forests, secondary growth, up to 900 m. Common resident.

นกกินแมลงหัวสีน้ำตาล

592. Moustached Babbler *Malacopteron magnirostre* S: 18

Distinguished by dark grey moustache (though often rather indistinct), greyish sides to head and by olive-brown crown which is no more than slightly darker than mantle. Strongly rufescent tail. Throat whitish; grey-brown wash across upper breast, sometimes appearing slightly streaked. Much heavier bill than Sooty-capped Babbler. **Juvenile:** in this and other *Malacopteron* species, shows uniformly flesh-coloured lower mandible. **Voice:** usually 4 or 5 rich, mournful whistles in descending sequence. Often followed by sharp *chwit* notes, given antiphonally by the mate. **Habitat:** evergreen forest, up to 900 m. Resident; usually the commonest *Malacopteron* of hill slopes in the Peninsula.

593. Sooty-capped Babbler *Malacopteron affine* S: 17 นกกินแมลงหัวสีคล้ำ

Distinguished from Moustached Babbler by absence of moustache, smaller size and by thinner bill. Almost blackish crown is noticeably darker than mantle. Underparts whitish with greyish wash across upper breast. **Juvenile:** crown paler, greyish, almost concolorous with mantle; wing feathers edged slightly rufous and lower mandible pale. **Voice:** song of about 8 hesitating whistles, undulating up and down the scale. Like primary song of Rufous-crowned but more rapid and stereotyped in delivery. Chattering notes are given antiphonally by the mate. Also a descending sequence of rapidly repeated double notes; *sweetoo, sweetoo, sweetoo.* **Habitat:** edges of evergreen forests of the level lowlands; peat swamp forest. Resident; now rare due to deforestation.

นกกินแมลงหัวแดงเล็ก

594. Scaly-crowned Babbler *Malacopteron cinereum* S: 17

Rufous crown and black nape (nape patch lacking or indistinct in birds from eastern Thailand). Black scales on crown are usually difficult to discern. Tail rufescent. From Rufous-crowned Babbler by smaller size, pinkish legs and by unstreaked brownish grey wash on otherwise whitish underparts. **Voice:** up to 6 wheezy, high-pitched whistles in ascending sequence. Also 3–4 clear whistles, with the middle or second note lowest; sharp *whit* notes are given simultaneously by the mate. Harsh, buzzing *tszi-jip* calls in alarm. **Habitat:** evergreen forests from plains to 800 m. Resident. Common in the Peninsula; uncommon elsewhere.

นกกินแมลงหัวแดงใหญ่

595. Rufous-crowned Babbler *Malacopteron magnum* S:18

Noticeably larger and clumsier than Scaly-crowned with greyish legs and slight grey streaking on breast. Lacks scales on the crown. **Voice:** a slow series of up to 12 rich whistles, somewhat undulating but in a mainly ascending sequence and often followed by a descending sequence. This is followed by a series of chattering notes, some of which are given antiphonally by the mate. The secondary song is a descending sequence, usually more rapid than the similar notes of Moustached Babbler. **Habitat:** evergreen forests of the extreme lowlands and foothills. Local and uncommon resident, much reduced due to lowland deforestation.

เหล่านกระวังไพร

SCIMITAR-BABBLERS: Genus *Pomatorhinus*. Have long, decurved bills and long tails. Usually in groups of one to three birds, often associating with laughingthrushes. Search for food in undergrowth and on the forest floor, though occasionally frequenting higher trees. Shy and quick to hide when alarmed. Most species have rather similar, soft rattling alarm calls in addition to diagnostic songs. Build domed nests on the ground or in low bushes.

นกระวังไพรปากยาว

596. Large Scimitar-Babbler *Pomatorhinus hypoleucos* S: 28

Large size and massive, horn-coloured bill. White-streaked supercilium and brown ear coverts with a rusty neck patch. Grey streaks on sides of breast and flanks. Often feeds on the ground. **Voice:** a distinctive, mellow triple hoot, *hu-hu-peh.* A pattern of 5–6 notes when two birds call antiphonally; *hu-hu-peh, hu-pi-hu.* **Habitat:** evergreen and mixed deciduous forest, bamboo, from plains to at least 1000 m. Fairly common resident.

นกระวังไพรแก้มสีน้ำตาล

597. Rusty-cheeked Scimitar-Babbler *Pomatorhinus erythrogenys* S: 26

Lacks supercilium; brownish bill. Cheeks, sides of breast, flanks and under tail coverts bright rusty. **Voice:** a mellow *plew-ip.* Also a pattern of 5–6 notes when two birds call antiphonally, a little reminiscent of the call of Large Scimitar-Babbler. **Habitat:** grassland, scrub and open hill evergreen forest from 1200 to 2000 m. Common resident.

Plate 95 Jungle Babblers II

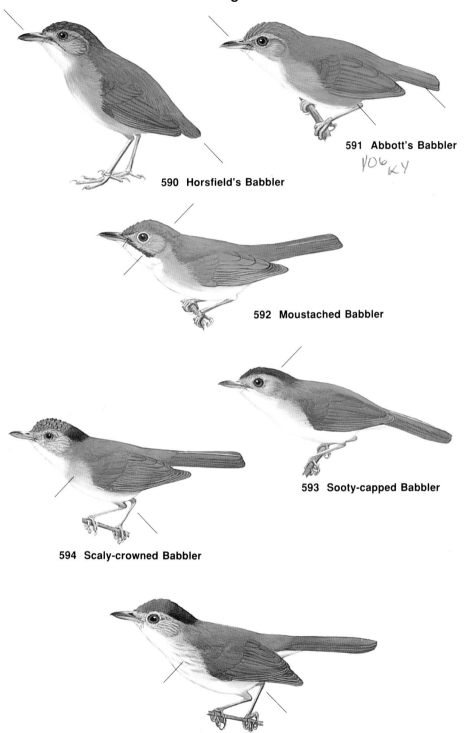

590 Horsfield's Babbler

591 Abbott's Babbler

592 Moustached Babbler

593 Sooty-capped Babbler

594 Scaly-crowned Babbler

595 Rufous-crowned Babbler

282

นกระวังไพรปากเหลือง

598. White-browed Scimitar-Babbler *Pomatorhinus schisticeps* S: 23

Diagnostic pale yellowish bill. Broad white supercilium contrasts with black mask. Upperparts brownish olive, becoming almost slaty on the crown. Band of rufous extends from hind ear coverts around back of neck. Throat, breast and belly white; flanks and under tail coverts olive-brown. **Voice:** a series of 3–6 mellow hooting notes, *hup-hup-hup*, uttered at varying rates; also a fluty *trew-tree* and dry rasping or rattling notes. **Habitat:** deciduous and evergreen forests, bamboo, scrub and grassland from plains to 2000 m. Very common resident.

นกระวังไพรปากแดงยาว

599. Red-billed Scimitar-Babbler *Pomatorhinus ochraceiceps* S: 24

Long, slender and strongly decurved red bill and uniformly bright rufescent upperparts. Breast and belly white. Frequently found in bird waves; more arboreal than other scimitar-babblers and often associates with White-hooded Babbler (648). **Voice:** a deep, liquid *tu-lip* and a hollow double hoot, *hoop-hoop*. Scolding, metallic rattle is harsher than equivalent notes of White-browed. **Habitat:** evergreen forests, bamboo between 600 and 1600 m. Uncommon resident.

นกระวังไพรปากแดงสั้น

600. Coral-billed Scimitar-Babbler *Pomatorhinus ferruginosus* S: 25

Relatively short and thick coral-red bill. From Red-billed by breast and belly suffused pinkish buff and by darker, olive-brown upperparts. Shows thin black line above white supercilium. Often favours groves of wild bananas in steep gulleys. **Voice:** a harsh churring rattle, similar to that of White-browed and a mellow, upward-inflected, disyllabic whistle. **Habitat:** hill evergreen forest, 1200 – 2000 m. Rare resident.

เหล่านกจู๋เต้น

WREN-BABBLERS: Genera *Kenopia, Napothera, Pnoepyga*. Short-tailed, with strong legs and bills and streaked or scaly plumage. Primarily ground-dwelling, favouring moist areas where they feed in leaf-litter or among fallen logs and boulders. Some species may sing from low trees.

601. Striped Wren-Babbler *Kenopia striata* S: 14   นกจู๋เต้นลาย

Striking whitish ashy sides of head, white throat and breast contrast with blackish, white-streaked crown. Rest of upperparts rufous-brown with prominent white streaks on upper back and wing coverts. Orange-buff lores and rufous flanks; whitish sides of breast scaled blackish. **Voice:** a clear, whistle, *ti-ki-tiii*. First note highest; last note long and stressed. Rhythmically repeated in a long sequence. **Habitat:** evergreen forests of plains and extreme lower hill slopes, rarely up to 300 m. Rare resident; threatened due to lowland deforestation.

602. Large Wren-Babbler *Napothera macrodactyla* S: 19   นกจู๋เต้นตีนใหญ่

Black sides to head and neck, white lores, narrow greyish white supercilium and unmarked white throat. Shows prominent buff streaks and dark scales on brownish upperparts and has white-streaked, greyish underparts. **Voice:** varied phrases of loud whistles, often with a distinctive, rippling quality; *aaah-peowrrr...* **Habitat:** evergreen forests of plains and extreme lower foothills, usually below 200 m. Rare resident; threatened by deforestation.

Plate 96 Scimitar-Babblers

596 Large Scimitar-Babbler

8 White-browed Scimitar-Babbler

597 Rusty-cheeked Scimitar-Babbler

600 Coral-billed Scimitar-Babbler

599 Red-billed Scimitar-Babbler

603. Limestone Wren-Babbler *Napothera crispifrons* S: 19   นกจู๋เต้นเขาปูน

Moderate length tail. Dark brown upperparts with scaling less contrasted than in Streaked Wren-Babbler. Differs also in having bolder black streaks which give a more strongly chequered appearance to white throat; lacks any pale spotting on greater coverts. Often shows a greyish supercilium behind the eye. Race *crispifrons* of north and west Thailand usually has blackish brown breast and flanks, with a paler belly. Race *calcicola* from Saraburi province has rufescent brown underparts, and thin pale shaft streaks on upperparts, resembling Streaked Wren-Babbler. **Voice:** a loud, undulating, rich whistling, uttered almost continuously; *tuu-wii-chuu, tuu-wii-chuu......* **Habitat:** evergreen and mixed deciduous forest and scrub of limestone hill country; usually among boulders and steep crags in shady, moist areas, below 900 m. Locally common resident.

604. Streaked Wren-Babbler *Napothera brevicaudata* S: 13–17   นกจู๋เต้นหางสั้น

Smaller than Limestone Wren-Babbler with stronger scaling on back, nape and crown formed by bolder black margins and paler centres to feathers of upperparts. Shows more blurred, less boldly streaked throat pattern and has tiny white tips to feathers of greater coverts. Underparts warm, rufescent brown. **Voice:** varied shrill whistles; most often *pew-ii* with emphasis on the higher, second syllable or *pew-ii-uu.* Also a plaintive, falling tone *piu.* Hard churring or rattling notes in alarm, often in conjunction with a soft piping note. **Habitat:** evergreen forest from foothills to 1600 m, often near damp gullies or rocky outcrops. Occurs also in those limestone areas which are outside the range of Limestone Wren-Babbler. Fairly common resident.

605. Eye-browed Wren-Babbler *Napothera epilepidota* S: 11   นกจู๋เต้นคิ้วยาว

Much smaller and shorter-tailed than preceding species, with diagnostic long buffy supercilium, dark eye-line, strongly mottled ear coverts and breast. Bold whitish tips to wing coverts form two wing bars. **Voice:** a one-second long, drawn-out, falling tone whistle *peeeow.* Also has a squeaky, almost continuous, undulating chatter, a soft *schrt* and a louder, more prolonged churring when alarmed. **Habitat:** evergreen forest from 1000 to 2100 m. Occurs down to the foothills in the Peninsula. Common resident.

606. Pygmy Wren-Babbler *Pnoepyga pusilla* S: 9   นกจู๋เต้นจิ๋ว

Very small, appearing tailless, like a tesia (706–708) with dark plumage. Upperparts dark brown, scaled, but lacking strong contrast; buff speckling formed by tips of wing coverts. Underparts heavily marked with blackish scales on a whitish or buffy ground colour. Constantly flicks wings; usually on or close to the ground in moist, shady areas. Occasionally climbs trees up to about 2 m high, keeping to thicker, moss covered branches. Solitary. **Voice:** three measured, well-spaced whistles uttered in descending sequence; *three..blind..mice.* (Race in Peninsula only gives two whistles.) Calls with a sharp *tsick.* **Habitat:** evergreen forests and occasionally shady secondary growth, from 1200 m to the highest summits. Locally common resident.

Plate 97 Wren-Babblers

N.c. calcicola

c. crispifrons

605 Eye-browed Wren-Babbler

603 Limestone Wren-Babbler

606 Pygmy Wren Babbler

601 Striped Wren-Babbler

604 Streaked Wren-Babbler

602 Large Wren-Babbler

KAMOL
BANGKOK

286

เหล่านกกินแมลงป่าและพงหญ้า

TREE and TIT-BABBLERS: Genera *Stachyris, Macronous.* Somewhat arboreal, but also frequenting forest undergrowth, grass and bamboo. Characterised by short, straight bills and medium length tails. The smaller species are somewhat warbler-like in appearance. Active, roaming through the undergrowth in small flocks. Easily overlooked, due to skulking habits. (*Chrysomma* and *Timalia* are also placed here for convenience.)

607. Deignan's Babbler *Stachyris rodolphei* S: 13   นกกินแมลงเด็กแนน

Probably difficult to distinguish from Rufous-fronted Babbler in the field, but has duller, less rufescent upperparts and underparts; darker, greyish lores, darker bill and duller rufous cap. In hand, shows greyish underwing coverts, axillaries and bend of wing (these areas white in Rufous-fronted Babbler). **Voice:** undescribed. **Habitat:** bamboo forest, 1000 – 1700 m. Endemic resident, restricted to Doi Chiang Dao; probably rare.

608. Rufous-fronted Babbler *Stachyris rufifrons* S: 13   นกกินแมลงหน้าผากน้ำตาล

Rufous forehead and crown, with diffuse, pale grey area around the eye and whitish lores. Throat whitish, with fine black streaks and warm, brownish buff underparts. (Here treated as conspecific with Buff-chested Babbler *Stachyris ambigua*.) See Striped Tit-Babbler, Deignan's Babbler. **Voice:** a series of soft, mellow piping hoots with a slight pause after the first note; *hu, hu-hu-hu-hu-hu,* uttered at varying speeds. Also a soft rattling or churring and a descending wheezy trill, similar to one of the calls of Grey-throated Babbler. **Habitat:** grasslands, scrub, bamboo and open forest, from plains up to 2100 m. Very common resident.

609. Golden Babbler *Stachyris chrysaea* S: 13   นกกินแมลงหัวสีทอง

Bright golden-yellow underparts and fine black streaks on golden-yellow crown. Black of lores extends below eye to form a moustache. Upperparts golden-olive. From warblers by lack of a contrasting supercilium or eye-ring. Usually shows a vivid pink base to lower mandible. Mainly arboreal, in shrubs and middle storey. **Voice:** a soft piping, very similar to that of Rufous-fronted Babbler but usually slightly slower and lower in pitch. Also wheezy *pi-pi-pi* notes which inflected upwards. **Habitat:** evergreen forests from 900–2000 m. Fairly common resident.

610. Grey-throated Babbler *Stachyris nigriceps* S: 15   นกกินแมลงคอเทา

Warm olive-brown plumage with black and white-streaked crown, broad black lateral head stripes and whitish supercilium; broad white malar stripe and grey throat. Frequently found in bird waves; in northern Thailand often associates with flocks of Grey-cheeked Fulvettas. Usually keeps close to the ground in low herbage. **Voice:** a sweet and high-pitched tremulous song of slurred whistles, *ti-ti-hi-i-i-i,* descending in pitch. Calls with a drier wheezy descending trill and gives a soft churring rattle in alarm. **Habitat:** evergreen forests and secondary growth from plains to 1800 m. Common resident.

Plate 98 Tree Babblers I

607 Deignan's Babbler

608 Rufous-fronted Babbler

609 Golden Babbler

610 Grey-throated Babbler

611 Grey-headed Babbler

613 Chestnut-rumped Babbler

612 Spot-necked Babbler

288

611. Grey-headed Babbler *Stachyris poliocephala* S: 15   นกกินแมลงตาขาว

Grey head with fine white streaks on throat and forecrown. Body plumage rufous brown with bright, deep rusty tinge on breast. From Chestnut-winged Babbler by creamy whitish eye; lack of blue orbital skin. **Voice:** high-pitched wavering whistles, *chiu-wiu-wiu*, the second note highest in pitch. Also four spaced-out, descending whistles. **Habitat:** evergreen forests from foothills to 700 m. Uncommon resident.

612. Spot-necked Babbler *Stachyris striolata* S: 18   นกกินแมลงคอลาย

Bold, white streaked supercilium, white throat and crescent below eye; prominent white streaks or spots on sides of neck. Ear coverts blackish grey; black moustache. Underparts bright orange-rufous. Usually keeps to low undergrowth; very shy and skulking. **Voice:** a clear, high-pitched whistle, *tiu-tii*, the second note usually higher. **Habitat:** evergreen forests from foothills to 1500 m. Uncommon resident.

613. Chestnut-rumped Babbler *Stachyris maculata* S: 18   นกกินแมลงตะโพกแดง

Identified by bold black spotting on breast and by bright chestnut lower back and rump. Blackish throat; flanks and abdomen dull grey-brown. Has blue orbital ring and yellow iris. Pale blue patches on sides of throat usually exposed when singing. **Juvenile:** throat and breast greyish. **Voice:** a series of mellow-sounding notes, *po-lop po-lop po-lop....* or *ho-hup ho-hup ho-hup...* Occasionally a rapid series, *huup-up-up-up-up*, recalling Chestnut-winged Babbler but much louder, richer. **Habitat:** evergreen forests, mainly below 200 m. Uncommon resident; much reduced by lowland forest destruction.

614. White-necked Babbler *Stachyris leucotis* S: 15   นกกินแมลงหูขาว

White supercilium which joins white spots at hind margin of ear coverts. Lores buffy. From Spot-necked Babbler by black throat and dark grey underparts. From Black-throated Babbler by lack of white in malar region. **Voice:** a clear whistle, *chuu-chilu-diii* (last note highest, stressed). Evergreen forests of lowlands and hill slopes. Rare resident.

615. Black-throated Babbler *Stachyris nigricollis* S: 15   นกกินแมลงคอดำ

Large area of black on throat, which narrowly bordered with white speckling on lower margin. White malar spot and short white supercilium extending behind eye. Shows fine white streaking on forecrown. Upperparts bright rufous. Ear coverts, breast and belly dark grey. **Voice:** four to seven evenly-spaced, hollow, monotone *hoop* notes repeated at a rate of about 2 per second. Sometimes uttered in a faster version of up to 14 notes (M&W). **Habitat:** lowland evergreen forests, including primary peat swamp forest. Uncommon to locally common resident, threatened by habitat destruction.

Plate 99 Tree Babblers II

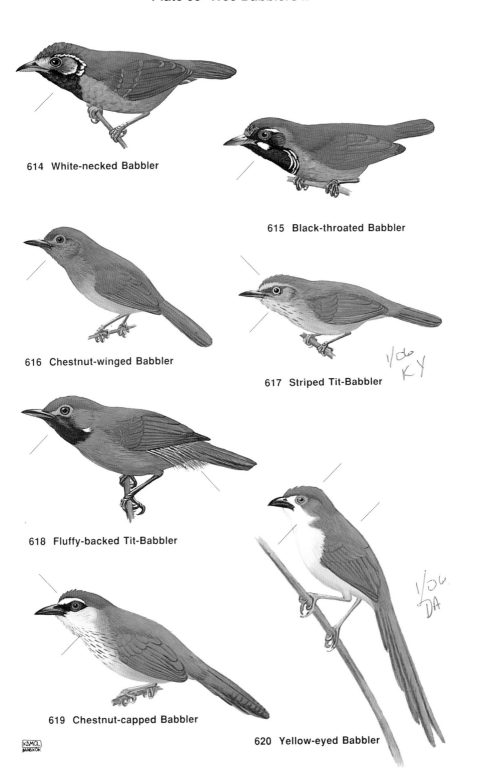

614 White-necked Babbler

615 Black-throated Babbler

616 Chestnut-winged Babbler

617 Striped Tit-Babbler

618 Fluffy-backed Tit-Babbler

619 Chestnut-capped Babbler

620 Yellow-eyed Babbler

KIMOL
BANGKOK

616. Chestnut-winged Babbler *Stachyris erythroptera* S: 14   นกกินแมลงปีกแดง

Broad blue orbital ring and rictal area; grey face and underparts contrasting with chestnut wings and tail. Usually in low trees. **Voice:** a series of *hoop* notes, lower pitched than the similar calls of Rufous-fronted Babbler or Black-throated Babbler and more rapidly delivered. Shows a diagnostic drop in pitch before the end (DRW). Also a querulous *piu* and harsh scolding. **Habitat:** evergreen forest, secondary growth from plains to 800 m. Fairly common resident.

617. Striped Tit-Babbler *Macronous gularis* S: 13   นกกินแมลงอกเหลือง

Pale yellowish underparts with fine streaks on throat and upper breast. Yellow supercilium and rufous crown blending into brownish olive upperparts. When seen from below, from warblers by contrast between yellowish underparts and rufescent underside of tail. Usually in low trees; frequently in bird waves. **Voice:** a monotonous, ringing *chonk chonk chonk...* Also rasping *pweesh-pwaash* call and various soft churring notes. **Habitat:** deciduous and evergreen forests, scrub, bamboo and secondary growth from plains to 1500 m. Very common resident.

618. Fluffy-backed Tit-Babbler *Macronous ptilosus* S: 17   นกกินแมลงหลังฟู

Dark rufescent brown plumage, with chestnut cap, black throat, turquoise orbital skin and white spot on sides of throat which is often visible when calling. Has unusual elongate, white-shafted plumes on lower back and flanks which can often be seen protruding from beneath folded wings. **Voice:** high-pitched, hollow-sounding *pong* notes, together with harsh calls, usually delivered by 2 birds when duetting. These of similar rasping quality to the call of Striped Tit-Babbler but usually 3 or 4 syllables in a distinctive rhythm instead of 2 syllables. **Habitat:** forest edge, secondary growth, swamp forest and bamboo of the level lowlands. Uncommon to rare resident, now much reduced.

619. Chestnut-capped Babbler *Timalia pileata* S: 18   นกกินแมลงกระหม่อมแดง

Shape recalls Yellow-eyed in having stubby black bill and long tail, but upperparts dull olive-brown with bright chestnut cap. Striking facial pattern of black mask, white supercilium and throat. Fine black streaks on white breast. Usually in small flocks, often occurring together with Yellow-eyed. Skulking. **Voice:** a fluty call of 2–4 notes, rapidly uttered in ascending sequence, *tu-twi-twii*, usually followed by grating notes. Also a series of wheezy calls in ascending sequence, *psii-psii-psii*, and a metallic *pwit*. Duets. **Habitat:** scrub, thickets and tall grass from plains up to 1400 m. Very common resident.

620. Yellow-eyed Babbler *Chrysomma sinense* S: 19   นกกินแมลงตาเหลือง

Easily recognised by sturdy black bill, long tail, uniformly rufescent brown upperparts and clean white underparts. Short white supercilium in front of eye; bold red orbital ring. **Voice:** a loud, warbling song with short, strident phrases; also a plaintive, piping series of falling tone notes, *piu, piu, piu...* and an explosive chattering. **Habitat:** open grassland, scrub and secondary growth from plains up to 1800 m. Very common resident.

เหล่านกกะราง

LAUGHINGTHRUSHES: Genus *Garrulax*. Large and robust birds with strong bills and long tails. Highly gregarious and usually found in flocks. Feed mostly on the ground. Most have loud, discordant calls. Build cup-shaped nests. Sometimes placed in a separate subfamily from babblers.

นกกะรางหัวหงอก

621. White-crested Laughingthrush *Garrulax leucolophus* S: 30

Easily identified by white head, throat, breast and erectile crest contrasting with black mask. Upperparts bright rufous, separated from white of head by a grey band across hindneck. **Voice:** distinctive scolding cackles and a chorus of hysterical laughter. **Habitat:** mixed deciduous and evergreen forests, bamboo, secondary growth from plains to 1200 m. Common resident; usually the commonest laughingthrush in lowland habitats.

นกกะรางสร้อยคอเล็ก

622. Lesser Necklaced Laughingthrush *Garrulax monileger* S: 30

Distinguished from Greater Necklaced Laughingthrush by lack of black moustache along the lower border of the ear coverts. Warm olive-brown upperparts, white supercilium and black eye-line. Outer tail feathers tipped whitish, with broad black subterminal band. Often in mixed flocks with White-crested and Black-throated Laughingthrushes. **Voice:** mournful, piping laughter in a descending cadence; also high-pitched, scolding rattles. **Habitat:** mixed deciduous and evergreen forests from plains to 1200 m. Common resident.

นกกะรางสร้อยคอใหญ่

623. Greater Necklaced Laughingthrush *Garrulax pectoralis* S: 33

Distinguished from Lesser Necklaced by complete black moustache which separates ear coverts from throat. Also by whitish lores and by brownish black primary coverts which contrast with rest of folded wing. Note range. Often in mixed flocks with Lesser Necklaced or White-crested Laughingthrushes. **Voice:** mournful descending laughter, *kow-ow-ow-ow*. **Habitat:** mixed deciduous and evergreen forests, bamboo, from plains up to 1200 m. Fairly common resident.

นกกะรางอกสีน้ำตาลไหม้

624. White-necked Laughingthrush *Garrulax strepitans* S: 30

Overall appearance dark, with a large white spot on side of neck which grades into an indistinct, diffuse, greyish neck collar. Warm brown crown and rusty ear coverts; blackish face and upper breast. **Voice:** high-pitched, maniacal laughter recalling White-crested, but differs in incorporating longer trills. Outbursts are usually preceded by dry *chuk* notes. **Habitat:** evergreen forests from 500 m to 1800 m. Uncommon to locally common resident.

292

625. Black-throated Laughingthrush *Garrulax chinensis* S: 30

Distinctive face pattern of slaty-grey crown, black mask and throat and striking white cheeks. Body plumage dark greyish olive. When in mixed flocks with White-crested and Lesser Necklaced, it is the least numerous of the three. **Voice:** an outstanding songster. Has a repetitive, thrush-like song of fluty whistles interspersed with high-pitched squeaky notes. **Habitat:** mixed deciduous and evergreen forests, secondary growth and scrub from plains to 1400 m. Fairly common resident.

626. Spot-breasted Laughingthrush *Garrulax merulinus* S: 27　นกกะรางอกลาย

Olive-brownish, with short buffy supercilium extending behind eye and bold black spots on buffy throat and breast. Little known; very highly skulking and keeps inside dense tangles. **Voice:** song rich and varied. **Habitat:** hill evergreen forest and secondary growth, 1800 m. Rare resident; so far recorded only from Doi Pha Hom Pok.

627. White-browed Laughingthrush *Garrulax sannio* S: 27　นกกะรางคิ้วขาว

Very distinctive. Dark, rufescent brown plumage with broad, creamy-white supercilium and malar patch which meet in front of the eye. Rusty under tail coverts. Much less shy than other laughingthrushes, and reputedly a pest of crops, fruit orchards. **Voice:** harsh ringing and buzzing calls. **Habitat:** open grasslands, secondary growth, scrub; often near cultivation, above 1000 m. Locally common resident.

นกกะรางหัวแดง

628. Chestnut-crowned Laughingthrush *Garrulax erythrocephalus* S: 27

Distinctive bright golden-olive wings and tail and dark chestnut crown. Pale silvery-grey cheeks. Black primary coverts and chestnut-tipped greater coverts form a striking pattern on leading edge of wing. Body plumage dark olive-grey (tinged chestnut in race *peninsulae* of the south). Favours dense undergrowth. **Voice:** fluty whistles, *che-ree to-ee.* Also calls with a high-pitched, laughing *hee-hee-hee-hee...* which increases gradually in volume and a soft, plaintive mewing. **Habitat:** evergreen forests of the higher mountains, from 1300 m to the highest summits. Locally common resident.

629. Red-tailed Laughingthrush *Garrulax milnei* S: 27　นกกะรางหางแดง

Diagnostic bright crimson-red wings and tail and bright rufous crown and nape. Mantle greyish olive with indistinct blackish scaling; underparts greyish, blacker on throat. Cheeks silvery-grey. **Habitat:** evergreen forest, secondary growth, above 1800 m. Rare resident.

Plate 100 Laughingthrushes

1 White-crested Laughingthrush

622 Lesser Necklaced Laughingthrush

3 Greater Necklaced Laughingthrush

624 White-necked Laughingthrush

25 Black-throated Laughingthrush

626 Spot-breasted Laughingthrush

27 White-browed Laughingthrush

628 Chestnut-crowned Laughingthrush

9 Red-tailed Laughingthrush

630 Red-faced Liocichla

KAMOL BANGKOK

เหล่านกกินแมลงนักร้อง

SONG-BABBLERS: A diverse grouping of ten genera of mainly arboreal babblers, many of which have bright plumage. Some species include much fruit in their diets; most build open, cup-shaped nests.

630. Red-faced Liocichla *Liocichla phoenicea* S: 24   นกกะรางแก้มแดง
Diagnostic bright red face, sides of head and neck, with red wing patches. Crown greyish. Tail blackish from above, orange-brown to black underneath with the individual feathers being tipped pale orange. Under tail coverts black with broad orange tips. Highly skulking, in dense undergrowth. Favours moist, shady areas. **Voice:** a loud, fluty song of 3–4 notes, either in descending sequence *tu-reew-reew* or with the last note higher, *tu-reew-ri*. Gives scolding rattles in alarm, rather sibia-like though shorter and less harsh. **Habitat:** evergreen forest, secondary growth and scrub from 1400 m to at least 2200 m. Uncommon resident.

631. Rufous-winged Fulvetta *Alcippe castaneceps* S: 11   นกมุ่นรกหัวน้ำตาลแดง
Dark chestnut crown and nape with narrow buffy streaks; whitish supercilium which curves around rear margin of mottled ear coverts. Blackish moustache and broad dark line behind eye. Contrasting wing pattern formed by black primary and greater coverts and bright, rufous-edged primaries. One of the commonest and noisiest species in bird waves of the highest elevations; often feeds on vertical trunks. **Voice:** song is a rich, undulating and descending warble, *ti-du-di-du-di-du-di* (JS). Usual call is a wheezy, descending trill, *tsi-tsi-tsi-tsi-tsirr* ; also a quiet *chip*. **Habitat:** evergreen forests from 1200 m to the highest summits. Common to locally very common resident.

632. Rufous-throated Fulvetta *Alcippe rufogularis* S: 12   นกมุ่นรกคอแดง
Slightly larger and stouter-billed than Rufous-winged Fulvetta. Distinctive chestnut gorget across lower throat and paler, brighter, chestnut crown bordered laterally with broad black coronal bands. Broad white supercilium. Shy; keeps to dense herbage of forest floor on, or close to, the ground. **Voice:** a sweet *chi-chu-one-two-three*, the last 3 notes in ascending sequence. **Habitat:** evergreen forests from plains to 900 m. Rare resident.

633. Brown Fulvetta *Alcippe brunneicauda* S: 15   นกมุ่นรกสีน้ำตาล

Nondescript; distinguished from similar peninsular race of Brown-cheeked Fulvetta by whitish, grey-tinged underparts, lacking any buff suffusion. Sides of head and neck grey or brownish grey; rest of upperparts rufescent brown. Grey eye. **Voice:** a descending series of 5–7 high-pitched, tinkling whistles, *ti-ti-ti-ti-tiu*, the last note falling in tone. Also a distinctive metallic *swit* call. Arboreal, usually keeping to lower middle storey. **Habitat:** evergreen forests from lowlands up to 900 m. Often close to streams. Fairly common resident.

Plate 101 Fulvettas, Yuhinas

631 Rufous-winged Fulvetta

632 Rufous-throated Fulvetta

633 Brown Fulvetta

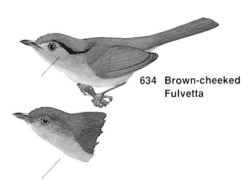

634 Brown-cheeked
     Fulvetta

636 Grey-cheeked Fulvetta

635 Mountain Fulvetta

637 Striated Yuhina

638 Whiskered Yuhina

639 Burmese Yuhina

640 White-bellied Yuhina

296

634. Brown-cheeked Fulvetta *Alcippe poioicephala* S: 16   นกมุ่นรกตาขาว
Lacks eye-ring and has warm, uniformly buffy underparts and pale brown sides to head which, in northern races *haringtoniae* and *alearis*, are sharply demarcated from clear grey of crown and nape by a long black line. Black head stripes reduced in race *karenni* of southwest Thailand and lacking in race *davisoni* of the Peninsula, while demarcation between brown and grey on head is also less sharp. Eye grey or whitish (brown in juvenile), but difficult to discern. **Voice:** a sweet, slurred whistling; *joey joey dii-wiu*, the penultimate note highest. Various squeaking and buzzing notes with a more bubbling quality than those of Grey-cheeked Fulvetta. **Habitat:** evergreen and mixed deciduous forest, secondary growth and bamboo from plains to 1100 m. Common resident.

635. Mountain Fulvetta *Alcippe peracensis* S: 16   นกมุ่นรกภูเขา
Differs from both Brown-cheeked and Grey-cheeked Fulvettas in having whitish underparts with slight greyish buff wash across upper breast. Grey crown and sides of head are sharply demarcated from olive-brown upperparts as in Grey-cheeked but head-stripe is bolder and whitish eye-ring is thinner and much less distinct. Eye grey or brown. Note range. **Voice:** a short, weak *chi-chi-chu-chui*, very like song of Brown-cheeked but last note highest. **Habitat:** evergreen forests from foothills to 1200 m. Local and uncommon resident.

636. Grey-cheeked Fulvetta *Alcippe morrisonia* S: 15   นกมุ่นรกตาแดง
Blackish line on side of head and distinct white eye-ring. Grey crown and sides of head sharply demarcated from olive-brown upperparts. Underparts warm buffy. Eye dark crimson (brown in juvenile). Not shy; usually the commonest component species in bird waves in the hill evergreen forests of the west and north. Keeps to middle storey and low undergrowth. **Voice:** a sweet whistling, *ji-ju ji-ju*, usually followed by a peculiar, quiet, undulating and drawn-out squeaking note. Also a harsh buzzing, *beez-eez-eez*, and a high-pitched, incessant buzzing or trilling which fluctuates in volume, reminiscent of a squeaking wheel bearing. **Habitat:** evergreen forests from 900 m to the highest elevations. Very common resident.

637. Striated Yuhina *Yuhina castaniceps* S: 14   นกภูหงอนหัวน้ำตาลแดง
Distinguished from other yuhinas by proportionately longer, more rounded tail which is conspicuously white-tipped. Short crest. Greyish crown, chestnut ear coverts and dull brownish upperparts with faint white streaks. Underparts whitish. In race *torqueola* of provinces bordering Laos, the chestnut of the ear coverts continues as a broad band across back of neck. Usually in large, noisy, single species flocks. Arboreal. **Voice:** loud chattering and ringing notes. **Habitat:** evergreen forest, open woodland, secondary growth, usually 900 – 1800 m. Common resident.

638. Whiskered Yuhina *Yuhina flavicollis* S: 14   นกภูหงอนวงตาขาว
High pointed crest; tail appears square-ended. Shows dark greybrown crown, black moustache, white eye-ring and bright rufous nuchal collar. Streaked brown sides, tawny brown flanks and under tail coverts. Arboreal. **Voice:** a thin, squeaky *swii swii-swii* ; also a metallic ringing note. **Habitat:** evergreen forests from 1200 m to 2200 m. Locally common resident.

297

639. Burmese Yuhina *Yuhina humilis* S: 14 นกภูหงอนพม่า

Very like Whiskered Yuhina, with which it is sometimes considered conspecific, but shows silvery whitish nuchal collar and greyish flanks and under tail coverts. **Habitat:** evergreen forests above 1200 m. Local and uncommon resident.

640. White-bellied Yuhina *Yuhina zantholeuca* S: 13 นกภูหงอนท้องขาว

From warblers by crest and by lack of supercilium. Bright yellowish green upperparts and strikingly white underparts with contrasting yellow under tail coverts. Bill pinkish. Usually active in middle storey, frequently in bird waves. Often hangs upside down, like a tit. **Voice:** sings with a short, high-pitched, ascending trill *si-i-i-i-i-i*; calls with scolding tit-like notes. **Habitat:** evergreen and mixed deciduous forests from plains to 1800 m. Very common resident.

นกเสือแมลงหน้าสีตาล
641. Chestnut-fronted Shrike-Babbler *Pteruthius aenobarbus* S: 11

Small; from warblers by short, thick bill and stocky appearance. White eye-ring; lacks black mark behind ear coverts. **Male:** yellow underparts with dark chestnut throat and forecrown, narrowly bordered yellow above. Two broad white wing bars. **Female:** drab; whitish underparts and more uniformly olive-green upperparts with rufous forecrown and cinnamon wing bars. ◆ Usually encountered in pairs; found frequently in bird-waves. **Voice:** sings with a rhythmic, prinia-like *ka-chip, ka-chip, ka-chip...* Other calls include a drawn-out chatter, *chr-r-r-r-uk*, and a sharp *pwit*. **Habitat:** evergreen forest, usually from 900 m to 1700 m; occasionally as high as 2500 m. Fairly common resident.

642. Black-eared Shrike-Babbler *Pteruthius melanotis* S: 11 นกเสือแมลงคอสีตาล

Both sexes distinguished from male Chestnut-fronted by black mark behind ear coverts. White eye-ring and yellow underparts. **Male:** from male Chestnut-fronted by paler, pinkish rufous throat and by yellowish forecrown. **Female:** entire underparts, including throat, yellow. Wing bars cinnamon instead of white. **Juvenile:** from female by whitish underparts and duller, more brownish, upperparts. From female Chestnut-fronted by black mark behind ear coverts. **Habitat:** evergreen forests, 1600 – 2200 m. Uncommon resident.

นกเสือแมลงปีกแดง
643. White-browed Shrike-Babbler *Pteruthius flaviscapis* S: 17

Much larger than other shrike-babblers; plump and relatively short-tailed with whitish underparts. **Male:** black head with a broad white supercilium; black wings with a large, reddish golden patch on tertials; white-tipped primaries and black tail. **Female:** grey head, with a less distinct greyish white supercilium and a bright greenish olive wing patch. Tail bright olive with whitish yellow tips to outer tail feathers. ◆ Forages along larger horizontal limbs. **Voice:** a monotonously repeated phrase of (usually) 4 notes; *chi-chewp, chi-chewp*, with *chewp* notes stressed. Also a short *pink*; grating *churr* notes in alarm. **Habitat:** evergreen forests from 800 m to 2200 m. Very common resident.

644. Blue-winged Minla *Minla cyanouroptera* S: 16   นกศิวะปีกสีฟ้า

Distinctive long, square-ended tail which, appears white with a narrow black margin; whitish underparts and supercilium. Features of upperparts (blue wings and tail, blue crown; light grey-brown mantle, rump and upper tail coverts) often difficult to see owing to arboreal habits. Whitish eye. Race *sordidior* of peninsular Thailand has brownish crown and much reduced blue in wings and tail. **Voice:** a clear, whistled *pi-piu* with emphasis on first note. Last note with falling tone. Also a loud *swit*. **Habitat:** hill evergreen forests, 900 – 2000 m. Common resident.

645. Chestnut-tailed Minla *Minla strigula* S: 17   นกศิวะหางสีตาล

Long, square-ended tail. Yellow underparts with black-barred throat and black and orange patches in wings and tail. Whitish tail-tip and edges to tertials. Rest of upperparts greyish olive with rufescent golden crown and yellowish eye-ring. Noisy and gregarious, feeding both in tree-tops and in low herbage. **Voice:** a slurred whistle, *jo-ey*, *jo-ey dii*, the last note highest. Also a ringing, metallic *chew*. **Habitat:** evergreen forests above 1600 m, though common only above 2000 m. Locally common resident.

646. Cutia *Cutia nipalensis* S: 19   นกขัติยา

Plump, short-tailed appearance; white underparts with bold black barring on sides of breast and flanks. Slaty-blue patches in black wings and black-tipped tail. **Male:** slaty-blue crown, black mask and uniform rufous mantle, rump and upper tail coverts. **Female:** upperparts olive-brown with large black spots; sides of head dark brown. ◆ Moves rather slowly along epiphyte-covered tree trunks and larger boughs. **Voice:** a long *cheeeet*, uttered with rising inflection. **Habitat:** evergreen forests from 1200 m to 2100 m. Rare resident.

647. Silver-eared Mesia *Leiothrix argentauris* S: 18   นกกะรองทองแก้มขาว

Black cap and moustache, silvery ear coverts and bright orange-yellow throat and breast. Primaries and secondaries edged orange-yellow, with red patch at base. Mantle, wing coverts and tail greyish olive. **Male:** red upper and under tail coverts. **Female:** dull orange-yellow upper and under tail coverts. ◆ Sometimes in flocks, though may be difficult to see, often keeping to dense bushes and grass. **Voice:** a series of slurred whistles in descending sequence; *cheer-ii*, *chu-ii*, *chu-ii-uu*. Loud and cheerful. Also various chattering and buzzing notes. **Habitat:** hill evergreen forest, secondary growth and scrub, 1300 m to 2000 m. Fairly common resident.

648. White-hooded Babbler *Gampsorhynchus rufulus* S: 24   นกเสือแมลงหัวขาว

Easily recognised by white head contrasting with rufous-brown body; long tail. Some birds show a blackish necklace across upper breast. Tail feathers tipped whitish. Bill pinkish. **Juvenile:** head browner. ◆ Often seen in association with Red-billed Scimitar-Babbler or in bird-waves. **Voice:** a distinctive, loud harsh chatter, *chr-r-r-r-uk*. **Habitat:** evergreen forests, bamboo from 500 – 1400 m. Uncommon resident.

Plate 102 Shrike-Babblers, Minlas, Cutia, Mesia

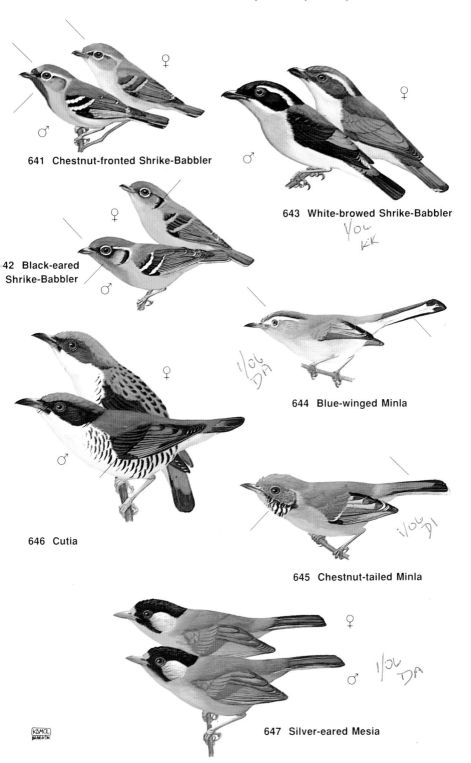

641 Chestnut-fronted Shrike-Babbler

♂ ♀

643 White-browed Shrike-Babbler

42 Black-eared Shrike-Babbler

♀ ♂

644 Blue-winged Minla

646 Cutia

♀ ♂

645 Chestnut-tailed Minla

♀ ♂

647 Silver-eared Mesia

KIMOL
BANGKOK

300

649. Spectacled Barwing *Actinodura ramsayi* S: 24   นกปีกลายตาขาว
A long-tailed brownish bird with a conspicuous white eye-ring and fine black barring on wings and tail. Shows rufous in the wings, black primary coverts and a white-tipped tail. Underparts tawny, paler than dull olive upperparts; lores blackish, ear coverts and sides of head greyish. Slight crest. **Voice:** a series of (usually) 7 sibilant whistled notes, the last two dropping suddenly in pitch; somewhat reminiscent of the song of Black-headed Sibia. Sometimes accompanied by nasal *piu, piu* calls, given antiphonally. **Habitat:** evergreen forest, secondary growth, grass and scrub, 1200 – 2100 m. Locally common resident.

650. Rufous-backed Sibia *Heterophasia annectens* S: 19   นกหางรำหลังแดง
Black head and black, white-streaked nape contrasting with bright rufous back and rump. Flight feathers of wings blackish, white-edged. Tail black with broad white tips. Shows rufous-buff suffusion on flanks and under tail coverts. Mostly arboreal, typically moving along the larger limbs of trees and sometimes on vertical trunks. **Voice:** usually 3–4 whistled notes, *chip, chu chu-ii*. A harsh chatter in alarm. **Habitat:** evergreen forest, 1000 – 2000 m. Common resident.

651. Black-headed Sibia *Heterophasia melanoleuca* S: 23   นกหางรำดำ
Slightly longer-tailed than preceding species, with pure white underparts. Upperparts entirely black, glossier on head and wings than on mantle. White tips to tail feathers. In flight, shows white patch at base of primaries (invisible when perched). Usually active in small flocks. Mainly arboreal, but frequently enters low herbage in order to feed on berries. **Voice:** a long, wavering, musical whistle, often with a sudden drop in pitch at the end. A dry rattle in alarm. **Habitat:** hill evergreen forests from 1000 m to the highest summits. Common resident.

652. Long-tailed Sibia *Heterophasia picaoides* S: 30   นกหางรำหางยาว
Much longer-tailed than Black-headed Sibia with dark grey upperparts and only slightly paler grey underparts. Tail feathers tipped greyish white; white patch in secondaries is usually visible both at rest and in flight. Usually in single species flocks; often feeds on nectar in flowering trees. **Voice:** single, musical piping notes. Also a dry rattling, similar to that of Black-headed Sibia. **Habitat:** evergreen forest, secondary growth, 900 – 1800 m. Fairly common resident.

Plate 103 White-hooded Babbler, Barwing, Sibias

648 White-hooded Babbler

649 Spectacled Barwing

650 Rufous-backed Sibia

651 Black-headed Sibia

652 Long-tailed Sibia

juvenile

adult

653 Malaysian Rail-babbler

302

RAIL-BABBLERS: Subfamily *Cinclosomatinae*. An Australasian subfamily of terrestrial, mainly insectivorous birds with long necks and long legs which are unrelated to the babblers. World: 13 species. Thailand: one species.

653. Malaysian Rail-babbler *Eupetes macrocerus* S: 29 นกคอสามสี
Long bill and tail, bright rufescent plumage. Broad white supercilium and black band on side of head. Forecrown rufous-buff; crown, nape and throat deep chestnut. Blue skin on sides of neck usually visible when bird calling. **Juvenile:** shows sharp contrast between white throat and dark grey-brown underparts. Forehead greyish.
◆ Usually solitary, shy; stays on the ground, walking with measured gait and jerking head like a chicken. **Voice:** a drawn out monotone whistle of about 1.5 to 2 seconds duration. Purer in tone and higher-pitched than the similar whistle of Garnet Pitta and sometimes with an almost imperceptible drop in pitch at the end. Popping, frog-like notes given in alarm. **Habitat:** evergreen forests from plains to 900 m. Uncommon resident.

วงศ์นกปากนกแก้ว

PARROTBILLS: Family *Panuridae*. Have short, deep bills with sharp cutting edges which are used for tearing up bamboo stems, etc. Very soft plumage. Usually encountered in small flocks. Most species are highly skulking and feed deep inside patches of grass and scrub. Build deep cup nests. World: 20 species. Thailand: 5 species.

นกปากนกแก้วอกลาย

654. Spot-breasted Parrotbill *Paradoxornis guttaticollis* S: 20
Shows large yellow bill, large black spot on ear coverts and black arrowhead markings on throat and breast. Rufous cap. **Voice:** harsh *chit-chit-chit* notes. **Habitat:** grass and scrub of mountains, 1200 – 2100 m. Local and uncommon resident.

655. Black-throated Parrotbill *Paradoxornis nipalensis* S: 10 นกปากนกแก้วหูเทา
Tiny, with bright orange-rufous upperparts, black throat and broad white malar stripe. Ear coverts and sides of neck grey. Some individuals show a short black brow behind the eye. **Voice:** squeaky, rattling trills. **Habitat:** bamboo, forest edge and secondary growth, from 1200 m to 2000 m. Uncommon resident.

656. Short-tailed Parrotbill *Paradoxornis davidianus* S: 10 นกปากนกแก้วหางสั้น
Tiny. Shorter-tailed than Black-throated, with a uniformly rufous head, black throat and drab olive-brown upperparts. **Habitat:** grassland and bamboo above 600 m. Rare resident.

303

657. Lesser Rufous-headed Parrotbill *Paradoxornis atrosuperciliaris* S: 17

Bright rufous head with short black eyebrow; unmarked olive-brown upperparts and pale buffy underparts. Bill pale grey. **Habitat:** bamboo and forest edge, from 1200 m to 2000 m. Rare resident.

658. Grey-headed Parrotbill *Paradoxornis gularis* S: 19   นกปากนกแก้วหัวเทา

Orange bill and grey head with black chin and eyebrow. White eye-ring and lores and diffuse malar stripe. Rufescent olive upperparts and silky whitish underparts. Much more arboreal and less skulking than other parrotbills. **Voice:** a rapidly uttered phrase of about four loud, ringing notes, *chiu-chiu-chiu-chiu*, together with harsh chattering. **Habitat:** hill evergreen forest and secondary growth, from 1200 m to 1800 m. Uncommon resident.

วงศ์นกกระจ้อยป่าโกงกาง

AUSTRALO-PAPUAN WARBLERS: Family *Acanthizidae*. Formerly placed with Old World Warblers, but now considered to belong to a separate superfamily. Build hanging, purse-shaped nests. World: 63 species. Thailand: one species.

659. Flyeater *Gerygone suphurea* S: 9   นกกระจ้อยป่าโกงกาง

Small and relatively short-tailed. Grey-brown upperparts and pale yellowish underparts. Dark sides of head sharply demarcated from yellow throat. Whitish lores and subterminal tail spots. **Juvenile:** whiter underparts. ◆ Much smaller than Mangrove Whistler. (See flowerpeckers 859–868.) **Voice:** a series of up to 10 long, wheezy high-pitched *zwee* notes in a rising sequence or descending cadence. **Habitat:** chiefly mangroves, coastal scrub. In the Peninsula, occurs also in plantations, lowland secondary growth and forest. Common resident.

วงศ์นกกระจ้อยและนกกระจิ๊ด

OLD WORLD WARBLERS: Family *Sylviidae*. Small, active, insectivorous birds with thin bills. Unlike thrushes, have unspotted juvenile plumage. Have weaker legs than babblers. The family includes many long-distance migrants. Sexes usually similar. World: 362 species. Thailand: 58 species.

660. Lesser Whitethroat *Sylvia curruca* S: 14   นกคอขาวน้อย

Dark grey head, with lores and ear coverts darker than crown, and grey-brown back, together with square tail and white outer tail feathers. Underparts whitish. Legs dark blue-grey. (See Grey-breasted Prinia, 695.) **Voice:** a quiet, repeated *tuc*. **Habitat:** scrub, secondary growth from plains to at least 1300 m. Rare winter visitor.

เหล่านกกระจ้อย

FLYCATCHER-WARBLERS: Genera *Seicercus, Abroscopus*. So-called because they have generally broader bills than leaf-warblers, which they somewhat resemble. Plumage generally brighter, with distinctive head markings and yellow underparts. *Seicercus* build globular nests while *Abroscopus* build cup-shaped nests.

661. Golden-spectacled Warbler *Seicercus burkii* S: 13   นกกระจ้อยวงตาสีทอง
Distinguished from leaf-warblers by lack of supercilium; sides of head greenish with thin yellow eye-ring. Crown greyish with broad black lateral head stripes. Bright yellow underparts and white outer tail feathers. Sometimes shows one faint wing bar. Inhabits middle and lower storey; flycatches, often returning to the same perch and frequently accompanies bird waves. **Voice:** a flat *tissheep*, very like the call of Two-barred Warbler (672), and a soft *trrip*. Also has a strident, slurred, undulating song of 5–7 notes. **Habitat:** evergreen and mixed deciduous forest from plains to 1800 m. Also occurs in mangroves, gardens on passage. Common winter visitor.

662. Grey-cheeked Warbler *Seicercus poliogenys* S: 12   นกกระจ้อยแก้มสีเทา
Distinguished from Golden-spectacled Warbler by darker grey head with less sharply defined head stripes, distinct yellow wing bar, and a white spectacle. Greyish white lores and chin. Shows white outer tail feathers. **Habitat:** evergreen forest above 1200 m. Very rare winter visitor.

นกกระจ้อยกระหม่อมแดง
663. Chestnut-crowned Warbler *Seicercus castaniceps* S: 10
Tiny. Chestnut cap, white eye-ring, greyish throat, upper back and sides of head. Black lateral crown stripes and yellow wing bars. Hovers frequently, showing conspicuous yellow rump and white in outer tail feathers. Very active; usually accompanies bird waves, keeping chiefly to middle and lower storeys. See Mountain Tailorbird (705). **Voice:** very high-pitched, thin, metallic, glissading song. **Habitat:** evergreen forest above 1200 m. Uncommon to locally common resident.

664. Yellow-bellied Warbler *Abroscopus superciliaris* S: 11   นกกระจ้อยคอขาว
Greyish head, white supercilium and dark eye-line. Bright olive-green upperparts, white throat and upper breast. Often in small parties. Much shorter-tailed than Yellow-bellied Prinia. **Voice:** a thin, tinkling song of usually 3–6 notes. Short, dry *trrit* calls. **Habitat:** bamboo brakes in evergreen and deciduous forests, secondary growth from plains to 1500 m. Common resident.

Plate 104 Parrotbills, Flyeater, Flycatcher-Warblers

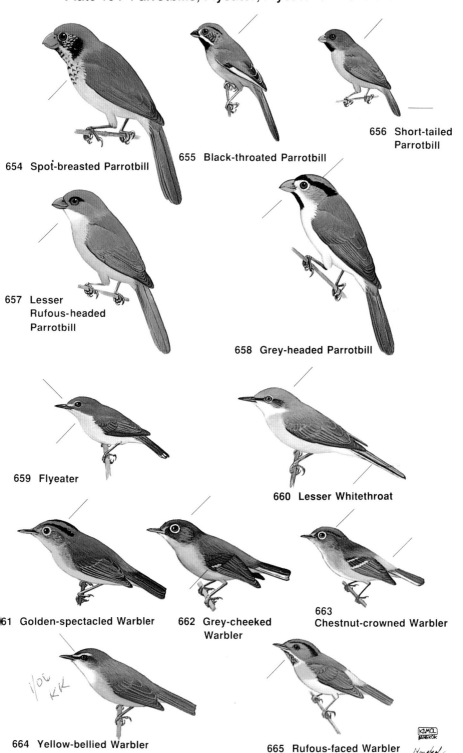

654 Spot-breasted Parrotbill

655 Black-throated Parrotbill

656 Short-tailed Parrotbill

657 Lesser Rufous-headed Parrotbill

658 Grey-headed Parrotbill

659 Flyeater

660 Lesser Whitethroat

661 Golden-spectacled Warbler

662 Grey-cheeked Warbler

663 Chestnut-crowned Warbler

664 Yellow-bellied Warbler

665 Rufous-faced Warbler

Mongkol

306

665. Rufous-faced Warbler *Abroscopus albogularis* S: 10   นกกระจ้อยคอดำ

 Distinguished from Chestnut-crowned Warbler by rufous sides of head and duller, olive crown and by lack of eye-ring. Throat streaked black and white; yellow on underparts confined to a band across upper breast. Belly whitish; rump whitish yellow. **Voice:** sings with a high-pitched, scraping *trrrrr* (JS). **Habitat:** evergreen forests from 800 m to at least 1400 m; favours bamboo. Rare resident.

เหล่านกกระจิ๊ด

LEAF-WARBLERS: Genus *Phylloscopus*. All species show a conspicuous pale supercilium and a dark eye-line, preventing confusion with other small perching birds such as white-eyes, female sunbirds, etc. The genus encompasses both arboreal and understorey-inhabiting forms. Although much less difficult to identify than is generally supposed, a keen eye for both structural and plumage detail is necessary, especially as their active feeding habits often make prolonged observation difficult. Voice is a useful aid to identification. Only two species breed in Thailand. The leaf-warblers have been arranged into four groups to aid in making the basic distinctions.

GROUP 1. Plain brownish above, lacking wing bars, crown stripes or rump patch. Comparatively short-winged and long-tailed. Favour undergrowth and low bushes, often feeding on or near the ground.

666. Buff-throated Warbler *Phylloscopus subaffinis* S: 11   นกกระจิ๊ดท้องสีน้ำตาล

 Distinctive bright, uniformly yellowish buff underparts which concolorous with broad supercilium. Upperparts with greenish olive tinge. Bill and legs mainly dark. **Voice:** a soft, cricket-like *chirrip*. **Habitat:** scrub and herbage of open areas, usually above 1200 m. Uncommon to fairly common winter visitor.

667. Dusky Warbler *Phylloscopus fuscatus* S: 12   นกกระจิ๊ดสีคล้ำ

Long, whitish supercilium, often with a slight rusty tinge behind eye; also rusty-tinged ear coverts and sides of neck. Upperparts dark grey-brown; underparts dirty whitish, suffused dull, pale brownish on flanks and under tail coverts. Bill with mainly pale lower mandible; legs dark pinkish brown. Both bill and legs markedly thinner than in Radde's Warbler; lacks contrasting tawny vent. **Voice:** a hard, repeated *tac* or *chac*. **Habitat:** low trees and bushes of open areas, often near water; mangroves. Usually inhabits plains and foothills, though found on the higher mountains on migration. Very common winter visitor.

Plate 105 Leaf-Warblers I

666 Buff-throated Warbler

667 Dusky Warbler

668 Yellow-streaked Warbler

669 Radde's Warbler

670 Pale-legged Leaf-Warbler

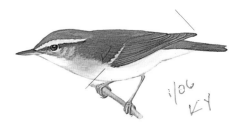

671 Arctic Warbler

672 Two-barred Warbler

673 Greenish Warbler

308

668. Yellow-streaked Warbler *Phylloscopus armandii* S: 13

Plumage almost identical to Radde's Warbler in having breast and belly appearing buffy, and contrasting with brighter tawny under tail coverts. (Fine, yellow streaking on throat, breast and belly is discernible only at very close range.) Distinguished from Radde's by voice and by thinner bill and legs and small size. From Buff-throated Warbler by contrast between duller buffy underparts and whiter supercilium; pale lower mandible and legs. From Dusky Warbler by lack of rusty colouration around head and neck. From all by distinctive call-note. **Voice:** a sharp, metallic, bunting-like *zic*. **Habitat:** low herbage and scrub of dry, deciduous woodlands, secondary growth and open areas; from plains and foothills to 1300 m (occasionally up to 2500 m on passage). Fairly common winter visitor.

669. Radde's Warbler *Phylloscopus schwarzi* S: 14 นกกระจิ๊ดปากหนา

Larger than any other leaf-warbler; both bill (with pale lower mandible) and legs (pinkish or straw-coloured) are noticeably thick. Upperparts dull olive-brown, usually with slightly brighter, greenish olive edgings to wing feathers. Supercilium whitish, becoming yellow-tinged in front of eye. Underparts dull, pale brownish buff contrasting with brighter tawny under tail coverts; belly often yellow-tinged. Often holds tail slightly above horizontal. From Aberrant Bush-Warbler (713) by stronger face pattern and square-ended tail. **Voice:** usually a low, quiet *prrit*, frequently repeated. Also a deep *tuc* or *whut*. **Habitat:** undergrowth of more open forests, both deciduous and evergreen; forest edge, open areas of scrub and grassland, from plains and foothills up to 2000 m. Common winter visitor.

GROUP 2. Slimmer and longer-winged than preceding group, with more arboreal habits. Greenish olive to olive upperparts, with narrow (occasionally highly indistinct) single or double wing bars. Lack crown stripes or other adornment. Lower mandible either entirely pale or with only very slight dark tip.

670. Pale-legged Leaf-Warbler *Phylloscopus tenellipes* S: 13 นกกระจิ๊ดขาสีเนื้อ

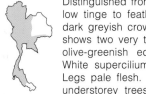

Distinguished from Arctic and Greenish Warblers by lack of any yellow tinge to feathers of both upperparts and underparts. Uniform dark greyish crown contrasts slightly with olive upperparts. Usually shows two very thin, indistinct buffy wing bars and slightly brighter olive-greenish edges to primaries; rump tinged rufescent olive. White supercilium and underparts; broad, heavy blackish eye-line. Legs pale flesh. Usually close to the ground, in undergrowth and understorey trees; often along streamsides. **Voice:** a diagnostic, short, high-pitched, metallic *tink*. **Habitat:** mixed deciduous and evergreen forests, secondary growth from plains to 1500 m. Also mangroves. In gardens on passage. Common winter visitor.

671. Arctic Warbler *Phylloscopus borealis* S: 13   นกกระจิ๊ดขั้วโลกเหนือ

Distinguished from Two-barred and Greenish Warblers by slightly larger size, longer and more pointed wings, and heavier bill which often appears slightly upturned. Closely resembles Eastern Crowned Warbler in proportions. Upperparts olive-green, usually with slight greyish cast, especially on the crown. Wing feathers may be edged brighter greenish. Usually shows one, occasionally two, thin yellow-white wing bars. Underparts whitish with slight yellow suffusion and usually a suggestion of grey streaking on upper breast. Legs pale horn. Mainly arboreal. **Voice:** a loud, hard *dzip*, resembling one of the calls of Olive-backed Sunbird. **Habitat:** mixed deciduous and evergreen forests, secondary growth, gardens, mangroves; usually in lowland areas, but has been recorded up to 1800 m. Abundant passage migrant, wintering mainly in the southern part of the country.

นกกระจิ๊ดเขียวปีกสองแถบ

672. Two-barred Warbler *Phylloscopus plumbeitarsus* S: 12

Very similar to Greenish Warbler, with which it may be conspecific, but distinguished by slightly broader wing bar on greater coverts and by second, median covert wing bar which though difficult to discern on worn birds, is usually visible at close range. In fresh plumage, in early autumn and late spring, shows broader wing bars, resembling Inornate Warbler, but differs in longer bill with entirely pinkish lower mandible, slightly longer tail and lack of pale tertial tips. Legs usually fleshy or horn coloured. Mainly arboreal. See under Arctic Warbler for distinctions from that species. **Voice:** a flat-sounding, rather dry, disyllabic *tissheep*. **Habitat:** deciduous and evergreen forests, secondary growth and bamboo of lowland areas and hills up to at least 800 m. Common winter visitor.

673. Greenish Warbler *Phylloscopus trochiloides* S: 12   นกกระจิ๊ดเขียวคล้ำ

Duller, more greyish green on upperparts than the Crowned Leaf-Warblers (674–678) though, as in these species, the bill appears long and fine with an entirely pinkish lower mandible. One rather indistinct whitish wing bar and a yellowish white supercilium. Underparts whitish, sullied with a slight greyish tinge on upper breast, tending more towards yellowish on the belly. Legs usually dark. Mainly arboreal. See Arctic Warbler. **Voice:** call-note identical to that of Two-barred Warbler. **Habitat:** evergreen forest, bamboo and secondary growth of hills of moderate and higher elevation. Fairly common winter visitor.

GROUP 3. Bright olive-green above with one or two yellow wing bars and a pale mesial crown stripe. Lack both tertial markings and rump patch. Bill long with entirely orange-pink lower mandible. Favour upper branches and tree-tops, often associated with bird waves.

310

674. **Eastern Crowned Warbler** *Phylloscopus coronatus* S: 13 นกกระจี๊ดหัวมงกุฎ
Size and shape as Arctic Warbler, but distinguished by crown stripe, brighter green upperparts and whiter breast and belly. Larger and longer-winged than Blyth's or White-tailed Leaf-Warblers with a single, thinner wing bar. Clean, silky-white breast and belly contrast with pale lemon-yellow under tail coverts. **Voice:** a harsh *zweet*; various slurred, sweeter-sounding notes given in subsong. **Habitat:** evergreen and mixed deciduous forests, chiefly of lowlands, but occasionally up to 1800 m. Occurs in mangroves and gardens on migration. Common passage migrant in continental Thailand; the commonest leaf-warbler of lowland, primary forest in the Peninsula, where it winters.

675. **Blyth's Leaf-Warbler** *Phylloscopus reguloides* S: 12 นกกระจี๊ดหางขาวใหญ่
Two broad, yellowish wing bars. Almost identical to White-tailed, but separable at close range, when folded tail viewed from below, by narrow whitish border to innermost web of outermost tail feathers. Less yellow on supercilium and underparts. Frequently behaves like a nuthatch, clinging to tree trunks. **Voice:** sings with a strident, undulating *pitchewee-pitchewee-pitchewee*; calls with a slurred *tisshoo-eet*, similar to call of White-tailed but generally much less vocal than this species. **Habitat:** evergreen forests, usually above 600 m to highest summits, but occasionally in the plains. Common winter visitor.

676. **White-tailed Leaf-Warbler** *Phylloscopus davisoni* S: 11 นกกระจี๊ดหางขาวเล็ก
Separated from Blyth's Leaf-Warbler by entirely whitish inner web to outermost tail feathers, visible at close range when folded tail viewed from below. White in tail visible, with difficulty, in flight or when tail flicked. Supporting characters are the brighter golden-yellow supercilium, more yellowish underparts and slightly smaller size. (Note: race in south-east Thailand shows tail pattern like Blyth's.) Builds a domed nest on the ground. **Voice:** song *tis-seechewee-tisseechewee-tiss* (also described as *witchety-witchety...*), slightly sweeter, more metallic and slurred than Blyth's, but with similar undulating quality; call-note similar to Blyth's. **Habitat:** evergreen forest above 1000 m. Very common resident.

677. **Yellow-vented Warbler** *Phylloscopus cantator* S: 11 นกกระจี๊ดคิ้วดำท้องขาว
Very distinctive; yellow mesial crown stripe and supercilium contrast sharply with broad, black lateral coronal bands. Bright yellow throat and under tail coverts contrast sharply with white lower breast and belly. See white-eyes (869–872). **Habitat:** evergreen forests, from foothills to 1700 m. Rare winter visitor.

นกกระจี๊ดคิ้วดำท้องเหลือง

678. **Sulphur-breasted Warbler** *Phylloscopus ricketti* S: 11
Very distinctive; differs from Yellow-vented Warbler in having entire underparts bright yellow. From Golden-spectacled Warbler (661) by yellow supercilium, yellow mesial crown stripe and by black eye-line. **Voice:** in late winter, gives subsong of sweet, descending cadence *sweety-sweety-sweety-swee*. **Habitat:** evergreen and mixed deciduous forests up to 1200 m. Fairly common winter visitor.

Plate 106 Leaf-Warblers II

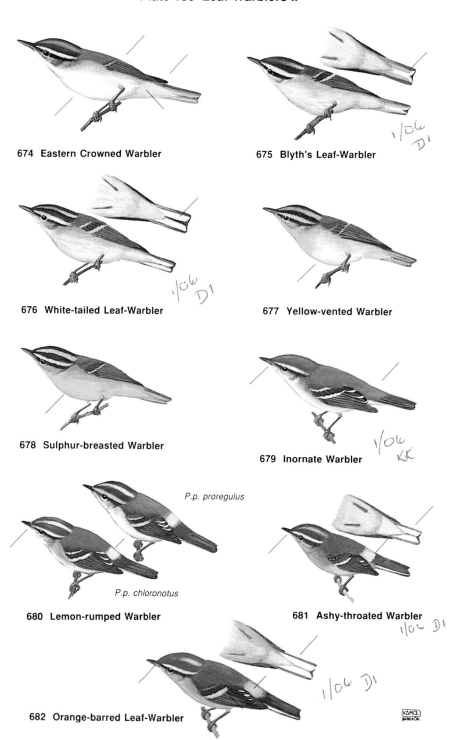

674 Eastern Crowned Warbler

675 Blyth's Leaf-Warbler

676 White-tailed Leaf-Warbler

677 Yellow-vented Warbler

678 Sulphur-breasted Warbler

679 Inornate Warbler

P.p. proregulus

P.p. chloronotus

680 Lemon-rumped Warbler

681 Ashy-throated Warbler

682 Orange-barred Leaf-Warbler

KIMOL
BANGKOK

312

GROUP 4. Olive-green upperparts with prominent wing bars and whitish tips to tertials. All but Inornate Warbler have mesial crown stripe and yellow rump patch. Have smaller, shorter bills than birds in groups 2 or 3. Feed both in canopy and in low herbage.

679. Inornate Warbler *Phylloscopus inornatus* S: 11   นกกระจิ๊ดธรรมดา

Lacks rump patch and crown stripe usually absent or very faint. Two broad, yellowish white wing bars; underparts dirty whitish, suffused faintly with fine greyish and yellowish streaking. From Two-barred Warbler by slightly shorter bill, with pale chiefly confined to basal half of lower mandible; shorter tail, whitish tips to tertials and by broader, more contrasting wing bars. Race *mandelli*, found in the mountains of the north, differs from the much more common *P. i. inornatus* on call and in having greyer crown usually showing a pale mesial crown stripe. **Voice:** a distinctive disyllabic *we-eest*, with rising inflection on second syllable. Race *mandelli* calls with a flat-sounding *schewp* somewhat like Greenish Warbler. **Habitat:** forests, secondary growth, scrub and all manner of wooded areas, including gardens, from extreme lowlands up to 2000 m. Very common and widespread winter visitor.

นกกระจิ๊ดตะโพกเหลือง

680. Lemon-rumped Warbler *Phylloscopus proregulus* S:10

Distinguished from Inornate Warbler by yellowish mesial crown stripe and lemon rump patch (though latter can be surprisingly difficult to see). From all except Ashy-throated Warbler by very short, fine bill which appears all black in the field. Wing bars yellowish. Commoner wintering race (*P. p. chloronotus*) has drab plumage tones, resembling Inornate; race *proregulus* is brighter, more yellow-green above with a yellower supercilium and cleaner, more silky white underparts. Frequently hovers. **Voice:** a sharp *swit*. **Habitat:** evergreen forests, secondary growth, usually above 1200 m. Uncommon to locally common winter visitor.

681. Ashy-throated Warbler *Phylloscopus maculipennis* S: 9   นกกระจิ๊ดคอสีเทา

Even smaller than Lemon-rumped Warbler, with which it shares a small and fine all-blackish bill. Distinguished by greyish throat and upper breast contrasting with pale yellowish lower breast and belly. Long, thin whitish supercilium and dark grey crown with paler grey mesial stripe; two thin sharply defined yellow wing bars. In flight, shows obvious white outer tail feathers and lemon rump. Builds nest hanging from a low branch. **Voice:** a high-pitched *zip*; song is a repeated *sweechoo, sweechoo*, similar in quality to song of White-tailed. **Habitat:** hill evergreen forest. Found only on the upper slopes of Doi Inthanon, where very common above 2000 m. Resident.

นกกระจิ๊ดแถบปีกสีส้ม

682. Orange-barred Leaf-Warbler (Buff-barred Warbler) *Phylloscopus pulcher* S:11

The only leaf-warbler, other than Ashy-throated, to show very obvious white outer tail feathers in flight, but distinguished by slightly larger size and longer bill with pale base to lower mandible. Upperparts dark, dull olive; median covert wing bar dull orange, often not easily visible, though greater covert wing bar is broad, pale orange-yellow. Mesial crown stripe usually indistinct, visible as a pale greyish patch on the nape. Underparts dull, pale yellowish, suffused with greyish on throat and upper breast and olive-buff on flanks. Frequently takes nectar from flowering trees. **Voice:** a high-pitched, thrush-like, staccato *tsi-i-i-i-i*; also a thin *sit*, sharper and more strident than similar call of Ashy-throated Warbler. In late winter, sings with slurred notes similar to those of White-tailed but interspersed with a distinctive long, dry trill. **Habitat:** evergreen forests above 1500 m (though most frequent above 2000 m). Uncommon to locally common winter visitor.

เหล่านกพง

REED-WARBLERS: Genus *Acrocephalus*. Have somewhat rounded tails and moderately long under tail coverts. All species occurring in Thailand have unstreaked upperparts and some are difficult to separate in the field. Inhabit reeds and grass, usually in marshy areas. Skulking. No species breed.

683. Thick-billed Warbler *Acrocephalus aedon* S: 20   นกพงปากหนา

Relatively large. Similar to Great Reed-Warbler in size and colouration but has noticeably thicker, shorter bill, shorter wings and longer tail. Large dark eye stands out on relatively unmarked face; whitish lores. More rufous than any bulbul and has a pale, orange-flesh lower mandible. **Voice:** a hard *chack*, recalling Dusky Warbler but much louder; a harsh chatter. **Habitat:** scrub growth, grass and reeds of both marshy and drier areas from plains up to 1500 m. Common winter visitor.

นกพงใหญ่พันธุ์อินเดีย

684. Clamorous Reed-Warbler *Acrocephalus stentoreus* S: 20

Relatively large. Very like Great Reed-Warbler but distinguished with care by slightly longer bill and usually buffier underparts which lack any suggestion of breast streaking. **Habitat:** marshy areas of lowlands. Very rare; status uncertain, but probably winter visitor.

685. Great Reed-Warbler *Acrocephalus arundinaceus* S: 20 นกพงใหญ่พันธุ์ญี่ปุ่น

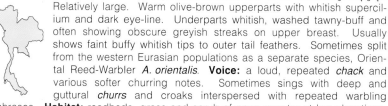

Relatively large. Warm olive-brown upperparts with whitish supercilium and dark eye-line. Underparts whitish, washed tawny-buff and often showing obscure greyish streaks on upper breast. Usually shows faint buffy whitish tips to outer tail feathers. Sometimes split from the western Eurasian populations as a separate species, Oriental Reed-Warbler *A. orientalis.* **Voice:** a loud, repeated *chack* and various softer churring notes. Sometimes sings with deep and guttural *churrs* and croaks interspersed with repeated warbling phrases. **Habitat:** reedbeds, grass and scrub of open country at low elevations. Usually close to water. Often feeds in low trees. Very common winter visitor.

314

686. Black-browed Reed-Warbler *Acrocephalus bistrigiceps* S: 14 นกพงคิ้วดำ
Long and broad, buffy supercilium bordered above with a black lateral crown stripe which contrasts strongly with pale olive-brown centre to crown. Rufescent olive-brown upperparts with brighter rufous rump and buffy underparts. **Voice:** a soft, repeated *chuc*, much quieter than calls of Great Reed-Warbler. Often sings before spring departure. **Habitat:** grass, reeds and scrub of marshy areas, lakesides and paddyfield margins. Occasionally in drier locations up to 800 m on passage. Very common winter visitor.

687. Paddyfield Warbler *Acrocephalus agricola* S: 14 นกพงนาหิมาลัย
Difficult to separate from Blunt-winged Warbler, but has a longer, more distinct supercilium which broadens behind the eye and which sometimes shows a faint suggestion of a dark upper border. Race *agricola*, known from the far north, is usually noticeably smaller-billed than Blunt-winged Warbler. Colouration usually pale grey-brown above, slightly more rufous on rump and upper tail coverts, and silvery-whitish underneath (when in worn plumage, for most of the winter); or bright rufous above with tawny-rufous wash on flanks (when in fresh plumage in autumn and late spring). Race *tangorum* has a larger bill and a slight, but noticeable, black brow above the whitish supercilium. In fresh plumage is bright olive-rufous above and tawny below resembling nominate race. When worn is duller, more grey-brown above (darker than nominate race) and whiter below, resembling Black-browed Reed-Warbler, but distinguished by longer, thinner tail; longer bill and by reduced contrast between shorter black brow and darker centre to crown. **Habitat:** grass and reeds of lowland marshes, lakesides. Rare winter visitor.

688. Blunt-winged Warbler *Acrocephalus concinens* S: 14 นกพงนาพันธุ์จีน
Longer-billed than Paddyfield Warbler, with less rufescent, deeper olive-brown upperparts. Sides of breast, flanks and under tail coverts washed brownish buff. Unlike Paddyfield, never shows a grey plumage phase. Lacks the black lateral head stripe of Black-browed and supercilium, though well-marked, is shorter and thinner than in Paddyfield. **Voice:** a short quiet *tcheck*; also a soft, drawn-out *churrr*. Sometimes gives scratchy warbling subsong before northward departure in spring. **Habitat:** primarily grass and reedbeds close to water, but also dry grassland of hills up to at least 800 m. Uncommon winter visitor.

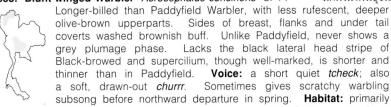

Oriental Reed-warbler
1/06 SP

Plate 107 Reed-Warblers, Grasshopper-Warblers

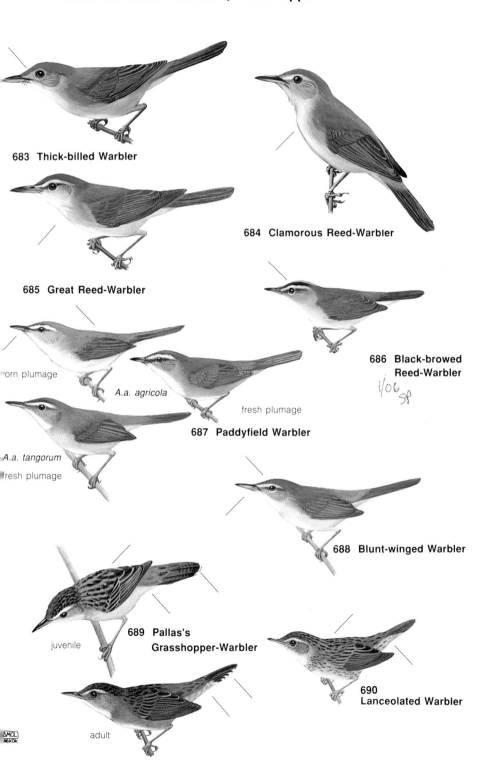

683 Thick-billed Warbler

685 Great Reed-Warbler

684 Clamorous Reed-Warbler

orn plumage

A.a. agricola

fresh plumage

687 Paddyfield Warbler

686 Black-browed
Reed-Warbler

i/06
SP

A.a. tangorum

fresh plumage

688 Blunt-winged Warbler

juvenile

689 Pallas's
Grasshopper-Warbler

690
Lanceolated Warbler

adult

เหล่านกพงตั๊กแตน

GRASSHOPPER-WARBLERS: Genus *Locustella*. Strongly rounded tails which appear broad or heavy at base and which, when held folded, taper slightly towards the tip. Long, graduated under tail coverts are longer than outermost tail feathers. Highly skulking. Both species known from Thailand are streaked forms. Winter visitors.

นกพงตั๊กแตนท้ายทอยสีเทา

689. Pallas's Grasshopper-Warbler (Pallas's Warbler) *Locustella certhiola* S: 15
Distinguished from Lanceolated Warbler by larger size, tail pattern and by unstreaked flanks and under tail coverts. Brownish olive upperparts with black streaks, rufescent lower back and rump; conspicuous whitish supercilium. Dense blackish streaking on crown often gives a capped appearance. Underparts and under tail coverts washed buffy-brown. Tail appears blackish distally with white tips to individual feathers (most easily visible on underside). **Juvenile:** underparts and under tail coverts washed yellowish buff; slight gorget of brown spots on upper breast. ◆ Less skulking than Lanceolated Warbler and, after being flushed, often perches in view for a few seconds before dropping down into thick ground cover. See Zitting Cisticola (693). **Voice:** an explosive, metallic *pwit*; a rattling trill, *rit-tit-tit-tit...* and an excited reed-warbler-like chacking. Slurred, trilling subsong is heard frequently throughout the winter. **Habitat:** reeds and grass of marshes, lakesides. Almost always close to water. Common winter visitor.

690. Lanceolated Warbler *Locustella lanceolata* S: 13   นกพงตั๊กแตนอกลาย
Smaller than the preceding species and lacking any rufescent tinge. Much more heavily streaked blackish on entire upperparts; also on upper breast, flanks and under tail coverts. Lacks capped appearance of Pallas's Grasshopper-Warbler; supercilium shorter and less distinct. Very highly skulking; usually only flushes when virtually underfoot. **Voice:** a diagnostic, explosive *rink-tink-tink*. Other calls are similar to preceding species; an explosive *pwit*, a *rit-tit-tit-tit* trill and an excited chacking when alarmed. **Habitat:** grass and scrub of marshes, paddy margins, open areas (including dry grasslands) from plains up to at least 1800 m. Very common winter visitor.

เหล่านกพงหญ้าและนกยอดข้าวหางแพน

GRASS-WARBLERS: Genera *Megalurus, Graminicola, Cisticola*. Streaked warblers with longish tails and short under tail coverts. Resident, building cup-shaped or purse-shaped nests and often delivering song in a display flight.

691. Striated Warbler *Megalurus palustris* S: 25   นกหางนาค
The largest warbler, with a long, graduated and pointed tail. Broad black streaks on buffy-brown upperparts; underparts paler and more finely streaked. Whitish throat and supercilium. Sings both from exposed perches and during a short, gliding, song-flight. **Voice:** a rich, fluty warbling song, which carries for long distances. Calls with an explosive *pwit*. **Habitat:** wet grasslands and marshes of lowlands. Favours the more open areas with scattered clumps of tall grass or reedmace. Locally common resident.

692. Large Grass-Warbler *Graminicola bengalensis* S: 17 นกพงหญ้า

Larger with a longer, broader tail and much shorter under tail coverts than the **Locustella** warblers and having a short, heavy bill. Upperparts rufous-brown with blackish streaks contrasting with unstreaked rufous rump and blackish, white-tipped tail. Unmarked whitish underparts. Little known. **Habitat:** reedy areas of marshy lowlands. Not recorded since 1923 and probably extinct in Thailand due to drainage and cultivation of its former haunts.

693. Zitting Cisticola *Cisticola juncidis* S: 11 นกยอดข้าวหางแพนลาย

Much smaller and shorter-tailed than Pallas's Grasshopper-Warbler with a fine bill. Streaked brown upperparts, rump rufous. Underparts whitish with rufous-buff flanks and under tail coverts. Tail shows broad white tips and blackish brown subterminal markings. From female or non-breeding Bright-capped by thin whitish supercilium contrasting with dull brown to rufous brown hindneck, whiter tips to tail feathers and by call. **Voice:** a hard *dik-ik*, *dik-ik*, much repeated, given in weak undulating display flight. **Habitat:** paddy-fields, marshland, grass and scrub in lowland, wet open country. Very common resident.

694. Bright-capped Cisticola *Cisticola exilis* S: 11 นกยอดข้าวหางแพนหัวแดง

Breeding male: diagnostic sandy-golden crown; short tail. **Non-breeding male and female:** distinguished from Zitting Cisticola by extensive rufous-golden nape and sides of neck concolorous with supercilium; by longer tail and by duller, brownish white tips to tail feathers. **Voice:** diagnostic; a high-pitched, nasal *pzeeew*. Song is delivered both in a high, towering songflight and from low perches; a musical, bulbul-like chuckle alternates with repetition of the nasal call. **Habitat:** tall grass and scrub of marshes and drier areas; occasionally dryland crops, from plains to 800 m. Requires longer grass than Zitting Cisticola. Common resident.

เหล่านกกระจิบหญ้า

PRINIAS: Genus *Prinia*. Small, resident warblers with long, strongly graduated tails which are sometimes held cocked. Build deep cup- or purse-shaped nests.

695. Grey-breasted Prinia *Prinia hodgsonii* S: 12 นกกระจิบหญ้าอกเทา

Dark grey crown and ear coverts and (usually) lack of white super-cilium; greyish breast band on otherwise whitish underparts. Some individuals out of breeding dress may resemble Rufescent Prinia in having browner head, whitish breast and a slight, short whitish eyebrow in front of the eye, but are always distinguished by call, thinner bill, less rufescent upperparts and by whiter tips to tail feathers. **Voice:** a diagnostic, laughing, high-pitched *hee-hee-hee-hee*. A metallic, rhythmically undulating song; *tirr-irr-irr-irr*. **Habitat** dry grassland, scrub and secondary growth, including roadside verges, from plains up to 1500 m. Very common resident.

696. Rufescent Prinia *Prinia rufescens* S: 12   นกกระจิบหญ้าสีข้างแดง

Distinguished from Grey-breasted Prinia by slightly thicker bill, whitish supercilium and by diagnostic call. Upperparts more rufescent; rufous-buff flanks and under tail coverts; pale brownish grey tips to tail feathers. **Breeding:** slaty grey head. **Non-breeding:** head brownish. ◆ Smaller and shorter-tailed than Plain Prinia. **Voice:** a buzzing *peez-eez-eez-eez*; song a rhythmic *chewp, chewp, chewp* **Habitat:** often in more wooded situations than Grey-breasted; undergrowth of deciduous and open evergreen forests; secondary growth, grassland up to 1600 m, but generally favouring low to moderate elevations. Very common resident.

697. Yellow-bellied Prinia *Prinia flaviventris* S: 13   นกกระจิบหญ้าท้องเหลือง

Small, slim and long-tailed with yellow belly and under tail coverts contrasting with whitish throat and breast. Slaty grey head usually with thin whitish supercilium; dark greenish olive upperparts. **Voice:** a soft, drawn-out, mewing *pzeeew*; song is a short, descending musical chuckle, *didli-idli-u* (DRW). **Habitat:** grass and scrub of marshes and drier situations of lowlands and hills up to at least 800 m. Also the landward edge of mangroves. Very common resident.

698. Plain Prinia (Tawny-flanked Prinia) *Prinia inornata* S: 15   นกกระจิบหญ้าสีเรียบ

Larger and longer-tailed than Rufescent Prinia with longer broad or whitish creamy supercilium. Upperparts sandy-brownish; crown sometimes tinged greyish. Underparts creamy with pale tawny flanks. Race *blanfordi* of northern Thailand is a warmer brown above with deeper, more uniformly buff supercilium and underparts. **Voice:** a rattling or buzzing *jirt-jirt-jirt-jirt*, uttered both from perch and in flight. **Habitat:** almost always associated closely with wet areas; reeds, grass and scrub of marshes, ponds, canals, paddyfield and mangrove margins. Occasionally in drier areas of hills up to 800 m. Very common resident.

699. Brown Prinia *Prinia polychroa* S: 18   นกกระจิบหญ้าสีน้ำตาล

Noticeably larger than Plain Prinia with a usually indistinct supercilium and slightly streaked upperparts. Underparts buffy-white. Gape blackish (pinkish orange in Plain Prinia). **Voice:** a loud, strident *cheep* or *cho-eep*, repeated; alarm note an insistent *chup, chup*. **Habitat:** undergrowth of open, usually dry dipterocarp, woodlands of the plains and lower hills up to 800 m. Uncommon to locally common resident.

700. Hill Prinia *Prinia atrogularis* S: 18   นกกระจิบหญ้าคิ้วขาว

Very long tail like Brown and Plain Prinias, but easily distinguished by grey ear coverts and dark streaks on sides of breast. Whitish supercilium; underparts whitish with tawny brown flanks. **Voice:** a loud repeated *cho-eep, cho-eep* song; calls with loud *chup* notes. **Habitat:** grass and scrub of open ridgetops, forest clearings, above 900 m. Common resident.

Plate 108 Grass-Warblers, Cisticolas, Prinias

691 Striated Warbler

692 Large Grass-Warbler

693 Zitting Cisticola

♀ and non-breeding

♂ breeding

694 Bright-capped Cisticola

breeding

non-breeding

695 Grey-breasted Prinia

1/06 KY

breeding

non-breeding

1/06 DA

696 Rufescent Prinia

697 Yellow-bellied Prinia

P.i. herberti

P.i. blanfordi

1/06 SP

698 Plain Prinia

KAMOL BANGKOK

320

TAILORBIRDS: Genus *Orthotomus*. Small warblers with long bills which frequently cock their tails. Rufous caps. Build purse-like nests stitched beneath leaves.

701. Common Tailorbird *Orthotomus sutorius* S: 12   นกกระจิบธรรมดา
Rufous forecrown and short whitish supercilium; green upperparts. Frequently shows some dark grey flecking on throat. From Dark-necked by less extensive rufous on cap and whitish under tail coverts. **Male:** elongate central tail feathers. **Juvenile:** crown greenish as rest of upperparts. **Voice:** an explosive *chee-yup*, *chee-yup*, incessantly repeated. **Habitat:** gardens, scrub, open areas, open deciduous woodlands and mangroves. From lowlands up to 1500 m. Very common resident.

702. Dark-necked Tailorbird *Orthotomus atrogularis* S: 11   นกกระจิบคอดำ
Distinguished from Common Tailorbird by more extensive rufous crown, brighter green upperparts and yellow under tail coverts. **Male:** black patch on side of neck, lacking in female. **Juvenile:** crown greenish, as rest of upperparts. **Voice:** a nasal, staccato high-pitched *kri-i-i-i-i* and a short *tew*. Also calls with a dry *prrrp-prrrp,* reminiscent of the ringing tone of a telephone. **Habitat:** ever-green and mixed deciduous forests, mangroves and well-watered scrublands from plains to 1200 m. Rarely in such dry, open situations as Common Tailorbird. Very common resident.

703. Ashy Tailorbird *Orthotomus sepium* S: 12   นกกระจิบหัวแดง
Distinguished from all other tailorbirds by rufous which extends on to sides of head and chin. Tail grey-brown, with white feather tips and black subterminal markings. **Male:** grey breast and belly. **Female:** paler underparts than male, with breast pale grey and belly whitish. **Juvenile:** chin and underparts whitish. **Voice:** a drawn-out *chee-er*; also a dry squeaky trill. **Habitat:** chiefly mangroves, coastal scrub and peat swamp forest. Occasionally in inland forest of the plains. Fairly common resident.

นกกระจิบกระหม่อมแดง

704. Rufous-tailed Tailorbird *Orthotomus sericeus* S: 12
Distinguished from Ashy Tailorbird by sharp contrast between rufous crown and buffy white cheeks; from all other tailorbirds by grey-brown back contrasting with rufous tail. **Voice:** a loud *tee-cher, tee-cher*, with both syllables equally stressed. **Habitat:** forest edge, secondary growth and clearings from plains to at least 400 m. Common resident.

Plate 109 Prinias, Tailorbirds, Tesias

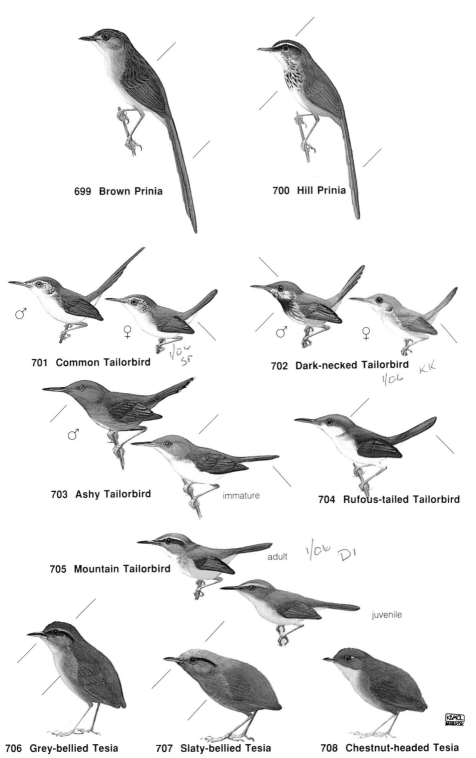

699 Brown Prinia

700 Hill Prinia

♂ ♀ 701 Common Tailorbird

♂ ♀ 702 Dark-necked Tailorbird

♂ 703 Ashy Tailorbird immature

704 Rufous-tailed Tailorbird

705 Mountain Tailorbird adult juvenile

706 Grey-bellied Tesia

707 Slaty-bellied Tesia

708 Chestnut-headed Tesia

322

705. Mountain Tailorbird *Orthotomus cuculatus* S: 12   นกกระจิบภูเขา
Bright yellow lower breast and belly, rufous orange forecrown and white supercilium. Does not usually cock tail like other tailorbirds. From Chestnut-crowned Warbler (663) by longer bill, lack of white eye-ring, yellow rump or wing bars. **Juvenile:** uniform dull olive upperparts; dull yellow supercilium and entire underparts. **Voice:** a thin, high-pitched and melodious whistle of 4 to 6 notes, glissading up and down the scale. Calls with dry *trrit* notes. **Habitat:** hill evergreen forest, forest edge and scrub from 1000 m to at least 2200 m. Favours areas with bamboo understorey. Fairly common resident.

เหล่านกจุนจู๋

TESIAS: Genus *Tesia.* Apparently tailless warblers inhabiting lush undergrowth of hill evergreen forests. Vocal and inquisitive.

706. Grey-bellied Tesia *Tesia cyaniventer* S: 10   นกจุนจู๋ท้องเทา

Very similar to Slaty-bellied Tesia but distinguished by dull, olive-green crown which contrasts with brighter, golden-olive supercilium. Underparts slightly paler grey with indistinctly whitish centre to belly and paler, more yellowish lower mandible. **Voice:** diagnostic song. Sibilant, piercing whistles followed by an almost nightingale-like flourish; *tji tji tju tju tju-chewit.* **Habitat:** evergreen forests above 1000 m. Very rare resident.

707. Slaty-bellied Tesia *Tesia olivea* S: 10   นกจุนจู๋

Olive-green above with a brighter, golden-washed crown. Underparts uniformly dark slate-grey with a broad, black eye-line. Lower mandible orange. Often bounds from side to side on low, horizontal twigs. **Voice:** 4 to 6 measured whistles followed by a sudden explosive, tuneless jumble of notes, recalling those of Pale-footed Bush-Warbler. **Habitat:** low herbage of evergreen forests from 900 m to the highest summits; especially in damp areas such as along stream courses. Uncommon to locally common resident.

708. Chestnut-headed Tesia *Tesia castaneocoronata* S: 10   นกจุนจู๋หัวสีตาล
Similar shape and habits to preceding species, but easily recognised by yellow underparts, chestnut head and white spot behind eye. Even more skulking than Slaty-bellied, usually staying on the ground. **Voice:** sings with an explosive rapid jumble of notes, somewhat recalling Slaty-bellied, but more hurried, lacking the preliminary whistles. Calls with an explosive *whit.* **Habitat:** undergrowth of evergreen forests above 1600 m. Uncommon resident.

เหล่านกกระจ้อยพงหญ้า

BUSH-WARBLERS: Genera *Cettia, Bradypterus.* Brownish, unstreaked and highly skulking warblers with rounded wings and (usually) longish tails which chiefly inhabit grassy areas and scrub, usually on or near the ground. Most are winter visitors.

Genus **Cettia**. Have tails of 10 feathers which appear either square-ended or characteristically notched. Some species slightly resemble the ground-feeding leaf-warblers, *Phylloscopus*. Generally in more woody or scrubby areas than *Bradypterus* and hop rather than run.

709. Stub-tailed Bush-Warbler *Cettia squameiceps* S: 11 นกกระจ้อยหัวลาย
Short tail which square-ended with rounded corners. Scale markings on crown rarely visible in the field though mottled, grey-scaled ear coverts and sides of throat usually evident. Long, creamy supercilium and dark eye-line. Dark brownish upperparts with rufescent tinge; whitish underparts. Pale flesh legs and pale lower mandible. Usually feeds on the ground. **Voice:** a sharp *stit* in alarm. **Habitat:** evergreen and mixed deciduous forests, bamboo from foothills up to 2000 m. Favours sloping banks. Uncommon winter visitor.

710. Pale-footed Bush-Warbler *Cettia pallidipes* S: 13 นกกระจ้อยสีไพล
Longer-tailed than Stub-tailed Bush-Warbler but shape and pattern of markings otherwise similar, with strongly contrasted face pattern and square-ended tail. Lacks any scaling on head; upperparts lack rufescent tinge. Whitish underparts. Legs pale flesh; pale lower mandible. **Voice:** an explosive jumble of notes recalling Slaty-bellied Tesia, but lacks preliminary whistles. **Habitat:** grassland, scrub from foothills up to 1800 m. Uncommon resident; (records at low elevations may possibly involve altitudinal migrants).

นกกระจ้อยนักร้อง
711. Manchurian Bush-Warbler *Cettia canturians* S: 18 (male); 15 (female)
Bright rufescent upperparts with slightly brighter rufous crown. Long, broad, buffy supercilium and dark eye-line. Long tail appears distinctly notched; usually held slightly cocked. Somewhat resembles a large, rufescent version of Radde's Warbler. **Voice:** a rich musical chuckle which starts off with a low trill and ends with a louder terminal flourish; *tu-u-u-teedle-ee-tee*. **Habitat:** scrub of secondary growth, forest edge from plains up to 1500 m. Rare winter visitor.

712. Chestnut-crowned Bush-Warbler *Cettia major* S: 13 นกกระจ้อยใหญ่
Similar to Pale-footed Bush-Warbler, with almost square-ended tail and strong face pattern, but has chestnut-brown crown and nape which contrasts with dark olive-brown upperparts. Underparts with brownish wash on breast and flanks. **Voice:** calls with a very sharp, metallic and high-pitched *tzip*. **Habitat:** scrub and forest undergrowth, 1500 – 2200 m. Very rare winter visitor.

713. Aberrant Bush-Warbler *Cettia flavolivacea* S: 13 นกกระจ้อยเหลืองไพล
Tail moderately long, notched and usually held slightly cocked. Olive upperparts, with slight greenish tinge; dark eye-line and dull buffy supercilium with slight yellowish tinge. Underparts dull olive buffy; slightly yellow-tinged, though browner on breast and flanks. Legs and base of lower mandible pale. **Voice:** contact note is a soft, dry *trrik*, repeated incessantly. Gives a more prolonged churring in alarm; also a soft, falling tone, plaintive whistle. **Habitat:** forest edge, clearings, secondary growth and scrub from 1200 m to the highest summits. Uncommon winter visitor.

324

Genus **Bradypterus**. Have strongly rounded tails of 12 feathers: under tail covert patterns often aid identification. Juveniles are yellow-tinged on underparts. Very highly skulking and almost impossible to flush, usually running along the ground like mice. When excited or alarmed, have rapid **Acrocephalus**-like chacking and explosive **pwit** notes. Usually in more open grassy situations than **Cettia.**

714. Spotted Bush-Warbler Bradypterus thoracicus S: 13   นกกระจ้อยอกเทา

Slightly shorter-tailed than other **Bradypterus** (recalling Lanceolated Warbler in shape) and distinguished by dark brown centres and sharply contrasted broad white tips to feathers of under tail coverts. (In field, these can appear mainly white with bold dark chevron markings.) Shows slight to pronounced black speckling on upper breast. Two forms occur: race **B. t. thoracicus** (rare) usually has all dark bill, greyish supercilium and sides of breast with heavy dark speckling and is strongly rufous-tinged above. Commoner form (**B. t. shanensis**) is duller brownish above with a pale lower mandible, whiter supercilium and underparts and lighter breast speckling. Recalls Chinese Bush-Warbler, from which distinguished by under tail covert pattern, shorter tail and (usually) by speckling on the breast. **Voice:** in addition to chacking and **pwit** notes described for the genus, gives a long, drawn-out, harsh **tzee-eenk.** **Habitat:** scrub and herbage of open areas, including marshes, from plains to 1400 m. Common winter visitor.

715. Chinese Bush-Warbler Bradypterus tacsanowskius S: 14 นกกระจ้อยพันธุ์จีน

Longer-tailed than Spotted Bush-Warbler with whiter underparts; under tail coverts are less contrasted, appearing mainly whitish, the paler buffy-brown feather centres being less sharply demarcated from the broad whitish tips. Lower mandible pale. Rarely shows slight throat speckling. **Habitat:** grass, reeds and scrub of the plains and foothills. Very rare winter visitor.

716. Brown Bush-Warbler Bradypterus luteoventris S: 14   นกกระจ้อยสีน้ำตาล

Warm, rufescent brown upperparts; pale, uniformly buffy-brown under tail coverts which lack any pale tipping; buffy-white supercilium. Breast and flanks variable, washed pale to dark buffy-brown. Sometimes shows slight spotting on upper breast. Lower mandible pale fleshy horn. **Voice:** calls with excited chacking notes typical of the genus. Also gives a metallic **pink.** Monotonous, continuous reeling song, **tic-tic-tic-tic...** not usually given in Thailand. **Habitat:** grasslands, scrub above 800 m. Rare winter visitor.

717. Russet Bush-Warbler Bradypterus seebohmi S: 14   นกกระจ้อยเขาสูง

Warm rufescent brown upperparts; warm brownish wash on flanks and sides of breast. Very like Brown Bush-Warbler but distinguished by under tail coverts which show very dark brown centres and whitish tips, recalling Spotted Bush-Warbler. Lower mandible blackish and bill appears rather thick. Usually shows slight greyish spotting on upper breast. From Spotted Bush-Warbler by longer tail; more rufescent upperparts and flanks; slightly less sharp white tipping on under tail coverts. **Voice:** sings with a monotonous, metallic and buzzing **zree-ut zree-ut....** uttered in a long series of notes. Calls with an excited chacking and also an explosive Lanceolated Warbler-like call of up to 7 syllables **rink-tink-tink.... Habitat:** open grassy hillsides above 1200 m. Locally common resident.

Plate 110 Bush-Warblers

709 Stub-tailed Bush-Warbler

710 Pale-footed Bush-Warbler

711 Manchurian Bush-Warbler

♀

♂

712 Chestnut-crowned Bush-Warbler

713 Aberrant Bush-Warbler

B.t. shanensis

B.t. thoracicus

714 Spotted Bush-Warbler

715 Chinese Bush-Warbler

716 Brown Bush-Warbler

717 Russet Bush-Warbler

KAMOL
BANGKOK

วงศ์นกเขน, นกกางเขนและนกเดินดง

THRUSHES: Family *Turdidae.* A huge, cosmopolitan family of mainly insectivorous birds, which show considerable variation in structure and habits. Generally have longer, heavier tarsi than either warblers or flycatchers. Differ from both warblers and babblers in having spotted juvenile plumages. Build cup-shaped nests. Often highly migratory. World: 316 species. Thailand: 49 species.

เหล่านกปีกสั้น

SHORTWINGS: Genus *Brachypteryx.* Non-migratory, highly skulking inhabitants of the forest floor with short tails and short, rounded wings. Have sweet, warbling songs.

718. Lesser Shortwing *Brachypteryx leucophrys* S: 13   นกปีกสั้นเล็ก

Reminiscent of a babbler; very short-tailed with prominent black bill. Unmarked dark rufescent brown upperparts; underparts usually appear buffy-brown in field, often with soft mottling on upper breast, and whitish throat and centre to belly. Slight buffy eye-ring. White supercilium is often concealed, but may be noticeable when the bird is excited. Long, slim, pale flesh legs. An inveterate skulker, keeping on or close to the forest floor. **Voice:** a brief, melodious warbling song of about 10 or 12 notes. The first few notes alternate up and down and then accelerate into a rapid jumble. Call-notes are a quiet, hard, *tack* or *tuck* and a plaintive piping whistle. **Habitat:** evergreen forests from 1000 m to 2000 m. Locally common resident.

719. White-browed Shortwing *Brachypteryx montana* S: 15   นกปีกสั้นสีน้ำเงิน

Somewhat longer-tailed than Lesser Shortwing with dark legs. **Male:** uniform dull, dark blue with prominent white supercilia which almost meet on forehead when expanded. **Female:** dark brown upperparts and diagnostic bright ferruginous forehead, lores and short, slight supercilium. **Immature male:** brown body plumage and white supercilium. Always separated from Lesser Shortwing by dark legs, darker underparts and longer tail. ◆ Usually on or close to forest floor but occasionally as high as 8–10 m on the larger, horizontal limbs of trees. **Voice:** a rich, loud and explosive, warbling song, usually introduced by one to three characteristic whistled *wheez* notes. Call-note a hard *tack*. **Habitat:** evergreen forests of the higher mountains, above 1400 m. (Most common above 2000 m.) Uncommon to locally common resident.

เหล่านกเขนน้อย

ROBINS: Genera *Erithacus, Luscinia, Tarsiger, Copsychus, Cinclidium.* Small to medium. Most species are shy and secretive, keeping to dense undergrowth. The majority are winter visitors.

720. Japanese Robin *Erithacus akahige* S: 15   นกเขนน้อยพันธุ์ญี่ปุ่น

Male: orange-rufous face and upper breast with narrow blackish breast band and greyish flanks. Upperparts rufescent brown with chestnut tail. **Female:** slightly duller, lacking breast band and with lower breast and flanks tinged brownish. ◆ Cocks tail. Highly secretive, keeping to dense undergrowth. **Habitat:** hill evergreen forests at 1500 m. Very rare winter visitor; so far only one record.

Plate 111 Shortwings, Robins

1/06 KY

719 White-browed Shortwing

♂

♀

718 Lesser Shortwing

immature ♂

720 Japanese Robin

♂

♀

722 Siberian Rubythroat

♂

♀

721 Rufous-tailed Robin

723 White-tailed Rubythroat

♂

♀

KAMOL
BANGKOK

328

721. Rufous-tailed Robin *Luscinia sibilans* S: 14   นกเขนน้อยหางแดง

Sexes similar. From female Siberian Blue Robin by whiter underparts which boldly scaled on upper breast and by contrast between rufous upper tail coverts and tail and olive-brown wings and mantle. Shows buffy whitish eye-ring and supraloral patch. See female Black-throated Robin. **Habitat:** forest undergrowth and moist, shady secondary growth, chiefly of plains but occasionally up to 1200 m. Rare winter visitor.

722. Siberian Rubythroat *Luscinia calliope* S: 16   นกคอทับทิม

Heavily built and fat-bodied. From Bluethroat by lack of chestnut in tail and by face pattern. **Male:** red throat bordered by broad white moustache and black malar stripe; blackish lores and white supercilium. **Female:** whitish throat contrasting with brownish breast band. Otherwise facial pattern similar to male but more subdued, with buffy-whitish supercilium and moustache, blackish brown lores and malar stripe. ◆ Highly skulking; most inclined to come out into the open in evening and early morning. **Voice:** a loud, faltering or falling tone whistle and a soft, deep *tschuck*. Also a *se-ic* note, like Siberian Blue Robin. Occasionally gives sweet warbling song before migrating north in spring. **Habitat:** scrub, thickets and grassland from plains up to 1800 m, usually near water. Very common winter visitor.

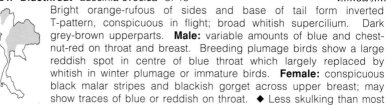

723. White-tailed Rubythroat *Luscinia pectoralis* S: 16   นกคอทับทิมอกดำ

Both sexes from Siberian Rubythroat by white tips to outer tail feathers. **Male:** facial pattern similar to male Siberian, but darker, greyer upperparts and blackish breast. White bases and tips to outer tail feathers. **Female:** greyer crown and upperparts than female Siberian. Tail blackish brown with white tips to outer feathers. **Habitat:** dense scrub of marshy plains. Very rare winter visitor; only one record.

724. Bluethroat *Luscinia svecica* S: 15   นกคอมรกต

Bright orange-rufous of sides and base of tail form inverted T-pattern, conspicuous in flight; broad whitish supercilium. Dark grey-brown upperparts. **Male:** variable amounts of blue and chestnut-red on throat and breast. Breeding plumage birds show a large reddish spot in centre of blue throat which largely replaced by whitish in winter plumage or immature birds. **Female:** conspicuous black malar stripes and blackish gorget across upper breast; may show traces of blue or reddish on throat. ◆ Less skulking than most other robins, often running around on open muddy areas. **Voice:** a twanging *dzyink* and a low, hard *tuck*. **Habitat:** marshes, paddyfields, well-watered open areas of plains. Very common winter visitor.

725. Black-throated Robin *Luscinia obscura* S: 15   นกเขนน้อยหัวดำ

Relatively short-tailed, like Siberian Blue Robin and probably shares distinctive tail-flickering habit. **Male:** differs from male Siberian Blue in having throat and breast black and by conspicuous white sides to tail. **Female:** from female Siberian Blue by unscaled underparts, buffy under tail coverts and by slightly rufescent tail. **Habitat:** moist secondary growth, scrub of plains or foothills. Very rare winter visitor; so far only one record.

Plate 112 Robins II

♂ ♀

724 Bluethroat

♂

♀

725 Black-throated Robin

♂
adult

imm. ♀

adult ♀

immature ♂

726 Siberian Blue Robin

♂

♀

♀

727 Orange-flanked Bush-Robin

♀

♂

728 Golden Bush-Robin

KAMOL
BANGKOK

330

726. Siberian Blue Robin *Luscinia cyane* S: 15   นกเขนน้อยไซบีเรีย

Relatively short-tailed; almost always shows distinctive, rapid tail-flickering habit when alarmed. Legs coloured pale flesh. **Adult male:** dark, dull blue upperparts and white underparts with black sides to throat and breast. **Adult female:** cold olive-brown upperparts, buffy throat and breast scaled with dark brown. Dull bluish rump, upper tail coverts and tail. **Immature male:** shows mottled blue and brown feathering on wing coverts and mantle. Blue rump, upper tail coverts and tail and warm rufous-buff underparts. **Immature female:** may lack any bluish tint on rump and tail; often shows pale buffy tips to greater coverts. ◆ Keeps to ground or low shrubs. **Voice:** a quiet, hard *tuck*, frequently repeated; also a loud *se-ic*. **Habitat:** mixed deciduous and evergreen forest, bamboo and moist, shady secondary growth; chiefly in plains and lower hills, but occasionally up to 1500 m. Occurs in mangroves or gardens on passage. Common winter visitor and passage migrant.

727. Orange-flanked Bush-Robin *Tarsiger cyanurus* S: 15   นกเขนน้อยข้างสีส้ม

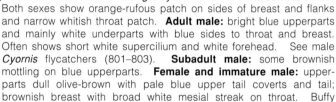

Both sexes show orange-rufous patch on sides of breast and flanks and narrow whitish throat patch. **Adult male:** bright blue upperparts and mainly white underparts with blue sides to throat and breast. Often shows short white supercilium and white forehead. See male *Cyornis* flycatchers (801–803). **Subadult male:** some brownish mottling on blue upperparts. **Female and immature male:** upperparts dull olive-brown with pale blue upper tail coverts and tail; brownish breast with broad white mesial streak on throat. Buffy eye-ring. From Siberian Blue Robin by blackish legs and longer tail which is irregularly flicked downwards at intervals. ◆ Usually keeps to low bushes within a few centimetres of the ground. **Voice:** a quiet, deep, croaking *churk*. **Habitat:** evergreen forest, secondary growth above 1200 m. Favours ridges, mountaintops. Uncommon to locally common winter visitor.

728. Golden Bush-Robin *Tarsiger chrysaeus* S: 15   นกเขนน้อยสีทอง

Diagnostic orange-yellow patches in sides of tail delineate inverted T-pattern, black in male, brown in female. **Male:** deep orange-yellow underparts, shoulder patches, supercilium and rump; black face mask. **Female:** entire upperparts greenish olive; underparts duller, a slightly paler, more golden-yellow than in male; usually slight dark mottling on upper breast. Faint buffy eyebrow in front of eye. ◆ Highly skulking. **Voice:** a hard, grating, *chit-t-tit*. **Habitat:** undergrowth of evergreen forest above 1900 m. Rare winter visitor.

นกกางเขนบ้าน

729. Oriental Magpie-Robin (Magpie Robin) *Copsychus saularis* S: 23

Large for a robin, with striking black and white plumage. **Male:** glossy black upperparts, head and breast. **Female:** black of upperparts and breast replaced with dark grey. **Juvenile:** shows distinct brownish mottling on breast. ◆ Confiding and conspicuous; often cocks tail sharply. **Voice:** loud, melodious whistled song. Calls with a long, plaintive whistle (similar to Siberian Rubythroat, but with rising tone) and gives a harsh, rasping and drawn-out *che-e-e-e-h* in alarm. **Habitat:** open woodlands, clearings, mangroves, cultivation, gardens, towns and cities, from plains to 1800 m. Very common resident.

Plate 113 Robins III

729 Oriental Magpie-Robin

730 White-rumped Shama

31 Rufous-tailed Shama

732 White-tailed Robin

733 Blue-fronted Robin

734 White-bellied Redstart

332

730. White-rumped Shama *Copsychus malabaricus* S: 22   นกกางเขนดง

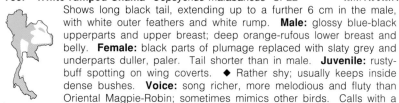

Shows long black tail, extending up to a further 6 cm in the male, with white outer feathers and white rump. **Male:** glossy blue-black upperparts and upper breast; deep orange-rufous lower breast and belly. **Female:** black parts of plumage replaced with slaty grey and underparts duller, paler. Tail shorter than in male. **Juvenile:** rusty-buff spotting on wing coverts. ◆ Rather shy; usually keeps inside dense bushes. **Voice:** song richer, more melodious and fluty than Oriental Magpie-Robin; sometimes mimics other birds. Calls with a harsh *tschack*. **Habitat:** evergreen and mixed deciduous forests, secondary growth, bamboo up to 1500 m. Very common resident.

731. Rufous-tailed Shama *Copsychus pyrropygus* S: 22   นกกางเขนดงหางแดง

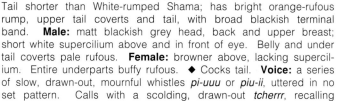

Tail shorter than White-rumped Shama; has bright orange-rufous rump, upper tail coverts and tail, with broad blackish terminal band. **Male:** matt blackish grey head, back and upper breast; short white supercilium above and in front of eye. Belly and under tail coverts pale rufous. **Female:** browner above, lacking supercilium. Entire underparts buffy rufous. ◆ Cocks tail. **Voice:** a series of slow, drawn-out, mournful whistles *pi-uuu* or *piu-ii*, uttered in no set pattern. Calls with a scolding, drawn-out *tcherrr*, recalling Oriental Magpie-Robin. **Habitat:** lowland rainforest, including primary peat swamp forest. Rare resident.

732. White-tailed Robin *Cinclidium leucurum* S: 18   นกเขนสีฟ้าหางขาว

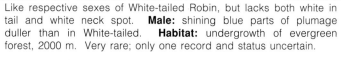

Moderately long, broad tail which appears slightly rounded and shows conspicuous white lateral patches when fanned. **Male:** blue-black plumage with shining blue forehead and bend of wing. White spot on neck usually concealed. **Female:** dark olive-brown plumage, slightly paler on underparts than upperparts, with whitish or buffy patch on throat. ◆ Keeps close to the ground. **Voice:** a loud, clear jangling whistled song of about 7–8 notes. Somewhat hurried; slightly reminiscent of Lesser Shortwing. Gives a thin 1–2 note whistle in alarm. Also a low *tuc*. **Habitat:** thick undergrowth of ever-green forests, usually above 1000 m but occasionally dispersing lower in winter. Very often close to small streams. Uncommon resident.

733. Blue-fronted Robin *Cinclidium frontale* S: 20   นกเขนน้ำเงิน

Like respective sexes of White-tailed Robin, but lacks both white in tail and white neck spot. **Male:** shining blue parts of plumage duller than in White-tailed. **Habitat:** undergrowth of evergreen forest, 2000 m. Very rare; only one record and status uncertain.

REDSTARTS: Genera *Hodgsonius, Phoenicurus, Rhyacornis, Chaimarrornis.* A rather heterogeneous grouping of birds with chestnut-orange flashes in the tail. Most are less skulking than robins. Some species frequent streams.

734. White-bellied Redstart *Hodgsonius phaenicuroides* S: 18 นกเขนแปลง
Longer-tailed than other redstarts with quite different actions and behaviour. **Male:** plumage dull, slaty-blue, with striking white belly patch and white flecking at bend of wing. Rump concolorous with mantle. Tail, long and graduated, usually held slightly cocked and fanned, with conspicuous, clear-cut, orange-rufous patches in basal half. **Immature male:** like female, but shows orange-rufous tail patches. **Female:** brownish olive upperparts and brownish buff throat and underparts. Lacks strong facial contrast. Tail uniform dull rufescent brown. Best distinguished by long-tailed, long-legged appearance and horizontal stance typical of some *Luscinia* spp. ◆ Usually shows conspicuous yellowish flesh gape flange and flesh-coloured legs. Highly skulking. **Voice:** a very deep, quiet, hard *tuk.* **Habitat:** dense low herbage of forest clearings and scrub in open country above 1200 m. Uncommon winter visitor.

735. Blue-fronted Redstart *Phoenicurus frontalis* S: 16 นกเขนสีฟ้าท้ายสีน้ำตาล
Distinctive tail pattern of mostly orange-rufous outer feathers contrasting with inverted 'T' formed by black (male) or dark brown (female) central feathers and terminal band. Longer-tailed than Daurian Redstart; pumps rather than shivers tail. **Male:** dark blue head, upperparts, throat and upper breast. Shining blue patch on forecrown; rufous-orange rump, upper tail coverts and abdomen. **Female:** from female Daurian by tail pattern; lack of white in wing. **Habitat:** evergreen forest, forest edge and scrub above 1400 m. Rare winter visitor.

736. Daurian Redstart *Phoenicurus auroreus* S: 15 นกเขนท้องแดง
Diagnostic white wing patch, rufous rump and tail with black (male) or dark brown (female) central feathers. **Male:** clean grey crown and hindneck, black back, black throat and orange-rufous breast and abdomen. **Female:** brown upperparts; underparts deep, buffy brownish, tinged rufous on abdomen. Buffy eye-ring. Shows distinctive, jerky shivering of tail. **Voice:** a hard, deep *tuck* and a short, sharp whistle. **Habitat:** understorey of open forests, secondary growth and scrub from 300 m to the highest summits. Uncommon to locally common winter visitor.

737. Plumbeous Redstart *Rhyacornis fuliginosus* S: 14 นกเขนเทาหางแดง
Male: dark slaty plumage with bright reddish chestnut upper and under tail coverts and tail. From other redstarts by habitat and lack of dark central tail feathers. Rounded tip to tail. **Female:** striking black and white tail pattern. Underparts whitish, scaled grey. **Juvenile:** like female, but tinged brownish, with buffy spotting on wing coverts and underparts. ◆ Often in apparent association with River Chat. **Voice:** a short, sharp whistle. **Habitat:** rocky, rushing streams from foothills to high mountains. Uncommon to locally common resident. Probably also a winter visitor and altitudinal migrant, occurring at lower elevations in winter.

738. River Chat *Chaimarrornis leucocephalus* S: 19   นกเขนหัวขาวท้ายแดง
Sexes similar.   Blackish plumage with striking white crown and chestnut-red rump and tail with black terminal band.   **Juvenile:** browner with black scales on crown. ◆ Often cocks tail.   **Voice:** a loud, sharp whistled *peeek*.   **Habitat:** rocky, rushing streams from foothills up to highest elevations.   Uncommon; status uncertain, but probably winter visitor.

เหล่านกกางเขนน้ำ

FORKTAILS: Genus *Enicurus*.   Long scissor-tails and striking black and white plumage.   Inhabit streams, usually keeping to the edge or hopping from rock to rock and feeding on aquatic invertebrates.   Fly low over stream course, uttering shrill notes when alarmed.   Build large cup nests of moss, rootlets, etc., placed under banks or in crevices among boulders, tree roots, or plastered on to rock with mud.

739. Chestnut-naped Forktail *Enicurus ruficapillus* S: 20   นกกางเขนน้ำหลังแดง
Male: distinguished from other forktails by chestnut crown and back of neck and by black scaling on breast.   **Female:** similar, but entire back chestnut.   **Voice:** shrill whistles, like Slaty-backed.   **Habitat:** rocky streams in evergreen forest from foothills to 900 m.   Uncommon resident.

740. Black-backed Forktail *Enicurus immaculatus* S: 23   นกกางเขนน้ำหลังดำ
Black head and back.   From White-crowned Forktail by smaller size, white breast and white on head confined to a narrow band on forecrown.   **Juvenile:** resembles Slaty-backed, having a slaty to sooty-brown back; slight grey scaling on breast.   **Voice:** a short whistle; weaker, less piercing than in Slaty-backed.   **Habitat:** rocky streams of wooded foothills.   Uncommon resident.

741. Slaty-backed Forktail *Enicurus schistaceus* S: 25   นกกางเขนน้ำหลังเทา
From other forktails by slaty-grey crown, hindneck and mantle.   **Juvenile:** slaty parts replaced by dark brown; shows scaling on breast.   **Voice:** a sharp, metallic *teenk*.   **Habitat:** rocky streams of wooded areas from 400 m to at least 1800 m.   Common resident.

742. White-crowned Forktail *Enicurus leschenaulti* S: 28   นกกางเขนน้ำหัวขาว
Larger than other forktails with black back and black breast.   White oval patch of feathers on forecrown rises to a slight crest.   **Juvenile:** all black crown. ◆ Very shy.   (Race in Peninsula is smaller and shorter-tailed.)   **Voice:** a harsh *scree*, or frequently *scree, chit-chit-chit* with almost exactly the same quality as the call of Blue Whistling Thrush (752).   Also has an elaborate, high-pitched whistling song, rarely heard.   **Habitat:** small streamlets and moist areas in evergreen and mixed deciduous forests up to 2000 m (though apparently restricted to level lowlands in the Peninsula).   Fairly common resident.

Plate 114 Redstarts, Forktails

735 Blue-fronted Redstart
♂
♀

736 Daurian Redstart
♂
♀

737 Plumbeous Redstart
♂
♀

738 River Chat

739 Chestnut-naped Forktail
♂
♀

740 Black-backed Forktail

741 Slaty-backed Forktail

742 White-crowned Forktail

Mongkol

336

COCHOAS: Genus *Cochoa*. Large, arboreal thrushes with broad bills and conspicuous pale bluish wing patches. Mainly frugivorous. Quiet and unobtrusive, sometimes sitting still in the shade of middle storey for long periods. Often sing from exposed limbs near forest edge.

743. Purple Cochoa *Cochoa purpurea* S: 30   นกปีกแพรสีม่วง

Pale blue crown and blackish sides to head; wing patch and tail pale lavender-purple. **Male:** dull, dark purplish brown body plumage. **Female:** rusty brown body plumage, darker on upperparts than on underparts. (Sometimes shows whitish throat.) ◆ Inhabits lower canopy and middle storey; often in fruiting trees with thrushes or bulbuls. **Habitat:** hill evergreen forest usually from 1000 m to 1800 m (though one record at 400 m). Rare resident.

744. Green Cochoa *Cochoa viridis* S: 28   นกปีกแพรสีเขียว

From Purple Cochoa by green body plumage, bright blue crown and nape. Pale blue wing patch and upperside of tail. **Female:** some green feathering in wing patch. ◆ Inhabits canopy and middle storey. **Voice:** a pure, monotone whistle of about 2 seconds duration. Of similar pitch to song of Black-headed Sibia (651) but lacks wavering quality. **Habitat:** usually hill evergreen forest above 1200 m, though occasionally descending as low as 400 m Uncommon resident.

CHATS: Genus *Saxicola*. Small. Inhabit open country where they perch in exposed positions such as low bushes, with a relatively upright posture. Often flick tails and jerk wings. Drop to the ground to feed.

745. Stonechat *Saxicola torquata* S: 14   นกยอดหญ้าหัวดำ

Male: black head and throat contrasting with orange-rufous breast and belly and white neck patch. Upperparts predominantly blackish with white patch on upper tail coverts and on inner wing coverts. **Female and immature:** much paler than female Pied Bushchat with well-marked dark streaks on brownish upperparts and pinkish buff rump and upper tail coverts. Often shows buffy supercilium and usually a white wing patch. Underparts pale rufous-buff, sometimes almost whitish. **Voice:** a sharp, continual *chack, chack, chack*, like two pebbles being struck together. **Habitat:** open country, grasslands and cultivated areas up to 2000 m. Recently found breeding above 1600 m in the far north-west. Very common winter visitor; local resident.

746. Pied Bushchat *Saxicola caprata* S: 14   นกยอดหญ้าสีดำ, นกขี้หมา

Male: all black with conspicuous white rump, upper tail coverts and wing patch (not always visible at rest). **Female:** uniformly dark brown, with indistinct streaks on upperparts and rusty rump and upper tail coverts. Lacks white in wing. **Juvenile:** body spotted with buff. (Immature males show white in wing and on upper tail coverts before assuming black body colouration of adult.) **Voice:** short whistling song, usually with a harsh ending; call notes a soft *chack, chack* and a plaintive whistled *hew*. **Habitat:** grasslands, scrub country and cultivated areas from plains up to 1600 m. Common resident.

Plate 115 Cochoas, Chats

743 Purple Cochoa ♂ ♀

744 Green Cochoa ♂ ♀

745 Stonechat ♂ ♀

746 Pied Bushchat ♂ ♀

747 Jerdon's Bushchat ♂ ♀

748 Grey Bushchat ♂ ♀

Mongkol

338

747. Jerdon's Bushchat *Saxicola jerdoni* S: 16 นกยอดหญ้าหลังดำ

Appears longer-tailed than other chats. **Male:** has glossy black upperparts and clean white underparts. **Female:** from female Grey Bushchat by shorter, less distinct supercilium and longer, slightly more rounded tail. ◆ Shy; more skulking than other chats. **Voice:** a short, plaintive whistle; higher-pitched than similar notes of other chats. **Habitat:** tall grass and scrub of riverine floodplains. Rare resident.

748. Grey Bushchat *Saxicola ferrea* S: 16 นกยอดหญ้าสีเทา

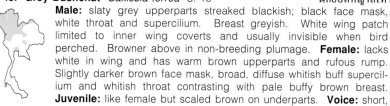

Male: slaty grey upperparts streaked blackish; black face mask, white throat and supercilium. Breast greyish. White wing patch limited to inner wing coverts and usually invisible when bird perched. Browner above in non-breeding plumage. **Female:** lacks white in wing and has warm brown upperparts and rufous rump. Slightly darker brown face mask, broad, diffuse whitish buff supercilium and whitish throat contrasting with pale buffy brown breast. **Juvenile:** like female but scaled brown on underparts. **Voice:** short, warbling song; alarm call is a soft *churr* followed by a plaintive piping *hew*. Also has a harsher note, *bzech*. **Habitat:** grass and scrub of open areas. Occurs down to plains in winter. Recently found breeding above 1600 m. Common winter visitor and local resident.

เหล่านกกระเบื้อง

ROCK-THRUSHES: Genus *Monticola*. Large chats. Some species perch in open country while others frequent forest edge and canopy.

749. White-throated Rock-Thrush *Monticola gularis* S: 19 นกกระเบื้องคอขาว

Smaller and slimmer than Chestnut-bellied and Blue Rock-Thrushes. **Male:** bright blue crown and nape; blackish, brown-scaled mantle; and blackish brown wings with small white patch. Orange-rufous rump, upper tail coverts and underparts with diagnostic white median throat stripe. **Female:** brownish above and whitish below with bold black scaling on both upperparts and underparts. Shows white median throat stripe. **Habitat:** evergreen and deciduous forest, and forest edge from plains to 1200 m. Uncommon winter visitor.

นกกระเบื้องท้องแดง

750. Chestnut-bellied Rock-Thrush *Monticola rufiventris* S: 25

Larger and longer-tailed than Blue Rock-Thrush. **Male:** distinguished from *philippensis* race of Blue Rock-Thrush by brighter, glossy blue crown contrasting with blackish sides to head; more glossy-blue upperparts. Unscaled, deep chestnut breast, belly and under tail coverts. **Female:** distinguished by broad whitish buff crescent behind dark ear coverts. Also from Blue Rock-Thrush by white throat stripe and submoustachial stripe and bolder, more contrasted underparts. ◆ Flicks tail upwards slightly. Often perches on exposed snags of taller trees. **Voice:** song of short whistled phrases, *tii-teru*, given from permanent perch. A longer version given in song flight. Call notes a thin *sit, sit* and a deep, croaking *churr*. **Habitat:** edge of evergreen forest, scrub country with rocky outcrops above 1200 m. Uncommon winter visitor; also resident on upper slopes of Doi Inthanon.

Plate 116 Rock-Thrushes, Thrushes

749 White-throated Rock-Thrush

750 Chestnut-bellied Rock-Thrush

M.c. caeruleus

752 Blue Whistling Thrush
1/06 KK

751 Blue Rock-Thrush
i/06 KY

M.s. philippensis

753 Chestnut-capped Thrush

754 Orange-headed Thrush

Mongkol

340

751. Blue Rock-Thrush *Monticola solitarius* S: 23   นกกระเบื้องผา

Male: dark grey-blue with narrow whitish and blackish scale-markings all over body. Blue Whistling Thrush is much larger and longer-tailed, with iridescent dark blue plumage. Male of race *philippensis* shows chestnut lower breast, belly and under tail coverts and more uniform, brighter blue upperparts, throat and upper breast. **Female:** heavily scaled, dark grey-brown (sometimes with bluish cast), lacking strong contrast on face or underparts. ◆ Stands erect on prominent perches; often bobs body downwards while tail flicked up after landing. Usually solitary. **Voice:** a low clucking sound. **Habitat:** towns (often perched on roofs or ledges of buildings), rocky seacoats, limestone outcrops and open areas from plains up to 1600 m. Common winter visitor; race *madoci* breeds in peninsular Thailand.

เหล่านกเอี้ยงถ้ำ

WHISTLING THRUSHES: Genus *Myiophoneus*. Large, dark bluish thrushes with glossy spangles in plumage. Inhabit moist, shady forests, rushing streams. Shy; loud, piercing calls. Take many aquatic invertebrates, and snails. Build cup-shaped nests in crevices of banks or fallen trees.

752. Blue Whistling Thrush *Myiophoneus caeruleus* S: 33   นกเอี้ยงถ้ำ

Large size, with broad, rounded tail. Sexes similar. Dark, purplish blue plumage with lighter iridescent spots and streaks. Bill usually yellow, but black in one of the migrant races, *M. c. caeruleus*. **Immature:** duller, lacking iridescent spots. ◆ Shy and retiring. **Voice:** a loud, harsh *scree*, very like the call of White-crowned Fork-tail; occasionally a shrill whistle. Also has a rich song combining both mellow fluty and harsh scratchy notes. **Habitat:** wooded streams and moist, shady areas of undergrowth; at the base of cliffs or gullies, especially in limestone areas; cave mouths. From lowlands to the highest elevations. Common resident and winter visitor.

เหล่านกเดินดง

TYPICAL THRUSHES: Medium to large. Rather shy birds of wooded habitats. Bound along the forest floor, feeding on insects, worms or fallen fruit. Many also take fruit and occasionally nectar from the tree-tops.

เหล่านกเดินดง 1

Genus *Zoothera*. Have broad white bands on the underwing, which are conspicuous in flight. Usually solitary or in pairs, feeding mostly on the ground and flying up to perch inconspicuously in understorey trees when disturbed. Some are resident.

753. Chestnut-capped Thrush *Zoothera interpres* S: 18   นกเดินดงหัวน้ำตาลแดง

Comparatively small and short-tailed. Sexes similar. Colouration superficially resembles that of Chestnut-naped Forktail (739) but black of throat extends to upper breast; back and rump dark slaty grey and tail almost entirely dark with white tips to outer feathers. Shows conspicuous white shoulder patch and black spotting on lower breast. White spot on ear coverts. Very shy and secretive. **Voice:** short, repeated, rich fluty phrases recalling White-rumped Shama but interspersed with very high notes. **Habitat:** evergreen forests, possibly up to 750 m but probably mainly confined to lowlands, foothills. Rare resident.

754. Orange-headed Thrush *Zoothera citrina* S: 22 นกเดินดงหัวสีส้ม

Diagnostic bright orange-rufous head and underparts. Upperparts blue-grey in male, olive-brown in female. Extreme lower belly and under tail coverts whitish. Race *gibsonhilli*, breeding in south-west, has whitish tips to medium coverts. **Juvenile:** head and mantle dull orange-brown, spotted and scaled; underparts pale orange-buff with dark scales or bars. Shows one or two dark bars on side of head. ◆ Feeds both on ground and in fruiting trees. **Voice:** a rich, sweet and variable song of short, frequently repeated strophes. A thin *tzzeet* in flight and a quiet deep, guttural *tjuck* in alarm. **Habitat:** evergreen forests, secondary growth up to 1500 m. Uncommon resident and winter visitor.

755. Siberian Thrush *Zoothera sibirica* S: 24 นกเดินดงสีเทาดำ

Male: slaty plumage with broad white supercilium. Center of belly either grey or whitish; under tail coverts scalloped. **Female:** from other *Zoothera* thrushes by long, buffy supercilium which curves around behind ear coverts; dark lores and bold dark eye-line contrasting with paler, streaked, ear coverts. Upperparts rufous-brown; underparts buffy with dark brown scale-markings. From *Turdus* thrushes by white-tipped tail feathers and by the typical *Zoothera* white stripe on underwing. ◆ Legs strikingly pale, fleshy or straw coloured. Shy. Often feeds in flocks with Eyebrowed Thrushes in fruiting trees and shrubs. **Voice:** a quiet *tsit*, thinner and shorter than similar note of Eyebrowed Thrush. **Habitat:** evergreen forests from lowlands to over 2500 m (mostly hills). Uncommon passage migrant; may possibly winter in the mountains of the south.

756. Long-tailed Thrush *Zoothera dixoni* S: 28 นกเดินดงหลังสีไพล

Sexes similar. From Scaly Thrush by uniform olive-brown upperparts with buff-tipped wing coverts forming two wing bars. Prominent buffy whitish lores and eye-ring and prominent blackish crescent on ear coverts. Underparts buffy white with short, transverse black bars. Whitish tips to outer tail feathers. Often associates with mixed thrush flocks; usually feeding on the ground. **Habitat:** evergreen forests above 1400 m. Rare winter visitor.

757. Scaly Thrush *Zoothera dauma* S: 28 นกเดินดงลายเสือ

Diagnostic bold black and golden-buffy scaling on both upperparts and underparts; markings are especially dense around the head. Black crescent on ear coverts. Prominent buffy white lores and white-tipped outer tail feathers. **Voice:** a soft, drawn-out, monotone whistle of about 0.75 seconds duration (AvdB). Calls with a thin, short, *tzeet*. **Habitat:** evergreen and occasionally mixed deciduous forests from foothills to the highest elevations. Uncommon resident and winter visitor.

758. Dark-sided Thrush *Zoothera marginata* S: 25 นกเดินดงเล็กปากยาว
Noticeably long, slightly decurved bill and plump-bodied, short-tailed appearance. Upperparts dark rufescent brown. Rufous-tinged patch on primaries contrasts slightly with dark primary coverts. Diffuse pale area on lores, sides of head and dark crescent on ear coverts, but contrast is more muted than in other *Zoothera* spp. Upper breast and flanks olive brown; lower breast and belly whitish, scaled olive-brown. Whitish throat. **Immature:** has buffy wing bars. ◆ Very shy. Keeps to ground, usually frequenting moist areas close to streams and digging in soft mud with long bill. **Voice:** sings with a thin whistle, like Scaly Thrush but softer and shorter (0.5 seconds); inflected downwards (AvdB). Calls with a soft, deep, guttural *tchuck*. **Habitat:** evergreen forest from plains to the highest elevations. Uncommon resident.

เหล่านกเดินดง 2

Genus *Turdus*. Exclusively winter visitors. Many are irruptive in occurrence, large numbers occuring in some years with comparatively few in others. Often in mixed flocks which may comprise 2 or 3 species, feeding in fruiting trees or shrubs, or on the forest floor.

759. Black-breasted Thrush *Turdus dissimilis* S: 23 นกเดินดงอกดำ
Slightly smaller than the other *Turdus* thrushes, with rufous wing lining. **Male:** black head and breast, slaty grey upperparts and orange rufous upper belly and flanks. **Female:** brownish head and upperparts. From Eyebrowed Thrush by lack of supercilium and by boldly streaked breast band. Bill yellow or orange. **Voice:** a sharp, resounding *tock*, *tock*, *tock*, *tock* (Smythies). **Habitat:** evergreen forests above 1000 m. Rare and irregular winter visitor.

760. Grey-winged Blackbird *Turdus boulboul* S: 28 นกเดินดงดำปีกเทา
Male: blackish plumage with conspicuous greyish white wing patch, formed by greater coverts, secondaries and tertials. Orange bill and orbital ring. **Female:** warm olive-brown plumage, with a paler rufous-brown wing patch. Duller, yellowish bill. ◆ Small numbers occasionally seen with flocks of Eyebrowed Thrushes. **Habitat:** evergreen forest above 1000 m. Rare winter visitor, a few occurring in most years.

761. Common Blackbird *Turdus merula* S: 28 นกเดินดงสีดำ
Male: entirely blackish plumage with orange-yellow bill and orbital ring. **Female:** darker brown than female Grey-winged Blackbird and lacks pale wing patch. Throat buffy, usually slightly streaked. Bill dusky yellowish to blackish brown. **Habitat:** open country, scrub of lowlands. Very rare winter visitor; only one record.

Plate 117 Thrushes II

♀ Siberian Thrush in flight to show typical *Zoothera* underwing pattern

755 Siberian Thrush ♂ ♀

757 Scaly Thrush

756 Long-tailed Thrush

758 Dark-sided Thrush

759 Black-breasted Thrush ♂ ♀

760 Grey-winged Blackbird ♂ ♀

761 Common Blackbird ♀ ♂

344

762. Chestnut Thrush *Turdus rubrocanus* S: 28 นกเดินดงสีน้ำตาลแดง

Large size. Deep chestnut back, rump and underparts and dark grey head, throat and neck. Under tail coverts whitish with bold, blackish streaks. Wings and tail black. **Female:** duller, with dark brownish wings and tail. ◆ Yellow bill, orbital ring and dusky yellow feet. **Voice:** a hard *chook-chook* and rapid, strident *sit-sit-sit*. **Habitat:** evergreen forest above 1200 m. Rare winter visitor, irruptive in occurrence.

763. Grey-sided Thrush *Turdus feae* S: 24 นกเดินดงอกเทา

Wing lining greyish white. Resembles Eyebrowed Thrush in having whitish supercilium and mark below eye, but rufous of underparts replaced with grey, and entire upperparts, including crown, are bright rufescent olive. **Male:** shows a more extensive, purer grey on breast and flanks than does female. **Immature:** shows pale tips to greater coverts. ◆ One or two birds often associate with feeding flocks of Eyebrowed Thrush. **Habitat:** evergreen forest above 1000 m. Uncommon winter visitor of annual occurrence.

764. Eyebrowed Thrush *Turdus obscurus* S: 24 นกเดินดงสีคล้ำ

Wing lining greyish white. White supercilium, white patch below eye and whitish chin. Flanks and lower breast pale orange-rufous. **Male:** grey head, throat and upper breast. **Female:** head olive-brown, showing little or no contrast from rest of upperparts; whitish throat and duller orange-rufous on underparts than in male. ◆ Bill basally yellowish. Usually the commonest thrush; often in large flocks. **Voice:** a thin, drawn-out *tseep*. Flocks often give a chuckling subsong before their northward departure in spring. **Habitat:** evergreen and deciduous forests, secondary growth from plains up to the highest elevations. (Most abundant above 1000 m.) In mangroves, gardens on passage. Common winter visitor and passage migrant of annual occurrence.

765a. Red-throated Thrush *Turdus ruficollis ruficollis* S: 25 นกเดินดงคอแดง

Pale rufous wing lining. From other thrushes by rufous in outer tail feathers. **Male:** rufous face, throat and breast, finely mottled with white in winter; white underparts. Upperparts grey-brown, grey tinge especially pronounced on crown and sides of neck. **Female:** very variable, but supercilium and throat usually buffy; rufous on breast much paler, sometimes lacking; mottled with white and spotted with black. Upperparts more olive, less grey-toned than in male. **Immature:** breast brownish grey, with dark streaks or spots. Buffy supercilium. From Dusky Thrush by less contrasting face pattern and relatively uniform wings, lacking any pale panel. Bill basally yellowish. **Voice:** flight note a thin *tseep*; gives a soft, throaty chuckle in alarm. **Habitat:** evergreen forests of high elevations. So far recorded only from the summit of Doi Inthanon. Very rare winter visitor.

Plate 118 Thrushes III

762 Chestnut Thrush ♂

763 Grey-sided Thrush ♂

immature ♀

64 Eyebrowed Thrush ♂

immature

765b Black-throated Thrush ♂

765a Red-throated Thrush ♂ ♀

immature

immature ♀

immature ♂

766 Dusky Thrush

Mongkol

346

765b. Black-throated Thrush *Turdus ruficollis atrogularis* S: 25   นกเดินดงคอดำ
Conspecific with preceding species.   Pale rufous wing lining, but lacks rufous in tail.   **Male:** black face, throat and upper breast, finely mottled with white in winter.   Rest of underparts whitish.   Upperparts grey-brown.   **Female and immature:** grey-brown upperparts with whitish supercilium; upper breast and sides of throat boldly streaked blackish.   Rest of underparts whitish with pale brown streaks on flanks.   Usually from Red-throated by lack of rufous in tail, but intergrades occur.   **Habitat:** evergreen forests above 1000 m.   Very rare winter visitor.

766. Dusky Thrush *Turdus naumanni* S: 25   นกเดินดงอกลาย
Wing lining pale rufous.   **Male:** striking black ear coverts, contrasting with white throat and partial collar, white supercilium.   Rufous wing patch formed by coverts and inner secondaries and a whitish notch at base of primaries on leading edge of wing.   Tail blackish.   Heavy black spotting and scaling on upper breast (often forming a double breast band) and flanks.   **Female and immature:** duller and browner, with less contrasting facial pattern; wing panel paler, biscuit-coloured.   Scaling on underparts browner, less bold.
Voice: a soft, slightly musical, squawking *chuk-chuk* or *which-which*.   Also a *swic*.
Habitat: evergreen forests, secondary growth, scrub; chiefly of higher elevations but also plains.   Rare winter visitor.   Occurence irregular, irruptive.   Occasionally in large flocks like Eyebrowed.

วงศ์นกจับแมลง

FLYCATCHERS: Family *Muscicapidae*.   A large and diverse family, characterised by flattened, broad-based bills with long rictal bristles and short, slender legs.   Sexes often differ, with bright-plumaged males being more readily identifiable than duller, brownish females.   Juvenile plumages are spotted or mottled.   Mainly insectivorous.   Many species show an upright posture, sit on exposed perches, and make brief sorties after flying insects while others feed close to the ground in forest undergrowth, gleaning insects from foliage.   Most have harsh call-notes and sweet, warbling songs.   Build small, cup-shaped nests placed in branches or in tree cavities, or in bankside hollows.   World: 182 species.   Thailand: 38 species.   (See also under Additions, page 401.)

เหล่านกจับแมลงป่า

JUNGLE FLYCATCHERS: Genus *Rhinomyias*.   Brownish plumage with rufescent tails.   Rounded heads, long and heavy bills, comparatively short wings and moderate length tails which frequently held cocked.   In shape and actions resemble female Blue Flycatchers (*Cyornis* spp.) and, like them, inhabit middle storey and understorey of forest.   Sexes similar.

767. Fulvous-chested Flycatcher *Rhinomyias olivacea* S: 15 นกจับแมลงอกสีเนื้อ

Olive-brown upperparts with rufescent tail and upper tail coverts.   Whitish throat and belly, with a broad, brownish buff band across upper breast.   Bill black and legs pale flesh.   From female *Cyornis* flycatchers by whitish throat and lack of orange on breast.   From Jungle Babblers (585–595) by much thinner, weaker tarsi.   **Immature:** shows buffy tips to greater coverts and tertials.   **Voice:** very like that of Hill Blue Flycatcher (802), but song weaker, simpler, more tinkling with fewer trilling notes.   Harsh *tac* and *trrt* calls.   **Habitat:** evergreen forest from plains to 900 m.   Common resident.

768. Brown-chested Flycatcher *Rhinomyias brunneata* S: 15

Distinguished from other *Rhinomyias* by yellowish lower mandible. Appears very long-billed. Usually shows slight dark scaling on whitish throat which is not strongly demarcated from brownish breast band. Legs pale fleshy. From Brown-breasted Flycatcher (774) by larger size, longer bill and less contrasted face pattern. **Immature:** shows dark tip to lower mandible; rusty buff tips to greater coverts and tertials. **Habitat:** evergreen and mixed deciduous forests of plains and lower hill slopes. Rare passage migrant.

769. Grey-chested Flycatcher *Rhinomyias umbratilis* S: 15　　นกจับแมลงอกเทา

Distinguished from Fulvous-chested Flycatcher by gleaming white throat, contrasting with grey or olive-grey breast band. Bill black; legs pale flesh. From Moustached Babbler (592) by weaker tarsi, browner sides of head and different actions. **Immature:** rusty-buff tips to greater coverts and tertials. **Voice:** song high-pitched, richer, more varied than in Fulvous-chested. **Habitat:** evergreen forests of lowlands and hills to 900 m. Uncommon or rare resident in the extreme southern provinces.

เหล่านกจับแมลงสีน้ำตาล

BROWN FLYCATCHERS: Genus *Muscicapa*. Long wings and erect posture. Usually frequent exposed perches, such as dead tree limbs, from which they make dashing sallies after flying insects. Plumage brownish, often with slight streaking on underparts. Show thin whitish or buffy wing bars and tertial edges in fresh plumage. Sexes similar. Quiet, thin, tuneless songs and hard calls.

770. Dark-sided Flycatcher *Muscicapa sibirica* S: 13　　นกจับแมลงสีคล้ำ

Dark grey-brown above, like Asian Brown Flycatcher, but separated by shorter bill, appearing all dark or with only a small pale area at base of lower mandible; very long wings, reaching 2/3 of the way down the tail. Underparts appear dark grey-brown, due to heavy, blurred streaking across upper breast and on flanks, with a broad white median stripe extending down the centre of the breast and on to the belly. Most, but not all, show a clear white throat and half collar. Whitish or buffy eye-ring and indistinct pale loral patch. Shows thin buffy-white wing bar and whitish tertial edges. **Voice:** calls with a distinctive, short metallic tinkle (not as harsh and dry as the call of Asian Brown Flycatcher). **Habitat:** evergreen and mixed deciduous forests (mostly edges and clearings), secondary growth, from plains up to 2000 m. Occurs in gardens, mangroves on passage. Common winter visitor, particularly in the Peninsula.

771. Ferruginous Flycatcher *Muscicapa ferruginea* S: 13 นกจับแมลงสีน้ำตาลแดง

Shape like Dark-sided, with very short bill which appears mainly dark; wings not quite so long. Rufous-brown back, bright orange-rufous rump and upper tail coverts and slaty-grey head with a bold white eye-ring. Bright orange-rufous edges to tertials and greater coverts. Lores appear dark, or show no more than a small buffy patch. White throat and (usually) half collar. Flanks and under tail coverts rusty-buff; breast darker, more brownish and centre of belly whitish. Favours small forest clearings such as those caused by tree falls and along streams. **Habitat:** evergreen forest, from plains to 2000 m. Uncommon passage migrant and winter visitor.

772. Asian Brown Flycatcher *Muscicapa dauurica* S: 13   นกจับแมลงสีน้ำตาล

Bill longer than either Dark-sided or Ferruginous Flycatchers; basal half of lower mandible pale (fleshy to yellowish) and tip dark. Wingtips fall about half way down tail. Dull grey-brown above and whitish underneath, with pale grey-brown suffusion across upper breast. Whitish or buffy eye-ring. In fresh plumage, often shows slight, blurred, breast streaking but, unlike Dark-sided, lacks any sharply contrasted underparts pattern. In fresh autumn plumage, shows thin but distinct whitish wing bar and tertial edges; these gradually abrade due to wear throughout the winter. Typical wintering form is easily recognised by extensive, diffuse whitish area in front of eye. This is much reduced in resident forms of north-west and western Thailand, which are slightly warmer brownish, with brown-washed throat and upper breast. **Voice:** sharp, dry *tit-tit-tit-it* rattling calls. Has a quiet, thin song. **Habitat:** migrant race inhabits open woodlands, forest edge and clearings, gardens and mangroves; from plains to 1500 m. Resident form so far known from deciduous and open hill evergreen forests, pines, from 600 m to 1400 m. Very common winter visitor; local and uncommon resident.

นกจับแมลงสีน้ำตาลท้องลาย

773. Brown-streaked Flycatcher *Muscicapa williamsoni* S: 13

Shape as Asian Brown Flycatcher, with medium to long wings and a heavy, broad-based, bill. Lower mandible yellowish with dark tip (sometimes lacking). Upperparts warmer than Asian Brown (milk-chocolate brown) with rufescent upper tail coverts, buffy eye-ring and indistinct off-white loral patch. Thin, buffy wing bar and rufous-buff tertial edges. Throat and upper breast whitish to pale buffy-brown, with blurred brownish streaks. Pale brownish sides and flanks; whitish lower breast, belly and under tail coverts. In worn plumage (May–June), ventral streaking may be reduced to a soft mottling while wing and face pattern and rufescent colouration of upperparts may be lost. Habits chiefly as Asian Brown, with which often considered conspecific, though in the breeding season frequently drops to the ground in order to collect food. **Voice:** song and calls as Asian Brown. **Habitat:** wooded gardens, forest edge from plains to 1300 m. In breeding season, frequents gardens and parkland with short ground vegetation, and new slash-and-burn clearings. Local and uncommon resident and passage migrant.

774. Brown-breasted Flycatcher *Muscicapa muttui* S: 14   นกจับแมลงอกสีน้ำตาล

Bill slightly longer than in Asian Brown and lower mandible entirely yellowish. Upperparts warm brown, with rufescent edges to flight feathers and coverts of wings; slightly rufescent upper tail coverts and tail. Underparts unstreaked, with brownish to grey-brown breast band. Shows a more sharply defined white submoustachial stripe than Asian Brown or Brown-streaked. Whitish lores and eye-ring; whitish throat and dark malar stripe. From Ferruginous Flycatcher by markedly less rufous plumage and by larger bill. **Voice:** calls with a thin *sit*. **Habitat:** hill evergreen forest at 1400 m. Very rare; status uncertain but possibly resident.

Plate 119 Jungle Flycatchers, Brown Flycatchers

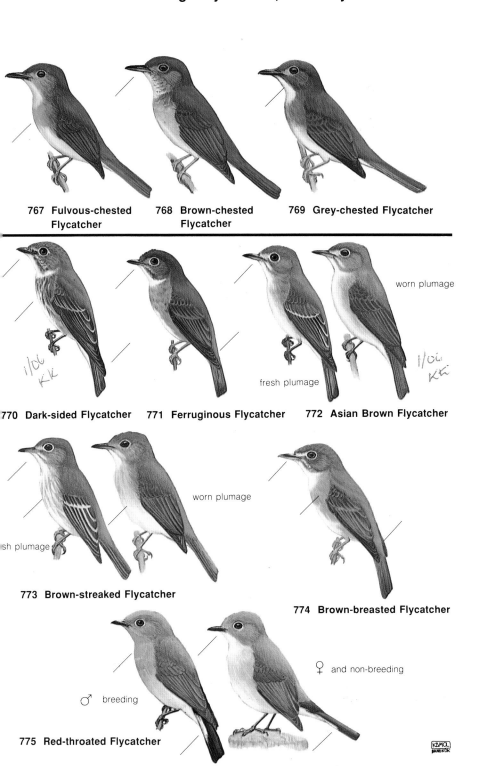

767 Fulvous-chested Flycatcher

768 Brown-chested Flycatcher

769 Grey-chested Flycatcher

770 Dark-sided Flycatcher

771 Ferruginous Flycatcher

fresh plumage

772 Asian Brown Flycatcher

worn plumage

773 Brown-streaked Flycatcher

sh plumage

worn plumage

774 Brown-breasted Flycatcher

♂ breeding

♀ and non-breeding

775 Red-throated Flycatcher

350

TYPICAL FLYCATCHERS: Genera *Ficedula, Muscicapella*. Small flycatchers, many of which are sexually dimorphic in plumage. Often identified by combinations of distinctive features such as wing bars, tail patches and distinctive body colours. Longer-winged forms are arboreal while shorter-winged forms inhabit undergrowth. The Grey-headed Flycatcher *Culicicapa ceylonensis* is atypical and belongs with the fantails (Family *Rhipiduridae*) but is placed here for convenience.

775. Red-throated Flycatcher *Ficedula parva* S: 13   นกจับแมลงคอแดง

Distinguished from Asian Brown by black upper tail coverts and tail, with white lateral patches which are often visible in flight and while tail cocked. Also by almost entirely dark lower mandible and by lack of obvious pale loral patch. **Male breeding:** small, orange-rufous throat patch, contrasting with grey sides of head and upper breast. **Female and immature/winter male:** head grey-brown, as rest of upperparts; underparts whitish, with a slight grey-brown wash on upper breast. ◆ Frequently drops to the ground to feed. The most common flycatcher in open areas, scrub. **Voice:** a distinctive, hard, grating *trrrt*; a much less frequent metallic *tic*; also a harsh *ze-it*. **Habitat:** forest edge, open woodlands, gardens and scrub from plains up to 2000 m. Very common winter visitor.

                                                  นกจับแมลงแถบคอสีส้ม

776. Rufous-gorgetted Flycatcher *Ficedula strophiata* S: 14

Tail pattern similar to Red-breasted Flycatcher, but distinguished by bright olive wings and by dark greyish face and upper breast. Shows whitish forehead and a small orange gorget which is often difficult to discern. Face pattern of male is usually brighter than in female. Usually in middle storey and undergrowth, sometimes dropping to feed on the ground. **Voice:** a harsh *trrt*, rather deeper than note of Red-breasted. Also a metallic *pink*. **Habitat:** hill evergreen forest, particularly in the more open woodlands, from 900 m to the highest summits. Fairly common winter visitor.

777. Mugimaki Flycatcher *Ficedula mugimaki* S: 13   นกจับแมลงดำอกสีส้ม

Distinguished from Rufous-chested by much longer wings, reaching more than half way down tail and by short, fine, bill. **Adult male:** dark slaty-grey or blackish upperparts with a large white wing patch and a short white eyebrow behind eye. Throat, breast and most of belly rich orange-rufous. Small, inconspicuous white patch at base of tail. **Immature male:** from female by more conspicuous wing bar. **Female:** upperparts olive-brown with one or two narrow, whitish buff wing bars. Throat and breast dull orange-buff. ◆ Often feeds high in the canopy. **Habitat:** evergreen forest, chiefly from 800 m to 1800 m. On passage also in wooded gardens, secondary growth, down to the plains.

Plate 120 Flycatchers II

776
Rufous-gorgetted Flycatcher

777 Mugimaki Flycatcher

778
Yellow-rumped Flycatcher

779 Narcissus Flycatcher

780
White-gorgetted Flycatcher

781
Rufous-browed Flycatcher

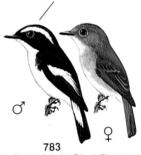

783
Little Pied Flycatcher

782 Rufous-chested Flycatcher

352

778. Yellow-rumped Flycatcher *Ficedula zanthopygia* S: 13

Adult male: black upperparts with white supercilium, bold white wing patch and yellow rump. Bright yellow underparts contrasting with white under tail coverts. Bill all black. **Immature male:** like female, but shows blackish upper tail coverts. **Female:** dull brownish olive upperparts and bright yellow rump patch (though difficult to see at rest). Shows one or two thin whitish wing bars and also usually a thin whitish streak in inner secondaries. Underparts pale buffy-yellowish, with faint olive scaling on throat and breast. Usually shows pale base to lower mandible. From warblers by more erect posture and lack of white in outer tail feathers. ◆ Long-winged. Mainly arboreal, usually keeping just below canopy. **Voice:** a deep grating *tr-r-r-rt.* **Habitat:** evergreen and mixed decidous forests from plains to at least 800 m; gardens, mangroves. Fairly common passage migrant; rare in midwinter.

779. Narcissus Flycatcher *Ficedula narcissina* S: 13

Only birds of the green-backed race, *F. n. elisae,* recorded. **Male:** grey-green upperparts with yellow rump, short yellow eyebrow and eye-ring and broad white wing patch. Bright yellow underparts. Tail blackish. **Female:** plumage subdued. From female Yellow-rumped by more greenish upperparts, lacking yellow rump patch, yellower underparts, faint yellowish wing bars, and yellowish olive eye-ring. Has a slightly rufescent tinge to tail. ◆ Keeps to middle storey and understorey. **Habitat:** evergreen forest of plains, especially along streams and tracks; mangroves. Rare winter visitor.

780. White-gorgetted Flycatcher *Ficedula monileger* S: 13

Sexes similar. Distinctive, black-bordered white throat patch, white forehead and short supercilium. Upperparts olive-brown, tinged rufescent on upper tail coverts and tail. Shy and skulking, feeding close to the forest floor in lush, dense herbage of moist areas, particularly along small streamlets. **Voice:** a thin, very high-pitched, whistling song; a metallic *dik*; a metallic scolding rattle and short, plaintive whistle. **Habitat:** evergreen forest, from 900 m to at least 1900 m. Uncommon resident.

781. Rufous-browed Flycatcher *Ficedula solitaris* S: 13

Sexes similar. From White-gorgetted Flycatcher by rufous forehead, lores and eye ring and by lack of black border to white throat patch. Proportions and habits similar to White-gorgetted, usually frequenting lush, low herbage along forest streams. **Voice:** gives very high-pitched, thin, short, undulating song phrases. In alarm, usually calls with 3 descending notes (*"three blind mice"*) and harsh churrs. **Habitat:** evergreen forests of hill slopes from 400 m to at least 1400 m. Uncommon resident.

782. Rufous-chested Flycatcher *Ficedula dumetoria* S: 12   นกจับแมลงอกสีส้ม

Plumage of both sexes resembles that of Mugimaki Flycatcher but shape and habits entirely different. Much shorter-winged, less elongate appearance and proportionately longer bill. **Male:** blackish upperparts with white supercilium; wing marking takes the form of a long white streak along the secondaries. Breast with orange-rufous wash, sometimes whiter on the throat, usually sharply demarcated from white belly. **Female:** brown above, with thin buffy wing bar and prominent buffy streak along edges of secondaries. Underparts slightly duller than in the male, and often paler on throat than on breast. ◆ Frequents low herbage and forest understorey, usually along streamsides. **Voice:** very high-pitched, 3–4 note song, glissading up and down the scale. **Habitat:** evergreen forests from plains to at least 800 m. Uncommon resident.

783. Little Pied Flycatcher *Ficedula westermanni* S: 12   นกจับแมลงเล็กขาวดำ

Male: black upperparts with very broad, long white supercilium; white wing patch and white at base of the outer tail feathers. White underparts. (Bar-winged Flycatcher-shrike, 486, is longer tailed and lacks supercilium.) **Female:** rather nondescript. Light greyish olive upperparts with a rufescent tinge on rump, upper tail coverts and tail. Often shows a slight buffy wing bar. From female Slaty-backed by whiter centre to breast and belly, tending towards a white median stripe which contrasts somewhat with greyer sides of breast. ◆ Frequents canopy and upper middle storey. **Voice:** song is sweet and high-pitched; a sharp *swit* followed by a harsh *trrrt* and a sequence of tinkling *swee-swee-swee* notes. **Habitat:** hill evergreen forest, particularly in more open woodlands; forest edge from 700 m to the highest summits. Common resident.

784. Snowy-browed Flycatcher *Ficedula hyperythra* S: 11 นกจับแมลงหน้าผากขาว

Small, short-winged and short-tailed. **Male:** upperparts dull, dark slaty-blue with browner flight feathers of wings. From other small blue and orange flycatchers by short, but prominent, white supercilia which almost meet on the forehead. Small amount of white at the base of the outer tail feathers is usually difficult to discern. **Female:** appears rather dark. Identified by relative lack of contrast between uniform, dull olive-brown upperparts and warm, buffy-brown underparts. Shows rusty-buff forehead, eyebrow and eye-ring. Legs pale flesh. From shortwings (718, 719) by smaller size and much thinner, weaker tarsi. ◆ Keeps to low undergrowth, close to the forest floor. **Voice:** a quiet, high-pitched and wheezy song of about 4 notes; *tsit-sit-si-sii.* Calls with a repeated thin *sip.* **Habitat:** evergreen forests from 800 m to the highest summits. Uncommon to fairly common resident.

785. Slaty-backed Flycatcher *Ficedula hodgsonii* S: 13   นกจับแมลงหลังสีเทา

Slim and long-winged, with a very short bill. **Male:** dull bluish slate upperparts. White bases to outer tail feathers are usually obvious in flight. Bright orange-rufous throat and breast grade into whitish belly. From Hill Blue Flycatcher (802) by duller plumage without any iridescence, smaller size, longer wings and shorter bill. **Female:** rather nondescript; dull olive upperparts, often with slight rufescent tinge to rump and upper tail coverts and paler, buffy-olive throat, breast and flanks (may appear whitish). Often shows a thin, buffy wing bar. From female Sapphire Flycatcher by duller underparts, lacking any orange suffusion. From female Little Pied by even suffusion across centre and sides of breast, lacking any suggestion of a whitish median stripe. ◆ Frequents middle storey, understorey. **Voice:** calls with a hard *tchrt*. **Habitat:** hill evergreen forests, particularly in more open areas; forest edge and secondary growth from 900 m to the highest summits. Fairly common winter visitor.

786. Ultramarine Flycatcher *Ficedula superciliaris* S: 12   นกจับแมลงสีคราม

Male: broad white band down centre of throat and breast, white abdomen and dark blue sides to head, neck and breast. Usually shows an iridescent blue forehead and short eyebrow. Small white patch at base of tail is usually difficult to see in the field. **Female:** buffy-white band down throat and breast with grey-brown sides to breast. Upperparts dull brownish grey, with rufous-brown tinge on forecrown. Many individuals show grey-blue on upper tail coverts and tail and some may also show prominent white wing bar and white tertial edges. ◆ Arboreal. **Voice:** a low grating rattle, *t-r-r-r-r-t*, recalling Sapphire. **Habitat:** open dry dipterocarp woodlands and stands of pines, from foothills to at least 1700 m. Uncommon or rare winter visitor.

787. Slaty-blue Flycatcher *Ficedula tricolor* S: 13   นกจับแมลงหน้าดำคอขาว

Male: triangular buffy throat patch contrasts slightly with greyer buff breast. Upperparts dark slaty-blue with brighter blue forecrown and blackish sides to head. Shows prominent white patches at sides of tail. **Female:** upperparts olive-brown with rufescent rump, strongly rufous tail and upper tail coverts, and buffy eye-ring. Underparts brownish buff, with paler triangular buff throat patch (not always easy to discern). Some individuals also show a thin rufous-buff wing bar. ◆ Skulks in dense cover, close to the ground; frequently cocks tail and drops to the ground like a Red-breasted Flycatcher. **Voice:** usual call is a metallic rattle, like Asian Brown Flycatcher; *tit-it-it-it*. Also gives a high-pitched whistle and a short warbling phrase. **Habitat:** scrub and secondary growth, from 1200 m to the highest elevations. Uncommon; status uncertain and may be only a winter visitor.

Plate 121 Flycatchers III

**784
Snowy-browed Flycatcher**

♂ ♀

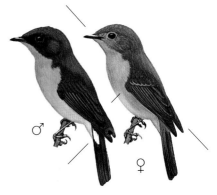

♂ ♀

785 Slaty-backed Flycatcher

♂ ♀

786 Ultramarine Flycatcher

♀

♂

787 Slaty-blue Flycatcher

♂ ♂ ♀

788 Sapphire Flycatcher

♂ ♀

789 Pygmy Blue Flycatcher

1/06
KK

790 Grey-headed Flycatcher

356

788. Sapphire Flycatcher *Ficedula sapphira* S: 11 นกจับแมลงหัวสีฟ้า
Small, with a tiny bill. **Male:** shining blue upper tail coverts and tail.
Some also show shining blue crown and back, but in most individuals these parts are olive-brown. Blackish primaries; centre of throat and upper breast bright rufous-orange; sides of throat and breast brownish. **Female:** from female Slaty-backed by strongly rufescent upper tail coverts and tail and by bright rufous-buff centre of throat and upper breast. ◆ Arboreal, usually in middle storey. **Voice:** a low *tit-it-it-it* rattle; deeper and slower than similar calls of all other small flycatchers except Ultramarine. **Habitat:** hill evergreen forest, especially in more open woodlands, above 1200 m. Uncommon winter visitor.

789. Pygmy Blue Flycatcher *Muscicapella hodgsoni* S: 10 นกจับแมลงสีฟ้าจิ๋ว
Tiny size and very small bill, long wings and short tail all combine to give a flowerpecker-like shape. **Male:** upperparts slightly duller blue than in male Sapphire, with shining blue restricted to forecrown, and yellower orange-rufous throat and breast. **Female:** plumage similar to female Sapphire, but brighter rufescent rump and upper tail coverts. ◆ Often flicks wings open and cocks tail. Frequents both middle storey and canopy. **Habitat:** hill evergreen forests, above 1200 m. Rare; status uncertain; possibly winter visitor.

790. Grey-headed Flycatcher *Culicicapa ceylonensis* S: 13 นกจับแมลงหัวเทา
Dark grey head, throat and upper breast; yellow lower breast and belly and bright olive-green upperparts. From similar warblers by lack of supercilium or eye-ring. Frequents middle storey; active and dashing, making flycatching sallies but frequently returning to the same perch. Often accompanies bird waves. **Voice:** a sweet rising sequence, *chilu-chili-chi*, with upward inflection on the last note. Also sharp metallic trills and twitters. **Habitat:** evergreen and deciduous forests from plains to the highest summits. Occurs in mangroves, wooded gardens on passage or in winter. Common resident; some populations are migratory.

เหล่านกนิลตวา

NILTAVAS: Genus *Niltava*. Most are larger and plumper than the Blue Flycatchers, *Cyornis* spp. (798–803), with proportionately shorter bills. The males usually show shining blue crown and rump patches while the females are chiefly brownish. In most species, both sexes also show a shining blue neckspot. Some eat small fruits in addition to insects. The Blue-and-White Flycatcher *Cyanoptila cyanomelana* is included out of sequence here, because of its similarly large size.

นกจับแมลงสีฟ้าท้องขาว

791. Blue-and-White Flycatcher *Cyanoptila cyanomelana* S: 18
Male: larger than Hainan Blue Flycatcher (800) with shining blue crown and bend of wing. Sharp demarcation between dull, dark blue breast and whitish belly. Blue parts of plumage turquoise-blue and sides of head blackish blue (race *cumatilis*) or deeper, cobalt blue and black respectively (race *cyanomelana*). **Female:** grey-brown upperparts with warmer brownish wings and tail (though much less deep rufous upper tail coverts and tail than female Pale Blue Flycatcher (798). Shows a fairly clear demarcation between brownish buff of upper breast and whitish abdomen. Crown appears slightly peaked. **Habitat:** evergreen forests, from plains to at least 1800 m. Uncommon passage migrant.

357

792. Large Niltava *Niltava grandis* S: 21   นกนิลตวาใหญ่

Relatively large. **Male:** dark blue plumage with shining blue crown, shoulder patch, rump and neck spot; black face. In poor light, often appears all blackish and might be confused with a Lesser Racket-tailed Drongo (550) lacking tail streamers. From Blue-fronted Robin (733) by shorter, weaker tarsi, more glossy plumage and arboreal habits. **Female:** olive-brown plumage with rufescent wings, triangular buffy throat patch and blue neck spot. Buffy-rufous forecrown and greyish hindcrown. **Juvenile:** upperparts speckled buff; juvenile male shows bluish wings and tail in combination with speckled brownish body plumage. ◆ Usually frequents middle storey but occasionally drops to ground. **Voice:** usually an ascending cadence of 4 softly whistled notes; may be given by both sexes in the context of alarm. Also a soft *chu-ii*, second note higher, and scolding rattles. **Habitat:** hill evergreen forest from 900 m to the highest summits. Common resident.

793. Small Niltava *Niltava macgrigoriae* S: 14   นกนิลตวาเล็ก

Resembles respective sexes of Large Niltava, but very much smaller; shining blue neck spot of both sexes brighter. **Male:** dark blue of upper breast fades into grey lower breast and belly. **Female:** lacks a clearly defined pale throat patch; blue spot on sides of neck. ◆ Shy and difficult to observe, keeping to dense undergrowth of moist areas. **Voice:** a very thin, high-pitched and wheezy song, *twii-twii-ii-twii*, rising in pitch to the second note and then falling. Metallic scolding and churring notes. **Habitat:** hill evergreen forest from 900 m to the highest summits. Uncommon resident.

794. Fukien Niltava *Niltava davidi* S: 18   นกนิลตวาท้องสีส้มพันธุ์จีน

Both sexes resemble those of Rufous-bellied Niltava and very difficult to distinguish. Neck spot brighter blue. **Male:** duller, darker blue on crown than Rufous-bellied, with shining blue feathers limited to forecrown. Rest of upperparts also darker, more purplish blue and orange of underparts becomes noticeably paler on lower belly and under tail coverts. **Female:** belly slightly whiter than in female Rufous-bellied Niltava, but indistinguishable in the field. ◆ Note range. **Habitat:** hill evergreen forests, above 900 m. Local and rare winter visitor.

795. Rufous-bellied Niltava *Niltava sundara* S: 18   นกนิลตวาท้องสีส้มคอดำ

Plump, large-headed appearance. **Male:** entire crown shining blue, giving capped appearance; neck spots, shoulder patches and rump shining blue. Face and throat black, without an obvious indentation on lower margin. Rest of underparts orange-rufous. **Female:** shows white gorget on lower throat and (usually, but not always) blue neck spots, but both features may be difficult to see, especially when posture hunched. Upperparts warm olive-brown with rufescent wings and tail; underparts grey-brown with indistinct white belly patch. ◆ Usually inhabits undergrowth and lower storey; often eats small fruits. **Voice:** a hard, robin-like *tic*. **Habitat:** hill evergreen forest, usually above 900 m. Common winter visitor.

796. Vivid Niltava *Niltava vivida* S: 19 นกนิลตวาท้องสีส้ม

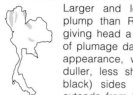

Larger and longer-winged, appearing more elongate and less plump than Rufous-bellied Niltava. Crown feathers often raised, giving head a slightly peaked appearance. **Male:** bright blue parts of plumage darker and duller than in Rufous-bellied. Lacks capped appearance, with shining feathers mainly restricted to forecrown; duller, less shining blue rump, and more blue-black (rather than black) sides of throat. Variable-sized wedge of orange-rufous extends from breast on to lower throat. **Female:** from females of Large and Rufous-bellied by lack of neck spot or white gorget and by more peaked crown. Colouration otherwise close to that of female Large, with greyish hindcrown and narrow buffy-white throat patch. ◆ Much more arboreal in habits than Rufous-bellied, usually in upper middle storey and canopy, among larger branches. **Habitat:** evergreen forests from 750 m to the highest elevations. Uncommon winter visitor.

เหล่านกจับแมลงสีฟ้า

BLUE FLYCATCHERS: Genus *Cyornis*. Rather short, rounded wings and comparatively long tails and long, heavy bills. Sexually dimorphic, with the shining parts of the male blue plumage restricted to forecrown and bend of wing. Most inhabit middle storey and understorey. Often cock their tails to above horizontal. Most species have sweet, melancholy warbling songs and in some, both sexes will sing in the context of alarm. The Verditer Flycatcher *Eumyias thalassina* is also included here in order to facilitate its separation from Pale Blue Flycatcher *Cyornis unicolor*.

797. Verditer Flycatcher *Eumyias thalassina* S: 17 นกจับแมลงสีฟ้า

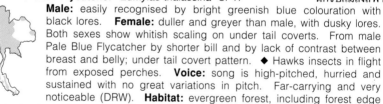

Male: easily recognised by bright greenish blue colouration with black lores. **Female:** duller and greyer than male, with dusky lores. Both sexes show whitish scaling on under tail coverts. From male Pale Blue Flycatcher by shorter bill and by lack of contrast between breast and belly; under tail covert pattern. ◆ Hawks insects in flight from exposed perches. **Voice:** song is high-pitched, hurried and sustained with no great variations in pitch. Far-carrying and very noticeable (DRW). **Habitat:** evergreen forest, including forest edge and clearings, from plains to highest summits. Occurs in mangroves and wooded gardens on passage or in winter. Common resident and winter visitor.

798. Pale Blue Flycatcher *Cyornis unicolor* S: 18 นกจับแมลงสีฟ้าอ่อน

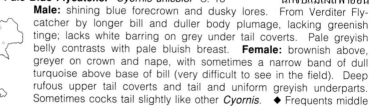

Male: shining blue forecrown and dusky lores. From Verditer Flycatcher by longer bill and duller body plumage, lacking greenish tinge; lacks white barring on grey under tail coverts. Pale greyish belly contrasts with pale bluish breast. **Female:** brownish above, greyer on crown and nape, with sometimes a narrow band of dull turquoise above base of bill (very difficult to see in the field). Deep rufous upper tail coverts and tail and uniform greyish underparts. Sometimes cocks tail slightly like other *Cyornis*. ◆ Frequents middle and upper storey. **Voice:** sings with rich, melodious, descending sequences, *chi, chuchichu-chuchichu-chuchi*, usually ending with a harsh *chizz*. Loud and thrush-like; quite different from other *Cyornis* spp. **Habitat:** evergreen forests from plains up to at least 1600 m, often favouring the more open areas. Uncommon resident.

Plate 122 Niltavas

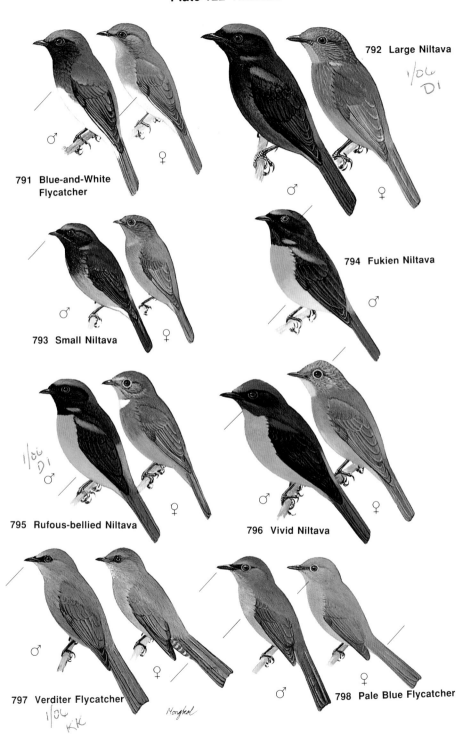

791 Blue-and-White Flycatcher
♂ ♀

792 Large Niltava
♂ ♀

793 Small Niltava
♂ ♀

794 Fukien Niltava
♂

795 Rufous-bellied Niltava
♂ ♀

796 Vivid Niltava
♂ ♀

797 Verditer Flycatcher
♂ ♀

798 Pale Blue Flycatcher
♂ ♀

Mongkol

799. White-tailed Flycatcher *Cyornis concreta* S: 19 นกจับแมลงสีคล้ำหางแถบขาว
Larger than other *Cyornis* but shape and actions are typical for the genus. Both sexes show white patches in spread tail. **Male:** markings similar to those of male Hainan Blue Flycatcher, but slightly darker blue. From male White-tailed Robin (732) by paler colouration and by white lower belly and under tail coverts. **Female:** rich, warm brown colouration, with a triangular white gorget on buffy brown throat and breast. **Voice:** variable piercing sibilant whistles of usually 2 or 3 syllables: *tii-tuu-tii-tuu-tii*; *huiiee* and *tuu-tii*. Also a harsh *scree* in alarm. **Habitat:** evergreen forests from foothills to 1000 m, often close to streams, shady gullies. Rare resident.

800. Hainan Blue Flycatcher *Cyornis hainana* S: 15 นกจับแมลงอกสีฟ้า
Male: dark blue upperparts, throat and upper breast, grading into greyish white abdomen. Shining blue on forecrown and shoulder. Smaller and darker, deeper blue than males of either Pale Blue or Blue-and-White. Occasionally may show a wedge of white extending up the throat. See male Ultramarine. **Female:** from females of following species (801–803) by duller, buffy-rufous throat and breast, becoming brownish laterally. **Voice:** calls with a hard *tic* (rather than *tac* as in following species). Song weaker, less complex than in Hill Blue Flycatcher. **Habitat:** mixed deciduous and evergreen forests, bamboo, from plains to 800 m. Fairly common resident.

นกจับแมลงคอสีน้ำเงินเข้ม
801. Blue-throated Flycatcher *Cyornis rubeculoides* S: 15
Male: distinguished from male Hill Blue and Tickell's Blue by dark blue throat, often with a narrow wedge of orange-rufous extending up from breast. (Usually no more than a small indentation, but sometimes extends almost to base of bill.) Male of wintering race *glaucicomans* (sometimes treated as a separate species, Chinese Flycatcher) always shows this feature. Varying amount of orange on breast, but usually shows a moderately clear demarcation from white of belly. **Female:** from female Hill Blue by more strongly rufescent upper tail coverts and tail; grey-brown sides of head and throat grade into more washed-out orange-rufous of centre of throat and breast. (Female *glaucicomans* shows a whitish throat demarcated from a buffy-orange breast band.) **Voice:** short, sweet, song phrases, recalling Tickell's Blue, but delivery more rapid and higher-pitched, with more trilling notes. Hard *tac* and *trrt-trrt* calls. **Habitat:** mixed deciduous forest and bamboo brakes of foothills to about 1000 m. Wintering birds usually inhabit evergreen forests of the plains; on passage also in mangroves, gardens and in hill evergreen forest up to 1700 m. Fairly common resident; uncommon winter visitor.

Plate 123 Blue Flycatchers

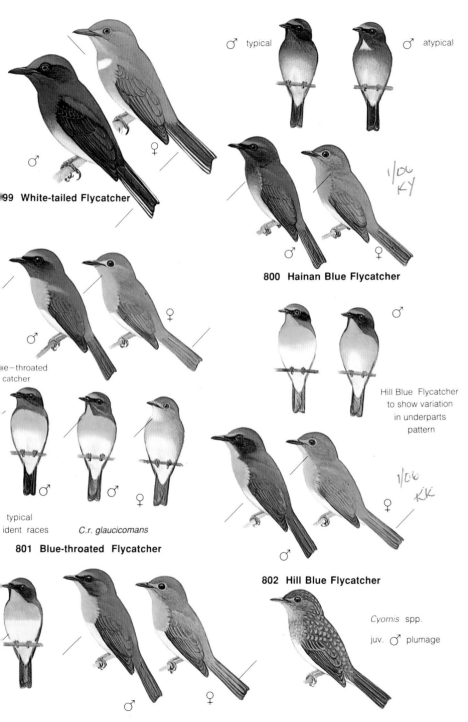

♂ typical   ♂ atypical

♂

99 White-tailed Flycatcher

♀

♂   ♀

800 Hainan Blue Flycatcher

1/06 KY

♂   ♀

e–throated
catcher

♂

Hill Blue Flycatcher
to show variation
in underparts
pattern

♂   ♂   ♀

typical
ident races   C.r. glaucicomans

801 Blue-throated Flycatcher

1/06 KK

♀

♂

802 Hill Blue Flycatcher

Cyornis spp.

juv. ♂ plumage

♂   ♀

803 Tickell's Blue Flycatcher

Mongkol

802. Hill Blue Flycatcher *Cyornis banyumas* S: 15   นกจับแมลงคอน้ำตาลแดง
Both sexes from those of Tickell's Blue Flycatcher by orange-rufous of throat and breast grading into white belly, without sharp demarcation. Extent of orange suffusion varies considerably and on many birds is restricted to the throat and upper breast. **Male:** from male Blue-throated by entire chin, throat and upper breast orange-rufous. See Mangrove Blue Flycatcher (915). **Female:** from female Blue-throated by sharp demarcation between grey-brown sides of head and deeper orange-rufous throat. Upper tail coverts and tail almost always rufescent brown. **Voice:** sweet, melancholy warbling song with longer, more complex phrases and more rapid delivery than in Tickell's Blue. Both sexes give a briefer, more simplified version of the song, especially in alarm. Hard *tac* and scolding *trrt-trrt-trrt* calls. **Habitat:** evergreen forests of the hill slopes from 400 m to 2100 m. Wintering or passage birds may be found in the plains. Very common resident; also winter visitor and passage migrant.

803. Tickell's Blue Flycatcher *Cyornis tickelliae* S: 15   นกจับแมลงอกส้มท้องขาว
Both sexes from those of Hill Blue by orange-rufous of throat and breast sharply divided from white belly. **Male:** upperparts slightly paler blue than in male Hill Blue. **Female:** upperparts somewhat greyer, less rufescent than in female Hill Blue and tinged blue in race *C. t. sumatrensis* of the Peninsula. Tail usually grey-blue; only rarely rufescent. **Voice:** song phrases shorter than those of Hill Blue, usually 5–7 notes per phrase; delivery slower. Both sexes sing, especially in alarm context. Hard *tac* and *trrt-trrt* notes. **Habitat:** mixed deciduous forests, bamboo, secondary growth and evergreen forests from the plains to 600 m. Common resident.

วงศ์นกอีแพรด

FANTAILS: Family *Rhipiduridae*. Have long, broad tails, often held cocked and fanned, and short, rounded wings. Inhabit undergrowth and middle storey and often found among bird waves. Sexes similar. Build cup-shaped nests. Are unrelated to the flycatchers and are now thought to belong with the crows and drongos. World: 42 species. Thailand: 5 species.

804. Yellow-bellied Fantail *Rhipidura hypoxantha* S: 13   นกอีแพรดท้องเหลือง
Small. The only fantail with yellow forehead, supercilium and underparts and dark face mask (black in male; dark olive-green in female). **Voice:** sweet, thin, high-pitched trilling notes. **Habitat:** evergreen forests, secondary growth and forest edge above 1500 m. Locally common resident.

805. White-throated Fantail *Rhipidura albicollis* S: 19   นกอีแพรดคอขาว
Entire body blackish grey, apart from white supercilium, throat and tip of tail. **Voice:** a measured song of 5–6 whistled notes in chiefly descending sequence. Calls with a squeaky *cheek*. **Habitat:** evergreen forests above 600 m. Common resident.

806. White-browed Fantail *Rhipidura aureola* S: 18 นกอีแพรดคิ้วขาว

Broader, longer white supercilium than other fantails and underparts mainly white, usually with dark throat. **Voice:** usually 4 ascending and 2–3 descending, well-spaced, melodious whistled notes. **Habitat:** dry dipterocarp and mixed deciduous forests below 900 m. Uncommon resident.

807. Spotted Fantail *Rhipidura perlata* S: 18 นกอีแพรดอกลาย

Easily identified by large white spots on dark grey throat and breast. Narrow white supercilium. **Voice:** a melodious two-phrase sequence, the second phrase rising sharply, *chilip*, *pechilip-chi* (M&W). **Habitat:** evergreen forest of the lowlands and foothills. Uncommon or rare resident.

808. Pied Fantail *Rhipidura javanica* S: 18 นกอีแพรดแถบอกดำ

Underparts with broad black breast band, white throat and white belly. Black sides to head with narrow whitish supercilium. **Voice:** song of measured, squeaky whistling notes, *chew-weet*, *chew-weet*, *chew-weet-chew*, last note with falling inflection. Squeaky chattering and squawking calls. **Habitat:** lowland woodlands, scrub, mangroves and other coastal cover, gardens, usually close to water. Very common resident.

วงศ์นกแซวสวรรค์

MONARCHS: Family *Monarchidae*. Rather large, robust flycatcher-like birds, with strong, broad bills and bright plumage. Sexually dimorphic. Mostly glean insects from foliage of middle or lower storey. Build cup-shaped nests. Not related to the true flycatchers and thought to be closely allied to the crows and drongos. World: 94 species. Thailand: 5 species.

809. Black-naped Monarch *Hypothymis azurea* S: 17 นกจับแมลงจุกดำ

Somewhat resembles the fantails in shape and habits, often with horizontal posture and long tail slightly fanned. Blue head and whitish belly; indistinct pale tips to tail feathers. Bluish bill and yellow gape. **Male:** bright blue plumage with conspicuous black nape and gorget. **Female:** blue duller, restricted to head; greyish breast, grey-brown back, wings and tail. **Voice:** a ringing song, *pwee-pwee-pwee-pwee*, uttered at a rate of about 3 notes per second. Also a rasping, disyllabic note. **Habitat:** deciduous and evergreen forests, open woodlands, secondary growth from plains up to 1200 m. In winter, found also in gardens, mangroves. Very common resident and partial migrant.

นกจับแมลงปีกน้ำตาลแดง

810. Rufous-winged Flycatcher *Philentoma pyrhopterum* S: 18

Rufous wings and tail in both sexes. Red eye. **Male:** pale blue head, breast and back. (Uncommon blue morph male has entirely pale blue plumage.) **Female:** greyish head, brown back and buffy underparts. From Asian Paradise-flycatcher by lack of crest and by dark leading edge to wing. **Juvenile:** from female by orange-rufous breast, brownish head and mantle. **Voice:** a soft, whistled *tu-huuuu* with emphasis on the lower, second syllable; also a rising tone whistle, *tew-ii*, and various harsh scolds. **Habitat:** evergreen forest from plains to 800 m. Fairly common resident.

811. Maroon-breasted Flycatcher *Philentoma velatum* S: 20   นกจับแมลงอกแดง

Relatively large. Dull, dark indigo-blue plumage which appears blackish in dim forest light. Red eye. **Male:** black throat and sides of head; maroon breast. **Female:** duller than male, lacking breast patch and with slaty sides of head and throat. See female Asian Fairy-bluebird, drongos. ◆ Wings make loud fluttering noise in flight. **Voice:** clear, bell-like whistles uttered in a long series. A loud, harsh, squirrel-like *chuck-uk.* **Habitat:** evergreen forest from plains to 1000 m. Uncommon resident.

นกแซวสวรรค์หางดำ

812. Japanese Paradise-flycatcher *Terpsiphone atrocaudata* S: 20

(Elongate tail of male extends up to a further 23 cm.) **Male:** glossy blackish plumage, with white belly. May lack long tail when moulting. **Female:** from Asian Paradise-flycatcher by darker, much duller rufescent brownish upperparts and tail. Duller, sooty crown, contrasting less with sides of head. **Habitat:** lowland forest, mangroves. Rare passage migrant and winter visitor.

813. Asian Paradise-flycatcher *Terpsiphone paradisi* S: 21   นกแซวสวรรค์

(Elongate tail of male extends up to a further 23 cm.) **Male:** two colour morphs; either white, with glossy back head and throat, or rufous with variable amounts of glossy black or grey on throat and sides of head. **Female and moulting or immature male:** lacks long central tail streamers, but from female Japanese by brighter, more orange rufous upperparts and tail and by glossier black crown. **Voice:** both ringing song and rasping calls somewhat similar to those of Black-naped Monarch. More strident, with a longer interval between notes than the similar song of Large Wood-shrike (488). **Habitat:** evergreen and mixed deciduous forests, secondary growth, from plains to 1500 m. In winter or on passage also in mangroves, gardens. Fairly common resident and winter visitor.

Plate 124 Fantails, Monarchs, etc.

804 Yellow-bellied Fantail

805 White-throated Fantail

806 White-browed Fantail

807 Spotted Fantail

808 Pied Fantail

809 Black-naped Monarch

♂ blue morph

♂ typical   ♀

810 Rufous-winged Flycatcher

white morph   ♂ rufous morph

♂   ♀

812 Japanese Paradise-flycatcher

813 Asian Paradise-flycatcher

811 Maroon-breasted Flycatcher

814 Mangrove Whistler

366

วงศ์นกโกงกางหัวโต

WHISTLERS: Family *Pachycephalidae*. Robust, with large, rounded heads and strong bills. Glean insects from foliage. Territorial; usually solitary or in pairs. Melodious whistling songs; males and females duet. Build cup-shaped nests. World range centred on New Guinea and Australia. World: 46 species. Thailand: one species.

814. Mangrove Whistler *Pachycephala grisola* S: 17   นกโกงกางหัวโต

Distinguished from most babblers and flycatchers by entirely black bill and black gape. Uniformly grey-brown upperparts (slightly greyer on crown) without any rufescent tinge. Silky-white underparts with slight greyish breast band. See Brown Fulvetta (633). **Voice:** a series of loud, ringing whistles, more deliberate and uttered less rapidly than call of Black-naped Monarch and with last note either markedly higher or lower; *pwee-pwee-pwee-pwee-pwit.* **Habitat:** mangroves, dry woodlands of coastal areas and islands. Uncommon to locally common resident.

วงศ์นกอีเสือ

SHRIKES: Family *Laniidae*. Medium sized, predatory passerine birds with stout hooked bills, large heads and long tails. Inhabit mainly open country and prey on insects, frogs, lizards, small rodents and sometimes small birds by pouncing on them from an exposed perch. Many species impale their prey on thorns. Solitary and territorial, even in winter quarters. Have harsh, scolding calls. Build bulky, cup-shaped nests placed in tall bushes and low trees. World: 70 species. Thailand: 5 species.

815. Brown Shrike *Lanius cristatus* S: 20   นกอีเสือสีน้ำตาล

Lacks obvious white in wings or tail (a few individuals rarely show a small white patch at base of primaries). **Adult:** upperparts rufous-brown to grey-brown, depending on race, with sharply contrasted face pattern of black mask, white supercilium and whitish forehead. Rump, upper tail coverts and tail brighter rufous than rest of upperparts. **Juvenile:** feathers of upperparts scaled with thin blackish subterminal bars and edged buffy. Shows some dark scaling on sides of breast and flanks. Mask blackish brown and supercilium buffy, usually not extending on to forehead. ◆ Adults of race *L. c. lucionensis* are duller grey-brown on back, with an ashy-grey crown and nape, less sharply defined from supercilium and forehead, and with rump and upper tail coverts pale rufous. In immature, pattern similar, but more subdued. From Grey-backed Shrike by smaller, slimmer appearance and by pale rufous-buff instead of rich tawny-rufous wash on flanks. **Voice:** a harsh, staccato *chak-ak-ak-ak-ak*; also high-pitched squawking notes. Occasionally gives soft, chuckling subsong. **Habitat:** open country, including both dry areas and paddies, marshes; scrub country, gardens. Chiefly lower elevations but up to 2000 m on passage. Very common winter visitor.

Plate 125 Shrikes, Wood-swallow

juvenile

adult

L.c. lucionensis

815 Brown Shrike

820 Ashy Wood-swallow

1/06 KY

juvenile

adult ♂

816 Tiger Shrike

1/06 KY

♀

♂

817 Burmese Shrike

1/06 KY

818 Grey-backed Shrike

juvenile

adult

819 Long-tailed Shrike

Mongkol

368

816. Tiger Shrike *Lanius tigrinus* S: 19   นกอีเสือลายเสือ

Noticeably shorter tail and heavier bill than Brown Shrike; lacks white in wings or tail. **Male:** chestnut upperparts, narrowly barred blackish; clean grey crown and nape; black mask and forehead. Shining white underparts. **Female:** slightly duller, with short dark bars on flanks. May show thin white eyebrow extending from above eye on to lores. **Juvenile:** upperparts rufous brown, with bold black barring on both upperparts and underparts. From immature Brown Shrike by lack of contrast in facial pattern, showing barred ear coverts and only a short buffy eyebrow visible above eye. Buffy lores. Frequently shows a pale crescent on ear coverts and also an obvious pinkish base to the bill. **Habitat:** deciduous forests and evergreen forest edge, clearings and secondary growth from plains to at least 300 m. Also in mangroves, gardens. Fairly common passage migrant.

817. Burmese Shrike *Lanius collurioides* S: 20   นกอีเสือหลังแดง

Proportionately slimmer and longer-tailed than preceding species. Chestnut upperparts, with crown, nape and upper back grey. Black mask; lacks supercilium. Small white patch at base of primaries is usually only visible in flight; white outer feathers to blackish tail. **Male:** extensive area of black on forehead. **Female:** black on forehead less extensive and admixed with white. **Juvenile:** shows barred upperparts, but otherwise like female. **Voice:** a staccato rattle, recalling Brown Shrike. **Habitat:** breeds in scrub and open woodlands of mountains, 900 – 1800 m; winters to plains, where often in paddies, cultivation. Local and uncommon resident; common winter visitor.

818. Grey-backed Shrike *Lanius tephronotus* S: 24   นกอีเสือหลังเทา

Large size; slightly shorter tail than Long-tailed Shrike. Grey upperparts with rusty-fulvous rump and upper tail coverts; black mask. May show a thin whitish supercilium (usually lacking). Shows rich tawny rufous suffusion on flanks. Lacks white in wings or tail. **Adult:** black forehead. **Immature:** blackish brown mask on ear coverts only; upperparts tinged browner, scaled. Shows some narrow barring on flanks. From immature *lucionensis* Brown Shrike by larger size and heavier bill; deeper tawny-rufous on flanks. **Habitat:** open scrub country from plains up to 2000 m. Uncommon winter visitor.

819. Long-tailed Shrike *Lanius schach* S: 25   นกอีเสือหัวดำ

Very long blackish tail, lacking white (apart from narrow buffy-white tips to shortest outermost feathers, usually not visible in the field). Shows white patch in wing, visible in flight. **Adult:** black head. Back sandy-rufous; throat and breast white; belly and under tail coverts deep rufous buff. **Juvenile:** shows dark-barred, pale ashy grey crown contrasting with black mask. Back, coverts and flanks barred. **Voice:** usually a scolding, drawn-out *chaak-chaak*. Has a scratchy, warbling song. **Habitat:** open country, scrubland, paddies, marshes, from plains to at least 1800 m. Very common resident.

WOOD-SWALLOWS: Family *Artamidae.* Stocky, aerial-feeding birds with thick-based, pointed bills. Larger than true swallows. Glide on stiff, broad-based, triangular wings and have a short square tail. Build cup-shaped nests in trees. Seek exposed perches such as bare tree limbs and telegraph wires. World: 10 species. Thailand: one species.

820. Ashy Wood-swallow *Artamus fuscus* S: 18 นกแอ่นพง
Slaty-grey body with paler breast and belly and whitish upper tail coverts. Bill bluish. Gregarious, often perches in small, tight-knit groups. Often bobs and fans tail. **Voice:** a squawking, nasal *chreenk.* **Habitat:** open areas with scattered trees from plains to 1800 m (chiefly in lowlands). Common resident.

วงศ์นกเอี้ยงและนกกิ้งโครง

STARLINGS, MYNAS: Family *Sturnidae.* Stocky, medium-sized birds with strong bills and legs and relatively short tails. Strong, direct flight on pointed wings (small starlings), or broader, more rounded wings (larger starlings and mynas). Includes arboreal, woodland species as well as terrestrial, open country species, many of which are expanding their ranges with increased deforestation. Feed on insects, fruits, etc. Gregarious and noisy; often in huge, communal roosts. Have a large repertoire of calls and many are accomplished mimics. Build untidy stick nests in trees and palm crowns or nest in holes. World: 112 species. Thailand: 16 species.

821. Philippine Glossy Starling *Aplonis panayensis* S: 20 นกเอี้ยงดำปักษ์ใต้
Adult: blackish plumage, glossed green; red eye. **Juvenile:** entire underparts whitish with bold black streaks; upperparts blackish brown with slight gloss. **Voice:** a sharp, ringing whistle. **Habitat:** gardens, secondary growth, cultivation, roadsides, towns. Very common resident.

822. Spot-winged Starling *Saroglossa spiloptera* S: 19 นกกิ้งโครงปีกลายจุด
Small white patch at base of primaries in flight. **Male:** dark chestnut throat and black sides of head contrast with deep rufous breast. Black-scaled, greyish upperparts. Rufous-brown upper tail coverts and tail. **Female:** uniform dark brown above (slightly darker on sides of head); paler greyish, dark-scaled underparts. ◆ Often feeds on nectar in flowering trees, one or two birds joining flocks of Chestnut-tailed Starlings. **Habitat:** open deciduous woodland, cultivated areas of plains. Rare winter visitor.

823. Chestnut-tailed Starling *Sturnus malabaricus* S: 20 นกกิ้งโครงแกลบหัวเทา
Distinguished from White-shouldered Starling by chestnut-rufous outer tail feathers; rump and upper tail coverts not obviously paler than back and often tinged rufous. White on upperwing only on primary coverts. Striking blue base to yellow bill. Flanks washed warm, buffy-rufous. A small proportion of birds show uniformly bright tawny rufous suffusion on breast and belly, which contrasts with silky whitish head. Often in large flocks, feeding on nectar in red-flowered trees. **Habitat:** open deciduous woodlands and open country with scattered trees, from plains and foothills to 800 m. Common resident and winter visitor.

824. Brahminy Starling *Sturnus pagodarum* S: 21 นกเอี้ยงพราหมณ์
Black crown and long crest; salmon pinkish underparts and pale grey-brown upperparts; lacks any white in wing. **Habitat:** dry, lowland open country. Very rare visitor; only one record of 4 birds associating with White-shouldered Starlings, March 1977.

825. White-shouldered Starling *Sturnus sinensis* S: 20 นกกิ้งโครงแกลบปีกขาว
Distinguished from Chestnut-tailed by (usually) obvious white in wings and tail; blackish central tail feathers showing obvious contrast with pale rump and upper tail coverts. From Purple-backed by paler grey to grey-brown back; prominent white tips to tail feathers; pale, bluish white bill and whitish eye. **Male:** striking, wholly white upperwing coverts and scapulars. **Female:** white on upperwing reduced to a broad bar. **Immature:** brownish; youngest stages show little or no white in wing. **Habitat:** well-watered open country with scattered trees, cultivated areas, mangroves. Common winter visitor.

826. Purple-backed Starling *Sturnus sturninus* S: 19 นกกิ้งโครงแกลบหลังม่วงดำ
Sexes similar. **Adult:** from White-shouldered by metallic purple upperparts, two narrow white wing bars, sharply defined square white rump patch and lack of white tip to tail. Shows pale head with dark patch on nape. **Juvenile:** metallic areas of upperparts replaced with dark brown. ◆ Dark eye and bill. **Habitat:** secondary growth, forest edge and cultivation of lowlands. Uncommon passage migrant, wintering mainly in the south.

827. Common Starling *Sturnus vulgaris* S: 22 นกกิ้งโครงพันธุ์ยุโรป
Mainly dark plumage, with long, sharply pointed bill and lack of white in wing. **Breeding:** blackish, with violet and greenish gloss; slight spotting and scaling. Bill yellow. **Non-breeding:** duller, more heavily spotted plumage, with dark bill. **Habitat:** lowland open country. Rare winter visitor.

Plate 126 Starlings I

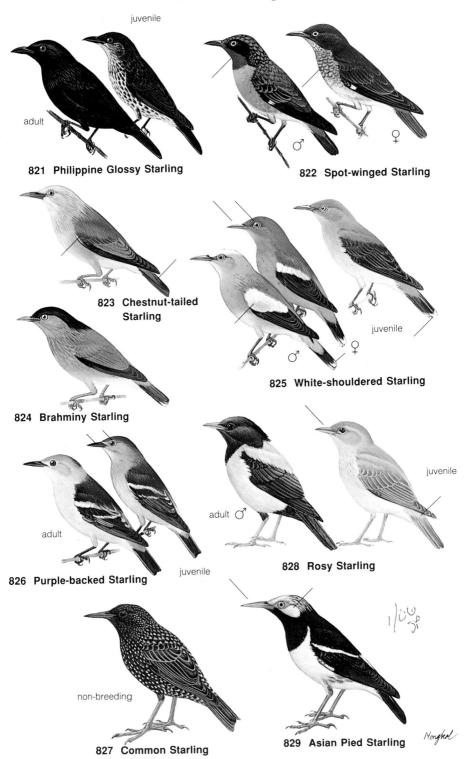

juvenile

adult

821 Philippine Glossy Starling

822 Spot-winged Starling ♂ ♀

823 Chestnut-tailed Starling

824 Brahminy Starling

♂ ♀ juvenile

825 White-shouldered Starling

adult

juvenile

826 Purple-backed Starling

adult ♂

juvenile

828 Rosy Starling

non-breeding

827 Common Starling

829 Asian Pied Starling

Mongkol

372

828. Rosy Starling *Sturnus roseus* S: 22   นกกิ้งโครงสีกุหลาบ

Adult: buffy pink body plumage with black wings, tail, head and throat. Black parts glossier and pink parts brighter in breeding plumage males; slightly duller in females and immatures. **Juvenile:** light sandy-brown above with paler rump; darker wings and tail. Underparts buffy. ◆ Bill yellowish with a dark tip. **Habitat:** open scrublands of the plains. Very rare winter visitor.

829. Asian Pied Starling *Sturnus contra* S: 24   นกเอี้ยงด่าง

Black head, throat and upper breast with white cheeks and forecrown. Base of bill and bare facial skin orange. In flight from Black-collared Starling by white underwing coverts, smaller size. **Habitat:** open lowlands, especially well-watered, cultivated areas, towns. Very common resident.

830. Black-collared Starling *Sturnus nigricollis* S: 28   นกกิ้งโครงคอดำ

Larger than Asian Pied Starling, with whitish head (usually soiled creamy or greyish), black bill, black collar, mainly blackish underwing and white tail-tip. **Juvenile:** lacks black neck collar. Dusky head and breast. **Voice:** very loud and jangling, with a characteristic quality like the squeaky hinge of a metal gate. **Habitat:** both dry and moist open country, scrub, towns and cities, from plains up to 1500 m. Very common resident, now extending its range into deforested areas of the Peninsula.

831. Vinous-breasted Starling *Sturnus burmannicus* S: 25   นกกิ้งโครงหัวสีนวล

Superficially resembles Black-collared, but distinguished by smaller size, lack of collar, vinous breast and belly, yellow bill with red base and, in flight, by white underwing coverts. **Juvenile:** duller, with brownish crown. ◆ Whitish eye. **Habitat:** usually drier open country, cultivation, with scattered trees. Favours well-watered short grass of lawns, playing fields. Uncommon to locally common resident.

832. Common Myna *Acridotheres tristis* S: 25   นกเอี้ยงสาริกา

The only dark myna with white underwing coverts and bright yellow facial skin. Dark brown body plumage with blackish grey head, throat and upper breast and white tail-tip. Lacks crest. Bill yellow; eyes red to brown. **Juvenile:** duller, with dark brown rather than blackish head and throat. **Habitat:** open country, cultivated areas, human habitations, up to 1500 m. Very common resident.

Plate 127 Starlings, Mynas

830 Black-collared Starling

adult

juvenile

831
Vinous-breasted Starling

832 Common Myna

833 Jungle Myna

adult

juvenile

834
White-vented Myna

G.r. religiosa

G.r. intermedia

836 Hill Myna

juvenile

835 Golden-crested Myna

♀

♂

Mongkol

833. Jungle Myna *Acridotheres fuscus* S: 24   นกเอี้ยงควาย

Distinguished from Common Myna by lack of yellow orbital skin, short crest, darker grey-brown body and by dark underwing coverts; white in wing restricted to a patch at base of primaries. From White-vented Myna by shorter crest; contrast between blackish head and throat and greyer body; yellow eye and blue base to bill. Lower belly whitish, grading into white vent. **Juvenile:** lacks crest; brownish head and pale throat. Bill may be entirely dull yellowish.
Habitat: paddyfields, open grassy areas usually around the margins of marshes and lakes. Occasionally forest clearings, mangroves. Uncommon resident.

834. White-vented Myna *Acridotheres javanicus* S: 25   นกเอี้ยงหงอน

Black plumage with conspicuous crest, white vent, white tail-tip and yellow bill. Eye dark red-brown. In flight, shows large white patch at base of primaries. Moulting birds often lack crest. **Habitat:** paddyfields, and well-watered open country, gardens, cities. Often associated with domestic cattle. Very common resident.

835. Golden-crested Myna *Ampeliceps coronatus* S: 22   นกเอี้ยงหัวสีทอง

Smaller than Hill Myna, with smaller pinkish bill which dark basally. Small, pale yellow wing patches in flight. **Male:** glossy black plumage with yellow crown, sides of head and throat. **Female:** like male, but yellow on head restricted to crown and to a diamond-shaped patch on throat. Sides of head black. **Juvenile:** head black, with yellowish white lores and throat patch; breast with faint whitish streaks. **Voice:** a higher-pitched, more metallic whistle than Hill Myna and a bell-like note. **Habitat:** evergreen and mixed deciduous forests from plains to 800 m. Uncommon resident.

836. Hill Myna *Gracula religiosa* S: 30   นกขุนทอง

Large and thickset. Glossy black body, with yellow face wattles and a large, thick, pinkish orange bill. Conspicuous white wing patches in flight. Race *religiosa* of peninsular Thailand is slightly larger with a complete dark bar of feathering across wattle. Often perches high up on dead branches. **Voice:** a loud, piercing whistle (*ti-ong*; DRW). Low croaking notes resembling the human voice. An excellent mimic. **Habitat:** deciduous and evergreen forests, partly cleared country, from plains to 1300 m. In the Peninsula, restricted to level lowlands and islands. Uncommon to fairly common resident, much reduced by capture and habitat loss.

วงศ์นกกินปลีและนกปลีกล้วย

SUNBIRDS AND SPIDERHUNTERS: Family *Nectariniidae*. Small, active, arboreal birds with long, curved bills. Males of many species show bright, orange or yellow pectoral tufts (usually only visible in display). Eat both nectar and small insects, spiders. Usually solitary or in pairs, though larger aggregations sometimes found in flowering trees. World: 117 species. Thailand: 22 species.

เหล่านกกินปลี

SUNBIRDS: Sexes differ, the males usually having bright, iridescent plumage and the females being drab-coloured. In some species, the males assume a mainly drab eclipse plumage after a post-nuptial body moult. Ecological counterparts of the New World hummingbirds, feeding mainly upon nectar, but less agile in flight, hovering much less. Call usually with short *chit* notes and sing with thin, high-pitched trills and twitters. Build hanging, purse-shaped nests.

Genus *Anthreptes*. Relatively straight, short bills. เหล่านกกินปลีปากสั้นหางสั้น

837. **Plain Sunbird** *Anthreptes simplex* S: 13 นกกินปลีสีเรียบ
Bright olive-green upperparts and drab, greyish olive underparts, with a relatively straight bill; tail appears square-ended. **Male:** dark iridescent blue-green patch above base of bill. **Habitat:** evergreen forest, forest edge and occasionally coastal scrub, up to 900 m. Fairly common resident.

838. **Brown-throated Sunbird** *Anthreptes malacensis* S: 14 นกกินปลีคอสีน้ำตาล
Male: distinguished by dull, light brown throat and sides of head; metallic purple shoulder patch. Never shows more than a small rufescent patch on upper wing coverts. **Female:** entire underparts bright yellowish. From female Olive-backed by larger size, straighter bill, lack of white in tail and by diffuse yellowish spectacle around eye. **Voice:** sings with a persistent, irregular *chiff-chaff-chiff-chiff-chaff...* **Habitat:** forest edge, mangroves, coastal scrub, gardens, fruit orchards, coconut palms of lowlands. Very common resident.

839. **Red-throated Sunbird** *Anthreptes rhodolaema* S: 13 นกกินปลีคอสีน้ำตาลแดง
Male: distinguished from Brown-throated by maroon-red sides of head and upper wing coverts, with only small metallic blue shoulder patch. Crown, nape and upper back iridescent greenish (predominantly purple-blue in Brown-throated). Throat light, dull reddish and underparts dull yellowish. **Female:** difficult to separate from female Brown-throated, but sides of breast duller, tinged greenish. In some, throat and occasionally breast and wing coverts tinged orange. **Habitat:** lowland evergreen forest and forest edge. Uncommon or rare resident.

840. Ruby-cheeked Sunbird *Anthreptes singalensis* S: 11   นกกินปลีแก้มสีทับทิม

Smaller and even straighter-billed than preceding species. **Male:** pale rufous throat and metallic copper-red ear coverts. Crown, body and covert feathers of upperparts metallic green. **Female:** diagnostic combination of dull olive-green upperparts, pale rufous throat and upper breast with otherwise yellow underparts. **Juvenile:** like female but lacks rufous on throat. **Voice:** disyllabic *wee-eest* call, with rising inflection, very like that of Inornate Warbler (679). **Habitat:** deciduous and evergreen forest, secondary growth and occasionally gardens, up to 900 m; also mangroves. Common resident.

นกกินปลีท้ายทอยน้ำเงิน

841. Purple-naped Sunbird *Hypogramma hypogrammicum* S: 15

Identified by relatively large size and streaked underparts. Smaller, shorter-billed than Streaked Spiderhunter. **Male:** metallic purple-blue on nape, rump and upper tail coverts. ◆ Frequents undergrowth and middle storey. **Voice:** a strident, prinia-like *schewp*. **Habitat:** evergreen forests below 900 m. Fairly common resident.

เหล่านกกินปลีปากยาวหางสั้น

Genus *Nectarinia*. Longer, more curved bills than preceding group. Male pectoral tufts are prominent in most species. Females show whitish tips to outer tail feathers and blackish upperside to tail.

842. Purple-throated Sunbird *Nectarinia sperata* S: 10   นกกินปลีคอสีม่วง

Male: distinguished from male Purple by clear-cut, iridescent green cap; from male Copper-throated by much smaller size and from both by iridescent purple throat and dull, maroon-red lower breast and belly. Lacks pectoral tufts. **Female:** duller, more whitish yellow underparts, with paler throat than female Olive-backed or Purple. Whitish tips to tail feathers are usually invisible in the field. **Habitat:** evergreen forest edge, secondary growth of moist lowlands up to 800 m. Uncommon resident.

นกกินปลีคอสีทองแดง

843. Copper-throated Sunbird *Nectarinia calcostetha* S: 14

Larger than Purple-throated, with relatively long tail (can appear square, but actually graduated). **Male:** bright iridescent green cap and shoulders, like Purple-throated, but has metallic, coppery throat and upper breast; iridescent violet-purple breast and belly. **Female:** greyish head, greyish white throat and upper breast grades into yellowish lower breast and belly; bold whitish tips to tail feathers. **Habitat:** mangroves, coastal vegetation; only occasionally inland. Uncommon resident.

Plate 128 Sunbirds I

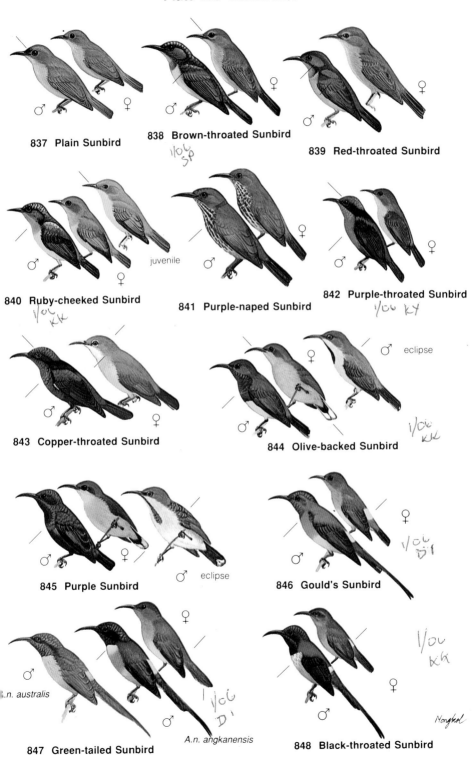

837 Plain Sunbird
♂ ♀

838 Brown-throated Sunbird
♂ ♀

839 Red-throated Sunbird
♂ ♀

840 Ruby-cheeked Sunbird
♂ ♀

841 Purple-naped Sunbird
juvenile ♂ ♀

842 Purple-throated Sunbird
♂ ♀

843 Copper-throated Sunbird
♂ ♀

844 Olive-backed Sunbird
♀ ♂ eclipse ♂

845 Purple Sunbird
♂ ♀ ♂ eclipse

846 Gould's Sunbird
♂ ♀

847 Green-tailed Sunbird
.n. australis ♂ ♀ A.n. angkanensis

848 Black-throated Sunbird
♂ ♀

Mongkol

844. Olive-backed Sunbird *Nectarinia jugularis* S: 11 นกกินปลีอกเหลือง
Uniform olive upperparts and bright yellow underparts in both sexes. **Male:** metallic blue-black throat. **Eclipse plumage male:** black reduced to a broad, mesial throat stripe. **Female:** from female Purple by bolder white tail feather tips with almost wholly white outer web to outermost tail feathers and brighter yellow underparts. From female Brown-throated by white in tail, lack of spectacle and sharp contrast between dark cheeks and yellow throat; more strongly curved bill. Some individuals show a faint yellow supercilium. **Voice:** a loud *sweet*, with rising inflection. **Habitat:** deciduous woodlands, open country, gardens, cultivation, mangroves and coastal scrub, up to 900 m. Very common resident.

845. Purple Sunbird *Nectarinia asiatica* S: 11 นกกินปลีสีดำม่วง
Male: appears mostly dark blue-black at a distance. At close range, head, upperparts and upper breast glossed green; throat blackish and separated from sooty-black belly by a maroon band across breast. **Eclipse male:** from eclipse male Olive-backed by iridescent blue wing coverts. **Female:** like female Olive-backed but narrower white tips to tail feathers; slightly paler yellowish underparts. **Habitat:** deciduous woodlands and open scrub country; coastal scrub. Common resident.

เหล่านกกินปลีหางยาว

Genus *Aethopyga*. Males mostly have a yellow rump patch and elongate tail feathers in nuptial dress. Female tails graduated or rounded. Strongly curved bills.

846. Gould's Sunbird *Aethopyga gouldiae* S: 11 นกกินปลีหางยาวคอสีฟ้า
Male: from male Green-tailed by entirely scarlet upper breast, brighter red mantle, red on sides of head and nape and metallic blue crown, throat, ear coverts and tail. Elongate tail extends up to a further 4 cm. **Eclipse male:** retains scarlet upper breast and yellow lower breast and belly. **Female:** from female Green-tailed by yellow rump. From female Black-throated by brighter, yellower lower breast and belly contrasting with greyish throat and upper breast. Whiter tips to tail feathers. **Habitat:** evergreen forest and secondary growth above 1200 m. Fairly common winter visitor.

847. Green-tailed Sunbird *Aethopyga nipalensis* S: 11 นกกินปลีหางยาวเขียว
Male: dark metallic green head, throat and tail; maroon mantle. Race *angkanensis* (endemic to Doi Inthanon) has yellow upper breast and scarlet lower breast. Race *australis* (endemic to mountains of Peninsula) has all yellow breast with slight red streaking. Elongate tail extends up to a further 3 cm. **Female:** bronze-green upperparts, lacking yellow rump; greenish yellow underparts and white tips to outer tail feathers. **Habitat:** evergreen forest above 1500 m (Doi Inthanon) or above 900 m (Peninsula). Locally common resident.

848. Black-throated Sunbird *Aethopyga saturata* S: 11 นกกินปลีหางยาวคอดำ
Male: dark metallic blue head and tail; dark maroon mantle. Throat usually mixed metallic blue and black. Lower breast and belly pale yellowish. In dim forest light appears drab; blackish above and creamy below. Elongate tail extends up to a further 3 cm. Race *anomala* in mountains of Peninsula lacks yellow rump band. **Female:** pale yellow rump; less obvious white tips to tail feathers and more drab body plumage than female Gould's. **Habitat:** evergreen forests from about 300 m to 1700 m. Common resident.

849. Crimson Sunbird *Aethopyga siparaja* S: 11 นกกินปลีคอแดง
Male: crimson mantle, throat and upper breast; drab, greyish belly and iridescent violet crown and tail. Tail extends up to a further 3 cm. **Eclipse male:** uniform dull olive, except for red on throat and breast. **Female:** drab, fairly uniform olive, lacking rump patch or white in tail. **Habitat:** evergreen and deciduous forest, forest edge, secondary growth, gardens up to 1000 m (commonest at low elevations). Fairly common resident.

850. Fire-tailed Sunbird *Aethopyga ignicauda* S: 12 นกกินปลีแดงหัวไพลิน
Male: from male Gould's by scarlet tail and mostly yellow underparts. Greatly elongate tail extends up to a further 7 cm. **Eclipse male:** body colouration like female, but retains scarlet tail. **Female:** like female Green-tailed, but lacks white tips to tail feathers. **Habitat:** evergreen forest of high elevations. Very rare winter visitor; only one record.

851. Scarlet Sunbird *Aethopyga temminckii* S: 11 นกกินปลีแดง
Male: from Crimson Sunbird by scarlet tail extending up to a further 3 cm. Red eyebrow and median line on forecrown with iridescent purple on head restricted to a horseshoe-shaped patch on sides of crown and nape. **Female:** scarlet fringes to wing and tail feathers; otherwise fairly drab, as female Crimson. **Habitat:** evergreen forest, up to 1500 m (mostly lowlands). Rare resident.

เหล่านกปลีกล้วย

SPIDERHUNTERS: Genus *Arachnothera*. Sexes similar, with mostly dull, yellow to olive plumage. Larger and more robust than sunbirds with extremely long bills and explosive chattering calls. Build cup-shaped nests sewn to the underside of large leaves with cobwebs or plant fibres.

852. Little Spiderhunter *Arachnothera longirostra* S: 16 นกปลีกล้วยเล็ก
Distinguished by small size and diffuse whitish cheek patch with pencil-thin dark moustache; whitish throat grades into yellow belly. Dull olive upperparts; white tips to outer tail feathers. Frequents understorey vegetation. **Voice:** a sharp *chit*. Sings with a rapidly repeated *chip-chip-chip*...., somewhat recalling Common Tailorbird (701), uttered from dense cover. **Habitat:** evergreen forests, forest edge and secondary growth, usually below 1000 m. Common resident.

380

นกปลีกล้วยปากหนา

853. Thick-billed Spiderhunter *Arachnothera crassirostris* S: 17

Close to Little Spiderhunter in size, but thicker bill. Shows no bold patterning on head though sometimes has a slight dark line through eye and a diffuse, broad, partial yellow spectacle. Throat and upper breast greyish olive, grading into bright yellow lower breast and belly. Yellowish tips to outer tail feathers. **Voice:** a chatter, *chit-chit-chit*, softer than similar call of Grey-breasted. **Habitat:** the canopy of lowland evergreen forest (though often descends to edges, clearings). Uncommon resident.

854. Long-billed Spiderhunter *Arachnothera robusta* S: 22 นกปลีกล้วยปากยาว

Large, with disproportionately long bill. Uniform dark olive-green sides of head, lacking eye-ring or ear patch. Throat and breast dusky yellow-green, vaguely streaked, grading into yellow belly. Whitish tips to outer tail feathers. Feeds mostly in canopy and nests in lower storey. **Habitat:** evergreen forest, forest edge of chiefly level lowlands though occasionally up to 1200 m. Rare resident.

นกปลีกล้วยหูเหลืองใหญ่

855. Spectacled Spiderhunter *Arachnothera flavigaster* S: 22

Slightly larger than Long-billed, but with shorter, exceptionally broad-based bill. Lacks pale tips to tail feathers. From Yellow-eared by much broader eye-ring and slightly less obvious ear patch. **Voice:** usually a loud, harsh, double note, *chi-chip*. **Habitat:** evergreen forest, forest edge, secondary growth below 600 m. Fairly common resident.

นกปลีกล้วยหูเหลืองเล็ก

856. Yellow-eared Spiderhunter *Arachnothera chrysogenys* S: 18

Eye-ring thinner and less conspicuous than in Spectacled; ear patch more conspicuous and base of bill when seen from below is much narrower. Greyish olive throat and upper breast grades into yellow belly and under tail coverts. Lacks pale tail-tips. **Juvenile:** lacks ear patch. **Voice:** often gives a single, high-pitched squeaky, *tchick*, reminiscent of the calls of some small woodpeckers. **Habitat:** evergreen forest, forest edge up to 900 m. Fairly common resident.

857. Grey-breasted Spiderhunter *Arachnothera affinis* S: 18 นกปลีกล้วยท้องเทา

Diagnostic combination of bright, olive-green upperparts and pale olive-greyish underparts; slight streaking on upper breast. **Voice:** a strident chatter. **Habitat:** evergreen forest, secondary growth from plains to 1100 m. Common resident.

Plate 129 Sunbirds, Spiderhunters

♂ eclipse

♀

♂ eclipse

849 Crimson Sunbird

850 Fire-tailed Sunbird

♀

♂

851 Scarlet Sunbird

852 Little Spiderhunter

853 Thick-billed Spiderhunter

854 Long-billed Spiderhunter

855 Spectacled Spiderhunter

856 Yellow-eared Spiderhunter

857 Grey-breasted Spiderhunter

858 Streaked Spiderhunter

Mongkol

382

858. Streaked Spiderhunter *Arachnothera magna* S: 19   นกปลีกกล้วยลาย

Distinguished from all other spiderhunters by boldly streaked upperparts and underparts. Feet orange-pink. See Purple-naped Sunbird (841). **Voice:** a strident chatter, very like one of the calls of Orange-bellied Leafbird (510). **Habitat:** evergreen forests, mixed deciduous forest and secondary growth from foothills to 1800 m. Common resident.

วงศ์นกกาฝาก

FLOWERPECKERS: Family *Dicaeidae.* Mostly very small birds, with short tails and short bills. Most species are sexually dimorphic, the females being duller and more difficult to identify. Juveniles of most species show pale or bright orange bills. Usually frequent canopy and forest edge, feeding in nectar-producing or fruiting trees. Most utter sharp, metallic notes. Build deep, hanging, purse-like nests suspended between twigs, usually high in the trees. World: 59 species. Thailand: 10 species.

นกกาฝากอกแดง

859. Scarlet-breasted Flowerpecker *Prionochilus thoracicus* S: 10

Thick bill. **Male:** black head and throat and large red breast patch; yellow belly and under tail coverts. In flight, shows yellow rump and upper tail coverts. **Female:** distinguished from female Crimson-breasted by greyer head, contrasting with olive-green upperparts; yellowish upper tail coverts and lack of whitish malar stripe. Shows more yellow on belly; has orange-tinged breast and yellow (not whitish) under tail coverts. **Juvenile:** duller; greyish olive underneath, lacking any yellow tinge. From juvenile Crimson-breasted by brighter, yellower bill. **Habitat:** mainly lowland forests, including swamp forest. Rare resident.

นกกาฝากอกเหลือง

860. Yellow-breasted Flowerpecker *Prionochilus maculatus* S:10

Thick bill. Diagnostic yellowish underparts with blurred olive-green streaks. Orange-red patch on crown. **Juvenile:** lacks crown patch; streaking on underparts less distinct. ◆ Frequents understorey. **Voice:** a rasping disyllabic note, reminiscent of the call of Black-naped Monarch (809); *tsweet-tsweet.* **Habitat:** evergreen forests, secondary growth, from plains to 1600 m. Common resident.

นกกาฝากอกสีเลือดหมู

861. Crimson-breasted Flowerpecker *Prionochilus percussus* S: 10

Thick bill. **Male:** bright yellow underparts contrast with slaty-blue upperparts. Shows red centre streak on breast, red crown patch and thin whitish malar stripe. **Female:** underparts show a bright yellow median stripe contrasting with olive-grey sides of breast and flanks; unstreaked. Shows indistinct whitish malar stripe. Upperparts dull olive-green, with an indistinct, dull orange median crown patch. **Juvenile:** duller, more uniformly olive; flesh-coloured bill. **Habitat:** evergreen forests, forest edge from plains and foothills to 600 m. Uncommon to fairly common resident.

Plate 130 Flowerpeckers, White-eyes

859 Scarlet-breasted Flowerpecker
♂ ♀

860 Yellow-breasted Flowerpecker

861 Crimson-breasted Flowerpecker
♂ ♀

862 Thick-billed Flowerpecker

863 Yellow-vented Flowerpecker

864 Yellow-bellied Flowerpecker
♂ ♀

865 Orange-bellied Flowerpecker
♂ ♀

866 Plain Flowerpecker

867 Scarlet-backed Flowerpecker
♂ ♀ juvenile

868 Buff-bellied Flowerpecker
D.i. cambodianum ♂
D.i. ignipectus ♂ ♀

869 Chestnut-flanked White-eye
pale individual

870 Japanese White-eye

871 Oriental White-eye
yellow morph

872 Everett's White-eye

Mongkol

384

862. Thick-billed Flowerpecker *Dicaeum agile* S: 10   นกกาฝากปากหนา

Thick bill, plain colouration and diagnostic habit of wagging broad tail from side to side. Whitish underparts show heavy, blurred greyish streaks; whitish-tipped tail feathers are difficult to see. Upperparts grey-brown with an olive-green wash on wings. Eye reddish to orange. **Juvenile:** flesh-coloured bill. ◆ Usually keeps to high canopy. **Voice:** a diagnostic, thin *pseeow*, usually uttered in flight. **Habitat:** mixed deciduous and evergreen forests, secondary growth from plains to 1500 m (mainly lowlands). Common resident.

นกกาฝากก้นเหลือง
863. Yellow-vented Flowerpecker *Dicaeum chrysorrheum* S: 10

Underparts white with bold, sharply defined black streaks; under tail coverts bright orange-yellow. Upperparts bright olive-green. **Juvenile:** paler yellow under tail coverts and less contrasted streaking. **Voice:** a short, harsh *dzeep* (like a short version of the call of Vernal Hanging Parrot). **Habitat:** mixed deciduous and evergreen forests, forest edge and secondary growth from plains to 1100 m. Fairly common resident.

นกกาฝากท้องเหลือง
864. Yellow-bellied Flowerpecker *Dicaeum melanoxanthum* S: 13

Larger than other flowerpeckers, with a distinctive broad white stripe extending down centre of throat and breast. **Male:** black upperparts, sides of throat and breast; yellow belly and under tail coverts. **Female:** duller grey-brown upperparts and greyish sides of throat and breast; yellow of belly paler than in male. **Habitat:** evergreen forest, forest edge above 1300 m. Uncommon; status uncertain, though possibly breeds above 2000 m.

นกกาฝากท้องสีส้ม
865. Orange-bellied Flowerpecker *Dicaeum trigonostigma* S: 9

Male: shows bright orange belly and under tail coverts, pale grey throat and breast. Upperparts slaty blue with orange back and rump. **Female:** pale grey throat and breast; dull yellowish belly and under tail coverts. Dark olive above, with dull orange-yellow rump patch. From female Scarlet-breasted by thin, slightly decurved bill. **Voice:** a harsh *dzip*. Sings with a slightly descending sequence, *tsi-si-si-si-sew*. **Habitat:** forest edge, secondary growth and wooded gardens, cultivation, from plains to 900 m. Common resident.

866. Plain Flowerpecker *Dicaeum concolor* S: 9   นกกาฝากสีเรียบ

Drab, unstreaked, with thin, slightly decurved, bill. Upperparts dull olive; underparts pale greyish, becoming creamy on centre of belly. From female Buff-bellied by sides of head which grade into paler throat, without any sharp demarcation. Bill often greyish, darker tipped. See juvenile Scarlet-backed. **Voice:** song is a *tsit, tsi-si-si-si-si*, recognisably different from both Scarlet-backed and Buff-bellied. **Habitat:** deciduous and more open evergreen forests, secondary growth from plains to 1700 m. Fairly common resident.

867. Scarlet-backed Flowerpecker *Dicaeum cruentatum* S: 9   นกสีชมพูสวน

Male: striking; red crown and nape extends in a broad band down back to upper tail coverts. Black sides to head, wings and tail; white underparts. **Female:** grey-brown above with red patch on rump and upper tail coverts; underparts buffy-grey. **Juvenile:** lacks red on rump and upper tail coverts; shows bright orange-red base to bill. **Voice:** a hard, metallic *dik*. Song is a thin, repeated, *tissit, tissit...* **Habitat:** deciduous woodlands, evergreen forest edge and open, cultivated country from plains to 1200 m. Even occurs in gardens in the heart of towns and cities. Very common resident.

868. Buff-bellied Flowerpecker *Dicaeum ignipectus* S: 9   นกกาฝากอกเพลิง

Male: glossy, dark blue-green upperparts, buffy underparts with a thin black line down centre of lower breast and belly. Scarlet patch on upper breast is lacking in race *cambodianum* of east and southeast Thailand, sometimes treated as a separate species, *D. beccarii.* **Female:** dark olive-brown above; very difficult to separate from Plain Flowerpecker but usually shows darker sides to head, more sharply demarcated from buffy throat and sides of breast. **Voice:** a sharp *dik*. Song like Scarlet-backed; *tissit, tissit....* **Habitat:** evergreen forest, secondary growth from 600 m to the highest summits. Very common resident; the most abundant flowerpecker at these elevations.

วงศ์นกแว่นตาขาว

WHITE-EYES: Family *Zosteropidae.* Small and active, greenish, warbler-like birds. All Thai species show bold white eye-rings. Mainly arboreal and usually in flocks, occasionally of mixed species. Feed mainly on nectar, small fruits and insects. Utter soft ringing and piping notes. Build small cup nests in the forks of horizontal branches. World: 84 species. Thailand: 4 species.

นกแว่นตาขาวข้างแดง

869. Chestnut-flanked White-eye *Zosterops erythropleurus* S: 12

Distinguished from other white-eyes by chestnut patch on flanks (in some individuals, shows as no more than a faint pinkish suffusion which is difficult to see). Cold green upperparts, lacking yellow on forecrown. **Habitat:** evergreen forests, secondary growth from foothills to the highest elevations; most often above 1000 m. Fairly common winter visitor.

870. Japanese White-eye *Zosterops japonicus* S: 12   นกแว่นตาขาวหลังเขียว

Distinguished from Oriental White-eye by darker, less yellow-green upperparts and edges on folded wing; by lack of a median yellow stripe on lower breast and belly. From both Oriental and poorly-marked Chestnut-flanked by contrast between narrow yellow-green band above base of bill and darker greenish crown. **Habitat:** forest, secondary growth and cultivated areas from the foothills to the highest elevations. Usually the commonest white-eye above 1000 m. Common winter visitor.

871. Oriental White-eye *Zosterops palpebrosus* S: 11   นกแว่นตาขาวสีทอง

Distinguished from Japanese by brighter, yellow-green upperparts and uniformly yellow-green crown. Shows a yellow median stripe on lower breast and belly, though distinctness varies. In western Thailand, many individuals show entirely yellow underparts. **Habitat:** deciduous and evergreen forests, secondary growth, mangroves, scrub and wooded cultivation from plains up to at least 1800 m. Very common resident.

872. Everett's White-eye *Zosterops everetti* S: 11   นกแว่นตาขาวสีเหลืองปักษ์ใต้

Distinguished from Oriental with difficulty by slightly darker grey sides of breast and flanks and colder green upperparts, particularly crown and rump. Note range and habitat. **Habitat:** evergreen forests, forest edge of mountain slopes from foothills to 1800 m. (In the Peninsula, where Oriental White-eye is restricted to scrub and mangroves, is the only white-eye in inland forest.) Uncommon resident.

วงศ์นกกระจอก

SPARROWS: Family *Passeridae.* Small to medium-sized birds with compact bodies and short, conical bills adapted to feeding on seeds and grain. Have notched tails. Build loose, dome-shaped nests placed either in holes or crevices, or in the branches of trees. Most are gregarious and are often found nesting or roosting in colonies. Many are sexually dimorphic in plumage. World: 43 species. Thailand: 4 species.

873. Eurasian Tree-Sparrow *Passer montanus* S: 15   นกกระจอกบ้าน

Sexes similar. Dark chestnut cap, whitish cheeks and partial neck collar with black ear patch and small black throat patch. Boldly streaked back. **Voice:** various harsh notes, *chirp* and *chissip*. **Habitat:** urban areas, villages, up to 1800 m, but mostly in lowlands. Very common resident.

874. Plain-backed Sparrow *Passer flaveolus* S:15   นกกระจอกตาล

Unstreaked upperparts in both sexes. **Male:** grey-green crown, back of neck and rump; chestnut mantle, scapulars and sides of head behind eye. Pale yellowish cheeks and underparts. **Female:** unstreaked, light brown upperparts and creamy-yellow underparts and long supercilium. **Voice:** a loud, clear *filip* (DRW); less harsh, but more metallic than Eurasian Tree-Sparrow. **Habitat:** open wooded country, cultivation and around the margins of towns and villages, up to 800 m. Very common resident.

875. Russet Sparrow *Passer rutilans* S: 14   นกกระจอกป่าท้องเหลือง

Male: much rustier above than Eurasian Tree-Sparrow, with cap, mantle and rump chestnut and lacking dark mark on ear coverts. Underparts usually tinged creamy-yellow (sometimes greyish white). **Female:** duller brownish above, heavily streaked black; sharp contrast between buffy supercilium and dark ear coverts. **Habitat:** open wooded country, cultivated areas from plains up to 2100 m. Rare winter visitor.

Plate 131 Sparrows, Weavers

873 Eurasian Tree-Sparrow

874 Plain-backed Sparrow

875 Russet Sparrow

876 House Sparrow

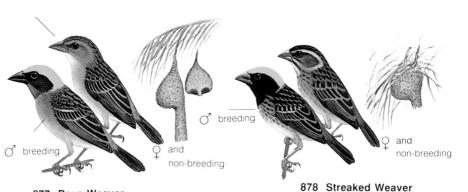

877 Baya Weaver

878 Streaked Weaver

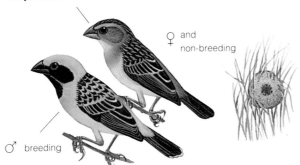

879 Asian Golden Weaver

Mongkol

388

876. **House Sparrow** *Passer domesticus* S: 15   นกกระจอกใหญ่

Male: distinguished from Eurasian Tree-Sparrow by grey crown and upper tail coverts, lack of black ear patch and by more extensive black on throat and upper breast. **Female:** distinguished from female Plain-backed by streaked upperparts, lack of yellow tinge on underparts. **Habitat:** villages, town margins, cultivated areas of plains. Local and rare resident; probably a recent colonist.

วงศ์นกกระจาบ

WEAVERS: Family *Ploceidae*. Similar to sparrows in shape, with heavy, conical bills adapted for eating seeds and grain. The Thai species all have rounded tails. Sexually dimorphic, the males having a distinctive nuptial plumage. Build elaborately woven nests, in colonies. World: 98 species. Thailand: 3 species.

877. **Baya Weaver** *Ploceus philippinus* S: 15   นกกระจาบธรรมดา

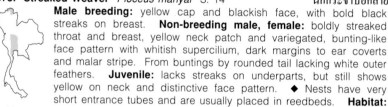

At all times from Asian Golden Weaver by less heavy bill, which noticeably longer than deep. **Male breeding:** yellow cap, blackish face mask and blackish brown throat. Blackish brown bill. **Non-breeding male, female:** underparts unstreaked or at most faintly streaked, and long buffy or tawny supercilum. Upperparts streaked. Bill horn-coloured, usually pinkish at base. ◆ Nests have long entrance tubes; suspended from trees. **Voice:** song of various chattering and wheezy notes. Harsh *chit-chit-chit* calls. **Habitat:** cultivated areas, secondary growth, both dry and well-watered open country up to 1200 m. Large numbers roost in reedbeds. Fairly common resident, though very much reduced due to human persecution.

878. **Streaked Weaver** *Ploceus manyar* S: 14   นกกระจาบอกลาย

Male breeding: yellow cap and blackish face, with bold black streaks on breast. **Non-breeding male, female:** boldly streaked throat and breast, yellow neck patch and variegated, bunting-like face pattern with whitish supercilium, dark margins to ear coverts and malar stripe. From buntings by rounded tail lacking white outer feathers. **Juvenile:** lacks streaks on underparts, but still shows yellow on neck and distinctive face pattern. ◆ Nests have very short entrance tubes and are usually placed in reedbeds. **Habitat:** cultivated areas, grasslands, marshes below 900 m (mostly plains). Uncommon resident.

879. **Asian Golden Weaver** *Ploceus hypoxanthus* S: 15   นกกระจาบทอง

Distinguished from Baya Weaver by massive and thick bill, as deep as it is long. **Male breeding:** yellow head and underparts with black mask and throat. Yellow streaking on upperparts. **Non-breeding male, female:** plumage almost identical to Baya; best identified by diagnostic bill shape. ◆ Builds dome-shaped nest with side entrance, usually placed low in reeds or tall grass. **Habitat:** marshy areas, paddyfields. Local and uncommon resident.

MUNIAS: Family *Estrildidae*. Mainly small and strikingly marked. Fly in close-packed flocks. Feed almost exclusively on seeds and can make local movements to areas of greatest food abundance, enabling them to breed year-round. Build globular nests, placed in low cover. World: 137 species. Thailand: 8 species.

880. Red Avadavat *Amandava amandava* S: 10   นกกระติ๊ดแดง
Male breeding: bright red plumage with white spots on wing coverts and underparts. **Non-breeding male, female:** red bill and upper tail coverts; otherwise brown plumage with small white spots on wing coverts, and a slight dark mask. **Juvenile:** lacks red on upper tail coverts. ◆ Easily overlooked when feeding in tall grass. Most often seen in rapid flight. **Voice:** a thin, shrill *pseep*. **Habitat:** open grassy areas and scrub, up to 1500 m (mainly lowlands). Uncommon resident.

881. Pin-tailed Parrotfinch *Erythrura prasina* S: 13   นกกระติ๊ดเขียว, นกไผ่
(Tail of male extends up to a further 2–3 cm.) Bright green upperparts in all plumages. **Male:** blue throat and sides of head; red rump, upper tail coverts and elongate central tail feathers. Underparts tawny-buff; most (but not all) birds show red on belly. **Female:** sides of head and throat green; without red on belly. Rump and upper tail coverts darker red; tail yellowish brown, lacking elongate feathers. **Habitat:** forest and forest edge, secondary growth and bamboo up to 1500 m. Partly nomadic, following the seeding of bamboos. Uncommon resident.

882. Java Sparrow *Padda oryzivora* S: 16   นกกระจอกชวา
Sexes similar. Easily identified by grey body, black head, white cheeks and red bill. **Juvenile:** browner above, buffier below. ◆ Introduced as a cagebird; an apparently viable colony exists in the northern suburbs of Bangkok. **Voice:** a soft *tup* given in flight. **Habitat:** cultivated areas, paddyfields of town margins. Uncommon resident.

883. White-rumped Munia *Lonchura striata* S: 11   นกกระติ๊ดตะโพกขาว
Plumage more contrasted than in Scaly-breasted Munia. **Adult:** blackish brown head, upper breast and upperparts with white rump and whitish belly. Dark parts of plumage faintly streaked and scaled. Bicoloured bill. **Juvenile:** paler than adult, with buffy-white rump. **Voice:** a tinkling, metallic *prrrit*. **Habitat:** secondary growth, scrub, grasslands, cultivation up to 1500 m. Very common resident.

884. White-bellied Munia *Lonchura leucogastra* S: 11   นกกระติ๊ดท้องขาว
Distinguished from White-rumped Munia by dark rump and by dull, pale yellowish upperside of tail and more extensive dark brown on breast and flanks. **Habitat:** evergreen forest, secondary growth, clearings, scrub and cultivation, below 500 m. Uncommon resident.

885. Scaly-breasted Munia *Lonchura punctulata* S: 11   นกกระติ๊ดขี้หมู
Adult: distinguished from White-rumped by less contrasted face and upperparts, concolorous rump and by bold scaling on breast and flanks. **Juvenile:** plain brown upperparts, rich buffy throat and entire underparts, lacking scaling. From juveniles of Chestnut and White-headed Munias by blackish grey bill. **Voice:** a piping, disyllabic *ki-dee* (DRW). **Habitat:** paddyfields, cultivation, scrub, secondary growth up to 1500 m. Very common resident.

886. Chestnut Munia *Lonchura malacca* S: 11   นกกระติ๊ดสีอิฐ
Adult: rich chestnut body, contrasting with black head, throat and upper breast. **Juvenile:** rich buffy brown, with more rufous under parts than juvenile Scaly-breasted; entirely bright blue-grey bill. **Habitat:** grassland, scrub, paddyfields, marshes of plains, including coastal flats. Uncommon resident.

887. White-headed Munia *Lonchura maja* S: 11   นกกระติ๊ดหัวขาว
Adult: white head, neck and throat contrasts with dark chestnut-brown body. Belly and under tail coverts blackish. Bright blue-grey bill. **Juvenile:** from juvenile Chestnut by more whitish-buffy sides of head and underparts. **Voice:** a thin, piping *puip* (M&W). **Habitat:** paddyfields, grasslands and scrub below 300 m. Uncommon resident.

วงศ์นกจาบปีกอ่อน

FINCHES: Family *Fringillidae*. Small to medium-sized birds, with thick conical bills and notched tails. Sexes usually differ, the males being more brightly coloured. Usually gregarious and often found in flocks. Feed on seeds and insects. Most species are migrant visitors to Thailand. World: 128 species. Thailand: 8 species.

888. Black-headed Greenfinch *Carduelis ambigua* S: 13   นกจาบปีกอ่อนเขียว
Bright yellow wing stripe and yellow wedges at base of tail conspicuous in flight. **Male:** black head, blackish wings and tail; yellowish underparts with blurred olive streaking. **Female:** duller and browner with dark grey-green head. **Juvenile:** underparts buffy-whitish. ◆ Usually in low trees and weedy growth. Often in small flocks. **Voice:** a wheezy *twzyee*, with rising inflection; hard *tit-tit, tit-tit* notes. **Habitat:** cultivated areas, secondary growth, usually above 1200 m. Rare winter visitor.

Plate 132 Munias

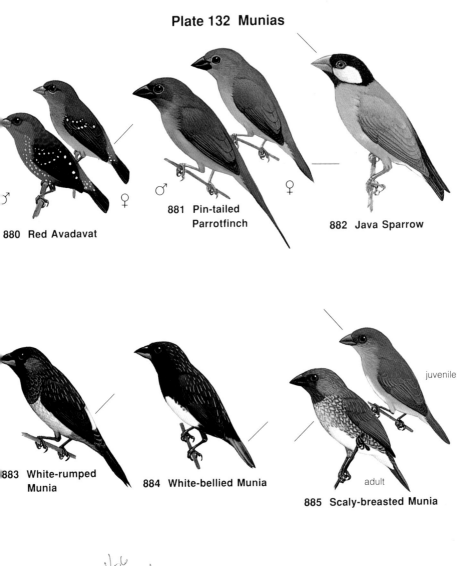

880 Red Avadavat
♂ ♀

881 Pin-tailed Parrotfinch
♂ ♀

882 Java Sparrow

883 White-rumped Munia

884 White-bellied Munia

885 Scaly-breasted Munia
juvenile
adult

886 Chestnut Munia
adult
juvenile

887 White-headed Munia
adult
juvenile

Mongkol

392

889. Dark-breasted Rosefinch *Carpodacus nipalensis* S: 16
Slightly longer, thinner bill than other rosefinches. **Male:** striking dark brown eye patch contrasts with pale pink supercilium and throat, bright crimson forecrown. Rosy underparts with darker, crimson-brown breast band. **Female:** uniform dark brown with paler, rufescent brown wing bars and tertial edges. ◆ Usually solitary, feeding mainly on the ground, favouring moist, shady areas. **Habitat:** evergreen forest, forest edge above 1900 m. Rare winter visitor.

890. Common Rosefinch *Carpodacus erythrinus* S: 16   นกจาบปีกอ่อนสีกุหลาบ
Male: crimson-rosy plumage, tinged brownish on back. Crimson-rosy rump. Sometimes shows brownish mask, but otherwise lacks any strongly contrasted plumage features. **Female:** streaked brownish upperparts with two buffy wing bars; buffy underparts with blurred dark streaks. Black eye stands out on relatively uniform, brownish, unmarked head; no white in tail. **Voice:** calls with a soft, quiet *sweep*. **Habitat:** forest edge, secondary growth, open scrub-land and cultivation from plains up to the highest summits. Common winter visitor.

891. Pink-rumped Rosefinch *Carpodacus eos* S: 15   นกจาบปีกอ่อนตะโพกชมพู
Male: distinguished from other rosefinches by fairly uniform, pale vinous-pink underparts; sharply contrasting pink supercilium and rump. Light brown upperparts show distinct dark streaks. **Female:** from female Common Rosefinch by whiter underparts with more sharply defined dark streaking. **Habitat:** open country, scrub growth. Very rare winter visitor; only one record, in plains.

892. Scarlet Finch *Haematospiza sipahi* S: 19   นกจาบปีกอ่อนสีแดง
Large, with pale bill. **Male:** brilliant scarlet plumage with black wings and tail. **Immature male:** from female by orange rump and dull orange-red upperparts. **Female:** scaly, dark olive upperparts with yellow rump; paler underparts. **Habitat:** forest edge, secondary growth and cultivation above 1200 m. Rare winter visitor.

893. Yellow-billed Grosbeak *Eophona migratoria* S: 20   นกกระติ๊ดใหญ่ปากเหลือง
Large yellow bill, greyish body and rufous flanks. Blackish wings with white tertial tips, white at base and tips of primaries. **Male:** glossy black hood, black tail. **Female:** head and throat grey-brown roughly concolorous with back; central tail feathers greyish. **Habitat:** secondary growth and clearings of the hills. Very rare winter visitor (one record from Khao Yai).

Plate 133 Finches

888 Black-headed Greenfinch

juvenile

♂

♀

889 Dark-breasted Rosefinch

♀

♂

890 Common Rosefinch

♂

♀

891 Pink-rumped Rosefinch

♀

♂

892 Scarlet Finch

♂

♀

893 Yellow-billed Grosbeak

♂

♀

894 Collared Grosbeak

♂

♀

895 Spot-winged Grosbeak

♂

♀

Mongkol

394

894. Collared Grosbeak *Mycerobas affinis* S: 24   นกกระติ๊ดใหญ่สร้อยคอเหลือง

Male: brilliant pattern of yellow underparts, neck collar, mantle and rump; black head, throat, wings and tail. From Black-hooded Oriole (556) by massive, blue-grey bill; all black wings. **Female:** dull, olive-green, with slightly brighter, yellow-tinged hindneck, rump and underparts. Grey head and throat, blackish wings and tail. **Habitat:** evergreen forests of higher mountains. Very rare visitor; one record from the summit of Doi Inthanon.

นกกระติ๊ดใหญ่ปีกลาย

895. Spot-winged Grosbeak *Mycerobas melanozanthos* S: 23

Massive, with pale grey bill; white patch at base of primaries conspicuous in flight. **Male:** black head and upper breast; yellow underparts. **Female:** boldly striped head pattern; body streaked both above and below. ◆ Usually feeds on fruits in tall trees, and often in large flocks. **Voice:** metallic trill given in flight. Feeding flocks give squeaky *tew-tew* notes. **Habitat:** hill evergreen forests and secondary growth, usually above 1400 m. Uncommon resident.

วงศ์นกจาบปีกอ่อนเล็ก

BUNTINGS: Family *Emberizidae*. Seed-eating birds with conical bills. Tails usually longer than in finches, often with white outer feathers. Head patterns important for identification. Brighter breeding plumage of males is obscured by pale feather tips in winter, which wear off gradually. Feed mainly on the ground. In Thailand, all are winter visitors, some species roosting in huge congregations in reedbeds or fields of sugar cane. World: 327 species. Thailand: 8 species.

896. Tristram's Bunting *Emberiza tristrami* S: 15   นกจาบปีกอ่อนหัวดำขาว

Strongly contrasted head pattern with whitish mesial, and dark lateral, crown stripes. Bright chestnut rump and upper tail coverts. Very conspicuous white in outer tail feathers. **Male:** black throat and ear coverts, lateral crown stripes, with white supercilium and submoustachial stripe. Broad, rufous-brown breast band. **Female:** throat buffy, bordered by dark malar stripe; black and white markings on head of male replaced by brown and buff. **Habitat:** evergreen forest, secondary growth, above 1500 m. Very rare winter visitor.

897. Chestnut-eared Bunting *Emberiza fucata* S: 16   นกจาบปีกอ่อนหัวเทา

Greyish crown and back of neck, greyish supercilium and striking white eye-ring. Chestnut ear coverts and shoulder patch, warm buffy-rufous rump and conspicuous white in outer tail feathers. Blackish malar stripes lead into a streaked gorget on upper breast. **Male:** ear coverts bright, fairly uniform chestnut; narrow pinkish chestnut band across breast. **Female:** duller, brownish chestnut ear coverts with slightly more obvious pale centre; more uniformly buffy lower breast and belly. **Voice:** calls like Yellow-breasted Bunting. **Habitat:** cultivated lowlands, especially fields of rice stubble. Occasionally in hills up to 1300 m. Locally common winter visitor.

Plate 134 Buntings

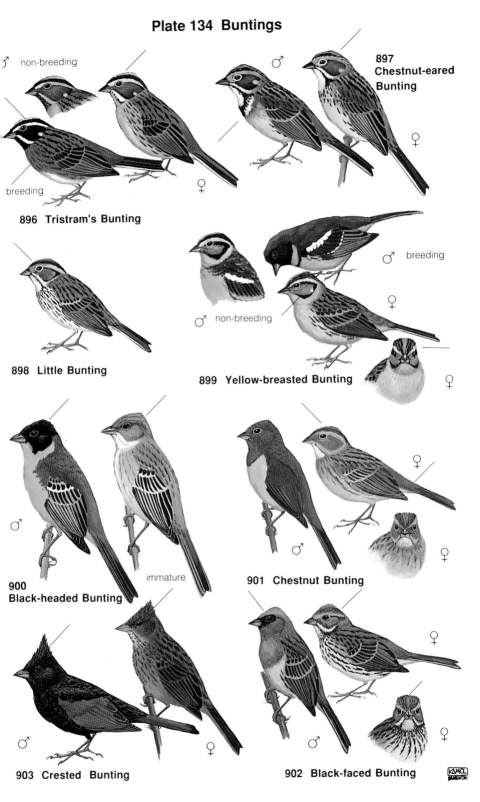

♂ non-breeding

breeding

896 Tristram's Bunting

♂

♀

897 Chestnut-eared Bunting

♀

898 Little Bunting

♂ breeding

♀

♂ non-breeding

899 Yellow-breasted Bunting

♀

♂

immature

900 Black-headed Bunting

♀

♂

901 Chestnut Bunting

♀

♀

903 Crested Bunting

♀

♂

902 Black-faced Bunting

♀

KAMOL BANGKOK

396

898. Little Bunting *Emberiza pusilla* S: 13   นกจาบปีกอ่อนเล็ก

 Broad area of chestnut on central crown, bordered by sharply contrasting blackish lateral crown stripes. Ear coverts chestnut with black hind border; conspicuous buffy supercilium. Cream eye-ring. Underparts whitish, streaked black on breast and flanks. Bill rather thin with straight culmen. Sexes similar, but female and winter male duller, less chestnut than breeding plumage male. **Voice:** a sharp metallic *tic*. **Habitat:** open scrubland and cultivation from plains up to 2000 m. Common winter visitor.

899. Yellow-breasted Bunting *Emberiza aureola* S: 15   นกจาบปีกอ่อนอกเหลือง

Male breeding: black face and throat, chestnut crown and breast band; bright yellow underparts and white shoulder patch. **Male non-breeding:** from female by white shoulder patch, usually darker face pattern and brighter yellow underparts. **Female and immature:** pale yellowish underparts; upperparts boldly streaked buffy-brown and black. From Chestnut Bunting by paler mesial crown stripe, paler supercilium; pale centre to ear coverts, contrasting sharply with dark margins. Also by white outer tail feathers and by lack of chestnut on rump and upper tail coverts. **Voice:** a short *tsip* or *tsic*. **Habitat:** open country, paddyfields, cultivation of plains. Often roosts in huge numbers in reedbeds. Common winter visitor.

900. Black-headed Bunting *Emberiza melanocephala* S: 18   นกจาบปีกอ่อนหัวดำ

Large size; unstreaked underparts and almost no white in outer tail feathers. **Male:** black head, yellow throat and entire underparts. Rufous back. **Female:** dark grey-brown head, lacking supercilium, malar stripes or other distinguishing features. Pale sandy-brown upperparts, streaked darker; buffy throat, pale yellow underparts. **Immature:** like female, but yellow on underparts usually confined to under tail coverts. Greyer above. **Habitat:** paddyfields, open areas of low elevations. Very rare visitor, so far known only from one market-purchased specimen.

901. Chestnut Bunting *Emberiza rutila* S: 15   นกจาบปีกอ่อนสีตาล

Lacks noticeable white in outer tail. **Male breeding:** chestnut upperparts, head, throat and upper breast with yellow belly. **Male non-breeding:** chestnut duller, partly obscured by pale feather tips. **Female and immature:** from Yellow-breasted by less contrasted head pattern and upperparts; rufous rump and upper tail coverts. ◆ Often feeds on seeding bamboo. **Voice:** thin *tseep*. **Habitat:** open deciduous and hill evergreen forests, scrub, secondary growth and open areas from foothills to 2500 m. Fairly common winter visitor.

902. Black-faced Bunting *Emberiza spodocephala* S: 15   นกจาบปีกอ่อนหน้าดำ

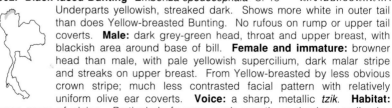 Underparts yellowish, streaked dark. Shows more white in outer tail than does Yellow-breasted Bunting. No rufous on rump or upper tail coverts. **Male:** dark grey-green head, throat and upper breast, with blackish area around base of bill. **Female and immature:** browner head than male, with pale yellowish supercilium, dark malar stripe and streaks on upper breast. From Yellow-breasted by less obvious crown stripe; much less contrasted facial pattern with relatively uniform olive ear coverts. **Voice:** a sharp, metallic *tzik*. **Habitat:** open areas of plains. Particularly favours scrub growth on riverine sandbanks. Local and rare winter visitor.

903. Crested Bunting *Melophus lathami* S: 17   นกจาบปีกอ่อนหงอน

Distinctive crest and dark plumage with rufous wings and tail. No white in outer tail feathers. **Male:** black body feathers, scaled olive-brown in winter. **Female:** olive-brown body plumage, with underparts slightly paler, streaked darker on breast and flanks. **Voice:** an explosive *tup* given in flight. **Habitat:** secondary growth, scrub, open areas and sometimes rice stubble from plains and foothills up to highest elevations. Locally common winter visitor.

LATE ADDITIONS

Family: *Procellariidae.*   วงศ์นกจมูกหลอด

904. Swinhoe's Storm-Petrel *Oceanodroma monorhis* S: 18   นกโต้คลื่นสีคล้ำ

A small seabird having dark brown plumage with an inconspicuous pale bar on upperwing coverts and a slightly forked tail (difficult to observe). Narrow, angled wings and a fast, erratic, swooping flight, dropping frequently to the water's surface. **Habitat:** open sea. Very rare passage migrant or winter visitor; only one record.

วงศ์นกร่อนทะเล

TROPICBIRDS: Family *Phaethontidae.* Medium-sized aerial seabirds with mainly white plumage and elongate central tail feathers. Have graceful, fluttering flight and feed by plunge-diving. World: 3 species. Thailand: one species.

905. White-tailed Tropicbird *Phaethon lepturus* S: 39   นกร่อนทะเลหางขาว

(Plus elongate tail of 36 cm.) Plumage mainly white with broad black diagonal bar across upperwing coverts, black patch at base of primaries and black eye-line. Yellowish to orange bill. **Juvenile:** shows black scalloping on upperparts and dull yellowish bill. Lacks tail streamers. **Habitat:** oceans, seacoasts. Very rare winter visitor or passage migrant. Only one record.

Family: *Ciconiidae.*   วงศ์นกกระสา

906. Milky Stork *Mycteria cinerea* S: 97   นกกระสาปากเหลือง

Shape like Painted Stork, but shows clean white body plumage, white scapulars and black flight feathers of wings and tail. Bill yellowish orange and legs pinkish. **Breeding:** brighter orange bill, red facial skin and legs. **Immature:** grey-brown upperparts, white rump and upper tail coverts. Grey legs. **Habitat:** mangroves, mudflats. Status uncertain; one old record. Probably once resident, but now extinct.

398

907. Storm's Stork *Ciconia stormi* S: 91 นกกระสาคอขาวปากแดง

Resembles Woolly-necked Stork but distinguished by black foreneck and sides of neck, with white mainly restricted to throat, nape and hindneck. Black outer tail feathers. Bill bright orange-flesh. In breeding dress, shows bright yellow orbital ring. **Habitat:** lowland evergreen forest. Very rare resident, now on the verge of extinction.

Family: *Anatidae.* วงศ์นกเป็ดน้ำ

908. Common Shelduck *Tadorna tadorna* S: 61 เป็ดเชลดัก

A large, mainly white duck with a dark, glossy green head and a broad chestnut band encircling upper breast and back. Broad blackish line down the centre of the underparts; blackish scapulars and flight feathers of wings. Reddish to pink bill and pink legs. **Male:** has a red knob at the base of the bill. **Habitat:** lakes and larger rivers. Very rare winter visitor; only one record.

909. Falcated Teal *Anas falcata* S: 51 เป็ดเปียหน้าเขียว

Medium-sized, with steep forehead and longish bill. **Male breeding:** pale grey body with greatly elongate black and white inner secondaries, narrow dark collar across foreneck. Head dark purple-chestnut with bronze-green patch on sides. Shows white spot above base of bill. In flight, shows grey forewing and black and green speculum. **Male eclipse:** like female, but retains paler grey upperwing. **Female:** uniformly dark brown, lacking crest or obvious face pattern. From female Eurasian Wigeon by longer bill, dark brown (not rufous) plumage; from female Gadwall by steeper forehead, dark bill. From both by dark belly. In flight, shows dark oily-green speculum and pale, greyish forewing. **Habitat:** marshes, lakes. Rare winter visitor.

Family: *Accipitridae.* วงศ์เหยี่ยวและนกอินทรี

910. White-tailed Eagle *Haliaeetus albicilla* S: 70–90 นกอินทรีหางขาว

Very large, somewhat vulture-shaped with broad, parallel-sided, deeply fingered wings, long protruding head and wedge-shaped tail. Wings always held slightly arched (horizontal or slightly raised when soaring and always horizontal when gliding). **Adult:** shows all white tail. Plumage medium brown but head, neck, upper breast and upperwing coverts paler, greyish. Bill yellow. **Juvenile:** tail appears dark. Darker, richer brown than adult, becoming darker on head and neck and rustier on breast and belly. Often shows a band of whitish flecking from axillaries across median underwing coverts. Older immatures begin to show whitish blotching on body. Bill mainly dark. **Habitat:** lakes, marshes. Very rare winter visitor. Known only from a captive bird said to have been caught in Nakhon Sawan province.

Plate 135 Late Additions

905 White-tailed Tropicbird

ad.

juv.

906 Milky Stork

adult

Swinhoe's Storm-Petrel

08 Common Shelduck

♀

♂

♀

907 Storm's Stork

909 Falcated Teal

immature underwing

910 White-tailed Eagle

immature

juvenile

adult breeding

adult underwing

912 Long-tailed Skua

911 Little Stint

breeding

913 Chinese Bulbul

n-breeding

♂

♀

914 Beautiful Nuthatch

915 Mangrove Blue Flycatcher

KAMOL
BANGKOK

Family: *Scolopacidae.* วงศ์นกอีก๋อย, นกชายเลน, และนกปากซ่อม

911. Little Stint *Calidris minuta* S: 16 นกสติ๊นท์เล็ก

Very like Rufous-necked Stint (194) but slightly longer legs and shorter, less projecting wing-tips give less elongate, more hunched appearance. Bill-tip finer. **Non-breeding:** upperparts have relatively broad, dark feather centres, contrasting with paler margins, giving browner, darker, more blotchy or scaled appearance than in Rufous-necked. Shows a brownish wash and fine, dark, streaks which usually extend right across the upper breast. (In Rufous-necked, breast band greyer, with streaking usually confined to the sides.) **Breeding:** face, head, neck and upper breast orange-rufous with dark streaking. Shows creamy lines at edges of mantle. Wing coverts and tertials broadly edged brownish rufous (greyer in Rufous-necked). **Juvenile:** shows more obvious whitish supercilium behind eye than juvenile Rufous-necked, contrasting more with bright rufous centre to crown. Obvious whitish lines at edges of mantle. **Voice:** a sharp *stit-it*, sharper, more metallic than call of Rufous-necked. **Habitat:** mudflats. Very rare winter visitor (only one record).

Family: *Stercorariidae.* วงศ์นกสกัว

912. Long-tailed Skua *Stercorarius longicaudus* S: 54 นกสกัวหางยาว

(Size includes elongate tail streamers of adult, ca. 15 cm.) Has proportionately longer, thinner wings than Arctic Skua (221), together with slimmer body, smaller head and bill. **Adult:** head and underparts pattern similar to that of Arctic Skua but differs in lacking obvious white wing flashes and shows contrast between pale upperwing coverts and dark trailing edge to wing. Tail streamers are approximately same length as body. **Juvenile:** from Arctic Skua by lack of obvious white on upperwing and paler, grey-brown plumage, lacking tawny coloration. Shows more conspicuous barring on upper and under tail coverts. **Habitat:** open seas. Very rare passage migrant or winter visitor.

Family: *Pycnonotidae.* วงศ์นกปรอด

913. Chinese Bulbul (Light-vented Bulbul) *Pycnonotus sinensis* S: 19 นกปรอดจีน

Identified by blackish head with broad white patch extending behind eye across nape. Olive-yellow wings and tail and whitish underparts with a slight, greyish, breast band. Lacks white in tail. **Habitat:** lowland scrub and woodland. Very rare winter visitor; only two records.

Family: *Sittidae.* วงศ์นกไต่ไม้

914. Beautiful Nuthatch *Sitta formosa* S: 18 นกไต่ไม้สีสวย

Identified by large size and vivid blue and black-patterned upper-parts. Shows two white wing bars. Underparts bright rufous-buff. **Habitat:** evergreen forests above 1800 m. Known only from the summit of Doi Pha Hom Pok. Very rare resident.

Family: *Muscicapidae.* วงศ์นกจับแมลง

915. Mangrove Blue Flycatcher *Cyornis rufigastra* S: 15 นกจับแมลงป่าโกงกาง

Shape, proportions and colouration like Hill Blue Flycatcher (802) but upperparts duller blue, almost lacking iridescence. Orange of underparts extends on to belly. **Male:** black lores and chin. **Female:** like male except for whitish lores and entirely buffy-orange chin and throat. **Voice:** a sweet warbling, somewhat reminiscent of Tickell's Blue Flycatcher, but slower and slightly deeper. **Habitat:** tall mangroves. Rare and local resident.

GLOSSARY

Aerial: pertaining to the air (e.g., an aerial feeder)
Antiphonal singing: duetting
Apical: refers to the apex or tip. See also distal
Aquatic: water-living
Arboreal: tree-living
Axillaries: the feathers in the axil (i.e., the 'arm-pit' beneath the base of the wing)
Back: term loosely applied to the mantle, scapulars and rump
Basal: refers to the base (of, e.g., the bill). See also 'proximal'
Breast band: a suffusion of colour forming a band across the upper breast
Cap: a distinct patch of colour covering all or most of the top of the head and which is sharply demarcated from the sides of the head
Carpal: pertaining to the bend of the wing or carpal joint. (*Carpal bar* – a line of usually dark colour along the leading edge of the wing extending between the body and the carpal joint; *carpal patch* – a contrasting marking near the carpal joint; either above or below the wing)
Casque: an enlargement of the upper part of the bill (e.g., as in hornbills)
Cheek: a colloquial term for the sides of the head, below the eye or on the ear-coverts
Collar: a band or bar of contrasting colour, either dark or light, passing around either the front or back of the neck
Coronal stripe: a stripe, either light or dark, on the crown (e.g., *lateral coronal stripe* on the side of the crown or *mesial coronal stripe* on the centre)
Cosmopolitan: a species which is widely distributed, having a near world-wide distribution
Crepuscular: active in the dim light of dawn and dusk
Crest: a tuft of (usually) elongate feathers on the top of the head which, in many species, may be raised or lowered
Decurved: curved downwards
Dimorphic: existing in two well-defined, genetically determined plumage types (e.g., in many species, males and females are sexually dimorphic). In some species, the dimorphism may be independent of sex (e.g., Sooty-headed Bulbul, in which individuals may have either red or yellow vents).
Dipterocarp: a tree belonging to the family Dipterocarpaceae
Distal: terminal or outer portion (opposite to 'proximal')
Diurnal: feeding and carrying out most activities during daylight hours
Duetting: male and female of a pair singing together, in response to each other and in a closely-coordinated manner
Ear patch: a well-defined patch of contrasting (usually dark) colour on the ear coverts
Echolocation: the ability to locate objects through the rapid emission of high frequency sounds and detection of the echoes. Used by cave-dwelling species (in Thailand, only by swiftlets *Aerodramus* spp.)
Eclipse plumage: a usually short post-nuptial plumage stage in which the distinctive breeding plumage is obscured. Shown by many ducks and also, apparently, by some sunbirds
Edgings: feather margins which are brighter or paler than the main body of the feather. Such edgings to primaries or secondaries can form a bright patch on the folded wing.

Endemic: referring to a species or subspecies which is totally confined to a particular area

Face: a term loosely applied to the sides of the head or the sides of the head, throat and forecrown

Facial skin: an extensive area of naked skin on the sides of the head

Feral: pertaining to formerly domesticated species or populations which have reverted to the wild and become self-supporting

First winter plumage: the plumage type shown by a bird in the winter of its first calendar year

First summer plumage: the plumage type shown by a bird which is approximately one year old (i.e., the plumage type succeeding the first winter plumage)

Flight feathers: the primaries, secondaries and tail feathers

Gape: the fleshy interior of the bill

Gape flange: enlarged, pale-coloured margins to the base of the bill, at the sides of the gape

Gliding: straight, level flight with wings oustretched or slightly swept back, without flapping

Gonys: a ridge on the lower mandible near the bill tip, formed by the fusion of the left and right sides of the bill or *rami*. A prominent feature in some gulls

Gorget: a necklet or distinctively coloured patch on the throat or upper breast

Granivorous: seed-eating

Gregarious: living in groups

Gular pouch: a loose, or elastic patch of skin on the throat

Hackles: long, pointed neck feathers; often slightly iridescent

Hand: applied to the spread primaries (those feathers attached to the bones of the wrist and hand). Especially used in descriptions of raptors in flight

Hepatic: literally 'pertaining to the liver'. Usually used as a label for the brown colour morph found in some cuckoos

Hindneck: the rear of the neck; lying posterior to the nape

Hood: a dark-coloured head and (usually) throat

Immature: all stages except adult (including juvenile unless described separately)

Jowl: the appearance of a heavy rounded cheek and throat (e.g., as in Cattle Egret)

Juvenile: the distinctive first plumage of a bird once it has left the nest

Leading edge: the forward edge of the wing

Lobe: a fleshy, rounded protruberance (usually on the feet, as an aid to swimming)

Mask: a dark mark on the side of the head, usually including the ear coverts (See ear patch)

Median / mesial: pertaining to the middle

Mid-wing panel: a panel, usually pale-coloured, formed by the wing coverts or bases to the flight feathers, in the middle of the wing, especially in gulls

Montane: pertaining to the mountains. In the context of this book, used only for areas above 1000 m elevation

Morph: a distinct, genetically determined plumage type or form which may coexist in the same breeding population as one or more other distinct forms

Nictitating membrane: a transparent fold of skin which can be drawn across the eye, forming a third eyelid

Nocturnal: active chiefly at night

Non-passerine: all orders of birds except for the Passerines

Nuchal: pertaining to the hindneck (e.g., nuchal collar is a collar across the back of the neck)

Ocellus: a round, iridescent spot (thought to mimic an eye) found on the tail feathers of peacock-pheasants and peafowl

Old World: The Palearctic, Afrotropical and Oriental zoogeographical regions

Oriental: referring to a zoogeographic region of the world extending from the Himalayas and the Yangtze River south through India and the mainland and islands of South-East Asia east to the Molucca Passage

Palearctic: referring to a zoogeographic region of the world, comprising the whole of Europe, northern Africa and Asia north of a line extending from the Himalayas to the Yangtze River

Passerine: those birds belonging to the Order Passeriformes, recognised by the structure of the foot and usually referred to as 'perching-birds'. The order includes all the typical songbirds (Oscines) as well as the Deutero-Oscines, which include pittas and broadbills.

Pelagic: frequenting the open ocean

Plume: a greatly elongate feather, usually used in display

Proximal: the near, or basal portion (of, e.g., the bill)

Race: a colloquial term for subspecies

Raptor: diurnal birds of prey (hawks, eagles and falcons)

Saddle: colloquial term for the centre of the back. Used especially to refer to a contrasting area of pigment

Shaft streak: a contrasting line of pigment along the midline of a feather which forms a pale or dark streak

Soaring: rising flight, riding updraughts to gain height without flapping; shown by many storks and broad-winged birds of prey

Speculum: a contrasting (often coloured or iridescent) square patch in the wing formed by the inner secondaries

Spur: use in two senses. A sharp projection which may be used in combat: found on the leg in some male pheasants and at the bend of the wing in River Lapwing. Also used to describe a sharply contrasting, hook-shaped marking on the plumage (e.g., as on the underwing of some frigatebirds)

Storey: a level of the forest (e.g., lower storey is used for undergrowth and ground cover; upper storey is used to mean the canopy)

Streamers: greatly elongate, ribbon-like tail feather or projections of the tail feathers

Subadult: a late immature stage of plumage in those species which take several years to reach full adult plumage (e.g., gulls)

Submontane: pertaining to the hill slopes, but below 1000 m

Subsong: a subdued version of the normal territorial song

Subspecies: a population, the members of which may be morphologically distinguished from other populations of the same species occurring in different geographical areas. By definition, distinct subspecies must occupy different and mutually exclusive breeding ranges.

Sundaic: pertaining to Sundaland, that part of the Oriental Region which includes peninsular Thailand, Malaysia and the islands of Sumatra, Java, Bali and Borneo (the Greater Sundas) which lie on the Asian continental plate and which were joined together during periods of lowered sea level. Rainforest is the climax vegetation over much of this subregion, which is characterised by a large number of birds (and other animal and plant species) which are confined within its limits.

Supraloral: above the lores

Termitarium: a termite nest structure

Terrestrial: ground-living

Trailing edge: the hind edge of the wing

Underparts: the entire under surface of the body, apart from the sides of the head

Underwing: the entire under surface of the wing, both coverts and flight feathers

Upperparts: the upper surface of the entire body including the scapulars

Upperwing: the entire upper surface of the wing, both coverts and flight feathers

Vent: strictly speaking, the cloaca, but often used to refer to the surrounding feathers of the lower belly and under tail coverts

Ventral: pertaining to the under surface of the body

Vermiculations: fine, wavy plumage markings

Wattle: a fleshy lobe of skin around the face or base of the bill which usually functions in the context of display

Web: used in two senses. Either a fold of skin stretched between the toes in some aquatic birds or the vane of a feather. (If used in the latter sense, the outer web refers to the vane on the external side of the feather shaft; the inner web that on the inner side of the shaft.)

Wing bar: a usually pale-coloured line across the wing, which, in perching birds, is usually formed by the tips to the greater coverts. (Some species also have an anterior wing bar formed by the tips of the median coverts.) In waders, the wing bar is usually formed by white bases to the primaries and secondaries.

Wing coverts: a general term used for all or part of the lesser, median and greater coverts of the upperwing or underwing

Wing panel: a contrasting area in the wing usually formed by pale or brightly coloured edges to the folded secondaries or primaries

Wing lining: a term loosely applied to the underwing coverts

Zygodactylous: having two toes directed forward and two backwards

406

SELECTED BIBLIOGRAPHY

The following is a list of some of the more useful works which may assist in the identification of Thai birds. Also listed are the more important or easily accessible works on taxonomy and distribution.

Ali, S. and Ripley, S.D. 1983. *A Pictorial Guide to the Birds of the Indian Subcontinent.* Oxford University Press, Delhi.

Ali, S. and Ripley, S.D. 1987. *Compact Handbook of the Birds of India and Pakistan.* 2nd edition. Oxford University Press, Delhi.

Clements, J. 1981. *Birds of the World: a Checklist.* Croom Helm, London.

Cramp, S. and Simmons, K.E.L. 1977–1988. *Handbook of the Birds of Europe, the Middle East, and North Africa; the Birds of the Western Palearctic.* Vols. 1–5. Oxford University Press, Oxford and New York.

Deignan, H.G. 1945. *The Birds of Northern Thailand.* U.S. Nat. Mus. Bull. 186. Smithsonian Institution, Washington, D.C.

Deignan, H.G. 1963. *Checklist of the Birds of Thailand.* U.S. Nat. Mus. Bull. 226. Smithsonian Institution, Washington, D.C.

Harrison, P. 1983. *Seabirds: an Identification Guide.* Croom Helm, London.

Hayman, P., Marchant, J. and Prater, A. 1986. *Shorebirds: an Identification Guide to the Waders of the World.* Croom Helm, London and Sydney.

Inskipp, C. and Inskipp, T. 1985. *A Guide to the Birds of Nepal.* Croom Helm, London and Sydney.

King, B., Dickinson, E.C. and Woodcock, M.W. 1975. *A Field Guide to the Birds of South-East Asia.* Collins, London.

Madge, S.C. and Burn, H. 1988. *Wildfowl: an Identification Guide to the Ducks, Geese and Swans of the World.* Christopher Helm, London.

van Marle, J.G., and Voous, K.H. 1988. *The Birds of Sumatra.* B.O.U. Check-list No. 10. British Ornithologists' Union, London.

Medway, Lord and Wells, D.R. 1976. *The Birds of the Malay Peninsula*, Vol. 5. Witherby and Penerbit Universiti Malaya, Kuala Lumpur.

Meyer de Schauensee, R. 1984. *The Birds of China.* Oxford University Press, Oxford.

Porter, R.F., Willis, I., Christensen, S. and Nielsen, B.P. 1976. *Flight Identification of European Raptors.* Poyser, Berkhamsted.

Ripley, S.D. 1982. *A Synopsis of the Birds of India and Pakistan.* 2nd edition. Bombay Natural History Society, Bombay.

Round, P.D. 1988. *Resident Forest Birds in Thailand: their Status and Conservation.* ICBP, Cambridge.

Sibley, C.G., Ahlquist, J.E., and Monroe, B.L. 1988. A classification of the living birds of the world based on DNA-DNA hybridization studies. *Auk* 105: 409–423.

Smythies, B.E. 1981. *The Birds of Borneo.* 3rd edition. The Sabah Society and the Malayan Nature Society, Kota Kinabalu and Kuala Lumpur.

Smythies, B.E. 1986. *The Birds of Burma.* 3rd (revised) edition. Nimrod Press, Liss, U.K.

Sonobe, K. and Robinson, J.W. 1982. *A Field Guide to the Birds of Japan.* Wild Bird Society of Japan, Tokyo.

Turner, A. and Rose, C. 1989. *A Handbook to the Swallows and Martins of the World.* Christopher Helm, London.

Voous, K.H. 1977. *List of Recent Holarctic Bird Species.* British Ornithologists' Union, London.

White, C.M.N. and Bruce, M.D. 1986. *The Birds of Wallacea.* B.O.U. Check-list No. 7. British Ornithologists' Union, London.

APPENDIXES

Appendix 1 Late additions to the list of Thai birds.

Three new species discovered for Thailand in 1989 were too late to be included in this book: Pied Avocet *Recurvirostra avosetta*, a non-breeding visitor, seen in April on the coast at Samut Sakhon, west of Bangkok; Malaysian Blue Flycatcher *Cyornis turcosa*, which is apparently resident in peat swamp forest in Narathiwat, close to the border with Malaysia; and Brambling *Fringilla montifrigilla*, a winter visitor from north Eurasia, seen on Doi Angkhang, Chiang Mai Province.

Appendix 2 Possible future additions to the list of Thai birds.

We have speculated on those other resident and migrant birds which may possibly be expected to occur in Thailand and list some of the likely contenders below. We have included all those Palearctic migrant species which are known from peninsular Malaysia or Singapore and which may be expected, therefore, to at least occasionally overfly Thailand during migration or vagrancy. We have also included those migrants which are thought to occur regularly in south and east Burma, South Yunnan and in Laos in winter and which could therefore overshoot into Thailand, as well as some of those which are common in Hong Kong. There are, in fact, a number of long distance migrant species which breed in north-east Asia and winter in south-east China or further south, in the Philippines or in Borneo, such as Grey-streaked Flycatcher, some of the thrushes and Pechora Pipit, listed below. These species would not normally be expected in Thailand, since they apparently pass well to the east. Nonetheless, occasional westward vagrancy might occur. For some species, sight records have been received although the details reported were considered to be insufficient to justify their inclusion on the Thai list. It is, of course, extremely difficult to predict which additional migrant species might be added to the Thai list, given such a great array of possibilities. Although we have concentrated mostly on those which have already been found in regions bordering Thailand, it is worth noting that some of the recent additions have been birds which had previously been found no closer than North-east Burma or the Indian Subcontinent.

Himalayan Griffon Vulture would seem to be an unlikely possibility, but is included on the strength of five different individuals, said to have been taken from the wild in Thailand, which were acquired by local bird traders.

It is rather unlikely that more than a few, if any, new resident species remain to be found but it is interesting to speculate on those which might have occurred in Thailand, before lowland habitats were so badly disturbed by man.

A few, such as Red-collared Woodpecker *Picus rabieri* and Grey-faced Tit-Babbler *Macronous kelleyi*, have been found in lowland forests just across the border, in Southern Laos, and it is conceivable that these species might have occurred in eastern Thailand in the recent past although it is virtually certain that insufficient forest habitat remains today. Another lowland forest species, Blue-rumped Pitta *Pitta nipalensis*, has likewise been found in Laos, just across the Mekong River from Chiang Rai province, in Northern Thailand.

A similar situation may apply to some peninsular Malaysian species in southern Thailand. The Crestless Fireback *Lophura erythrophthalma* has been recorded as far north as Kedah province of Malaysia and could conceivably have once occurred in the far southern Thai provinces. Unfortunately, however, its level lowland rainforest habitat has been totally destroyed in peninsular Thailand. We have, however, chosen to consider seven other resident Malaysian birds, for which there are either unconfirmed records or for which suitable habitat is present: among these, the Brown-capped Woodpecker inhabits mangroves, while the Short-toed Coucal and the Grey-chested Babbler could well occur in Thailand's last remnant of primary peat swamp forest at Pa Phru, Narathiwat province. In addition, the White-breasted Wood-swallow has recently colonised Malaysia from Java and one possible sighting in Thailand has been reported. Black-browed Barbet is listed because there is a possibility that it could occur in the Budo mountain range of the far south.

From the drier lowlands to the west, there is the White-tailed Buschat *Saxicola leucura* which, together with the wide-ranging Grass Owl *Tyto capensis*, is known to inhabit tall grass along riverine floodplains in Burma. Such species might well have once occurred in the plains of Thailand but again, since it is unlikely that any suitable habitat remains, neither appears in the table below.

Among the northern montane birds, there is perhaps a slight chance of adding one or two more resident species. Within the past few years, Black-tailed Crake, Beautiful Nuthatch and Burmese Yuhina have all been discovered in Thailand. In trying to determine which montane resident birds might have been hitherto overlooked, we have confined ourselves to listing all those recorded from both East and South Burma within an altitudinal range which corresponds to the elevation of mountains in Thailand. This would allow us to consider Red-tailed Minla, Brown-capped Fulvetta and Greater Rufous-headed Parrotbill, though unlikely, as being of possible occurrence.

Some possible future additions to the list of Thai birds

(R = resident; M = migrant. Malaya is used to indicate Peninsular Malaysia and Singapore)

Species	Seasonal status	Burma E	Burma S	Laos	S. China	Malaya	Other	Thai unconfirmed
Bulwer's Petrel *Bulweria bulwerii*	M					X	X	
Wilson's Storm-Petrel *Oceanites oceanicus*	M	X				X		
Red-billed Tropicbird *Phaethon aethereus*	M	X				X		
Eastern White Pelican *Pelecanus onocrotalus*	M					X		
Dalmatian Pelican *Pelecanus crispus*	M						X	
Red-footed Booby *Sula sula*	M					X		X
Indian Pond-Heron *Ardeola grayii* 1/6 ŭ	M	X	X					X
Oriental White Stork *Ciconia boyciana*	M						X	X
Fulvous Whistling-Duck *Dendrocygna bicolor*	R	X	X					
Baikal Teal *Anas formosa*	M						X	X
Mallard *Anas platyrhynchos*	M	X					X	

Species	Seasonal status	Burma E	S	Laos	S. China	Malaya	Other	Thai unconfirmed
Himalayan Griffon Vulture *Gyps himalayensis*	R/M							X
Western Marsh-Harrier *Circus aeruginosus*	M	X	X			X		X
Pallid Harrier *Circus macrourus*	M	X	X					
Steppe Eagle *Aquila nipalensis*	M					X		X
Lesser Kestrel *Falco naumanni*	M		X					X
Common Crane *Grus grus*	M	X			X		X	
Eurasian Oystercatcher *Haematopus ostralegus*	M		X				X	
Ringed Plover *Charadrius hiaticula*	M					X		
Yellow-wattled Lapwing *Vanellus malabaricus*	R/M					X		
Oriental Plover *Charadrius veredus*	M					X	X	X
Lesser Yellowlegs *Tringa flavipes*	M						X	
Pectoral Sandpiper *Calidris melanotos*	M					X	X	
South Polar/Antarctic Skua *Catharacta maccormicki/ antarctica*	M							X

Species	Seasonal status	Burma E	Burma S	Laos	S. China	Malaya	Other	Thai unconfirmed
Lesser Black-backed Gull *Larus fuscus*	M						X	X
Saunders' Gull *Larus saundersi*	M						X	
Relict Gull *Larus relictus*	M						X	
Long-tailed Parakeet *Psittacula longicauda*	R					X		
Rose-ringed Parakeet *Psittacula krameri*	R	X	X					
Pied Cuckoo *Clamator jacobinus*	M		X					
Short-toed Coucal *Centropus rectunguis*	R					X		
Giant Swiftlet *Hydrochous gigas*	R					X		
Black-browed Barbet *Megalaima oorti*	R					X		
Brown-capped Woodpecker *Picoides moluccensis*	R					X		X
Short-toed Lark *Calandrella brachydactyla*	M		X				X	X
Sand Lark *Calandrella raytal*	R/M		X					
Red-vented Bulbul *Pycnonotus cafer*	R	X	X					

Species	Seasonal status	Burma E	S	Laos	S. China	Malaya	Other	Thai unconfirmed
Black-billed Magpie *Pica pica*	R/M							X
Grey-breasted Babbler *Malacopteron albogulare*	R					X		
Red-tailed Minla *Minla ignotincta*	R	X	X	X				
Brown-capped Fulvetta *Alcippe brunnea*	R	X	X	X	X			
Greater Rufous-headed Parrotbill *Paradoxornis ruficeps*	R	X	X	X				
Rufous-headed Robin *Erithacus ruficeps*	M					X		
Grey-backed Thrush *Turdus hortulorum*	M				X		X	
Japanese Thrush *Turdus cardis*	M			X			X	
Brown-headed Thrush *Turdus chrysolaus*	M						X	
Pale Thrush *Turdus pallidus*	M						X	
Chiffchaff *Phylloscopus collybita*	M						X	
Tickell's Leaf-Warbler *Phylloscopus affinis*	M	X	X					
Large-billed Leaf-Warbler *Phylloscopus magnirostris*	M	X	X					

Species	Seasonal status	Burma E	Burma S	Laos	S. China	Malaya	Other	Thai unconfirmed
Blyth's Reed-Warbler *Acrocephalus dumetorum*	M	X	X				X	
Middendorff's Warbler *Locustella ochotensis*	M						X	X
Grey-streaked Flycatcher *Muscicapa griseisticta*	M						X	
Blyth's Pipit *Anthus godlewskii*	M		X				X	
Pechora Pipit *Anthus gustavi*	M						X	
Siberian Water-Pipit *Anthus japonicus*	M				X			X
White-breasted Wood-swallow *Artamus leucorhynchus*	R					X		X
Chestnut-cheeked Starling *Sturnus philippensis*	M					X	X	
Pale-billed Flowerpecker *Dicaeum erythrorhynchos*	R	X	X					
Yellow-browed Bunting *Emberiza chrysophrys*	M				X			X
Yellow-throated Bunting *Emberiza elegans*	M				X		X	
Rustic Bunting *Emberiza rustica*	M						X	

INDEX OF COMMON NAMES

The common names used in this book are listed below.   Where the name used in King et al. (1975) differs, this is also listed.   The numbers refer to the species numbers assigned in this book.

418

420

422

INDEX OF SCIENTIFIC NAMES

Scientific names are listed below by genera. Where the name used in King et al. (1975) differs, this is also listed. The numbers are the species numbers used in this book.

430

Species number		
Anthracoceros (continued)		
malayanus	373	
Anthreptes malacensis	838	
rhodolaema	839	
simplex	837	
singalensis	840	
Anthus cervinus	478	
hodgsoni	476	
novaeseelandiae	477	
roseatus	479	
Aplonis panayensis	821	
Apus acuticauda	453	
affinis	455	
pacificus	454	
Aquila clanga	99	
heliaca	101	
rapax	100	
Arachnothera affinis	857	
chrysogenys	856	
crassirostris	853	
flavigaster	855	
longirostra	852	
magna	858	
robusta	854	
Arborophila brunneopectus	129	
cambodiana	130	
charltonii	132	
chloropus	131	
rufogularis	128	
Ardea cinerea	15	
purpurea	16	
sumatrana	14	
Ardeola bacchus	17	
speciosa	18	
Arenaria interpres	192	
Argusianus argus	126	
Artamus fuscus	820	
Asio flammeus	325	

Species number	
Athene brama	317
Aviceda jerdoni	72
leuphotes	73
Aythya baeri	60
ferina	58
fuligula	61
nyroca	59
Bambusicola fytchii	136
Batrachostomus affinis (see javensis)	
auritus	326
hodgsoni	328
javensis	329
stellatus	327
Berenicornis comatus	366
Blythipicus pyrrhotis	414
rubiginosus	413
Botaurus stellaris	32
Brachypteryx leucophrys	718
montana	719
Bradypterus luteoventris	716
seebohmi	717
tacsanowskius	715
thoracicus	714
Bubo coromandus	320
nipalensis	318
sumatranus	319
Bubulcus ibis	19
Buceros bicornis	376
rhinoceros	375
Burhinus oedicnemus	217
Butastur indicus	84
liventer	83
Buteo buteo	82
Butorides striatus	25
Cacomantis merulinus	291
sepulcralis	292

432

Species number

Circus (continued)
   spilonotus 106
Cissa chinensis 563
   hypoleuca 562
   thalassina (see hypoleuca)
Cisticola exilis 694
   juncidis 693
Clamator coromandus 281
Coccothraustes
   (see Eophona, Mycerobas)
Cochoa purpurea 743
   viridis 744
Collocalia esculenta 450
   (see also Aerodramus)
Columba hodgsonii 263
   livia 262
   pulchricollis 264
   punicea 265
Copsychus malabaricus 730
   pyrropygus 731
   saularis 729
Coracias benghalensis 363
Coracina fimbriata 494
   melaschista 493
   macei 490
   novaehollandiae (see macei)
   polioptera 492
   striata 491
Corvus macrorhynchos 569
   splendens 570
Corydon sumatranus 428
Coturnix chinensis 140
   coromandelica 139
   japonica 138
Criniger bres 534
   finschii 536
   flaveolus 531
   ochraceus 533

Species number

Criniger (continued)
   pallidus 532
   phaeocephalus 535
Crocethia (see Calidris)
Crypsirina temia 567
Cuculus canorus 287
   fugax 285
   micropterus 286
   poliocephalus 289
   saturatus 288
   sparverioides 282
   vagans 284
   varius 283
Culicicapa ceylonensis 790
Cutia nipalensis 646
Cyanoptila cyanomelana 791
Cymbirhynchus macrorhynchos 429
Cyornis banyumas 802
   concreta 799
   hainana 800
   rubeculoides 801
   rufigastra 915
   tickelliae 803
   turcosa (see Appendix 1)
   unicolor 798
Cypsiurus balasiensis 451

Delichon dasypus 471
   nipalensis 472
   urbica 470
Dendrocitta formosae 566
   vagabunda 565
Dendrocygna javanica 67
Dendronanthus indicus 484
Dicaeum agile 862
   chrysorrheum 863
   concolor 866
   cruentatum 867

434

438

440

Species number			Species number	
Sturnus (continued)		Trichastoma abbotti	591	
sinensis	825	bicolor	589	
sturninus	826	malaccense	587	
vulgaris	827	rostratum	588	
Sula dactylatra	9	sepiarium	590	
leucogaster	10	tickelli	586	
Surniculus lugubris	296	Tringa erythropus	182	
Sylvia curruca	660	glareola	188	
Sylviparus modestus	573	guttifer	185	
Syrmaticus humiae	123	nebularia	184	
		ochropus	187	
Tachybaptus ruficollis	1	stagnatilis	186	
Tadorna ferruginea	66	totanus	183	
tadorna	908	Turdus boulboul	760	
Tarsiger chrysaeus	728	dissimilis	759	
cyanurus	727	feae	763	
Tephrodornis pondicerianus	489	merula	761	
virgatus	488	naumanni	766	
Terpsiphone atrocaudata	812	obscurus	764	
paradisi	813	rubrocanus	762	
Tesia castaneocoronata	708	ruficollis	765	
cyaniventer	706	Turnix suscitator	143	
olivea	707	sylvatica	141	
Thamnolaea (see Chaimarrornis)		tanki	142	
Threskiornis melanocephalus	43	Tyto alba	307	
Timalia pileata	619			
Treron apicauda	246	Upupa epops	365	
bicincta	255	Urocissa erythrorhyncha	564	
capellei	256			
curvirostra	250	Vanellus cinereus	163	
fulvicollis	252	duvaucelii	165	
olax	253	indicus	164	
phoenicoptera	257	vanellus	162	
pompadora	251			
seimundi	247	Xenorhynchus (see Ephippiorhynchus)		
sieboldii	249	Xenus cinereus	190	
sphenura	248			
vernans	254	Yuhina castaniceps	637	

	Species number		Species number
Yuhina (continued)		*Zoothera* (continued)	
flavicollis	638	*interpres*	753
humilis	639	*marginata*	758
zantholeuca	640	*sibirica*	755
		Zosterops erythropleurus	869
Zoothera citrina	754	*everetti*	872
dauma	757	*japonicus*	870
dixoni	756	*palpebrosus*	871

INDEX OF THAI NAMES
ดรรชนีชื่อนกภาษาไทย

444

446

448

450

452

456

NOTE